ISBN 978-1-5283-9215-0
PIBN 11005452

FB &c Ltd, Dalton House, 60 Windsor Avenue, London, SW19 2RR.
Company number 08720141. Registered in England and Wales.

For support please visit www.forgottenbooks.com

ACTS

OF THE

One Hundred and Seventeenth Legislature

OF THE

STATE OF NEW JERSEY,

AND

Forty-Ninth Under the New Constitution.

TRENTON, N. J.:
MacCrellish & Quigley, State Printers.

1893.

The following General Public Laws, passed by the One Hundred and Seventeenth Legislature, are compiled in accordance with the act entitled "An act relative to public printing," approved March 23, 1883, which provides "that the laws shall be collated under two heads of General Public Acts, Special Public and Private Acts."

The General Public Laws are printed in the front part of the volume.

The Joint Resolutions and Proclamations by the Governor are placed next after the General Public Laws.

The Special Public and Private Acts follow in the order of their approval, and, with table of Contents and Index of all the laws, complete the same.

HENRY C. KELSEY,

Secretary of State.

MEMBERS

OF THE

One Hundred and Seventeenth Legislature

OF NEW JERSEY.

SENATORS.

ATLANTIC, . .	SAMUEL D. HOFFMAN.
BERGEN, . .	HENRY D. WINTON.
BURLINGTON, .	MITCHELL B. PERKINS.
CAMDEN, . .	MAURICE A. ROGERS.
CAPE MAY, . .	LEMUEL E. MILLER.
CUMBERLAND, .	EDWARD C. STOKES.
ESSEX, . .	MICHAEL T. BARRETT.
GLOUCESTER, .	GEORGE H. BARKER.
HUDSON, . .	WILLIAM D. DALY.
HUNTERDON, .	WILLIAM H. MARTIN,
MERCER, . .	WILLIAM H. SKIRM.
MIDDLESEX, . .	ROBERT ADRAIN.
MONMOUTH, . .	HENRY S. TERHUNE.
MORRIS, . .	ELIAS C. DRAKE.
OCEAN, . .	GEORGE G. SMITH.
PASSAIC, . .	JOHN HINCHLIFFE.
SALEM, . .	JAMES BUTCHER.
SOMERSET, . .	WILLIAM J. KEYS.
SUSSEX, . .	JOHN McMICKLE.
UNION, . .	FREDERICK C. MARSH.
WARREN, . .	JOHNSTON CORNISH.

ASSEMBLYMEN.

ATLANTIC, . .	CHARLES A. BAAKE.
BERGEN, . .	SAMUEL G. H. WRIGHT,
	JOHN J. DUPUY.
BURLINGTON, .	HOWARD E. PACKER,
	MICAJAH E. MATLACK.
CAMDEN, . .	CLAYTON STAFFORD,
	GEORGE W. HENRY,
	WILLIAM J. THOMPSON.
CAPE MAY, . .	EDMUND L. ROSS.
CUMBERLAND, .	WILBER H. BAXTER,
	JOHN N. GLASPELL.
ESSEX, . .	WILLIAM HARRIGAN,
	JOHN L. ARMITAGE,
	JOSEPH P. CLARKE,
	JOSEPH M. BYRNE,
	THOMAS A. MURPHEY,
	DENNIS F. OLVANEY,
	WILLIAM J. KEARNS,
	JOHN H. PEAL,
	J. BROADHEAD WOOLSEY,
	TIMOTHY BARRETT,
	AUGUSTUS C. STUDER.
GLOUCESTER, .	SOLOMON H. STANGER.
HUDSON, . .	EBENEZER BERRY, JR.,
	MAX SALINGER,
	HENRY H. HOLMES,
	HUGH A. KELLY,
	ADAM J. DITTMAR,
	TIMOTHY J. CARROLL,
	MARTIN LAWLESS,
	STEPHEN V. W. STOUT,
	MICHAEL J. COYLE,
	CORNELIUS J. TAHEN,
	JOHN ZELLER.

HUNTERDON, .	JOSEPH L. CHAMBERLIN,
	BENJAMIN E. TINE.
MERCER, . .	BARTON B. HUTCHINSON,
	JAMES W. LANNING,
	CHARLES G. ROEBLING.
MIDDLESEX, . .	JOHN W. BEEKMAN,
	JOHN H. DALY,
	HEZEKIAH WARNE.
MONMOUTH, . .	REUBEN G. STRAHAN,
	JOHN D. HONCE,
	WILLIAM T. PARKER.
MORRIS, . .	THOMAS J. O'BRIEN,
	SYLVESTER UTTER.
OCEAN, . .	JOHN T. BURTON.
PASSAIC, . .	JOHN I. HOLT,
	JOHN F. SMITH,
	THOMAS FLYNN,
	FRANK GLEDHILL.
SALEM, . .	WILLIAM DIVER.
SOMERSET, . .	GEORGE H. CRAMER.
SUSSEX, . .	JACOB SWARTWOUT.
UNION, . .	TIMOTHY M. KELLY,
	THOMAS F. LANE,
	GEORGE KYTE.
WARREN, . .	L. MILTON WILSON,
	RICHARD H. SHEPPARD.

General Public Laws.

GENERAL PUBLIC ACTS

PASSED BY THE

ONE HUNDRED AND SEVENTEENTH LEGISLATURE

CHAPTER I.

An Act ceding to the United States of America jurisdiction over a lot of land situate in the city of Paterson, and exempting the same and its appurtenances from taxation.

WHEREAS, the United States of America have recently appropriated money for the erection of a building in the city of Paterson for the accommodation of the post office and other governmental offices of the United States; therefore,

1. BE IT ENACTED *by the Senate and General Assembly of the State of New Jersey*, That jurisdiction of the land and its appurtenances which have been purchased in said city of Paterson for the erection of the aforesaid building, be and the same is hereby ceded to the United States of America; *provided*, that all civil and criminal process, issued under the authority of this state, or any officer thereof, may be executed on said land in the same way and manner as if jurisdiction had not been ceded as aforesaid.

Lands ceded to United States

Proviso

2. *And be it enacted*, That the said land, with its appurtenances, and the building and other property thereon, shall forever hereafter be exempt from all state, county and municipal taxation and assessment so long as the

Lands ceded exempt from taxation.

same shall remain the property of the United States of America.

8. *And be it enacted,* That this act shall take effect immediately.

Approved January 18, 1898.

GEORGE T. WERTS,
Governor.

ROBERT ADRAIN,
President of the Senate.

THOMAS FLYNN,
Speaker of the House of Assembly.

CHAPTER II.

An Act in relation to warrants drawn to meet disbursements and expenditures made by boards in cities of the first class in this state in certain cases, and giving the common council or other governing body power in relation thereto.

Form and manner of drawing warrants on treasury of cities to be protected by ordinance.

1. BE IT ENACTED *by the Senate and General Assembly of the State of New Jersey,* That it shall be lawful for the common council or other governing body in any city of the first class of this state to provide by ordinance for the form and manner in which warrants upon the treasury of the said city for the purpose of meeting and discharging obligations incurred by the expenditure and disbursements of other boards therein shall be drawn, signed and paid, and all warrants made and signed for such expenditures and disbursements in accordance with an ordinance duly passed for that purpose in any such city shall be deemed and taken to be in all respects regular and lawful.

2. *And be it enacted*, That all acts and parts of acts inconsistent with this act be and the same are hereby repealed, and that this act shall take effect immediately.

Approved January 31, 1893.

CHAPTER III.

A Supplement to the act entitled "An act to facilitate proceedings in the prerogative court," approved February eleventh, one thousand eight hundred and eighty-eight.

1. BE IT ENACTED *by the Senate and General Assembly of the State of New Jersey*, That the fifth section of an act entitled "An act to facilitate proceedings in the prerogative court," approved February eleventh, one thousand eight hundred and eighty-eight, which fifth section reads as follows:

"5. *And be it enacted*, That the vice-ordinary or vice-surrogate general shall receive as compensation for the performance of the duties which shall be imposed upon him under this act, an annual salary of fifteen hundred dollars, in addition to his compensation as vice-chancellor, to be paid to him by the treasurer of the state in equal monthly or quarter-yearly payments, as he shall from time to time elect," be and the same is hereby repealed. Section repealed.

2. *And be it enacted*, That this act shall take effect immediately.

Approved January 31, 1893.

CHAPTER IV.

A Supplement to an act entitled "An act respecting the court of chancery," approved March twenty-seventh, one thousand eight hundred and seventy-five.

Annual salary of vice-chancellors.

1. BE IT ENACTED *by the Senate and General Assembly of the State of New Jersey,* That the vice-chancellors of this state shall each be entitled to receive an annual salary at the rate of nine thousand dollars and no more; said salaries shall be paid in equal monthly payments by the treasurer of this state on the warrant of the comptroller of the treasury, and shall be in full of all services to be rendered by said officers respectively, and neither of said officers shall be entitled to any per diem or other allowance over and above said salaries.

Repealer.

2. *And be it enacted,* That all acts or parts of acts inconsistent with the provisions of this act are hereby repealed, and that this act shall take effect immediately.

Approved January 31, 1893.

CHAPTER V.

An Act to amend an act entitled "A further supplement to an act entitled 'An act respecting the orphans' court, and relating to the powers and duties of the ordinary and the orphans' court and surrogate,'" approved March twenty-seventh, one thousand eight hundred and seventy-four.

Section to be further amended.

1. BE IT ENACTED *by the Senate and General Assembly of the State of New Jersey,* That section twenty-six of the act to which this act is a supplement, as the same was amended

by a supplement to said act, approved March seventeenth, anno domini one thousand eight hundred and eighty-two, and as further amended by a further supplement to said act, approved May eleventh, one thousand eight hundred and eighty-six, be and the same hereby is further amended, so as to read as follows:

26. *And be it enacted*, That when any will shall have been proved and recorded in any state or territory of the United States or the District of Columbia, or in any foreign state or kingdom, and any person shall desire to have the same recorded in this state, for the purpose of making title to lands or real estate in this state, it shall be lawful for any surrogate of any county in this state, upon an exemplified copy of such will and proof thereof being filed in his office, exemplified and attested as a true copy according to the provisions of the act of congress for exemplifying and certifying judicial records of any state, if it be the record of any state or territory of the United States or the District of Columbia, or in the manner required by the laws of the foreign state or kingdom in which such will shall have been proved and recorded, to make it legal evidence in such foreign state or kingdom, if it be the record of a foreign state or kingdom, to record such will and proofs and file the said copy in his office; and any such will and proofs and certificate, upon being so recorded, shall have the same force and effect, in respect to all lands and real estate whereof the testator died seized, as if said will had been admitted to probate and letters testamentary or of administration, with the will annexed thereon, had been issued in this state; and all conveyances of such real estate, heretofore or hereafter made, by any executor or executors, or administrator or administrators, with the will annexed, or the survivor or survivors of them, or by any devisee or devisees or their heirs, shall be as valid as if said will had been admitted to probate in this state, and such record or certified copies of said will and proof and certificate shall be received in evidence in all courts of this state. Section as amended.

2. *And be it enacted*, That this act shall take effect immediately.

Approved February 8, 1898.

CHAPTER VI.

A Further Supplement to an act entitled "An act to enable incorporated towns to construct water works for the extinguishment of fires, and supplying the inhabitants thereof with pure and wholesome water," approved March fifth, one thousand eight hundred and eighty-four, and enlarging the powers and authority of the commissioners appointed under said act.

Governing body provide by ordinance for control and management of sewer system.

1. BE IT ENACTED *by the Senate and General Assembly of the State of New Jersey*, That in all incorporated towns in this state, wherein a system of water works has been or shall be erected and put in operation under the provisions of an act entitled "An act to enable incorporated towns to construct water works for the extinguishment of fires and supplying the inhabitants thereof with pure and wholesome water," approved March fifth, one thousand eight hundred and eighty-four, and commissioners have been or shall be appointed and acting pursuant to the terms of said act, and in which a system of sewers has been or shall hereafter be constructed and put in operation under the laws of this state, it shall be lawful for the board of commissioners or other governing body of such incorporated towns to provide by ordinance or resolution, that the water commissioners appointed under the provisions of the act above recited shall take the control, charge and management of the sewer system of said town, and upon entering upon the discharge of their duties under this act, shall have power to authorize connections to be made therewith, and to establish rents for such connections and for the use of the said sewer system, and the time of payment thereof, as they may deem proper; and in their care and management of the said sewer system shall be governed by the same rules and regulations as are provided in the act above recited for the care and

government of the water system of said town, so far as the same shall be applicable thereto.

2. *And be it enacted*, That said water commissioners, after the passage of such ordinance or resolution, shall have authority to prescribe such rules, regulations, conditions and restrictions as to the connection with and use of the said sewer system as in their opinion may be proper or necessary, and shall have power to employ suitable and proper laborers, workmen, clerks, collectors and assistants in the conduct, management and care of said sewer system upon such terms as they may deem reasonable; *provided*, that no regular salaries shall be allowed or paid by said water commissioners to any employee until the agreement therefor shall have been first submitted to and approved by the board of commissioners or other governing body of said towns.

Commissioners authorized to prescribe rules and have power to employ laborers

Provided.

3. *And be it enacted*, That the rents for connections with and use of the said sewer system so fixed by the said water commissioners, shall draw interest from the time they become due, and shall be and remain, until paid, a lien upon the premises with which such sewer system shall be connected; and said water commissioners shall have similar remedies for the collection of said rents, with interest and costs, as the said towns have by law for collecting the expense of paving sidewalks in front of lots required to be paved in said towns, which remedies it shall be the duty of said water commissioners to enforce in all cases where the sewer rents shall be more than two years in arrear.

Rents draw interest from time due until paid, and are lien on premises

4. *And be it enacted*, That the said water commissioners shall cause a careful estimate to be made of the cost of managing, keeping in repair, and operating the said sewer system once in each and every year, and estimate approximately the rents to be collected therefrom, for the ensuing year, and shall report the same in writing to the board of commissioners or other governing body of said towns on the first Monday of April, each and every year.

Estimate to be made of cost of managing sewer system annually.

5. *And be it enacted*, That in case of any deficiency from the revenue of said sewer system to meet the expenses thereof and the principal and interest on the bonds issued to construct the same, as they may become due, then it shall be the duty of the board of commissioners or other

Case of deficiency three per centum to be added and assessed upon property governing body of said towns to add to such deficiency so reported three percentum of the cost of managing and keeping in repair and operating the said sewer system, to cover losses and contingencies, and to assess such deficiency and said three percentum so added as aforesaid, upon all the taxable property in said town in the same manner as other taxes are assessed, and said sums shall be collected by the collector and other officers of said towns, who are by law required to collect taxes, and if not paid by the time required by law for the payment of other town taxes, shall be collected by warrant, and by and in the same manner as other taxes are collected in said towns, and shall be a lien upon the property whereon the same are assessed in like manner as other taxes of the said towns.

Funds deposited in local banks.

6. *And be it enacted*, That it shall be the duty of the said water commissioners to keep all funds which may come to their hands on deposit with one or more of the banks located in said towns, and they shall draw said funds by checks to be signed by at least two of their members, which said checks shall specify briefly the purposes for which the same are drawn.

Receipts and disbursements, how kept open to inspection, &c.

7. *And be it enacted*, That it shall be the duty of the said water commissioners to keep an accurate account of the receipts and disbursements connected with said sewer system in proper books to be provided for that purpose, and which shall always be open for the inspection of the board of commissioners or other governing body of said town, and their authorized agents, and which accounts shall be annually, in the month of March, audited by a committee of said board of commissioners or other governing body and a short abstract thereof shall be published with the annual statement of the town finances.

Additional compensation of water commissioners.

8. *And be it enacted*, That in addition to the amount which the said water commissioners are now entitled by law to receive, they shall receive and be paid as full compensation for all time, attention, trouble, and labor bestowed by them upon said sewer system, the sum of fifty dollars each per year.

Repealer.

9. *And be it enacted*, That all acts and parts of acts inconsistent with this act be and the same are hereby repealed.

10. *And be it enacted*, That this act shall take effect immediately.

Approved February 8, 1893.

CHAPTER VII.

An Act concerning the location and erection of buildings for a city hall and the accommodation of the different officers and departments of the city government in cities of the first and second class in this state.

1. BE IT ENACTED *by the Senate and General Assembly of the State of New Jersey*, That all buildings, hereafter erected for a city hall and the accommodation of the different officers and departments of the city government in cities of the first and second class in this state, shall be so located and erected that there shall be an open and vacant space of ground of at least twenty-five feet in width on all sides of the same; *provided*, that this act shall not apply to the alteration and erection of additions to buildings now in use for such purposes. Buildings erected for a city hall shall have open and vacant space twenty-five feet in width on all sides

2. *And be it enacted*, That it shall not be lawful for the common council, board of aldermen, board of commissioners or other governing body having charge of the locating and erecting of any such buildings as are mentioned in section one of this act, in any city of the first and second class in this state, to expend any moneys for the erection and completion of the same unless the said buildings are located and erected as provided for in section one of this act. Not lawful for common council or other governing body to expend any moneys for erection of same unless as provided in section one

3. *And be it enacted*, That all acts or parts of acts inconsistent with the provisions of this act be and the same are hereby repealed in so far as their operation may conflict with this act. Repealer.

4. *And be it enacted*, That this act shall take effect immediately.

Approved February 13, 1893.

CHAPTER VIII.

An Act to authorize the boards of managers of cemetery associations to pass by-laws.

Board of managers, directors or trustees of cemetery associations may pass necessary by-laws, and may amend or repeal any by-laws.

1. BE IT ENACTED *by the Senate and General Assembly of the State of New Jersey*, That the board of managers, directors or trustees of any cemetery association, company or corporation of this state organized under any general or special law or laws, or the body having the management of any such cemetery, by whatever name such body may be known, may ordain, pass and put into execution such by-laws as they may judge to be necessary and convenient for carrying into effect the objects of the association and for regulating such association; and may amend or repeal any by-laws already in existence; *provided, however*, that no such change shall be made except by a vote of three-fourths of the total number of such managers, directors or trustees at a meeting thereof specially called to consider changes in the by-laws.

Proviso.

2. *And be it enacted*, That this act shall take effect immediately.

Approved February 14, 1893.

CHAPTER IX.

An Act to provide for the compensation of certain officers of the legislature.

1. BE IT ENACTED *by the Senate and General Assembly of the State of New Jersey*, That the second assistant engrossing clerk of the senate and the two assistant engrossing clerks of the house of assembly shall each receive as compensation, for the legislative session, the sum of six hundred dollars; the second assistant sergeant-at-arms of the senate, the sum of five hundred dollars for the legislative session; the assistant private secretary of the president of the senate the sum of five hundred dollars for the legislative session; the assistant bill clerk of the senate the sum of five hundred dollars for the legislative session; the clerks of the committees on judiciary, corporations, municipal corporations, revision of the laws, and railroads and canals, of the senate, the sum of three hundred dollars each for the legislative session; and to each assistant doorkeeper of the senate the sum of three hundred and fifty dollars each, and to such one of the assistant sergeants-at-arms of the house of assembly whose salary is not provided for by law, the sum of five hundred dollars; to each of the two assistant bill clerks of the house of assembly the sum of five hundred dollars; to the assistant private secretary of the speaker of the house of assembly the sum of four hundred dollars; the postmaster of the house of assembly, five hundred dollars; the officer assistant to the clerk of the house of assembly, four hundred dollars; to the clerks of the following committees of the house of assembly, viz, judiciary, corporations, bill revision, banks and insurance, boroughs and borough commissions, revision of the laws, railroads and canals, labor and industries, towns and townships, fisheries, ways and means, and municipal corporations, the sum of three hundred dollars each.

Fixing compensation of assistant engrossing clerks at $600

Second assistant sergeant-at-arms of senate at $500

Assistant private secretary of president of senate at $500

Assistant bill clerk of senate at $500

Clerks of senate committees at $300

Assistant doorkeepers of senate, $350

Assistant sergeant-at arms of the house of assembly at $500.

Assistant bill clerks of the house of assembly at $500

Assistant private secretary of the speaker at $400.

Postmaster of the house of assembly at $500.

Assistant to the clerk of the house of assembly at $400

Clerks of assembly committees at $300

To apply to the present session only.

2. *And be it enacted,* That this act shall take effect immediately, and shall apply to the present session of the legislature only.

Approved February 20, 1893.

CHAPTER X.

An Act in relation to the manner of paying teachers in the public schools of certain cities in this state, and giving the common council or other governing body power in relation thereto.

Governing body to provide by ordinance manner of payments to teachers of public schools.

1. BE IT ENACTED *by the Senate and General Assembly of the State of New Jersey,* That it shall be lawful for the common council or other governing body in any city of the first class of this state to provide by ordinance for the manner in which payments shall be made to teachers of the public schools in such cities, and for the form and manner in which warrants upon the public treasury of any such city shall be drawn and signed for this purpose; and all payments and disbursements made, and all warrants drawn in accordance with the terms of an ordinance duly passed for that purpose, in any such city, shall be deemed and taken to be in all respects regular and lawful.

Warrants drawn in accordance to terms of ordinance shall be lawful.

Repealer.

2. *And be it enacted,* That all acts and parts of acts inconsistent with this act be and the same are hereby repealed, and that this act shall take effect immediately.

Approved February 20, 1893.

CHAPTER XI.

An Act to amend an act entitled "An act respecting conveyances" (Revision), approved March twenty-seventh, one thousand eight hundred and seventy-four.

1. BE IT ENACTED *by the Senate and General Assembly of the State of New Jersey*, That section seventeen of the act to which this is amendatory be and the same is hereby amended to read as follows:

Section to be amended.

17. *And be it enacted*, That all such powers of attorney, being so acknowledged or proved and certified, shall and may be recorded with the clerks or registers of the several counties of this state, in suitable books to be provided for that purpose; and that the record of any such letters of attorney, heretofore made and executed, and acknowledged or proved, and certified and recorded as aforesaid, or hereafter to be made and executed, and acknowledged or proved, and certified and recorded as aforesaid and the transcript thereof, duly certified by the proper officer, shall be received in evidence in any court of this state, and have the same effect as if the original letter of attorney were then and there produced and proved.

Powers of attorney may be recorded with clerks or registers in suitable books provided for that purpose.

Transcript thereof duly certified shall be received in evidence in any court of this state.

2. *And be it enacted*, That this act shall take effect immediately.

Approved February 20, 1898.

CHAPTER XII.

An Act in relation to the state house and adjacent public grounds.

Superintendent of state house, how appointed and term.

1. BE IT ENACTED *by the Senate and General Assembly of the State of New Jersey*, That the state house and adjacent public grounds be and are hereby put under the care and safe keeping of some suitable person to be superintendent of the same, who shall be nominated and appointed by the governor, by and with the advice and consent of the senate, and commissioned by him, and shall continue in office for the term of five years from the date of his commission and until his successor is appointed and qualified.

Superintendent to have general supervision of buildings and grounds.

2. *And be it enacted*, That the doorkeepers of the two houses of the legislature, immediately after the legislature shall have adjourned, shall deliver to the said superintendent all the keys of their respective houses, which shall be safely kept in his office until the next meeting of the legislature; and when the courts held in the state house are not in session the keys of the respective court rooms shall be deposited with the said superintendent for safe keeping; that it shall be the duty of said superintendent to have the general supervision and care of the state house and said grounds, to preserve them from injury and to provide for their being kept in proper order; he shall also take care that the occupied parts of the state house be kept warm, ventilated, swept and cleaned, and he shall employ so many necessary assistants for that purpose, at such prices and upon such terms as the governor, attorney-general and state treasurer, or a majority of them shall approve; and he shall render monthly accounts to the state treasurer, and the state treasurer shall certify the same, and they shall thereupon be paid by the state treasurer on the warrant of the comptroller.

Shall employ assistants.

Render monthly accounts.

Distribution of laws, reports, &c.

3. *And be it enacted*, That hereafter the said superintendent shall have the distribution of the laws, law

reports, equity reports, the minutes, journal and proceedings of each house of the legislature and all other documents published under the authority or patronage of the state, and he shall transmit such copies to such person or persons as is now provided for by law, and he shall have the same supervision and control over such documents as the superintendent of the state house and adjacent public grounds now has.

4. *And be it enacted*, That the said superintendent shall receive an annual salary of three thousand dollars, to be paid by the treasurer upon the warrant of the comptroller out of the treasury of the state in monthly installments, to be computed from the day of the appointment of said superintendent. Annual salary.

5. *And be it enacted*, That the said superintendent before entering upon the execution of the duties of said office, shall take and subscribe the following oath, to wit: I, A. B., being appointed superintendent of the state house and adjacent public grounds, do solemnly promise and swear that I will justly and honestly keep the books, papers and writings to me committed, and to be committed by virtue of my said office, and that I will faithfully and honestly perform all the duties of the said office according to the best of my ability and understanding, so help me God. To take oath. Form of oath.

6. *And be it enacted*, That this oath, required by the preceding section of this act, shall be administered by a judge or justice of any court of record of this state. Oath, by whom administered.

7. *And be it enacted*, That the said superintendent, before entering upon the performance of the duties of his said office, shall enter into a bond to the state of New Jersey, with at least two sufficient sureties, being freeholders of this state, in the sum of five thousand dollars, conditioned for the faithful and honest performance of the duties of said office, the said bond to be approved by a judge or justice of any court of record of this state, and when so executed and approved, together with the oath or affirmation of office duly taken and subscribed, shall be recorded in the office of the secretary of state and filed in the same, to be by the secretary of state safely kept among the public papers of his office. To give bond. Bond to be approved, recorded and filed.

Repealer.

8. *And be it enacted*, That the act entitled "An act in relation to the state house and adjacent public grounds," approved February eighth, one thousand eight hundred and ninety-two, and all acts and parts of acts inconsistent with the provisions of this act, be and the same are hereby repealed.

9. *And be it enacted*, That this act shall be a public act, and shall take effect immediately.

Approved February 21, 1893.

CHAPTER XIII.

An Act to amend an act entitled "An act in relation to the appointment of sergeant-at-arms and criers to the several courts of the counties and fixing the salaries for the same," approved April seventh, one thousand eight hundred and ninety.

Section to be amended.

1. Be it enacted *by the Senate and General Assembly of the State of New Jersey*, That section one of the above entitled act be and the same is hereby amended to read as follows:

Supreme court justice authorized to appoint sergeant-at arms, also crier of circuit court.

1. Be it enacted *by the Senate and General Assembly of the State of New Jersey*, That the justice of the supreme court to whom a judicial district has been or may be assigned, and which judicial district comprises counties of the first class, is authorized to appoint in their respective judicial district a suitable person as sergeant-at-arms and also a suitable person as crier of the circuit court of said judicial district, to hold office during the pleasure of said justice, whose duties it shall be to attend daily upon the said courts in the county wherein appointed, during the several thereof, for which services the said sergeant-at-arms and said crier, in all counties of the first class having a population within their territorial limits exceeding

one hundred and fifty thousand inhabitants, shall each receive and be paid an annual compensation or salary of nine hundred dollars in lieu of any per diem compensation, such annual compensation or salary to be paid monthly by the county collector upon the certificate of the county clerk of such county; *provided, however*, that whenever it shall seem to be proper and advisable, under all the circumstances, to do so, the said justice of the supreme court may and hereby is authorized to order and fix, in lieu of the annual compensation herein provided for, for said sergeant-at-arms, such per diem allowance to him, not exceeding five dollars per day, as shall appear to said justice in the exercise of his discretion to be fair and reasonable to allow, but said per diem allowance shall be made and taken in lieu of all fees, perquisites and allowances whatever; same to be paid on certificate made as aforesaid, after a claim for the service rendered or claimed to be rendered by the claimant, verified by his oath, shall have been presented to such clerk.

Annual salary.

Paid monthly by county collector upon certificate of county clerk.

Supreme court justice may fix per diem allowance in lieu of annual salary.

How paid.

2. *And be it enacted*, That this act shall take effect immediately.

Approved February 21, 1893.

CHAPTER XIV.

An Act providing for the appointment of county collectors in the several counties of this state.

1. BE IT ENACTED, *by the Senate and General Assembly of the State of New Jersey*, That at the annual stated meetings of the board of chosen freeholders of the several counties of the first and second-class of this state, the said board shall appoint some fit person, being a freeholder and resident in such county, and not a member of such board, to the office of county collector, who shall hold his office for a term of three years and until his successor shall be

County collector to be appointed by board of chosen freeholders for term of three years.

To give bond. Proviso.

appointed and shall have given bond as required by law; *provided*, that the term of office of any person now holding the office of county collector of such county, shall continue until the expiration of the time for which such person was elected or appointed and no longer.

Vacancy, how filled.

2. *And be it enacted*, That in case any vacancy shall occur in the office of county collector, by death, removal, resignation, failure to give satisfactory bond or otherwise, the said board of chosen freeholders shall appoint a fit person as aforesaid to be such county collector, who shall hold said office until the next annual meeting of said board, and the appointment and giving bond by his successor.

Repealer.

3. *And be it enacted*, That all acts and parts of acts, general, special or local, inconsistent with the provisions of this act be and the same are hereby repealed, and this act shall be deemed a public act and shall take effect immediately.

Approved February 21, 1893.

CHAPTER XVI.

An Act concerning the maintaining of race courses in this state, and to provide for the licensing and regulating of the same.

Board of chosen freeholders or other body authorized to license owners of race courses.

1. Be it enacted *by the Senate and General Assembly of the State of New Jersey*, That the board of chosen freeholders of any county in this state, or the board of aldermen, common council, township committee or other body having general charge of the affairs of any city, township or municipal division of this state in which there is situated and maintained a race course for the racing, running, trotting or pacing of horses, mares or geldings for a purse, plate or other thing to be run, paced or trotted for by such horses, mares or geldings, shall

have power and is hereby authorized to license the owners of such race course to maintain and use the same for any running, racing, pacing or trotting of any horses, mares or geldings for any purse or stake, plate or other thing; such license shall be for a period of not more than five years, and no license shall be granted for the maintenance or use of a race course within the corporate limits of any city having a population of more than one hundred thousand people, according to the census last taken.

Period of license.

Owners, jockeys and trainers of horses allowed the privilege of entering, racing and training unless ruled off under rules or regulations.

2. *And be it enacted*, That the licenses provided for in this act shall be granted only upon the expressed condition that the owners and managers of the race course so licensed shall allow all owners, jockeys and trainers of horses, mares and geldings all the privileges of entering, racing and training horses, mares and geldings which shall be allowed to any other owners, jockeys or trainers, unless such owners, jockeys or trainers, or such horses, mares or geldings shall have been ruled off another race course within this state for fraudulent practices, or under some rule or regulation adopted by the owners of a majority of the licensed race courses in this state.

Unlawful to maintain or use a race course unless licensed.

3. *And be it enacted*, That it shall be unlawful for any person or incorporated body or association to maintain or use a race course in this state for the racing, running or trotting or pacing of horses, mares or geldings for a purse, plate or other thing, or to permit such running, racing, trotting or pacing upon any grounds owned or leased or controlled by such person or incorporated body or association unless a license for that purpose shall have been granted as in this act provided; any license granted under this act shall become void upon any breach of any condition upon which it shall be granted.

When license void.

Unlawful to maintain race course not used prior to January 1, 1893, unless file a resolution with secretary of state.

4. *And be enacted*, That it shall not be lawful for any person or incorporated body or association to maintain or use in this state for the running, trotting or pacing of horses, mares or geldings for a purse, plate or other thing to be run, paced or trotted for by such horses, mares or geldings any race course which was not used for such running, trotting or pacing prior to the first day of January, one thousand eight hundred and ninety-three, unless such person or incorporated body or association

shall first file with the secretary of state a certified copy of a resolution adopted by three-fourths of the members of the board of chosen freeholders of the county in which such race course is proposed to be maintained, which resolution shall declare that the maintaining of such race course is a public necessity.

Repealer

5. *And be it enacted*, That all acts and parts of acts inconsistent with this act are repealed, and this act shall take effect immediately.

Passed February 27, 1893.

CHAPTER XVII.

An Act to provide that betting and the practice and betting, commonly known as book-making, upon horse races within the enclosed grounds of any incorporate association or body in this state, or the keeping of a place or places within such grounds to which persons may resort for such betting, shall not constitute any misdemeanor or criminal offence when such association or incorporated body is not indictable for the carrying on of said races therein.

Book-making not a misdemeanor or criminal offence.

1. Be it enacted *by the Senate and General Assembly of the State of New Jersey*, That the practice, habitual or otherwise, of betting upon horse races, commonly known as book-making, or any of the acts of either betting or book-making upon horse races, or the keeping of a place or places to which persons may resort for such betting, shall not constitute a nuisance or the keeping of a disorderly house or a conspiracy or any other misdemeanor or criminal offence whatever, or the persons engaged therein be indictable when such betting or book-making is carried on or done within the exterior enclosure of the

grounds of any race course of any agricultural society or other incorporated body of this state, and wherein, for the running, racing, trotting or pacing of horses, mares or geldings for a purse, plate or other thing, the said society or incorporated body is not indictable; *and provided, further*, that such betting or book-making is carried on or done only on the days of the races of said society or body, and upon the races within such enclosure. Proviso.

2. *And be it enacted*, That all laws and parts of laws, both statutory and common, inconsistent with this statute, are hereby repealed, and that this act shall take effect immediately. Repealer.

Passed February 27, 1893.

CHAPTER XVIII.

Supplement to an act entitled "An act for the punishment of crimes" (Revision), approved March twenty-seventh, one thousand eight hundred and seventy-four.

1. BE IT ENACTED *by the Senate and General Assembly of the State of New Jersey*, That if any person or persons, or corporation or association shall within the exterior enclosure of the grounds of any race course of any licensed agricultural society or other licensed incorporated body of this state wherein, for the running, racing, trotting or pacing of horses, mares or geldings for a purse, plate or other thing, the said society or incorporated body is not indictable, shall in an indictable manner practice, habitually or otherwise, the betting upon horse races, commonly known as book-making, or any of the acts of either betting or book-making upon horse races within such enclosure or in an indictable manner keep a place or places within such enclosure to which persons may resort for such betting or book-making, such person or persons or corporation or asso- Book-making a misdemeanor punishable by fine not exceeding twenty dollars.

R—

ciation shall be deemed guilty of a misdemeanor, and shall upon conviction be punished by a fine not exceeding twenty dollars, but such person or persons, corporation or association shall not, for such practice, habitual or otherwise, of betting or book-making, or of keeping a place or places within such enclosure to which persons may resort for such book-making or betting, or for authorizing or permitting such book-making or betting within such enclosure, be deemed guilty of maintaining a disorderly house, or maintaining a nuisance, or of conspiracy or of any criminal offence whatever, except as in this section provided.

Persons who resort to book-making not guilty of maintaining a disorderly house

Repealer.

2. *And be it enacted*, That all parts of the act to which this is a supplement, and all laws and parts of laws, both statutory and common, inconsistent with the provisions of this statute, are hereby repealed, and that this act shall take effect immediately.

Passed February 27, 1893.

CHAPTER XIX.

A Further Supplement to an act entitled "An act authorizing the establishment of hospitals in the cities of this state," approved February twenty-third, one thousand eight hundred and eighty-three.

Management and control of hospitals vested in the board of health.

1. Be it enacted *by the Senate and General Assembly of the State of New Jersey*, That from and after the first day of May, one thousand eight hundred and ninety-three, the management and control of all hospitals established under the authority of the act to which this is a supplement, and all thereafter established, shall pass to and be vested in the board of health of the city or cities wherein any such hospital has been or may be established, and the term or terms of the present board of control or direction shall thereafter cease and determine.

2. *And be it enacted*, That all the power and authority given by the said act, or any act supplementary thereto, to such board of control or direction, shall thereafter pass to and be vested in such board of health, and such board of health shall be charged with all the duties by the said act or acts imposed upon such board of control or direction. Power and authority vested in board of health.

3. *And be it enacted*, That all acts or parts of acts inconsistent with this act be and the same are hereby repealed, and that this act shall take effect immediately. Repealer.

Passed February 27, 1893.

CHAPTER XX.

A Further Supplement to an act entitled "A further supplement to an act entitled 'An act to regulate elections,'" approved April eighteenth, one thousand eight hundred and seventy-six, which supplement was approved May twenty-eighth, one thousand eight hundred and ninety.

1. BE IT ENACTED *by the Senate and General Assembly of the State of New Jersey*, That in any township or borough in this state where the election districts have been renumbered, or the boundary lines of the same have been changed, or wherein new election district or districts have been formed by the township committee of any such township, or the governing body of any such borough, it shall be the duty of the county board of registry to immediately appoint, in the manner provided in section two of the act of which this is a supplement, a registry board for each election district in such township or borough, and said registry board so appointed shall hold office until the first day of June next ensuing, when their successors shall be appointed; and said board of registry, so ap- County board of registry to appoint a registry board for each election district. Term of office and when successors appointed.

pointed in each election district, shall proceed in the manner prescribed in the act to which this is a supplement, except that when the next election shall be an election for township or borough officers, then such board shall proceed to make a new register in the same manner as provided in the act to which this is a supplement, for the making a register of the voters at the election held for the members of the general assembly, which registry, when made, shall be used at such township or borough election.

Duties of said board of registry

2. *And be it enacted*, That this act shall take effect immediately.

Approved February 27, 1893.

CHAPTER XXI.

A Supplement to an act entitled "An act for the government and regulation of the State prison," approved April twenty-first; one thousand eight hundred and seventy-six.

Compensation of secretary of board of inspectors of state prison.

1. Be it enacted *by the Senate and General Assembly of the State of New Jersey*, That the secretary of the board of inspectors of the New Jersey state prison shall receive an annual salary of five hundred dollars for his services as secretary of said board, to be paid to him by the treasurer of this state, by warrant of the comptroller.

2. *And be it enacted*, That this act shall take effect immediately.

Passed February 27, 1893.

CHAPTER XXII.

An Act respecting the fees and compensation of the clerks of the several counties of this state, and repealing all acts providing for the payment of a fixed salary in lieu of fees.

1. BE IT ENACTED *by the Senate and General Assembly of the State of New Jersey*, That hereafter the clerks of the several counties of this state, and the clerks of the civil and criminal courts therein, shall be entitled to demand and receive such fees and compensation as are now established by law. Compensation of the clerks of counties of this state.

2. *And be it enacted*, That this act shall only apply to those clerks of the several counties of this state and the clerks of the civil and criminal courts therein whose term of office shall hereafter commence, or to those now in office who may file their assent in writing, under their hands, to the provisions of this act, in the office of the clerk of the county in which he is such clerk. Clerks may file their assent in writing

3. *And be it enacted*, That all acts and parts of acts which requires or permits the payment of a fixed and stated salary to any of such clerks in lieu of fees, whether such acts be general, special or local, or which are in conflict with this act, be and the same are hereby repealed. Repealer.

4. *And be it enacted*, That this act shall take effect immediately.

Approved February 27, 1893.

CHAPTER XXIII.

A Supplement to an act entitled "An act concerning the government of certain cities in this state and constituting a municipal board of public works and other officers therein, and defining the powers and duties of such boards and relating to the municipal affairs and departments of such cities placed under the control and management of such board and providing for the maintenance of said board," approved March twenty-third, one thousand eight hundred and ninety-two.

Section to be amended.

1. BE IT ENACTED *by the Senate and General Assembly of the State of New Jersey*, That section three of the act to which this is a supplement be and the same is hereby amended so as to read as follows:

Board to open, grade, pave and improve streets.

Power to make rules, regulations and ordinances to regulate, prevent and remove obstructions upon streets and sidewalks at expense of owner of premises, to provide for street improvements and to prevent tearing up of streets

3. *And be it enacted*, That the board of public works of any city herein authorized shall have power by ordinance to lay out, open, grade, pave, repave, improve and vacate the streets and alleys within the corporate limits of any such city in like manner as the same now are laid out, opened, graded, paved, repaved, improved and vacated in any such city by existing laws, and to make all sewer constructions, connections, alterations, repairs and improvements in like manner as the same now are constructed, connected, altered, repaired and improved in any such city by existing laws, and to construct, repair, maintain, control and operate all public works, and to control the public water supply and the distribution, sale and use of the water, and of the collection of water rents and charges of such city in like manner as the same now are constructed, repaired, maintained, controlled and operated, and said board shall have the power to make, alter and amend rules, regulations and ordinances to regulate, prevent and remove obstructions and encumbrances in and upon the streets and sidewalks; to enforce

the removal of snow and ice from the sidewalks and gutters thereof by the owners and occupants of the premises fronting thereon; to regulate and prevent the throwing and depositing of ashes, offal, dirt, garbage and other refuse and material in the streets; to regulate and prevent the erection and construction of any stoop, step, platform, cellar, area, sign, post or any obstruction or projection in, over and upon any street or avenue, and to remove the same at the expense of the owner or occupant of the premises; to provide for and regulate street improvements, cross-walks, curbstones, gutters and sidewalks; to regulate and prevent the tearing up of streets for the purpose of laying water, gas and sewer pipes, and making house connections therewith, and the laying of conduits for electric wires; to regulate the speed of vehicles; to grant franchises and licenses relating to the use of streets; and said board shall and may enforce obedience to all such ordinances relating to the above enumerated powers by the imposition of fines not exceeding fifty dollars or by imprisonment not exceeding thirty days, or by both; any ordinance of the city now in force relating to any of the above enumerated objects shall continue in force and operation until repealed or modified by said board.

Power to grant franchises and licenses.

Shall enforce obedience to all such ordinances by imposition of fines

2. *And be it enacted*, That section seven of the act to which this is a supplement be and the same is hereby amended so as to read as follows:

Section to be amended

7. *And be it enacted*, That it shall be the duty of the common council, board of aldermen or other governing body or board having charge of the finances of the cities subject to the provisions of this act, each and every year hereafter, to levy a tax of two and one-eighth mills on each dollar on all taxable property in such city, such tax to be levied and collected as and with the general taxes of the city, and to be known as the fund for the board of public works, and shall be used by said board of public works for the purpose of repairing, cleaning and improving streets, the repairing and cleaning of sewers, the repairing and building of receiving basins, for drains and sewers for sanitary purposes; and all repairing and cleaning of such other property entrusted to the care and custody of said board under this act and the supple-

Council to levy a tax on all taxable property, to be collected with the general taxes, to be known as the fund for board of public works, to be used for repairing, &c., property entrusted to care of said board.

Fund to be in lieu of all other appropriations

ments thereto; and said fund shall be in lieu of all other appropriations for the purposes aforesaid, to be made by such body or board, except that in case the public water-supply for the city is leased or obtained from a private corporation, then a sum equal to the amount paid for such supply for the last fiscal year shall also be inserted in the annual tax ordinance, and shall with the said fund be placed to the credit of said board of public works, and expended by them as provided in this act.

Repealer

3. *And be it enacted*, That all acts and parts of acts inconsistent herewith be and the same are hereby repealed, and that this act shall take effect immediately.

Approved February 28, 1893.

CHAPTER XXIV.

An Act to amend an act entitled "An act for suppressing vice and immorality" (Revision), Approved March twenty-seventh, one thousand eight hundred and seventy-four.

Not unlawful to print and sell newspapers, milk, &c., on the Sabbath.

1. BE IT ENACTED *by the Senate and General Assembly of the State of New Jersey*, That from and after the passage of this act it shall not be unlawful for any person or corporation, on the christian Sabbath, or first day of the week, commonly called Sunday, to print, publish and sell newspapers, to sell and deliver milk, or to walk, ride or drive for recreation, and to hire horses and carriages or other conveyances for riding or driving; *provided, however*, that the board of aldermen, common council, township committee or other governing body of the municipalities, or incorporated camp meeting associations of this state shall have the power to adopt such ordinances or rules as they may deem necessary and proper to regulate or prohibit the acts hereby made lawful, and may pre-

Governing bodies of municipalities or incorporated camp meeting associations have power to regulate or prohibit same and prescribe fines and penalties for violation of same.

scribe fines and penalties for the violation of the same, which shall be enforced and collected in the same manner as is now provided by law for the violation of other ordinances and rules of such municipalities or associations.

Repealer.

2. *And be it enacted*, That all acts or parts of acts inconsistent with the provisions of this act be and the same are hereby repealed.

3. *And be it enacted*, That this act shall take effect immediately.

Approved February 28, 1893.

CHAPTER XXV.

An Act to amend an act entitled "A supplement to an act entitled 'An act to regulate fishing with seines in Barnegat bay,'" passed February seventeenth, one thousand eight hundred and forty-two, passed April twenty-first, one thousand eight hundred and seventy-six.

Section to be amended.

1. BE IT ENACTED *by the Senate and General Assembly of the State of New Jersey*, That section two of the act entitled "A supplement to an act entitled 'An act to regulate fishing with seines in Barnegat bay,'" passed February seventeenth, one thousand eight hundred and forty-two, which said supplement was passed April twenty-first, one thousand eight hundred and seventy-six, be and the same is hereby amended so as to read as follows, to wit:

Unlawful to set or use any net, &c., for taking fish from waters of Barnegat bay, &c

2. *And be it enacted*, That it shall not be lawful for any person or persons to set or use any net or nets, or stationary device whatever, for the purpose of taking fish from the aforesaid waters of Barnegat bay, and its tributaries below a line across said tributaries two hundred and fifty yards from the mouths thereof.

Section to be amended.

2. *And be it enacted*, That section three of said act shall read as follows, to wit:

Unlawful to haul any seine, &c., for taking fish from waters of Barnegat bay, &c.

3. *And be it enacted*, That it shall not be lawful for any person or persons to haul any seine, or other moving net or device for the purpose of taking fish from the aforesaid waters of Barnegat bay, and its tributaries below a line across said tributaries two hundred and fifty yards from the mouths thereof.

Repealer.

3. *And be it enacted*, That all acts and parts of acts inconsistent with this act, be and the same are hereby repealed, and that this act shall take effect immediately.

Approved February 28, 1893.

CHAPTER XXVI.

An Act to amend an act entitled "An act providing for sewerage in and from certain towns in this state," approved April twentieth, one thousand eight hundred and eighty-six.

Section to be amended.

1. Be it enacted *by the Senate and General Assembly of the State of New Jersey*, That section five of an act entitled "An act providing for sewerage in and from certain towns in this state," approved April twentieth, one thousand eight hundred and eighty-six, be amended so as to read as follows:

Notice of filing reports, &c., to be published.

5. *And be it enacted*, That after the filing of said report and map or maps, said town council or other governing body shall cause a notice of the filing of said plans, maps, estimates and report to be given by publication in one or more daily or weekly newspapers circulating in the neighborhood of the lands in the said drainage area, for at least three weeks, once in each week, and posting a like notice in ten conspicuous places in the said drainage area for the same period; and that the owners of the lands in said town lying within said drainage area may or can within thirty days after the date of said notice, file with the clerk of said town their written dissent to said

Owners of land may dissent to proposed sewers, &c.

proposed sewer or sewers, laterals and appurtenances, and unless the owners of a majority of the lands in said town lying within said drainage area shall dissent thereto as aforesaid within said thirty days, the said town council or other governing body of said town shall have the right, if deemed for the best interests of said town or any portion or portions thereof, and all the necessary power and authority is hereby granted to make and enter into a contract or agreement in the name of said town, either with said owner or owners, or jointly with the said land owner or owners, with any other person or persons for the construction, by said land owner or owners or such other person or persons, of such sewer or sewers and necessary laterals and appurtenances, upon such conditions, in such manner and of such style, size, dimensions and details as set forth in said plans and maps, mutually determined upon as aforesaid and at such cost as may be agreed upon, and for the payment by said town to said land owner or owners, or such other person or persons of such proportionate part of the cost thereof as may also be agreed upon; *provided, however*, that the amount agreed to be paid by said town shall not exceed the proportion of the estimated cost which should be borne and paid by said town, as set forth in the aforesaid report made by said commissioners; *and provided, further*, that if in the progress of said work a change in the line of said sewer, as originally set and laid on the map and plans, filed as aforesaid, be considered advisable by the unanimous consent of all parties in interest, who shall have executed and delivered the said contract or agreement for the construction of the sewer or sewers therein specified, the town council or other governing body of said town shall have the necessary power and authority to agree to the change in the line of said sewer and in the terms and conditions of the contract or agreement aforesaid theretofore entered into, and shall have power and authority to enter into such further or additional contract or contracts, agreement or agreements, for the additional expense incurred by such change in the line of the sewer, as set out on said maps and plans so filed, and in the name of the town to enter into such additional contract or agreement, either with the land owner or

Town council may enter into contract for construction of sewers, &c.

Proviso.

Proviso.

owners, or jointly with the said land owner or owners, with any other person or persons, for the completion of said sewer originally contracted for on a line different from that originally proposed and set out in the plans theretofore filed, and upon such terms and conditions and in such manner and of such style, size, dimensions and details as to the work and material additionally to be contracted for, and such costs as may be mutually agreed upon between the parties to said original contract or agreement, and for the payment to said land owner or owners, or other person or persons contracted with, of such proportionate share thereof as shall have theretofore been fixed by the commissioners aforesaid; *and provided*, that said additional work and material shall not increase the proportionate share of the expense thereof to be borne by said town beyond thirty per centum of the amount agreed to be paid by the original contract or agreement; *and provided further*, that a map and plans of such intended change and the terms, conditions, details and price intended to be paid for such additional work and material, be filed in the office of the clerk of said town, there to remain at least thirty days, and that public notice of the filing of the map and plans, showing such intended change, and of the details, conditions, price and terms for which such additional contract or agreement is to be entered into, be given in one or more daily or weekly papers circulating in the neighborhood of the lands in the said drainage area, and for at least three weeks, once in each week, and that the owners of the lands in the said town within the drainage area may or can, within thirty days after the date of said notice, file with the clerk of said town their written dissent to said proposed change in the plans and contract, and unless the owners of a majority of the lands lying within said drainage area shall so dissent thereto within said thirty days, the said town shall have the right to enter into such contract or agreement for such additional labor and materials upon the terms, conditions, details and at the prices specified in said plans and specifications so filed as aforesaid as it may deem advisable, and may agree thereto jointly with the said land owner or owners, or other person or persons, jointly with them, anything in any law

Proviso

Proviso.

contained to the contrary notwithstanding; *and provided*, Proviso. that the expense of preparing the plans and specifications and other necessary expenses attending the said additional contract or agreement and change therein, be borne and paid by all parties interested, in the same proportion as payments are made to the contractor or contractors under said original contract or agreement aforesaid; *and provided further*, Proviso that any such sewer shall not be constructed so as to at any time empty into or discharge any of its contents into any creek, stream, lake, pond or water course, the waters of which are used for or connect with the waters of any river, creek, stream, lake, pond or water course used for the supply of water to any acqueduct, water-main or reservoir of any city, town, township or municipality in this state.

2. *And be it enacted*, That section six of said act be Section to be amended. amended so as to read as follows:

6. *And be it enacted*, That no contract, as provided for Contracts to be advertised. in section five of this act, shall be made and entered into between said town and said land owner or owners, jointly of the one part, and any other person or persons of the other part, excepting upon advertisements in one or more newspapers printed and published in the county wherein said town is located, for proposals for furnishing all the materials and doing all the required work, but said town and said land owner or owners shall be under no obligation to award the said contract to the lowest bidder, and may, if deemed for their best interest, reject all bids; *and provided further, however*, that no advertisement for Proviso proposals for furnishing such additional labor and material, caused by said change in the line of the sewer and in the plans and specifications for said sewer, as provided for in the preceding section, shall be necessary, but that the filing of said plans and specifications under said additional contract intended to be made, and the notice provided for by publication in the preceding section shall be sufficient to authorize, and hereby does authorize, said town to enter into such additional contract for said additional work and material according to said change and plans and the specifications filed.

3. *And be it enacted*, That all acts and parts of acts Repealer. inconsistent with this act be and the same are hereby

repealed, and that the provisions of this act shall apply to contracts or agreements made before this act takes effect, under which work has been partially performed.

4. *And be it enacted*, That this act shall take effect immediately.

Approved February 28, 1898.

CHAPTER XXVII.

An Act for the protection of certain kinds of birds, animals and fish, and to provide a procedure to recover penalties for the violation hereof.

When unlawful to kill and have in possession any buck, doe, &c.

1. BE IT ENACTED *by the Senate and General Assembly of the State of New Jersey*, That it shall not be lawful to pursue, take, kill or have unlawfully in possession any buck, doe, fawn or wild deer, except only between the fourteenth day of October and the sixteenth day of December in any year, under a penalty of one hundred dollars for each buck, doe, fawn or wild deer so killed, pursued or had unlawfully in possession.

Penalty.

When unlawful to kill, &c., any squirrel.

2. *And be it enacted*, That hereafter it shall not be lawful for any person or persons to capture, kill, or have unlawfully in possession after the same has been taken or killed, any gray, black or fox squirrel, except only between the fourteenth day of September and the sixteenth day of December in any year, under a penalty of twenty dollars for each gray, black or fox squirrel so taken, killed or had unlawfully in possession.

Penalty.

When unlawful to kill, &c., any quail, hare or rabbit.

3. *And be it enacted*, That hereafter it shall not be lawful for any person or persons to capture, kill, or have unlawfully in possession after the same has been taken or killed, any quail or any hare (commonly called rabbit) except only between the last day of October and the sixteenth day of December in any year, under a penalty of

twenty dollars for each quail or rabbit so taken, killed or had unlawfully in possession. Penalty.

4. *And be it enacted*, That hereafter it shall not be lawful for any person or persons to capture, kill, or have unlawfully in possession after the same has been taken or killed, any rufled grouse (commonly called partridge), except only between the last day of September and the sixteenth day of December in any year, under a penalty of twenty dollars for each ruffed grouse so taken, killed or had unlawfully in possession. When unlawful to kill, &c., ruffed grouse or partridge. Penalty.

5. *And be it enacted*, That hereafter it shall not be lawful for any person or persons to capture, kill, or have unlawfully in possession after the same has been taken or killed, any woodcock, except only during the month of July and between the last day of September and the sixteenth day of December in any year, under a penalty of twenty dollars for each woodcock so taken, killed or had unlawfully in possession. When unlawful to kill, &c., Woodcock. Penalty.

6. *And be it enacted*, That hereafter it shall not be lawful for any person or persons to capture, kill, or have unlawfully in possession after the same has been taken or killed, any Wilson snipe (commonly called English or gray snipe), except only during the months of March and April and also between the twenty-fifth day of August and the sixteenth day of December in any year, under a penalty of twenty dollars for each Wilson snipe so taken, killed or had unlawfully in possession. When unlawful to kill, &c., Wilson snipe, English or gray snipe. Penalty.

7. *And be it enacted*, That hereafter it shall not be lawful for any person or persons to capture, kill, or have unlawfully in possession after the same has been taken or killed, any reed bird, rail bird or any marsh hen, except only between the twenty-fifth day of August and the sixteenth day of December in any year, under a penalty of twenty dollars for each and every bird so taken, killed or had unlawfully in possession. When unlawful to kill, &c., any reed bird, rail bird or marsh hen. Penalty.

8. *And be it enacted*, That hereafter it shall not be lawful for any person or persons to capture, kill, or have unlawfully in possession after the same has been taken or killed, any upland or grass plover, except only between the last day of July and the sixteenth day of December in any year, under the penalty of twenty dollars for each When unlawful to kill, &c., any upland or grass plover. Penalty

upland or grass plover so taken, killed or had unlawfully in possession.

When unlawful to kill, &c., any pinnated grouse (prairie chicken) or wild turkey

9. *And be it enacted*, That hereafter it shall not be lawful for any person or persons to capture, kill, or have unlawfully in possession after the same has been taken or killed, any pinnated grouse (commonly called prairie chicken) or any wild turkey, except only between the last day of October and the sixteenth day of December in any year, under the penalty of twenty dollars for each pinnated grouse (commonly called prairie chicken) or wild turkey so taken, killed or had unlawfully in possession.

Penalty.

When unlawful to kill, &c., any hen European partridge, hen European grouse or hen European pheasant.

10. *And be it enacted*, That hereafter it shall not be lawful for any person or persons to capture, kill, or have unlawfully in possession after the same has been taken or killed, any hen European partridge, hen European grouse or hen European pheasant within five years after the passage of this act, under a penalty of twenty dollars for each hen European partridge, grouse or pheasant so taken, killed or had unlawfully in possession.

Penalty.

When unlawful to kill, &c., any male English pheasant, partridge or grouse.

11. *And be it enacted*, That it shall not be lawful for any person or persons to capture, kill, or have unlawfully in possession after the same has been taken or killed, any male English pheasant, European partridge or grouse, except only between the last day of October and the sixteenth day of December in any year, under a penalty of twenty dollars for each male bird aforesaid so taken, killed or had unlawfully in possession.

Penalty.

Unlawful to kill, &c., any night hawk, meadow lark, robin, &c.

12. *And be it enacted*, That hereafter it shall not be lawful for any person or persons to capture, kill, or have unlawfully in possession after the same has been taken or killed, or to trap or to expose for sale, any night hawk, whip-poor-will, thrush, meadow lark, finch, martin, barn swallow, wood-pecker, robin, oriole, red or cardinal bird, cedar bird, tanager or any other insectivorous bird, under a penalty of twenty dollars for every bird so killed, trapped, exposed for sale or had unlawfully in possession; *provided, however*, that nothing in this section shall be so construed as to prevent individuals from taking or killing English sparrows, cranes, hawks, crows, ravens, crow-black birds or king fishers; and this section shall not apply to persons killing birds for scientific purposes; *provided*,

Penalty.

Proviso.

Proviso.

they shall first have obtained a permit as hereinafter provided.

Unlawful to kill, take or capture, on own property or property of another, any doe, buck, &c., any partridge, quail, pheasant, &c , or snipe or reed bird, &c., by any trap, snare, &c

13. *And be it enacted*, That it shall not be lawful for any person or persons at any time, either on his own property or on the property of another, to kill, take or capture any doe, buck, fawn or other sort of deer whatsoever, or any partridge, quail, pheasant or grouse of any kind whatsoever, or any snipe, reed bird or rail bird, by means of any blind, trap, snare, net or device whatever, or to set the same for the purpose herein mentioned, under the penalty of twenty dollars for each and every animal or bird so trapped, snared or taken or for any trap, snare or net so set; *provided, however*, that nothing in this act shall be so construed as to prevent incorporated associations from gathering alive with nets or traps any animal or animals, bird or birds for the purpose of propagating or preserving them alive during the winter, providing that they be released again in this state the following spring, not later than the fifteenth day of April.

Penalty.

Proviso.

When persons liable to penalties.

14. *And be it enacted*, That no person or persons shall kill, shoot or hunt any of the birds or animals mentioned in this act on his own property or the property of any other person, except during the season and at such times and in such manner as provided in this act, and any person or persons so doing shall be liable to the penalties provided for by said act for violation thereof.

Unlawful to have, sell or have for sale any hare, rabbit, squirrel, &c , after same has been caught by means of any snare, trap, &c.

15. *And be it enacted*, That it shall not be lawful for any person or persons to have in possession, sell or have for sale, any hare, rabbit, squirrel, quail, pheasant, woodcock, reed bird, rail bird, plover or duck, after the same has been caught or trapped by means of any snare, snoods, trap or device of any account or description whatsoever, under the penalty of twenty dollars for every animal or bird had in possession, sold or exposed for sale.

Penalty.

Unlawful to hunt for rabbits with ferrets, &c.

16. *And be it enacted*, That it shall not be lawful for any person or persons to hunt for rabbits with ferrets, or to capture or kill any rabbit or hare by means of any ferret or ferrets, under a penalty of twenty dollars for each hare or rabbit so hunted or killed.

Penalty.

Unlawful to hunt with gun, &c , or to fish on the Sabbath, except.

17. *And be it enacted*, That it shall not be lawful for any person or persons to hunt with a gun, or with a dog and gun, or with any fire arms, or weapons, or to fish with

hook and line, or in manner whatsoever on the Sabbath day (commonly called Sunday), except those who observe the seventh day of the week as the Sabbath, hunting upon their own property, under a penalty of twenty dollars for each and every offence.

Penalty.

Unlawful to rob or destroy the eggs or nest of any wild birds. Penalty.

18. *And be it enacted*, That it shall not be lawful for any person or persons to rob or destroy the eggs or nest of any wild bird whatever, under the penalty of twenty dollars for each and every offence.

Fish commissioners may issue permits to collect birds' nests or eggs. Term of permit.

19. *And be it enacted*, That the fish and game commissioners of this state may issue permits to any properly accredited person of eighteen years or upwards, permitting the holder thereof to collect birds, their nests or eggs for strictly scientific purposes only; such permits shall be in force for one year from the date of issue, and shall not be transferable.

Unlawful to hunt geese, duck, &c., to place boat, &c., at distance more than one hundred feet from ice, marsh, &c., or to pursue them with light at night. Penalty.

20. *And be it enacted*, That it shall not be lawful for any person or persons hunting or gunning after geese, duck or brant to place the boat or sink box or other floating vessel in which he lies in wait to kill said geese, duck or brant at a distance of more than one hundred feet from ice, or from marsh, or meadow, or heaped seaweed, or sand bank not covered with water at high tide; neither shall it be lawful for any person with intent to capture or kill geese or ducks to hunt after or pursue them with a light at night, and every person so offending against the provisions of this section shall for each and every offense forfeit and pay the sum of twenty dollars.

Unlawful to shoot at any goose, duck &c., from any sail or steamboat or vessel anchored or staked. Penalty.

21. *And be it enacted*, That it shall not be lawful for any person or persons to sail for, to shoot or shoot at any goose, brant or duck from any boat or boats, vessel or vessels, propelled by steam or sail, or from any boat or boats, vessel or vessels, or similar structure or structures anchored or staked upon the waters of this state, under the penalty of twenty dollars for each and every offence.

Unlawful to kill any goose, duck, &c., with swivel or punt gun, or to set any net.

22. *And be it enacted*, That it shall not be lawful for any person or persons to kill any goose, brant or duck with any device or instrument known as a swivel or punt gun, or with any other gun than such guns as are held at arms' length and fired from the shoulder without other rests, or to use or set any net, device, instrument or gun other than such gun as aforesaid, with intent to capture

or kill any goose, brant or duck, under the penalty of twenty dollars for each and every offence.

23. *And be it enacted*, That it shall not be lawful for any person or persons to take, kill, shoot at, or expose for sale or have unlawfully in possession any goose, duck. brant or other web-footed wild fowl, except only between the last day of August and the first day of May in each and every year, under the penalty of twenty dollars for every goose, duck, brant or other web-footed wild fowl so taken, killed, shot at, exposed for sale or had unlawfully in possession.

Unlawful to kill any goose, duck, &c, except between last day of August and first day of May.

Penalty.

24. *And be it enacted*, That it shall not be lawful for any person or persons to catch, kill, take or have unlawfully in possession any black bass, or Oswego bass, except only between and including the thirtieth day of May and the first day of December in any year, under a penalty of twenty dollars for each fish so caught, killed, taken or had unlawfully in possession.

Unlawful to catch, kill, &c, any black bass or Oswego bass except only between and including thirtieth day of May and first of December.

Penalty.

25. *And be it enacted*, That it shall not be lawful for any person or persons to catch, kill or have unlawfully in possession any brook trout, except only between the first day of March and the fifteenth day of July in any year. under the penalty of twenty dollars for each fish so caught, killed, taken or had unlawfully in possession.

Unlawful to catch, kill, &c., any brook trout except between first day of March and fifteenth day of July.

Penalty.

26. *And be it enacted*, That it shall not be lawful for any person or persons at any time to catch, kill, sell, expose for sale, or have in possession, any black bass measuring less than nine inches in length, or any trout measuring less than six inches in length, except for the use of stocking waters of this state therewith, and on license in writing first obtained for that purpose under the hand of one of the fish and game commissioners of this state, under the penalty of twenty dollars for each fish so caught, killed, sold, or exposed for sale or had unlawfully in possession.

Unlawful to catch, kill, &c, any black bass less than nine inches in length or any trout less than six inches in length except for use of stocking waters of this state, &c.

Penalty.

27. *And be it enacted*, That it shall not be lawful for any person or persons, either on his own land or the land of any other person, at any time whatsoever, either by day or by night, to put, place or haul any gill, drift, fyke or other net or nets, or any eel pot or pots, basket or baskets, or any other contrivance whatever for the taking or catching of fish in any of the waters of this state above tide

Unlawful to place or haul gill or fyke nets, &c., above tide water, or waters inhabited by bass, pickerel, pike and trout, &c.

water, or to keep any gill, drift, fyke or other net or nets, or any eel pot or pots, basket or baskets, or any contrivance whatever for the taking or catching of fish in any of the said waters mentioned, or to catch or assist in taking or catching any fish in manner aforesaid, or to put, place, haul or keep, or assist in putting, placing, hauling or keeping in any of said waters any of the aforementioned contrivances therefor, or to spear any game fish in any of the aforesaid mentioned waters, or sell or expose for sale or have unlawfully in possession after the same has been killed, any fish caught by any contrivance prohibited by this section, or to place, keep or use any set line or lines in waters inhabited by bass, pickerel, pike or trout, under a penalty of not less than twenty dollars nor more than two hundred and fifty dollars for each and every offence, at the discretion of the justice of the peace, police magistrate or district court before whom said conviction is had; *provided*, that said penalty shall not apply to the legitimate catching of fish commonly called minnows for bait with a seine not over sixteen feet in length, if the young of bass, pickerel, perch, trout and other species of fish known as game fish be not destroyed thereby, or to the catching of fish at any time by or under the orders in writing of the fish and game commissioners of this state; or to the legitimate catching of minnows for bait with a net over sixteen feet in length, provided a special permit in writing be first obtained from the fish and game commissioners; *and provided further*, that this penalty shall not apply to the owners or lessees of private ponds which are in no manner runways for migratory fish; *and provided further*, that this section shall not apply to the river Delaware.

Penalty.

Proviso.

Proviso.

Proviso.

Unlawful to use boats, traps, nets, &c.

28. *And be it enacted*, That if any person or persons shall be found making use of any boat or boats, vessel or vessels, or of any seine, gill, drift, anchor or sink nets, fixed nets, trap, pot, pound, set line, fyke, weirs or other apparatus for the unlawful taking of fish in any waters within the jurisdiction of this state contrary to the intent and meaning of this act, he, she or they shall, in addition to the penalties prescribed, forfeit the boat or boats, vessel or vessels, seine or seines, net or nets, gill or gills, drift or drifts, draw net or nets, fyke or fykes, trap or

Additional penalties.

traps, pot or pots, pound or pounds, weir or weirs, set line or lines or other apparatus so unlawfully used; and it shall be the duty of any constable, sheriff, fish and game protector, deputy fish and game protector or fish warden, or it may be lawful for any other person or persons to seize and secure any of the aforesaid apparatus unlawfully had, and immediately thereafter to give notice to some justice of the peace, district court or other magistrate of the county where said seizure shall have been made, and said justice of the peace, district court or other magistrate is hereby required and authorized at such time and place as he shall appoint, to hear and determine in a summary manner whether the same was so unlawfully used, and if it shall appear to his satisfaction that the same was used unlawfully, to make an order directing that the same be declared confiscated and forfeited to the use of the game and fish commissioners of this state, who may destroy the same or sell the same at public outcry; the proceeds of such sale, after deducting all legal costs and charges, shall be paid one-third to the fish and game commissioners, one-third to the person making the complaint, and one-third to the person furnishing the necessary evidence.

29. *And be it enacted*, That it shall not be lawful for any person or persons to take or catch with hook, line and rod or with spoon or scroll in the manner usually known as trolling, or in any other manner, from any lake, pond or stream, any fish of the kind with which such lake, pond or stream of this state is or may hereafter be stocked by the fish and game commissioners of this state or by private individuals, for three years from the time such stock fish are introduced into such lake, pond or stream, under a penalty of twenty dollars for each fish so caught or taken.

Unlawful to fish by trolling in waters stocked by fish commissioners.

Penalty.

30. *And be it enacted*, That it shall not be lawful for any person or persons to place in any pond, lake, river, stream or in any of the waters of this state any dynamite, giant or electric powder or any explosive substance whatever, or any drug or medicated bait for the purpose of taking or killing fish, under a penalty of not less than one hundred dollars nor more than five hundred dollars for each and every offence, at the discretion of the justice

Unlawful to place in any pond, lake, &c., dynamite, giant powder, &c.

Penalty

of the peace, police magistrate or district court before whom said conviction is had.

No person or company shall allow any dye stuff, &c, to be turned into any waters of this state, either private or public

31. *And be it enacted*, That no person or persons, company, corporation or association shall allow any dye stuff, coal tar, saw dust, shavings, tan bark, lime, refuse from gas houses or other deleterious or poisonous substance to be turned or allowed to run into any of the waters of this state, either private or public, in quantities destructive to the life of or disturbing the habits of fish inhabiting the same, under a penalty of not less than one hundred dollars or more than five hundred dollars for each and every offence, at the discretion of the justice of the peace, police magistrate or district court before whom such conviction is had.

Penalty

Unlawful to draw off waters for taking fish

32. *And be it enacted*, That it shall not be lawful to shut off or draw off the water of any pond, stream or lake in this state for the purpose of taking, capturing or killing the fish therein, under the penalty of not less than twenty-five dollars nor more than two hundred and fifty dollars for each and every offence, at the discretion of the justice of the peace, police magistrate or district court before whom such conviction is had.

Penalty.

Licensed dealers of game or fish allowed ten days to dispose of same.

33. *And be it enacted*, That nothing in this act shall prevent any licensed or established dealer in game to dispose of such game or fish mentioned in this act for ten days after the expiration of the periods in which the same may be killed or caught; *provided*, that said game or fish shall not have been killed or caught in this state within the periods prohibited in this act, or shall have been purchased outside the limits of this state.

Proviso

In prosecutions of game carriers it shall be competent for them to show, &c

34. *And be it enacted*, That in all prosecutions of game carriers under this act it shall be competent for them to show that the prohibited article came in possession in another state or from beyond the United States at some place where this act did not apply.

Justices of the peace, &c., have jurisdiction to try persons violating this act.

35. *And be it enacted*, That hereafter justices of the peace, district courts and police magistrates in any city shall have jurisdiction to try and punish all person or persons guilty of violating any of the provisions of this act, and all the different penalties in this act prescribed for violation thereof may be enforced and recovered before any justice of the peace, district court or police

Penalties may be enforced and recovered

magistrate, either in the county where the offence is committed or where the offender is first apprehended or where he may reside.

36. *And be it enacted*, That such justice of the peace, district court or police magistrate in any city, upon receiving proof by affidavit or affidavits of one or more persons, of the violation of any of the provisions of this act, is hereby authorized and required, unless the accused is then before him, to issue a warrant under the hand and seal of said justice or police magistrate, or under the seal of such district court, as the case may be, directed to any constable, police officer, fish warden of the county, the fish and game protector of the state, or deputy fish and game protector, to cause such person or persons to be arrested and brought before such justice, district court or police magistrate, and shall thereupon in a summary way hear and determine the guilt or innocence of the person or persons so charged, and upon conviction of any such person or persons upon such hearing, the said justice, district court or police magistrate is hereby authorized and required to impose upon the offender and offenders so convicted the penalty or penalties prescribed, together with the costs of prosecution for such offence, and if any person or persons shall fail to pay the penalty or penalties so imposed, together with the costs of prosecution, the said justice, district court or police magistrate is hereby authorized and required to commit such offender to the common jail of the county for a period of not less than ten or more than thirty days, or until said penalty and costs are paid.

Justice of peace, upon affidavit of violation of this act, authorized to issue warrant, &c

Said justice authorized to impose the penalty prescribed, &c

37. *And be it enacted*, That for the violation of any of the sections of this act done in the view of any constable, police officer, fish warden, game and fish protector or deputy fish and game protector, such officer is hereby authorized, without warrant, to arrest the offender or offenders and to carry him or them before a justice of the peace, police magistrate or district court of the county wherein such arrest is made; and the justice, district court or police magistrate before whom such offender shall be taken shall have jurisdiction of the case, and is hereby authorized and required summarily to hear and determine the same, after receiving from the said officer

Constable, &c, authorized to arrest without warrant

an affidavit in writing of the commission of the offence for which the person or persons was or were arrested.

Actions for violation of this act to be in name of complainant.

38. *And be it enacted*, That all actions commenced for violation of this act shall be entitled and run in the name of the person making the complaint, and the prevailing party shall recover costs against the other; the same fees and costs shall be allowed therein as in trial before justice of the peace holding court for the trial of small causes.

Case under this may be adjourned.

39. *And be it enacted*, That any case begun under this act may be for good cause shown adjourned by the justice, district court or police magistrate not exceeding thirty days from the date of arrest of the defendant, but in such case it shall be the duty of the justice, district court or police magistrate to retain the defendant in custody unless he shall enter into bond unto the person making the complaint with at least one sufficient surety in double the amount of the penalty prescribed for the offence complained of, conditioned for his appearance at the adjourned day of trial, and thence from day to day until the case is disposed of, and then to abide by the judgment of the justice, district court or police magistrate or otherwise to demand and perfect an appeal to the court of common pleas of the county within ten days after rendering final judgment; and such bond if forfeited may be prosecuted in the name of the person making the complaint in any court of competent jurisdiction; all sums of money recovered for the violation of this act or the forfeiture of such bonds shall be paid, one-third to the person making the complaint, one-third to the game and fish commissioners and one-third to the person or persons furnishing the evidence necessary to secure conviction.

Bond to be given

Bond forfeited, person making complaint paid one-third.

May appeal from judgment or sentence of justice

40. *And be it enacted*, That any party to any proceeding instituted under this act may appeal from the judgment or sentence of the justice, district court or police magistrate, to the court of common pleas of the county in which the said trial shall take place; *provided*, that the party appealing shall within ten days from the rendering of judgment serve a written notice of appeal upon the person making the complaint and pay the costs adjudged against him, and deliver to the justice, district court or police magistrate a bond to the opposite party in double the amount of the penalty imposed, with at least one

Proviso

sufficient surety, conditioned to prosecute the appeal and to stand to and abide by such order or judgment of the court as may be made against him in the premises.

41. *And be it enacted*, That whenever an appeal shall be taken as aforesaid it shall be the duty of the justice, district court or police magistrate to send all the papers in the case to the next court of common pleas of the said county, which court shall receive and try and determine all such appeals in the same way and manner that appeals from the courts for the trial of small causes are now tried and determined in that court, except that on the trial of such appeals no notice of the production of any new evidence on behalf of either party shall be required.

Court of common pleas to hear appeal.

42. *And be it enacted*, That in cases under this act no state of demand or other pleading shall be required, but the preliminary affidavit shall specify among other things the section of this act claimed to have been violated.

No state of demand required.

43. *And be it enacted*, That the duly appointed fish and game protector, deputy fish and game protector and fish wardens of this state shall have the same powers and be entitled to the same fees for the service or process in cases instituted under this act that constables have and are entitled to receive in the courts for the trial of small causes.

Fees of fish and game protectors.

44. *And be it enacted*, That no person shall be excused from giving evidence in any action or proceedings taken or had under this act on the ground that the evidence might tend to convict such witness or to establish the liability of such witness under any provisions thereof, but such evidence shall not be received against such witness to recover any of the penalties mentioned in this act.

No person excused from giving evidence.

45. *And be it enacted*, That an act entitled "An act to amend and consolidate the several acts relating to game and game fish," approved March twenty-seventh, one thousand eight hundred and seventy-four, and the several supplements or further supplements thereto, approved respectively March seventeenth, one thousand eight hundred and seventy-five; March sixteenth, one thousand eight hundred and seventy-six; April fifteenth, one thousand eight hundred and seventy-six; March eighth, one thousand eight hundred and seventy-seven; April fifth, one thousand eight hundred and seventy-eight; March third, one thousand eight hundred and eighty;

Acts repealed hereby.

March tenth, one thousand eight hundred and eighty; March ninth, one thousand eight hundred and eighty-five; March first, one thousand eight hundred and eighty-six; March twentieth, one thousand eight hundred and eighty-six; February twenty-eighth, one thousand eight hundred and eighty-eight; May thirteenth, one thousand eight hundred and eighty-nine; April fourteenth, one thousand eight hundred and ninety-one, and the several acts entitled "A supplement to an act entitled 'An act to consolidate the several acts relating to game and fish in this state,'" approved respectively April third, one thousand eight hundred and eighty-nine; April second, one thousand eight hundred and ninety-one, and the act entitled "A further supplement to an act entitled 'An act to consolidate the several acts relating to game and fish in this state,'" approved April second, one thousand eight hundred and ninety-one, and an act entitled "A further supplement to an act entitled 'An act to amend and consolidate the several acts relating to game and game fish,'" approved March twenty-seventh, one thousand eight hundred and seventy-four, and the supplement thereto approved March eighth, one thousand eight hundred and seventy-seven, which act was approved March seventeenth, one thousand eight hundred and eighty-one, be and the same are hereby repealed.

Repealer. 46. *And be it enacted*, That an act entitled "An act for the protection of the fisheries of this state," approved March twenty-first, one thousand eight hundred and seventy-four, and the several supplements thereto, approved respectively March sixteenth, one thousand eight hundred and eighty-five, and April twentieth, one thousand eight hundred and eighty-six, be and the same are hereby repealed.

Repealer. 47. *And be it enacted*, That an act entitled "An act for the preservation of fish," approved April thirteenth, one thousand eight hundred and seventy-six, and the several acts supplementary thereto, approved respectively March eighth, one thousand eight hundred and seventy-seven; March tenth, one thousand eight hundred and eighty; March thirty-first, one thousand eight hundred and eighty-five; and an act entitled "An act for the preservation of fish," approved April fifth, one thousand eight hundred and seventy-eight, and the several acts supplementary thereto, approved respectively March fourteenth, one thousand eight hundred and seventy-nine; March eleventh, one thousand eight hundred and seventy-nine, March seventeenth, one thousand eight hundred and eighty-two; March tenth, one thousand eight hundred and eighty-four; March twenty-second, one thousand eight hundred and eighty-three, and June first, one thousand eight hundred and eighty-six, and an act entitled "An act to amend an act entitled 'A supplement to an act entitled "An act for the preservation of fish,"'" approved April fifth, one thousand eight hundred and seventy-eight, which said supplement was approved March seventeenth, one thousand eight hundred and eighty-two, which act was approved April first, one thousand eight hundred and eighty-seven; and also an act entitled "An act to amend an act entitled 'An act to amend an act entitled "A supplement to an act entitled 'An act for the preservation of fish,'"'" approved April fifth, one thousand eight hundred and seventy-eight, which said supplement was approved March seventeenth, one thousand eight hundred and eighty-two, approved April first, one thousand eight hundred and eighty-seven, which act was approved February fifteenth, one thousand eight hundred and eighty-eight, be and the same are hereby repealed.

48. *And be it enacted*, That an act entitled "An act for the protection of game and game fish," approved April fourth, one thousand eight hundred and seventy-eight, and an act entitled "A supplement to an act entitled 'An act for the protection of game fish,'" approved April fourth, one thousand eight hundred and seventy-eight, and other game laws of this state providing for the payment of fines into the county treasury, approved January twenty-eighth, one thousand eight hundred and eighty-five; and an act entitled "A further supplement to the act entitled 'An act for the protection of game and game fish,'" approved April fourth, one thousand eight hundred and seventy-eight, which act was approved February twenty-fifth, one thousand eight hundred and eighty-nine. Repealer.

49. *And be it enacted*, That an act entitled "An act for the protection and to limit the time and manner of killing European pheasants and other game birds of foreign Repealer.

origin," approved March twenty-second, one thousand eight hundred and eighty six, and the supplement thereof, approved March twenty-fourth, one thousand eight hundred and ninety-two, and an act entitled "An act for the preservation of squirrels," approved April twenty-eighth, one thousand eight hundred and eighty-six, be and the same are hereby repealed.

Repealer. 50. *And be it enacted*, That an act entitled "An act for the protection of black bass in the rivers of New Jersey," approved April twenty-first, one thousand eight hundred and seventy-six, and an act entitled "A supplement to an act regulating fisheries," approved March third, one thousand eight hundred and eighty-two, and an act entitled "An act to amend an act entitled 'Supplement to an act regulating fisheries,'" approved March third, one thousand eight hundred and eighty-two, which act was approved February fifteenth, one thousand eight hundred and eighty-six, be and the same are hereby repealed.

Repealer. 51. *And be it enacted*, That an act entitled "An act to provide a uniform method of procedure for the recovery of penalties for violation of the several laws relating to game and game fish," approved March sixteenth, one thousand eight hundred and eighty-five, be and the same are hereby repealed.

Repealer. 52. *And be it enacted*, That an act entitled "An act to provide for the better protection of the fishing interests of this state," approved April fifth, one thousand eight hundred and seventy-eight, and an act supplementary thereto, approved April fourteenth, one thousand eight hundred and ninety-one, and an act entitled "An act for the further protection of fisheries," approved March fourteenth, one thousand eight hundred and seventy-nine, and also an act entitled "An act to empower the fish wardens to enforce game laws," approved April fourteenth, one thousand eight hundred and eighty-four, and an act entitled "An act to amend an act entitled 'An act to empower fish wardens to enforce game laws,'" approved April tenth, one thousand eight hundred and eighty-five, be and the same are hereby repealed.

Repealer. 53. *And be it enacted*, That an act entitled "An act for the preservation of deer and other game, and to prevent trespassing with guns," approved April sixteenth, one thousand eight hundred and forty-six, and the several supplements thereof, approved respectively February fourteenth, one thousand eight hundred and fifty-two; March twenty-third, one thousand eight hundred and fifty nine; March twenty-sixth, one thousand eight hundred and sixty-six; March twenty-seventh, one thousand eight hundred and sixty-seven; March seventeenth, one thousand eight hundred and seventy; March twenty-first, one thousand eight hundred and seventy-three; April fourth, one thousand eight hundred and seventy-three, and March fourteenth, one thousand eight hundred and seventy-nine, be and the same are hereby repealed

54. *And be it enacted*, That "An act for the preservation of fish in the Hackensack river and its tributaries or branches within the counties of Bergen and Hudson," approved February twenty-first, one thousand eight hundred and eighty-eight, the supplement thereto approved April fourteenth, one thousand eight hundred and ninety-one, and an act entitled "An act relative to fishing in the Delaware river," approved April seventeenth, one thousand eight hundred and eighty-eight, and also an act entitled "An act to divide the counties of the state into two sections, to be known as game sections, and to fix the time for shooting certain game birds and animals therein," approved April second, one thousand eight hundred and eighty-eight, be and the same are hereby repealed. Repealer.

55. *And be it enacted*, That an act entitled "An act permitting the catching of fish by set lines and fish weirs in those tributaries of the Delaware river above tide water which are obstructed by dams," approved March thirteenth, one thousand eight hundred and eighty-three, be and the same are hereby repealed. Repealer.

56. *And be it enacted*, That an act entitled "An act to amend and partially consolidate the several game laws of this state,' approved March twenty-fourth, one thousand eight hundred and eighty-one, and the supplement thereto approved February eighth, one thousand eight hundred and eighty-three; and an act entitled "An act for the protection of fish," approved March twenty-fifth, one thousand eight hundred and eighty-one, and the supplement thereto approved April twenty eighth, one thousand Repealer.

eight hundred and eighty-six; and an act entitled "A supplement to an act to repeal the first section of an act entitled 'An act for the protection of fish,'" approved April sixteenth, one thousand eight hundred and eighty-four, which supplement was approved April sixteenth, one thousand eight hundred and eighty-six; and an act entitled "A further supplement to an act to repeal the first section of an act entitled 'An act for the protection of fish,'" approved April sixteenth, one thousand eight hundred and eighty-four, which supplement was approved March twenty-eighth, one thousand eight hundred and eighty-seven; and an act entitled "An act for the preservation of terrapin," approved March second, one thousand eight hundred and fifty-five, be and the same are hereby repealed.

Repealer. 57. *And be it enacted*, That all other acts or parts of acts, whether general or special, public or private, contrary to or inconsistent with the provisions of this act be and the same are hereby repealed.

58. *And be it enacted*, That this act shall take effect immediately.

Approved February 28, 1893.

CHAPTER XXVIII.

A Supplement to an act entitled "An act to authorize the boards of chosen freeholders of the respective counties of this state to issue bonds to raise money for state or county purposes, in anticipation of the arrearages of state or county taxation" (Supplement to Revision), approved March eighteenth, one thousand eight hundred and eighty-one.

Section to be amended. 1. BE IT ENACTED *by the Senate and General Assembly of the State of New Jersey*, That the first section of the act to which this is a supplement, and which section reads as follows (vide Supplement to Revision, page ninety-two), shall be amended so that the same shall read as follows:

1. BE IT ENACTED *by the Senate and General Assembly of the State of New Jersey*, That if in any county of this state there shall now exist, or hereafter shall exist arrearages of state and county taxes, owing and unpaid to the county collector, by the different cities, towns or townships in said county, by reason of any appropriation and levy of taxes for state or county purposes, or for errors in the apportionment or assessment of state school tax, heretofore made or hereafter to be made, that it shall be lawful at any time, or from time to time, for the board of chosen freeholders of any county of this state to borrow such sum or sums of money as they may deem necessary for the payment of any floating debt of such county, or for the payment of any temporary loans based upon such arrearages, or for the payment of any state or school tax which may be due from such county to this state, and to cause, by resolution, the bonds of such county, in the name of the board of chosen freeholders of such county, to be issued for the same in such sums each as they may deem proper; *provided*, that said board of chosen freeholders of such county shall not, in all, borrow to an amount exceeding the amount of arrearages of taxes owing to the county collector by the different cities, towns and townships in such counties; and such loans shall be made and such bonds issued only in anticipation of the collection of such arrearages of taxation; *provided, also*, that the first moneys realized from such bonds shall be paid into the state treasury in payment of such state taxes as may be then due.

Boards of chosen freeholders authorized to issue bonds to raise money for arrearages of state or county taxation.

Proviso.

Proviso

2. *And be it enacted*, That this act shall take effect immediately.

Approved February 28, 1893.

CHAPTER XXIX.

A Further Supplement to an act entitled "An act to enable counties which have no county hospital to assist in maintaining hospitals located in such county," approved April twenty-sixth, one thousand eight hundred and eighty-six.

Section to be amended

1. BE IT ENACTED *by the Senate and General Assembly of the State of New Jersey,* That section one of the act to which this is a supplement be amended so as to read as follows:

Freeholders authorized to make annual appropriations for maintenance of patients in hospitals.

1. BE IT ENACTED *by the Senate and General Assembly of the State of New Jersey,* That it shall and may be lawful for the board of chosen freeholders of any county of this state which has no hospital located therein maintained by such county, other than the hospital or sick ward of the county poorhouse, to make an appropriation of a sum of money not exceeding five thousand dollars each year in the same manner that appropriations for other county purposes are made, which sum so appropriated shall be included in the annual tax levy of such county, and collected in the same manner and at the same time as other county taxes, and shall be applied to the purpose of supporting and maintaining such patients as may be sent to any hospital or hospitals supported by private charity and located in such county; *provided,* the sum so appropriated be used and applied for the benefit, comfort and maintenance of such patients, inmates of such hospital, as are residents of said county at the time of being sent to said hospital; *provided,* that the provisions of this act shall not apply to counties of the first class.

Proviso.

2. *And be it enacted,* That this act shall take effect immediately.

Approved February 28, 1893.

CHAPTER XXX.

An Act to amend an act entitled "An act concerning legacies" (Revision), approved March twenty-seventh, one thousand eight hundred and seventy-four.

1. BE IT ENACTED *by the Senate and General Assembly of the State of New Jersey*, That section eight of the act above mentioned, to which this act is amendatory, be and the same hereby is amended to read as follows: Section to be amended.

8. *And be it enacted*, That whenever personal property is bequeathed to any person for life, or for a term of years, or for any other limited period, or upon a condition, or any contingency, the executor or administrator cum testamento annexo shall not be compelled to pay or deliver the property so bequeathed to the person having any such life interest, or other interest as aforesaid, until security shall be given to the orphans' court having jurisdiction of such executor's or administrator's accounts, in such sum and form as in the judgment of the said court shall sufficiently secure the interest of the person or persons entitled in remainder, whenever the same shall accrue or vest in possession; but where the person or persons next immediately in remainder shall be the lineal descendant of any such life tenant, or person having any limited estate as aforesaid, and such executor or administrator shall not have filed any security, such life tenant or other person having such limited interest or estate as aforesaid shall not be required to give security in a greater sum than fifty thousand dollars; *provided, however*, in every case where the executor or administrator is the person to whom any such life interest, or other interest as aforesaid, is bequeathed, then such executor or administrator, before receiving into his possession such personal property, notwithstanding that by the will it is or may be provided that no security shall be required of the executor, shall file with the surrogate of the county in which the will shall be or has been proved, or letters granted, a Security required from legatee for life or limited period. Amount of such security. Proviso.

bond to the ordinary of this state in double the amount of the money or the value of the property to be received, with two sufficient sureties, to be approved by the orphans' court, conditioned for the faithful conservation of said property, and until such a bond shall be filed it shall not be lawful for such executor or administrator to receive such money or personal property, but the orphans' court may, upon petition presented by any person in interest, and upon ten days' notice in writing to such executor or administrator, appoint some other fit person to receive and administer such property as trustees upon such security being given for the faithful discharge of his duties as to the said court shall seem proper.

Provisions of this act apply to all cases.

2. *And be it enacted*, That the aforesaid provisions of this act shall be held to apply as well to all cases where any will has already been proved as where it shall be proved; *provided, however*, that any such executor has not already received such personal property into his possession.

Repealer.

3. *And be it enacted*, That all acts and parts of acts, general, special or local, inconsistent with the provisions of this act, be and the same are hereby repealed, and that this act shall take effect immediately.

Approved February 28, 1893.

CHAPTER XXXI.

An Act authorizing the payment to the Heinz Printing Company of the sum of two thousand seven hundred and fifty dollars for work done for the state.

Preamble.

WHEREAS, The house of assembly on the first day of March, anno domini one thousand eight hundred and ninety-two, adopted the following resolution: "*Resolved*, That the Heinz Printing Company be authorized to print the following reports in the German language for the use of the members of this house: one thousand copies of the report of the bureau of statistics, one thousand copies of the report of the board of agriculture, one thousand copies of the report of the state geologist, all for the year one thousand eight hundred and ninety-one, to be paid at the same rate as the preceding year;" and, whereas, the Heinz Printing Company, in compliance with the aforesaid resolution, proceeded with the aforesaid work, and expended thereon the sum of four thousand dollars for the purchase of maps, drawings and printing, and also delivered a portion of said work to the state, when the said company discovered that the resolution was not such an authorization to do the work as required by law in order to make the state responsible for the payment of said work, and has received no pay for said work; therefore,

State treasurer authorized to pay upon warrant of comptroller

1. BE IT ENACTED *by the Senate and General Assembly of the State of New Jersey*, That the treasurer of the state, upon the warrant of the comptroller, is hereby authorized and required to pay to the Heinz Printing Company the sum of two thousand seven hundred and fifty dollars for such work and disbursements.

2. *And be it enacted*, That this act shall take effect immediately.

Approved February 28, 1898.

CHAPTER XXXII.

A Supplement to an act entitled "An act for the formation and government of boroughs," approved April second, one thousand eight hundred and ninety-one.

Mayor and council authorized to issue bonds styled "improvement bonds"

1. BE IT ENACTED *by the Senate and General Assembly of the State of New Jersey*, That whenever a majority of the legal voters of any borough incorporated under the provisions of the act to which this act is a supple-

ment, voting at a special election held for the purpose, pursuant to the provisions of any law of this state, shall or may hereafter have authorized the issue of "improvement bonds" for the construction of a system of water works and a sewage system, or any other public improvement for said borough, it shall and may be lawful for the mayor and council of said borough to issue bonds of the said borough, under the signature of the mayor and borough clerk, with the corporate seal affixed, to be styled "improvement bonds."

Amount of improvement bonds not to exceed ten per centum of assessed valuation shown by assessor's duplicate.

2. *And be it enacted*, That the aggregate amount of the "improvement bonds," authorized by section one of this supplementary act, shall not at any time exceed ten per centum of the amount of the assessed valuation of the property in the said borough, as shown by the assessor's duplicate for the preceding year; and the said bonds shall be issued in such sums, payable at such time or times, not longer than twenty years, and bear interest, payable semi-annually, at a rate not exceeding six per centum per annum, as the mayor and council of said borough shall by ordinance direct.

Bonds to be sold at not less than par value.

3. *And be it enacted*, That the said bonds hereby authorized shall be negotiated or sold at public or private sale, at not less than the par or the face value thereof, and the proceeds of said bonds shall be appropriated, by the mayor and council of said borough, only to the payment and cancellation of such indebtedness as shall or may be incurred for and in the erection and construction of the said system of water works and sewage system of said borough, and for such other necessary public improvements as shall be within the powers of the mayor and council of said borough, by virtue of the provisions of the act to which this act is a supplement, or such other and further acts applicable thereto as may be now or hereafter enacted.

Repealer.

4. *And be it enacted*, That all acts or parts of acts, inconsistent with this act, be and the same are hereby repealed, and this act shall take effect immediately.

Approved February 28, 1898.

CHAPTER XXXIII.

An Act to amend an act entitled "An act providing for the creation of a police department in cities of the second class in this state whose population now exceeds or may hereafter exceed fifty thousand, and vesting in such police department certain powers of management and appointment now vested in other departments or officers in said cities," approved March eleventh, one thousand eight hundred and ninety-two.

1. BE IT ENACTED *by the Senate and General Assembly of the State of New Jersey*, That section second of the act to which this is an amendment, which section reads as follows: Section to be amended.

"2. *And be it enacted*, That the commissioners of police appointed under this act shall be and they are hereby invested with and shall possess all the powers heretofore given to and perform all the duties now required of or imposed upon any board of aldermen or common council or other governing body, by whatever name called, in any such city of the second class in this state, concerning and appertaining to the appointment, powers, government and other matters relating to the police of such cities; they shall also adopt such rules and regulations as to the appointment, control, duties and dismissals of the members of the police force as to them shall seem expedient, and may alter the same at pleasure; *provided, however*, that no member of the said police force shall be removed except for cause and after trial therefor before said commissioners of police; the police force of such city shall not exceed one for each one thousand of population of such city, unless said commissioners by unanimous vote shall determine that a greater number is required," shall be amended so that said section shall read as follows:

2. *And be it enacted*, That the commissioners of police appointed under this act, together with the police justices Powers of commissioners, together with the police justices

of said cities, who shall be a full member of said board *ex-officio*, and entitled to a full vote on all proceedings therein, shall be and they are hereby invested with and shall possess all the powers heretofore given to and perform all the duties now required of or imposed upon any mayor or any board of aldermen or common council or other governing body, by whatever name called, in any such city of the second class in this state, concerning and appertaining to the appointment, powers, government and other matters relating to the police of such cities; they shall also adopt such rules and regulations as to the appointment, control, duties and dismissals of the members of the police force as to them shall seem expedient, and may alter the same at pleasure; *provided, however*, that no member of the said police force shall be removed except for cause and after trial therefor before said commissioners of police; the police force of such city shall not exceed one for each one thousand of population of such city, unless said commissioners by unanimous vote shall determine that a greater number is required; *provided further*, that said police justice shall not receive any additional compensation for his service as such commissioner.

Rules and regulations.

Proviso.

Section to be repealed.

2. *And be it enacted*, That section four of the act to which this is an amendment be and the same is hereby repealed.

Repealer.

3. *And be it enacted*, That all acts or parts of acts inconsistent with this act be and the same are hereby repealed, and that this act shall be a public act and shall take effect immediately.

Passed February 28, 1898.

CHAPTER XXXIV.

An Act concerning public roads and parks, and creating boards for the control and management of the same.

Township committee authorized by resolution to divide townships into road districts, and file maps.

1. Be it enacted *by the Senate and General Assembly of the State of New Jersey*, That the township committee in the respective townships of this state, or a majority of such committee, may, at their first regular meeting or at a special meeting, after this act shall have become a law, divide their respective townships into convenient road districts, cause maps thereof to be made and filed in the office of the clerk of the county in which said township is located, with the clerk of such township and with the clerk of the road board to be organized as hereinafter provided, with a copy of their resolution making such division.

Resolution adopted to be submitted to voters.

Notice of election.

Persons entitled to vote.

Ballot to contain the words.

2. *And be it enacted*, That the said committees shall, by resolution adopted at said meeting so held as aforesaid, submit the question of the acceptance or rejection of this act to the voters of such township at any general or special election to be held therein, whereof at least ten days' notice shall be given, in the manner now directed for the giving of notice of the annual township elections or town meetings; and if a majority of those who shall vote for the acceptance or rejection thereof shall be in favor of the acceptance of this act, then this act shall go into effect immediately, and the grant of power herein made to any such township shall be deemed accepted by such township, and such township shall be bound by the terms of this act; persons entitled to vote at any township election or town meeting, where this question is submitted to them, shall express their assent or rejection of this act by depositing ballots at such election in the election district of any township; and those who are in favor of the acceptance of this act and the grants and powers therein contained, shall deposit a ballot containing the words "road act of 1898 (with chapter number of

same) accepted," written or printed thereon, and those who are opposed, shall each deposit a ballot with the words "road act of 1893 (with chapter number of same) rejected," written or printed thereon; and this acceptance or rejection may be expressed upon the ballot on which are the names of the township officers, and no separate ballots shall be required for the purpose of this vote, if had at the general election; there shall be a canvass on the return of the votes upon this question of such acceptance or rejection made by the election officers, in the same way and manner as for officers voted for at such election; and if a majority of the ballots on which there shall be either the words "road act of 1893 (with chapter number of same) accepted" or "road act of 1893 (with chapter number of same) rejected," shall be found to be for the acceptance of this act it shall then, but no otherwise, go into effect and be binding upon such township wherein such vote shall have been taken; if a special election be held under the provisions of this act, the same shall be conducted in every respect as is now provided for the conduct of the general township election or town meeting.

Election officers canvass the votes.

Special election conducted same as general township election.

Township committee shall call an assembly of freeholders to elect road commissioner for term of three years.

3. *And be it enacted*, That the said township committee in each of said townships in which said act shall have been accepted in manner aforesaid, shall thereupon call an assembly in each of said districts into which said township has been divided as aforesaid, of the freeholders in said district, at such convenient place in said district, and within three weeks after the acceptance of this act as aforesaid, at four o'clock in the afternoon, as the said committee shall deem expedient, upon ten days' notice by printed hand bill or a hand bill partly printed and partly written, to be posted conspicuously in at least ten public places, in said district, and published in a newspaper printed and published in the said township, or where there is no such newspaper then in one printed and published in the county and circulating in said township, at which assembly after being duly organized, the said freeholders so assembled shall elect by ballot a suitable person, who shall also be a legal voter in the township and a freeholder and resident in the district for which he is nominated, as a road commissioner for said

district for the term of three years; and the said freeholders so assembled shall also have the same powers and authority in relation to the voting and raising of money for the making, maintaining and repairing the public highways within such district as the inhabitants of the said township now have or had in relation to the roads and highways therein when assembled in town meeting, and in addition thereto they shall also have the power of appropriating such sums of money as they may deem proper for keeping in repair or improving any public parks in said township now acquired or that may hereafter be acquired under any of the laws of this state, and also to appropriate moneys for the laying and constructing of sidewalks and keeping the same in repair, the said voters having the option of designating where said money so appropriated for sidewalks shall be expended; and they and their property, both real and personal, shall be in all respects liable for the same, in like manner as the inhabitants of the said township and their said property are now liable in respect to the roads therein; *provided*, that in making assessments for the purposes mentioned in this act, no deductions shall be made for debts owing by the owners of the real estate assessed, or for any mortgage thereon; *and provided*, that each of the said districts respectively shall make, maintain and keep in repair, under the direction of the board to be composed as hereinafter provided, the public highways within their respective limits, in the same manner, to the extent of each district respectively as the said township now is authorized and required to make, maintain and keep in repair the highways within its limits; *and provided further*, that all moneys so voted and raised by any district shall be applied by the said board to the use of the public highways and sidewalks in such district and not in any other district; that no decision, vote or appropriation shall be valid unless at least twelve freeholders of said district shall be present and take part therein; and if twelve freeholders of said district are not present on the day appointed as aforesaid, the said meeting shall be adjourned from day to day until said number of freeholders are present, and a majority of those present shall be necessary to give validity to a decision, vote or appro-

Powers and authority of said freeholders.

Proviso.

Proviso

Proviso.

priation; that a minute of the proceedings of said meeting shall be made by the secretary of said meeting, to be entered in the book of minutes of said district, which minute shall specify the names of at least twelve freeholders present at the assembly.

Commissioners to be known as the "public road board."

4. *And be it enacted*, That the said commissioners when so elected as aforesaid, and their successors to be thereafter elected, are hereby constituted a board of commissioners to be known as the "public road board" of the respective townships in which the same may be elected; that the said commissioners or a majority of them shall within ten days after their election, at two o'clock in the afternoon, assemble at such place as may be designated by said township committee by a resolution adopted for that purpose and of which written notice shall be given to each of said commissioners, and proceed to the organization of said board by the election of a president and such other officers as they shall see fit, who shall hold their offices for one year or until their successors are elected, and annually thereafter, on the first Monday in May, at the hour of two o'clock in the afternoon, said commissioners shall meet for such organization as aforesaid, and the said officers when so elected shall hold their offices for the period of one year, or until their successors are elected as hereinbefore provided.

Time when and how to organize said board.

Term of office.

5. *And be it enacted*, That the term of office of each commissioner elected after the expiration of the term of office of the commissioners hereinbefore provided for shall be three years; and that he shall be a legal voter of the township and a freeholder and resident of the district for which he is nominated and elected, and shall be elected as hereinafter provided; that all vacancies in said board arising from death, resignation, removal from the township, or any cause other than the expiration of the term of office, shall be filled by the said board within thirty days from the occurrence of the same, with a person who is a legal voter of the township and a freeholder and resident of the district for which he is named; that when any vacancy shall arise from other cause than the expiration of the term of office, then the remaining members of the board shall discharge the duties of the retiring member or members until his or their successor or

Vacancies to be filled by the board.

successors shall have been appointed; and each commissioner shall, before he enters upon the performance of the duties of his office, take an oath or affirmation before any officer of this state authorized to take the same, faithfully, fairly and impartially to exercise and perform the duties of said office, which oath or affirmation shall, within five days after taking the same, be filed with the clerk of said township. **To file oath**

6. *And be it enacted*, That the commissioners herein provided for shall within the limits of the district to which each shall from time to time be assigned, have the same duties, and be subject to the same penalties as overseers of the highways in the said township now have or heretofore had, perform or performed or are or were subject to within and for the said township, and that the board hereby created shall in addition to the other powers and duties conferred and enjoined by this act, have the same powers, perform the same duties, and be subject to the same obligations and penalties as the township committee now have, had, perform or performed or are or were subject to, in relation to the public highways; and in addition thereto shall have a general and exclusive supervision, control and management of the public highways and sidewalks in said township and of their repair or regulation, and of all parks and other lands in such township which have been or may be dedicated to the public or which may be acquired as now provided by law, and shall from time to time prescribe by the vote of the majority of said board the manner in which the public highways shall be worked, repaired, kept in order, regulated and named, and the time when the same shall be worked and repaired; and if any person shall desire to dedicate to public use, as a highway, any portion of his or her land, and twelve freeholders of the district in which said lands so proposed to be dedicated are situated, shall petition the said board to accept the same for public use, then upon grading the same and putting it in good condition as a highway and the execution of a deed of the same to the inhabitants of the said township with an acceptance in writing signed by a majority of the said board, endorsed thereon and recorded with the same in the office of the clerk of the county wherein said township is lo- **Duties and penalties.** **Have general and exclusive control of public highways, &c.**

cated, the land so dedicated and accepted shall be a public highway from the time of so recording said deed, with like effect as if the same had been opened under the provisions of any existing law.

Board to call annual assembly of freeholders.

7. *And be it enacted*, That the said board shall once in every year call an assembly in each of said districts of the freeholders in said district in the manner provided for in section three of this act; that at said assembly the commissioner of said district shall preside, and the said freeholders so assembled shall have the same powers and authority particularly enumerated and set out in said last-named section, and they and their property shall be subject to the like liability therein particularly stated; that the enactment in this section shall be subject to the three provisos in said last-named section particularly set out, and that no vote or appropriation shall be valid unless under circumstances detailed in said section, and that a minute of said meeting shall be kept and entered as therein provided.

Commissioner to preside.

Assembly to prescribe rules.

8. *And be it enacted*, That the said assembly shall be conducted according to such general rules as the said board may from time to time prescribe, and shall decide, vote and appropriate such sum or sums as they shall deem necessary and proper for the use of the public highways, sidewalks and parks in the district, and the tax so voted shall be assessed by the township assessor and collected by the township collector in the manner provided by law for the assessment and collection of taxes in the said township, and shall be paid over by the officer or officers receiving the same to the president of said board, to be by the said board applied to the purposes prescribed by this act.

Taxes, how assessed and collected.

Board authorized to employ surveyors, laborers, &c.

9. *And be it enacted*, That the said board may appoint, employ and discharge from time to time such surveyors, superintendents, engineers and laborers as they may deem necessary in order more effectually to carry out the intentions of this act, and pay them with compensation or wages as they may deem fair and reasonable; also to purchase or hire and to use for the said township such horses, cattle, implements and materials as they may deem proper.

10. *And be it enacted*, That the said board shall (subject only to the right of appeal and review hereinafter provided) have the full and exclusive power and authority to lay out, open, widen, alter, straighten, grade and vacate public highways in such townships; that whenever the said board, upon the written application of twelve freeholders in any of the said districts, shall deem it expedient to lay out, open, alter, widen, straighten, grade or vacate any public highway, or any number of connecting public highways in any such township, the said board shall cause a map of such proposed measures to be made and filed in their office, which map shall be open to inspection at all reasonable times by any person desiring to inspect the same, and shall thereupon cause notice to be given, as provided in section three of this act, and by printed hand bills, or hand bills partly printed and partly written, posted conspicuously in ten or more public places in such district, stating that such map is open for inspection and requiring all persons interested therein to appear before said board at a convenient time and place, to be specified in said notice, when and where the said board shall hear and weigh all arguments for or against said improvements; and if, at said time, any one or more parties interested desire an adjournment of the said hearing, and give notice in writing to said board of such desire, said hearing shall be adjourned to such other time as may be determined upon by said board; that after said hearing the commissioners shall appoint a committee of their number to examine the route of the proposed road, and to report upon the feasibility and advisability of the same, and what changes, if any, should be made therein, and thereupon the said board shall decide and determine upon the necessity of such proposed improvement, and if the said board shall decide and determine in favor thereof they shall make their decision in writing and shall award such damages as they may deem just to each and every person affected thereby, and assess such lands as may be benefited in proportion to the benefit received by the owners thereof, but in no case exceeding the same; that within five days after making such assessment as aforesaid, a printed or written or partly printed and partly written notice shall be addressed and mailed to each

Board shall have full and exclusive power.

Procedure for laying out roads, &c.

When map filed board to give notice thereof.

Commissioners appoint committee to examine routes, award damages and assess such lands in proportion to benefits received by owners thereof.

individual or party so assessed, directed to him or her at his or her post office address, if the same can be ascertained, stating the amount of said assessment against said individual or party for said improvement, and that said assessment will remain open at the office of said board for examination and inspection by all persons interested therein, at all reasonable times during the fifteen days next succeeding the mailing of said notices as aforesaid, and that said board will attend at their office on a day subsequent to the expiration of said fifteen days, and also on one or more evenings, not exceeding three evenings in all, if so required by any party or parties interested, to hear and weigh all objections thereto; that said board shall thereafter reconsider said assessment and make any alterations therein they may deem just, and thereupon they shall confirm said assessment, and within ten days after such confirmation file a map of the said improvement as finally determined on by them, with their afore said written decision and said assessment so confirmed aud award so made, in the office of the clerk of the county in which such township is located; that the said board shall give notice of such filing by publication in a newspaper printed and published in the said township, and where there is none published in said township then in one printed in the county in which said township is located and circulating in said township, once a week for four weeks, and the determination of the said board shall be final and conclusive in the premises, unless an appeal is taken to the court of common pleas in and for such county, within the time and manner provided for in this act, or in case of a proposed new road, a petition against the making of the same shall be presented to the board within twenty days from their determination in the matter, signed by the owners of a majority of lineal feet fronting on the proposed new road.

When map filed, board to give notice thereof.

Determination to be final unless appeal is taken to court of common pleas.

Board shall estimate for benefits as well as for damages.

11. *And be it enacted*, That all property taken under any provisions of this act shall be deemed taken for public use, and in estimating any award or assessment hereunder the said board shall estimate for benefits as well as for damages as aforesaid.

12. *And be it enacted*, That the said board shall (subject only to the right of appeal and review hereinafter pro-

vided) have the full and exclusive power and authority to construct sidewalks and gutters of such material as they shall deem proper along any public highway in said township, upon the application in writing of the owners of a majority of the lineal feet of lands fronting upon both sides of the highway whereon such improvement is to be made; that whenever the said board upon receiving such written application as aforesaid shall deem it expedient to construct such sidewalks and gutters as aforesaid, they shall proceed to a determination of said question in the same formal manner particularly enumerated and set out in section ten of this act; and if the said board shall decide and determine that said improvement is necessary and shall decide in favor thereof, they shall make their decision in writing, and shall assess such lands as may be benefited in proportion to the benefit received by the owners thereof, but in no case exceeding the same; that thereupon the said board shall give notice of said assessment in manner provided in said section ten of this act, and shall proceed in all things to the final determination thereof as is particularly provided in said last named section; that upon such final determination the same shall be final and conclusive unless an appeal be taken as provided for in this act.

Board shall have full and exclusive power to construct sidewalks, &c.

Procedure.

Shall assess lands in proportion to benefit received by owners thereof.

18. *And be it enacted*, That said public road board shall have full power and authority, upon the application in writing of twelve freeholders of any such townships for that purpose, to excavate, build and construct in any road, street or avenue, and with the consent of the owner in any private lands, such sewer or sewers as they may deem requisite or proper for purposes of drainage, and for the preservation of the public health; that whenever said board shall deem it advisable to construct such sewer or sewers, they shall proceed to a determination of said question in the same formal manner particularly prescribed and laid down by section ten of this act; and if the said board shall decide and determine that said improvement is necessary, they shall make their decision in writing and shall assess such lands as may be benefited in proportion to the benefits received by the owners thereof, but in no case exceeding the same; that there-

The public road board authorized to construct sewers for drainage.

Procedure.

upon the said board shall give notice of said assessment in manner provided in said section ten of this act; and shall proceed in all things to the final determination thereof as is particularly provided in said last-named section; that upon such final determination the same shall be final and conclusive, unless an appeal be taken as provided in this act.

Appeal to court of common pleas.

14. *And be it enacted*, That any person feeling himself or herself aggrieved by the action of said board under the tenth, twelfth and thirteenth sections of this act may, within, twenty days from the filing of the decision of the board in the office of the clerk of the county in which said township is located, appeal to the court of common pleas of such county by serving a notice in writing upon any member of the said board, and the said court shall have full power to hear, determine and review the proceedings of the board in the premises, and to confirm, alter, modify, set aside or reverse in whole or in part for errors, either of fact or law, and the said court shall have power to hear and try the same in a summary way and may summon a jury to determine any question of fact, and the said court may proceed in due course according to the power of the court in other cases, and the determination of the said court shall be final and conclusive in the premises and not subject to appeal or review, and the said court or any judge thereof may, until such determination, stay all proceedings in the matter, in reference to which the appeal may be taken until such final determination, and the like fees and costs shall be paid to the judges, jury, officers of the court and parties as are allowed in other causes of which the court has or may have jurisdiction, and the said court shall have power to make and prescribe all necessary forms, rules and regulations in the conduct of any proceeding to be taken under this act.

Trial by jury.

Fees and costs paid.

Rules and regulations.

Assessment lien on lands.

15. *And be it enacted*, That if no appeal shall be taken within the time and in the manner prescribed herein the action of the said board shall take effect, and the said board may proceed to carry out the same under this act, and any assessment laid by virtue hereof shall be a lien on the lands on which it is laid, and the said commissioners shall procure a certified copy of their award and the

judgment of the said court of common pleas, if any appeal shall have been taken, to be placed in the hands of the collector of taxes for the time being of any such township, and thereupon it shall be the duty of the collector to collect the said assessment within sixty days from the time of placing such copy in his hands, and to pay the same over to the president of the said board; and the said collector shall, in the collection of the assessment, be liable to the same pains and penalties and entitled to the same fees as in the collection of the annual township taxes, the said fees being reserved by him out of the amount so collected; *provided*, that the said collector, in each and every year before proceeding under this act, shall enter into bonds to the said board with such sureties and in such sums as the said board shall approve, conditioned for the faithful performance of his duties under this act; and the said president, before receiving any money from said collector, shall enter into bonds to the inhabitants of such township in their corporate name, with such sureties and in such sum as the said board shall approve, conditioned for the faithful performance of his duties as such president.

Collector to collect assessment.

Fees of collector.

Proviso.

16. *And be it enacted*, That in case any owner or owners of lands assessed for any of the purposes as aforesaid shall fail to pay the assessment laid thereon, within three months from the time of placing the certified copy of the award in the hands of the collector, then the lands upon which the said assessment is a lien shall be sold in the same manner as land is now authorized by law to be sold for unpaid taxes in any such township upon a warrant issued by said board of like character and form as that issued for the collection of said taxes, so as to raise a sufficient sum to pay the said assessment and the interest, at the rate of twelve per centum per annum, from the expiration of sixty days from the time of placing such copy in the hands of the collector, and the lawful costs and fees of collection and sale.

Lands to be sold if assessments remain unpaid for three months.

17. *And be it enacted*, That notwithstanding any mistake in the name or names of the owner or owners of any lands, tenements and real estate, in the said township in making awards or assessments, or in giving or addressing notice of the same, in pursuance of the tenth

Mistake in names of owners of lands does not invalidate assessment.

section of this act, such awards and assessments shall be valid and effectual in law against such lands, tenements and real estate, and the same may be proceeded against and sold in the manner prescribed in the sixteenth section of this act.

Board authorized to borrow money.

18. *And be it enacted*, That the said board is hereby authorized to borrow money in anticipation of the sums to be raised annually by tax for road purposes, in the several districts of said township, and thereupon if the commissioner of any district shall in writing require the said board of his township to advance the sum voted in such district, such board shall proceed to raise the same within thirty days after such requisition; the money so advanced to be repaid by the president of said board when he shall receive the amount levied by tax from the township collector.

Commissioners have general and exclusive control of sidewalks and gutters.

19. *And be it enacted*, That this act shall be construed so as to give the commissioners a general and exclusive supervision, control and management of all sidewalks and gutters along the public highways within their respective road districts, and to pay for their repair and regulation out of the moneys voted by the annual assemblies and raised by tax, as in this act provided.

Compensation of commissioners.

20. *And be it enacted*, That the said commissioners shall receive two dollars a day for each and every day's attendance upon and about the duties imposed upon them by this act, which shall be paid to them by the township collector upon the order of the president of the board, and there shall be levied and collected in each and every year, at the time and in the manner provided for the collection of taxes in such township, a sum sufficient to defray such fees, advertising expenses and such other general expenses, costs and charges as the said board may become liable for in performing their duties under this act, the amount of which shall be annually determined by said board and certified under seal to the assessor of said township; and that wherever the word "board" is used in this act it shall be considered as meaning a majority thereof.

Meaning of the word "board."

21. *And be it enacted*, That at each annual meeting or assembly, held as provided in this act, the commissioner presiding shall present his accounts, which shall give in

separate items a statement of work done, the location of it and the amount paid therefor and to whom paid, and also in separate items a statement of all other expenditures for the past year, which accounts shall be read to the meeting and be examined by it or by a committee of three persons appointed by said meeting; and within two weeks thereafter the commissioner presiding shall cause the said accounts to be published in full in a newspaper printed and published in the township, if there be one, and if not, then in a newspaper printed and published in the county in which such township is located.

At annual meeting the commissioner shall present an itemized statement of all expenditures.

Publication of accounts

22. *And be it enacted*, That this act shall take effect immediately; *provided, however*, that nothing in this act shall apply to or affect any street, avenue or highway under the charge or control of any county public road board in this state.

Proviso.

Approved March 1, 1893.

CHAPTER XXXV.

An Act concerning bailments.

1. BE IT ENACTED, *by the Senate and General Assembly of the State of New Jersey*, That it shall not be lawful in cities, towns or other municipalities of this state where there is located any corporation expressly authorized to receive on deposit for safe-keeping valuable property, for the officers or directors of any incorporated bank, savings bank, trust company, life or fire insurance company (not so expressly authorized) to take or accept for safe-keeping, stocks, bonds, jewelry, plate, money or other valuable property of any kind, unless such officers or directors shall have been specially authorized to take the same on such deposits by a vote of the majority in interest of all the stockholders of such bank or corporation, at a meeting of the stockholders of such bank or corporation called

When unlawful for incorporated banks, savings banks, &c., to receive valuables for safe-keeping.

for the purpose of vesting such authority in such officers or directors.

Approved March 1, 1893.

CHAPTER XXXVI.

A Supplement to an act entitled "An act for the punishment of crime" (Revision), approved March twenty-seventh, one thousand eight hundred and seventy-four.

Section to be amended.

1. BE IT ENACTED *by the Senate and General Assembly of the State of New Jersey*, That section sixty-eight of the act entitled "An act for the punishment of crime" (Revision), approved March twenty-seventh, one thousand eight hundred and seventy-four, which now reads:

"68. *And be it enacted*, That all murder which shall be perpetrated by means of poison, or by lying in wait, or by any other kind of wilful, deliberate and premeditated killing, or which shall be committed in perpetrating or attempting to perpetrate any arson, rape, sodomy, robbery or burglary, shall be deemed murder of the first degree, and all other kinds of murder shall be deemed murder of the second degree, and the jury before whom any person indicted for murder shall be tried shall, if they find such person guilty thereof, designate by their verdict whether it be murder of the first or second degree, but if such person shall be convicted on confession in open court the court shall proceed by examination of witnesses to determine the degree of the crime and give sentence accordingly;" be and the same is hereby amended to read as follows:

Murder

68. *And be it enacted*, That all murder which shall be perpetrated by means of poison, or by lying in wait, or by any other kind of wilful, deliberate and premeditated killing, or which shall be committed in perpetrating or attempting to perpetrate any arson, rape, sodomy, rob-

bery or burglary, shall be deemed murder of the first degree, and all other kinds of murder shall be deemed murder of the second degree, and the jury before whom any person indicted for murder shall be tried shall, if they find such person guilty thereof, designate by their verdict whether it be murder of the first degree or second degreee; and in no case shall the plea of guilty be received upon any indictment for murder, and if, upon arraignment, such plea of guilty should be offered it shall be disregarded and a plea of not guilty entered, and a jury, duly empaneled, shall try the case in manner aforesaid; *provided, however*, that nothing herein contained shall prevent the accused of pleading non vult or nolo contendere to such indictment; the sentence to be imposed, if such plea be accepted, shall be the same as that imposed upon a conviction of murder of the second degree.

Degrees of murder.

Proviso.

2. *And be it enacted*, That this act shall be a public act, and to take effect immediately.

Approved March 1, 1893.

CHAPTER XXXVII.

An Act concerning assessments for benefits and awards for damages in the opening of streets in cities of this state, and providing for a new assessment and award.

1. BE IT ENACTED *by the Senate and General Assembly of the State of New Jersey*, That in all cases where writs of certiorari may be brought to remove assessments for the costs and expenses of laying out or opening any street in any city of this state, it shall be lawful for the supreme court or one of the justices thereof, in term or vacation, on the application of the city to appoint three commissioners to make a new assessment of the costs and expenses thereof, and a new award of damages for the land taken in such improvement, and the commissioners so

In case of writ of certiorari justices of supreme court, upon application, may appoint commissioners to make new assessment and award

Proceedings to make a new assessment and award.

appointed shall proceed to make a new assessment and award upon the same principles and in the same manner as if they had been the original commissioners, and shall give such notice of a hearing before them, and of the time when they will present their report to such court or justice, when objections may be presented to such report, as the court or justice may direct, and said commissioners shall present their report in writing, signed by a majority of them, to such court or justice, and such court or justice, after hearing the parties to such certiorari, if they appear, and such other parties in interest as shall appear at the time fixed for the presentation of said report and hearing thereon, may modify and confirm such report as to the court or justice shall seem just, and such report, when so confirmed, shall be final, both as to the assessments for benefits and awards for damages therein contained, and shall be in lieu of the original report; and all such assessments shall be collected and awards for damages paid in the manner provided in the statutes for collecting such assessments and payments of awards for such improvements, and such assessments shall be due from the date of the confirmation of such report, which shall be filed, together with the other papers, with the person charged with the duty of the collection of such assessments in the respective cities.

Justice may modify and confirm report, which shall be final.

Report shall be filed.

Unpaid taxes and assessments due city on lands taken shall be deducted from the award

2. *And be it enacted*, That in all cases where awards for damages are made for land taken in the opening of any street in any city of this state, there shall be at the time of the making of such award unpaid taxes and assessments due to such city on the lands so taken, the amount so due for such unpaid taxes and assessments, with all interest, shall be deducted from the award at the time of payment or tender thereof by the officer charged with the payment thereof.

Compensation of commissioners.

3. *And be it enacted*, That such commissioners shall receive such compensation for their services as such court or justice shall order, to be paid by such city.

4. *And be it enacted*, That this act shall take effect immediately.

Approved March 1, 1893.

CHAPTER XXXVIII.

A Further Supplement to an act entitled "An Act concerning evidence," approved March twenty-seventh, one thousand eight hundred and seventy-four.

Public statutes or laws of foreign countries authorized to be published received as evidence in all courts of this state.

1. BE IT ENACTED *by the Senate and General Assembly of the State of New Jersey*, That the printed statute books and pamphlet session laws or other laws of any foreign country or of any province or subdivision thereof, printed and published by the direction or authority of such foreign country, province or subdivision thereof shall be received as evidence of the public statutes or laws of such foreign country, province or subdivision thereof in any and all courts of this state, and the court may determine whether any such book or pamphlet offered in evidence was so printed or published, either from the inspection of such book, or the knowledge of the court, or from testimony in support thereof, and no error shall be assigned for the rejection of any such book or pamphlet so offered, unless it be proven on error that such book or pamphlet offered as such in evidence is what it purports to be; nor shall any error assigned for the admission of such book or pamphlet be sustained unless it be shown in support thereof that the statute or law offered in evidence or some material part thereof was not in force in such foreign country, province, or subdivision thereof at the time of the transaction or matter to which it was offered as pertinent or material.

Court may determine as to authenticity.

2. *And be it enacted*, That this act shall take effect immediately.

Approved March 1, 1893.

CHAPTER XXXIX.

An Act to enable villages in this state to acquire lands and erect buildings for municipal uses and purposes.

Governing body of any village with three thousand population authorized to purchase lot and erect public hall

1. BE IT ENACTED *by the Senate and General Assembly of the State of New Jersey*, That it shall be lawful for the governing body of any village having a population of three thousand or over to purchase a suitable lot or tract of land within such village, and to erect thereon a building for a public hall for the use of the people thereof, to hold their public meetings and have their public offices located therein, and for such other purposes as the said governing body may deem for the interests of said village, the cost of which said lot and building shall not exceed the sum of twenty-five thousand dollars.

Authorized to issue bonds denominated "public building bonds."

Term bonds shall run.

Denomination of bonds

2. *And be it enacted*, That it shall be lawful for the governing body of such village to raise money for the purposes aforesaid by the issuing of the bonds of such village, which bonds shall be denominated "public building bonds," and shall state upon their face the purpose for which they were issued; and the term for which said bonds shall run shall not be longer than thirty years, and they shall be redeemable any time after the expiration of five years, at the option of the said village; and shall be of denomination of not less than five hundred dollars, and shall bear not exceeding the legal rate of interest, and shall not be sold at less than par.

Authorized to lease, rent or hire any part of said building not necessary for public uses exclusively.

3. *And be it enacted*, That for the purpose of paying the principal and interest of said bonds as the same shall become due, and for the further purpose of maintaining such building and for the general improvement of the same, said village is hereby authorized to lease, rent or hire, for any specified time, any part of said building not necessary for public uses exclusively, as in the judgment of the governing body thereof may deem proper, for such sum or sums of money as they may deem for the best interests of such village; that the money received from

such leases shall first be applied in payment of such necessary improvements and repairs as the governing body of such village shall have made from time to time, and the balance shall be applied to the payment of the interest and principal of said bonds as the same shall become due.

How money received from such leases to be applied.

4. *And be it enacted*, That at least one-twentieth of the principal sum of said bonds shall be raised each year by tax on all the taxable property in said village, and shall be applied in payment of the principal and interest of said bonds as the same shall fall due, and for no other purpose; that should no bonds or interest be due on which to apply said money as the same shall be raised, then in that case the governing body of such village shall appoint three responsible persons as sinking fund commissioners, who shall give bonds for the faithful discharge of their duties; that such commissioners shall have power and authority to invest said money in such manner and for such time as they shall deem for the best interests of such village, subject, however, to the approval of the governing body of such village.

One-twentieth of principal sum of said bonds shall be raised each year by tax on all taxable property.

When sinking fund commissioners shall be appointed.

5. *And be it enacted*, That this act shall take effect immediately.

Approved March 1, 1893.

CHAPTER XL.

An Act in relation to assessments of taxes in cities.

1. BE IT ENACTED *by the Senate and General Assembly of the State of New Jersey*, That in all incorporated cities of this state that now have or may hereafter have block maps, it shall be the duty of the taxing officer or officers in all cases, in making their assessments for taxes upon real estate, to describe the same by block and lot numbers as shown upon the assessment maps of the city.

Taxing officer in incorporated cities having block maps shall make assessments describing same by block numbers.

New owners of property shall have the change properly noted on the books and maps.

2. *And be it enacted*, That when any change occurs in the ownership of property in any such city, it shall be the duty of the new owner to present his deed, or other evidence of title, to the officer, officers or department having charge of the assessment of taxes therein, that the change of ownership may be properly noted on the books and maps kept by the said taxing officer or officers.

Deeds shall not be recorded unless it shall be duly certified thereon that the same have been presented at the office of the officer having charge of the assessment of taxes.

3. *And be it enacted*, That no register of deeds, county clerk or other officer whose duty it shall be to record deeds, shall record any deed which conveys any property in cities of this state that now have or may hereafter have block maps, unless it shall be duly certified thereon that the same has been presented at the office of the officer, officers, or other department having charge of the assessment of taxes, for the purpose of recording or noting such changes as may have been made thereby in the property lines and ownership of the property; *provided*, that nothing in this act shall prevent the recording of such deed in case a fee of twenty cents is paid at the time any such deed is deposited for record to the register of deeds, county clerk, or other officer whose duty it is to record the same, upon which payment having been made it shall be the duty of said register of deeds, county clerk or other officer, within five days thereafter to present such deed or an abstract thereof to the officer, officers or department having in charge the assessment of taxes, for the purpose of having such changes in lines of ownership as may be made thereby recorded or noted.

Proviso.

Repealer

4. *And be it enacted*, That all acts and parts of acts inconsistent with this act be and the same are hereby repealed, and that this act shall take effect immediately.

Approved March 1, 1893.

CHAPTER XLI.

An Act to provide for the regulation and licensing of keepers of employment agencies and intelligence offices.

Common council authorized to make rul s to regulate keepers of employment agencies, fix rates of compensation, require bonds, &c.

1. BE IT ENACTED *by the Senate and General Assembly of the State of New Jersey*, That the common council or the legislative body in any city of this state be and is hereby authorized and empowered to make, establish, publish, modify, amend and repeal ordinances, rules and regulations to license and regulate keepers of employment agencies or intelligence offices; to fix the rates of compensation to be allowed to them; to require them to furnish bonds to such city for the faithful observance by them of all the requirements and provisions of such ordinances, rules and regulations of such city; to prohibit unlicensed persons from keeping or maintaining any such employment agency or intelligence office; and to provide for the proper inspection and supervision of the said agencies or offices.

2. *And be it enacted*, That this act shall take effect immediately.

Approved March 1, 1893.

CHAPTER XLII.

An Act to provide an efficient fire alarm in cities of the first class.

In cities of first class duty of board of fire commissioners to provide perfect system of alarm.

1. BE IT ENACTED *by the Senate and General Assembly of the State of New Jersey*, That in cities of the first class in this state the board of fire commissioners or board having

charge of the department or branch of the city government to whose custody is committed all apparatus for the extinguishment of fires shall have power and it is hereby made its duty to provide and maintain a perfect system of alarm in case of fire.

When ordinary appropriation is insufficient, how to meet extraordinary expenditure.

2. *And be it enacted*, That in all cities wherein the present fire alarm system is uncertain or inadequate and the ordinary appropriation for this purpose is insufficient to meet any extraordinary expenditure in changing the present system or substituting the latest improved system the said board having charge as aforesaid may, with the concurrence of the board of finance or board having charge of the finances of any such city, expend for the purposes of this act such sum not exceeding twenty-five thousand dollars as said board may determine.

Board of finance authorized to borrow necessary amount and issue bonds.

3. *And be it enacted*, That for the purposes of this act the said board of finance or board having charge and control of finances as aforesaid shall be authorized to borrow the amount necessary for the purpose aforesaid and to issue bonds of the city therefor.

Bonds payable in thirty years, rate of interest five per cent.

4. *And be it enacted*, That the bonds to be issued under the provisions of this act shall be made payable in not exceeding thirty years from the date of issuing the same, and shall draw such rate of interest not exceeding five per centum per annum, and be in such sums as the board having charge and control of the finances of said city shall determine, which bonds shall be executed under the corporate seal of said city and the signature of the mayor, comptroller or other proper financial officer thereof, and may be either registered or coupon bonds, as said board may direct; *provided*, that said board may dispose of the bonds hereby authorized at public sale for the best price that can be obtained for the same but not less than par; *and provided further*, that in order to redeem the bonds issued under the provisions of this act at maturity it shall be the duty of the board having charge of the finances as aforesaid to establish a sinking fund, which shall be created by a special tax of not less than three per centum on the issue herein provided for to be raised in each annual tax levy.

Proviso.

Proviso.

Interest on bonds shall be levied and collected annually.

5. *And be it enacted*, That the interest on the bonds hereby authorized to be issued shall be raised and paid

by a special appropriation to be annually levied and collected as other taxes in such city are now or may hereafter be levied and collected, and the whole of each year's interest shall be so raised, levied, collected and paid within each year.

6. *And be it enacted*, That all acts and parts of acts inconsistent with this act be and the same are hereby repealed, and that this act shall take effect immediately. Repealer.

Approved March 1, 1893.

CHAPTER XLIII.

A Further Supplement to an act entitled "An act to provide for the incorporation of associations for the erection and maintenance of hospitals, infirmaries, orphanages, asylums and other charitable institutions," approved March ninth, one thousand eight hundred and seventy-seven.

1. BE IT ENACTED *by the Senate and General Assembly of the State of New Jersey*, That any training school, organized or to be organized under the act to which this is a supplement, or under any supplement thereto, may confer the degree of medical and surgical nurse upon any of its graduates, under such rules and regulations as such training school may prescribe; *provided*, that instruction be given in anatomy, physiology, hygiene, dietetics and medical, surgical, obstetrical and gynecological nursing.

Training school may prescribe rules and regulations to confer degree upon its graduates.

Proviso.

2. *And be it enacted*, That this act shall take effect immediately.

Approved March 7, 1893.

CHAPTER XLIV.

An Act to amend a supplement to an act entitled "An act for the preservation of clams and oysters" (Revision), approved April fourteenth, one thousand eight hundred and forty-six, which supplement was approved March twenty-ninth, one thousand eight hundred and ninety-two, chapter CCXXV.

Section to be amended.

1. BE IT ENACTED *by the Senate and General Assembly of the State of New Jersey*, That section two of the supplement to an act entitled "An act for the preservation of clams and oysters" (Revision), approved April fourteenth, one thousand eight hundred and forty-six, which supplement was approved March twenty-ninth, one thousand eight hundred and ninety-two, be amended to read as follows, to-wit:

Section as amended.

2. *And be it enacted*, That all acts and parts of acts inconsistent herewith be and the same are hereby repealed, and that this act shall take effect immediately.

Approved March 7, 1893.

CHAPTER XLV.

An Act to authorize the acquisition by the United States of a tract of land in the township of Middletown, in the county of Monmouth and state of New Jersey, to be used for the purpose of erecting and maintaining thereon fortifications and accessories for the defence of the southern entrance to New York harbor.

WHEREAS, the United States has acquired, by purchase, a tract or parcel of land situate, lying and being in the township of Middletown, in the county of Monmouth and state of New Jersey, and which is more particularly described as follows: beginning at the government stone monument in southwest corner of the United States light-house reservation for Bayside beacon, on the south shore of Raritan bay and southeast of Point Comfort; running thence north eleven degrees and forty-nine minutes west (N. 11° 49′ W.) in a straight line, passing through a monument two hundred and two and eight-tenths ($202\frac{8}{10}$) feet from the point of beginning, a distance of three hundred and sixty-seven and sixty-two hundredths ($367\frac{62}{100}$) feet; thence, south nineteen degrees and fifty-three minutes west (S. 19° 53′ W.), three hundred and eighty-five and five-tenths ($385\frac{5}{10}$) feet; thence, north, sixty-six degrees and forty-five minutes west (N. 66° 45′ W.), thirteen hundred and seventy-six (1376) feet; thence, south eleven degrees and fifty minutes east (S. 11° 50′ E.), fourteen hundred feet; thence, north seventy-eight degrees and ten minutes east (N. 78° 10′ E.), seven hundred and forty-three and three-tenths ($743\frac{3}{10}$) feet; and thence, north thirty-three degrees and fifty-nine minutes east (N. 33° 59′ E.), eight hundred and sixteen and five-tenths ($816\frac{5}{10}$) feet to the point or place of beginning, containing twenty-five and seven hundred and thirty-four thousandths ($25\frac{734}{1000}$) acres; therefore, Preamble.

State of New Jersey cedes lands to the United States for fortifications, &c

1. Be it enacted *by the Senate and General Assembly of the State of New Jersey*, That the consent of the state of New Jersey is hereby given to the acquisition by the United States of the tract or parcel of land above described, and the same is hereby ceded to the United States of America; upon the said land so acquired the United States may erect fortifications, barracks, and other public buildings, for the defence of the southern or main entrance to New York harbor, and the United States shall have, hold, occupy and own said land thus acquired, and exercise jurisdiction and control over the same and every part thereof subject to the restrictions hereafter mentioned; the same, however, not to be used for quarantine purposes.

Description to be filed in office of secretary of state.

2. *And be it enacted*, That the jurisdiction hereby ceded shall vest when a plat and description of the land thus acquired shall have been filed in the office of the secretary of state of the state of New Jersey; such jurisdiction shall continue no longer than the United States shall own such land, and such consent is given and jurisdiction ceded upon the express condition that the state of New Jersey shall retain concurrent jurisdiction with the United States in and over such land so far as that all civil processes in all cases, and such criminal and other processes as may issue under the laws or authority of the state of New Jersey against any person or persons charged with crimes, misdemeanors or criminal offences committed within the state may be executed thereon, in the same way and manner as if such consent had not been given or jurisdiction ceded, except so far as such processes may affect the real or personal property of the United States.

Not taxable by the state.

3. *And be it enacted*, That so long as such land thus acquired shall remain the property of the United States, and no longer, the same shall be and continue exonerated from all taxes, assessments and other charges which may be levied or imposed under the authority of the State.

4. *And be it enacted*, That this act shall take effect immediately.

Approved March 7, 1893.

CHAPTER XLVI.

A Supplement to an act entitled "An act incorporating the inhabitants of townships, designating their powers and regulating their meetings," approved April fourteenth, one thousand eight hundred and forty-six.

1. BE IT ENACTED *by the Senate and General Assembly of the State of New Jersey*, That the overseers of the poor and town clerks of the respective townships of this state elected after the passage of this act, shall hold their office for the term of three years. Term of office.

2. *And be it enacted*, That all acts or parts of acts inconsistent with the provisions of this act be and the same are hereby repealed, and that this act shall take effect immediately. Repealer.

Approved March 7, 1893.

CHAPTER XLVII.

An Act concerning the constitution of the common council, board of aldermen or other governing body of certain cities in this state.

1. BE IT ENACTED *by the Senate and General Assembly of the State of New Jersey*, That in all cities in this state that now have, or hereafter may have, a population of fifty thousand inhabitants or over, the common council, board of aldermen or other governing body thereof, shall consist of two members in and for each of the wards or aldermanic districts of such cities. In cities of fifty thousand inhabitants governing body shall consist of two members for each ward.

Term of office.

2. *And be it enacted*, That in all cities subject to the provisions of this act, where there now are or hereafter may be three or more members of the common council, board of aldermen or other governing body in and for each of the wards or aldermanic districts of such cities, the office as well as the term of office of every member of such common council, board of aldermen or other governing body in and for each of such wards or aldermanic districts, saving and excepting the oldest and next oldest members thereof, in point of service, having regard to the service of the now or then present terms only of all the members, shall immediately cease, determine and end, and then and from thenceforth the common council, board of aldermen or other governing body of such cities shall consist of but two members in and for each of the wards or aldermanic districts of such cities.

Manner of choosing second member where there is only one now.

3. *And be it enacted*, That in all cities subject to the provisions of this act, where there are now or hereafter may be one member of the common council, board of aldermen or other governing body in and for each of the wards or aldermanic districts of such cities, a second member thereof from each of such wards or aldermanic districts shall be chosen in like manner as though a vacancy existed in the office of members of the common council, board of aldermen or other governing body from each of the wards or aldermanic districts of such cities; or, if there be no provision for an election to fill a vacancy in such an office in any of such cities, then at the next succeeding annual city election in such cities.

Term of office.

4. *And be it enacted*, That hereafter in all cities subject to the provisions of this act, where the common council, board of aldermen or other governing body thereof, now or hereafter shall consist of two members in and for each of the wards or aldermanic districts of such cities, all members of such common council, board of aldermen or other governing body shall be elected for terms of two years each, and in any ward of any city subject to the provisions of this act, where there is or may be, more than one vacancy, one member of council or board of aldermen thereof shall be elected for one year only.

Term of office in case of vacancy.

Repealer.

5. *And be it enacted*, That all acts and parts of acts, general, special, public or local, inconsistent with the

provisions of this act, be and the same are hereby repealed.

6. *And be it enacted,* That this act shall take effect immediately.

Approved March 7, 1893.

CHAPTER XLVIII.

A Further Supplement to an act entitled "An act concerning mortgages," approved March twenty-seventh, one thousand eight hundred and seventy-four.

Chattel mortgages, &c., to be signed and executed by husband and wife and recorded.

1. Be it enacted *by the Senate and General Assembly of the State of New Jersey,* That every mortgage, bill of conditional sale or conveyance hereafter made upon, or for any household goods and furniture in the use and possession of any family in this state, not given to secure the purchase money for such goods and chattels thus in use and possession, shall be absolutely void and of no effect or validity, unless such mortgage, bill of conditional sale, conveyance or instrument in writing intended to affect such household goods and furniture, shall be first duly signed, sealed, executed and acknowledged, according to law, by the husband and wife of the family, and be duly recorded as provided by law, in the county where such household goods and furniture may be situate at the time of the execution of any such instrument intended as a lien or conveyance of or upon such goods and chattels as herein above specified.

2. *And be it enacted,* That this act shall take effect immediately.

Passed March 7, 1893.

CHAPTER XLIX.

An Act to amend an act entitled "An act to establish a system of public instruction" (Revision), approved March twenty-seventh, one thousand eight hundred and seventy-four.

Section repealed.

1. BE IT ENACTED *by the Senate and General Assembly of the State of New Jersey*, That section fifty-five of the act entitled "An act to establish a system of public instruction" (Revision), approved March twenty-seventh, one thousand eight hundred and seventy-four, be and the same is hereby repealed.

Section repealed.

2. *And be it enacted*, That section fifty-five a. of said act be and the same is hereby repealed.

3. *And be it enacted*, That section fifty-seven of said act be and the same is hereby amended to read as follows:

Section as amended.

57. *And be it enacted*, That each county shall be entitled to at least six times as many pupils in the school as it has representatives in the legislature; and in case any county is not fully represented additional candidates may be admitted from other localities on sustaining the requisite examination; the applicants shall give on admission a written declaration signed with their own hands, that their object in seeking admission to the school is to qualify themselves for the employment of public school teachers, and that it is their intention to engage in that employment in this state for at least two years or refund to the state the cost of their tuition.

4. *And be it enacted*, That section sixty of said act be and the same is hereby amended to read as follows:

Section as amended.

60. *And be it enacted*, That for the support of the normal school and to carry out the purpose and designs of this act, there is appropriated hereby the annual sum of twenty-eight thousand dollars, to be paid out of the income of the school fund upon the warrant of the comptroller.

5. *And be it enacted*,. That this act shall take effect immediately.

Approved March 7, 1898.

CHAPTER L.

An Act authorizing the state board of education to erect a suitable building on the grounds of the state normal school, providing additional class-rooms, etc.

1. Be it enacted *by the Senate and General Assembly of the State of New Jersey*, That the state board of education be and they are hereby authorized to erect upon the grounds of the state normal school a suitable building, of such size as the said board may deem proper, for providing additional class-rooms, rooms for instruction in manual training and for such other purposes as in the opinion of the said board may be necessary to increase the accommodations and facilities of the school; and the said board are hereby authorized to procure for the said building such furniture and apparatus as in their judgment may be necessary and requisite for the above-named purposes.

State board of education authorized to erect suitable building to increase accommodation and facilities of school.

2. *And be it enacted*, That the erection and furnishing of the said building shall be done by contract or otherwise, as the board shall deem for the best interest of the state, and the said board shall have power to employ architects, superintendents and mechanics, to advertise for proposals, to make a contract or contracts for the whole or any part of said work, and to incur all necessary expenses to carry out the provisions of this act; and for these purposes the sum of twelve thousand dollars, or so much thereof as may be necessary, is hereby appropriated from the income of the state school fund, the same to be paid by the treasurer of the state, on a warrant of the comptroller, from time to time, as payments shall become due, said payments to be made upon proper vouchers ap-

Building to be erected and furnished by contract or otherwise.

Amount appropriated.

proved and duly certified by the said board or such officers thereof as they may designate for that purpose.

Board to make detailed report.

3. *And be it enacted*, That the said board shall make to the legislature at its next session, and at each succeeding session until the said building is completed, a full and detailed report of their proceedings and expenditures under this act.

4. *And be it enacted*, That this act shall take effect immediately.

Approved March 7, 1898.

CHAPTER LI.

An Act providing for a chief clerk or secretary to the board of tax commissioners or board of assessment and revision of taxes in cities of the first class.

In cities of first class board of tax commissioners authorized to appoint secretary.

1. BE IT ENACTED *by the Senate and General Assembly of the State of New Jersey*, That in cities of the first class, the board of tax commissioners or board of assessment and revision of taxes shall have power to appoint a chief clerk

Term of office.

or secretary for a term of three years from the date of his appointment, at a salary to be fixed by such board at

Salary.

the time of such appointment, not less than eighteen hundred dollars nor more than twenty-five hundred dollars per annum, payable monthly.

Duties of secretary.

2. *And be it enacted*, That such chief clerk or secretary shall, in addition to such other duties as may be imposed upon him by said board, have charge of the records, books and papers of said department, subject, however, to the direction of said board.

Provision for payment of salary.

3. *And be it enacted*, That should there be no appropriation or fund for the payment of such salary, then and in such case the board, or other authority having the charge and control of the finances in any such city, shall make provision therefor in such manner as they may deem

proper, and if money is borrowed for such purpose the amount so borrowed shall be placed in the next tax levy of such city.

Passed March 7, 1893.

CHAPTER LII.

A Further Supplement to an act entitled "An act for the formation of borough governments," approved April fifth, one thousand eight hundred and seventy-eight.

WHEREAS, Doubts have arisen whether the legal voters, residents of boroughs formed under and by virtue of the act entitled "An act for the formation of borough governments," approved April fifth, one thousand eight hundred and seventy-eight, and the several supplements thereto, are entitled to vote in the township out of which or from which the several boroughs were formed, or in the borough of which they are residents; now, therefore, Preamble.

1. BE IT ENACTED *by the Senate and General Assembly of the State of New Jersey*, That the legal voters of all boroughs existing within any of the townships of this state and incorporated under the provisions of the act of which this is a supplement, shall hereafter in all elections vote within their several boroughs. Legal voters shall vote within their boroughs.

2. *And be it enacted*, That at the annual elections for borough officers, which are held on the same day that the town meetings are held in the various townships of this state, the legal voters of said boroughs shall not only be entitled to vote for such officers or appropriations as are authorized by the act entitled "An act for the formation of borough governments," approved April fifth, one thousand eight hundred and seventy-eight, and the several supplements thereto, but shall also be entitled to vote for a chosen freeholder for any township in which such borough is situated and of which it forms a part. Voters of boroughs entitled to vote for chosen freeholder.

County boards of registration appoint boards of registry and election for said boroughs.

3. *And be it enacted*, That the several county boards of registration shall appoint boards of registry and election and registry or poll clerks for the said boroughs of their respective counties, and that all elections held within the said boroughs shall be conducted under the provisions of the act entitled "An act to regulate elections," approved April eighteenth, one thousand eight hundred and seventy-six, and the several supplements thereto and amendments thereof.

Repealer

4. *And be it enacted*, That all acts and parts of acts inconsistent with the provisions of this act be and the same are hereby repealed.

5. *And be it enacted*, That this act shall take effect immediately.

Approved March 7, 1893.

CHAPTER LIII.

An Act relating to cities of the third class.

Mayor and council in cities of third class may elect clerk

1. Be it enacted *by the Senate and General Assembly of the State of New Jersey*, That from and after the passage of this act it shall be lawful in cities of the third class of this state, having a mayor and council, for said mayor and council of said cities to elect a clerk, to fix his compensation and his term of office, and by resolution define the duties to be performed by said clerk.

Repealer.

2. *And be it enacted*, That all acts or parts of acts inconsistent with this act be and the same are hereby repealed, and that this act shall take effect immediately.

Approved March 7, 1893.

CHAPTER LIV.

A Supplement to an act entitled "An act for the formation and government of boroughs," approved April second, one thousand eight hundred and ninety-one.

Preamble.

WHEREAS, Boroughs incorporated under the above mentioned act are empowered by said act to provide for the sewerage and drainage of such boroughs, but said act does not sufficiently set forth and define a manner of procedure for the exercise of the power so conferred by said act; now, therefore,

Council may pass resolution to cause sewers and drains to be constructed on petition of owners of property.

1. BE IT ENACTED *by the Senate and General Assembly of the State of New Jersey*, That whenever a petition in writing of any owner or owners of property interested shall be presented to the council of any borough asking for the construction of a sewer or sewers, drain or drains in such borough, the council of such borough may pass a resolution declaring its intention to cause such sewer or sewers, drain or drains to be constructed, and the said council shall cause public notice of such intention to be given by publishing the said notice of intention in a newspaper printed in the county for the space of two weeks, at least once in each week, briefly describing the character and location of the proposed work, and requesting such persons as may object thereto to present objections in writing to the clerk of the borough at or before the expiration of ten days from the date of such notice of intention, and if persons owning or representing more than one-half of the lineal feet of the land in front of which said proposed sewer or sewers, drain or drains is or are to be constructed shall so present their objections in writing, then such proceedings shall cease; but otherwise, and after the expiration of said ten days, it shall be lawful for such council to pass an ordinance for the construction of such sewer or sewers, drain or drains or such part or parts thereof covered by the notice of intention, as the council may deem advisable, and said ordinance

Publishing notice.

Council to pass an ordinance for construction of such sewer.

Publication of ordinance

so passed and approved by the mayor shall be published for the space of two weeks, at least once in each week, in a newspaper printed in the county in which said borough lies.

Council authorized to purchase lands.

2. *And be it enacted*, That the council shall have power to treat with the owner or owner of any lands across which any proposed sewer or drain is to be constructed for the purchase of the land necessary for the construction of said sewer or drain, or for the right to construct such sewer or drain across said lands, and the price paid for such land or paid for the right of way across said lands necessary for the construction of the sewer or drain shall form a part of the whole cost and expenses of said sewer or drain; and if the council cannot agree with the owner or owners as to the price to be paid, the council shall have the right to apply to the courts for the appointment of commissioners to condemn said land or right of way, and the proceed ngs in such case shall be those usually provided for by law in proceedings for condemnation.

May apply to the courts for appointment of commissioners to condemn land.

Shall advertise for bids.

3. *And be it enacted*, That after the passage of the ordinance and its approval by the mayor the council shall advertise for bids for constructing the work, and upon the basis of the bids received shall cause a preliminary assessment of the entire estimated cost of the work to be made upon the property fronting on said work covered by the ordinance, and when said preliminary assessment has been approved by the council each property owner so assessed shall be notified by the clerk of the borough and be requested to make an advance payment to the treasurer of the borough of the whole or any part of the amount assessed against said property owner on the above preliminary assessment, and said property owner shall receive from the treasurer a certificate or receipt of the amount so paid in as an advance payment on his sewer assessment, and when fifty-five per centum of the entire cost of the work is thus paid to the treasurer of the borough the council may award the contract and order the mayor to execute the same and the work may proceed, and if fifty-five per centum of the entire cost be not received by the treasurer of the borough before the expiration of sixty days after the approval by the council

Property to be assessed.

Owners notified to make advance payment.

Upon payment of fifty-five per cent of entire cost council may award the contract.

of the preliminary assessment the council shall rescind the ordinance, and the treasurer shall forthwith return to the several property owners the amounts respectively paid in, and all expenses for engineering, advertising and all other incidental expenses properly chargeable to the proposed work shall in that case be borne by the borough at large and included in the tax levy.

Council may borrow money, &c.

4. *And be it enacted*, That if upon completion of the work the treasurer has not sufficient money on hand from the advance payments made by the property owners interested to pay the entire cost and expenses of the work, or during the progress of the work to pay for any current estimate, he shall report the amount of the deficiency to the council; and it shall then be lawful for the borough to borrow the money necessary therefor, temporarily, upon promissory notes of the borough, or the borough may issue temporary improvement certificates, and said notes or certificates shall bear a rate of interest not exceeding six per centum per annum, and shall not be issued for a term exceeding three years.

Commissioners to be appointed

5. *And be it enacted*, That upon completion of the entire work authorized by the ordinance, and its acceptance by the council, the council shall appoint three commissioners who shall be disinterested freeholders, not owning or interested in any lands along the line of the improvement, residing in the county in which such borough lies, to revise the preliminary assessment on the basis of the whole cost and expenses of the work duly ascertained (said whole cost and expense of the work to include the expense of engineering, superintendence and assessment, and all other incidental expenses properly chargeable to the work), and the council shall have power to fill any vacancy in the office of the commissioner, occurring from any cause, and said commissioners shall take and subscribe before some person duly authorized to administer the same, an oath or affirmation that they will make such assessment required of them fairly, impartially and legally, according to their best skill and understanding, which oath or affirmation shall be attached to the report that they are hereinafter required to make; and said commissioners having thus qualified shall proceed to revise said preliminary assessment on the basis of the whole

Commissioners to take oath.

cost and expenses of the work duly ascertained, assessing upon the various plots and parcels of land and real estate which they deem benefited by the construction of said sewer or drain amounts proportionate to the benefits that have actually accrued to the various plots and parcels of land and real estate by reason of the construction of said sewer or drain, and in case the whole cost and expense of such work shall exceed the amount of the benefits so assessed upon the land and real estate, then the excess thereof shall be assessed upon and be paid by the borough at large, and be raised by general tax; and before signing the report of the assessment so made, the commissioners shall give public notice of the time and place when and where they will meet for the purpose of giving all persons interested in the same an opportunity to examine said assessment, and hearing any objections to the same that may be made, which notice is to be published in a newspaper printed in the county in which such borough lies for the space of two weeks, at least once in each week, and after such meeting the commissioners, having given due consideration to all objections that may be made, may amend the assessment in any manner they may deem just and equitable, and then shall proceed to complete such report of assessment by signing the same, and transmitting such report of assessment to the council, together with a map showing the various lots and parcels of land so assessed and the names of the owners of the various plots and parcels of land as far as they can be ascertained, with the amounts assessed against the same, and no error or omission in stating the name or names of the owner or owners of such lands shall invalidate the assessment; and the council shall then ratify the assessment so made without delay, and the same shall be final and conclusive as well upon the borough as upon the owners of land affected thereby; and such assessment shall be and remain a first lien upon the lands so assessed to the same extent as taxes and assessments are now a lien under the general laws of this state, and shall bear interest at the rate of six per centum per annum; and the council shall immediately give public notice that such assessment has been ratified.

Public notice to be given and published in a newspaper.

Council to ratify the assessment

Assessment shall be first lien on land.

6. *And be it enacted*, That no certiorari shall be allowed by any court to review any of the proceedings in relation to such work, nor to affect in any way any assessments made by such commissioners, after the lapse of thirty days from the ratification of the council of the borough of such assessment; and such writ of certiorari shall not be allowed unless the party applying for the same shall enter into bond to such borough in sum of two hundred dollars, with two good and sufficient sureties, conditioned that such applicant shall prosecute the said certiorari; and shall pay to the said borough the cost and charges incurred by said borough necessary under the proceedings of the certiorari, with interest, if the assessment shall stand; and said bond to be approved by the court to which the application is made.

Certiorari not allowed by court after thirty days from ratification of assessment.

Party applying for writ shall give bond.

7. *And be it enacted*, That after the ratification of the said assessment, the treasurer of the borough shall credit upon each lot or parcel of land and real estate assessed the amount of the advance payment that may have been made by the owner thereof, under section three of this act, and the balance remaining unpaid upon the assessment shall then be collected as hereinafter provided; and if any owner of land has paid to the treasurer on his advance payments an amount greater than the amount of the assessment against his property, as shown upon such ratified assessment, then the difference shall be refunded to said owner by the treasurer of the borough.

Treasurer to credit amount of advance payment.

8. *And be it enacted*, That if any assessment upon any plot or parcel of land remains unpaid after the expiration of two years from the ratification of the assessment, then the collector of the borough shall proceed to enforce the collection thereof as now required of township collectors in this state; *provided, however*, that when any lands shall be sold against which an unpaid assessment for benefits for construction of a sewer has been returned, the same shall be sold free and clear of all incumbrances and the title thereto shall become an absolute title in fee simple to any purchaser after the expiration of two years from the date of the certificate of such sale, issued by the collector of said borough, in the same manner that certificates of sale are now issued where lands are sold to raise and pay taxes assessed and levied under the general

Collector to enforce collection thereof after two years.

Proviso.

laws of this state, and all proceedings under this act to sell lands to pay such assessments shall be carried on in the same manner and subject to the same rules observed and provided in this state for making the general taxes a first lien upon real estate and providing for the sale of the same, except as herein otherwise provided.

Council authorized to order the assessor to include whole amount in next tax levy.

9. *And be it enacted*, That the council of any borough, in which part of the costs and expenses for building any sewer or sewers, drain or drains has been assessed upon the borough at large, shall have the power to order the assessor of the borough to include the whole amount so assessed upon the borough in the tax levy next following the ratification of the assessment; or such council can, in its discretion, order the amount so assessed against the borough to be assessed and collected in not more than three yearly tax levies next following the ratification of the assessments.

Proceedings under the act to which this is supplement legal

10. *And be it enacted*, That if any borough which is incorporated under the act to which this act is a supplement shall have already begun proceedings for the purpose of constructing sewers or drains, as they are empowered by said act to do, all such proceedings shall have as full legal effect as if they had been taken after the passage of this act; *provided*, they have been taken in a manner set forth in this act, and they are hereby confirmed.

Proviso.

11. *And be it enacted*, That this act shall take effect immediately.

Approved March 7, 1898.

CHAPTER LV.

An Act to amend an act entitled "An act authorizing municipalities governed by commissioners to pave and improve streets and avenues and provide for the payment thereof," approved March eleventh, one thousand eight hundred and ninety-two.

Section to be amended.

1. Be it enacted *by the Senate and General Assembly of the State of New Jersey*, That section one of said act be and the same hereby is amended so as to read as follows:

Governing body in municipality governed by commissioners may pass resolution providing for an election to decide whether street improvements shall be made.

1. Be it enacted *by the Senate and General Assembly of the State of New Jersey*, That whenever the governing body of any municipality, by whatever name the same may be known, and however created, governed by commissioners, shall be desirous of causing any street or streets, avenue or avenues, or portions thereof, lying within the limits of such municipality to be paved, macadamized or otherwise improved, it shall be lawful for such body, after the consent of a majority of the owners of real estate on the street or streets to be improved has been obtained in favor of such improvement, by a majority vote of all the members thereof, at any regular meeting thereof, to call an election of such voters of such municipality, by a resolution of such body, stating the time of holding such election; that the object is to obtain the consent of voters to the paving, macadamizing or improving of a street or streets, avenue or avenues (which shall be named in the resolution), or some portion thereof (which shall be described in the resolution), and to the assessment and collection of a portion of the cost of such improvement upon all the property adjoining and abutting on such improvement, and also the amount of money proposed to be expended for such improvement; and if it is proposed to issue the bonds mentioned in section eighteen of the act hereby amended, said resolution shall also state that it is proposed to issue bonds of said municipality,

Statement of contents of such resolution.

pledging the faith, credit and property thereof, for the payment, with interest, by the said municipality of the proportion (not exceeding three-fifths) of the cost of such improvement not assessed upon the property fronting thereon.

All contracts hereby legalized.

2. *And be it enacted*, That any and all contracts executed by any such municipality for paving, macadamizing or otherwise improving streets or avenues, or parts of them, are hereby legalized and confirmed, notwithstanding any informality in the proceedings.

Amendment not to affect proceedings.

3. *And be it enacted*, That no suit or proceedings in any court of record shall be defeated or affected by this amendment.

4. *And be it enacted*, That this act shall take effect immediately.

Approved March 7, 1893.

CHAPTER LVII.

A Further Supplement to an act entitled "An act relative to sales of lands under a public statute or by virtue of any judicial proceedings," approved March twenty-seventh, eighteen hundred and seventy-four.

Section to be amended.

1. Be it enacted *by the Senate and General Assembly of the State of New Jersey*, That the twelfth section of the act entitled "An act relative to sales of lands under a public statute or by virtue of any judicial proceedings," approved March twenty-seventh, eighteen hundred and seventy-four, be and the same is hereby amended so as to read as follows:

In case of death or disqualification of a master in chancery or sheriff after sale, the court out of which execution issued may appoint another to make deed, &c.

12. *And be it enacted*, That if any master in chancery or the sheriff of any county who hath made or shall make sale of any lands, tenements, hereditaments and real estate by virtue of an execution against the same shall abscond or depart from the state or be disqualified by law or shall die or have died, or in any way become in-

capable of making a deed or conveyance for the same, it shall be lawful for the court out of which the said execution issued, upon satisfactory proof that such sale has been fairly and legally made, to appoint another master in chancery or the then sheriff of the county, who shall have full power on tender of the purchase money, or if the purchase money or any part of it has been paid, then on proof of such payment and on tender of the residue if any there be, to sign, seal and deliver to the said purchaser or his legal representative a deed or conveyance of the lands, tenements, hereditaments and real estate so sold, which deed shall be as good and valid and have the same force and effect as if the master or sheriff who made such sale had signed, sealed and delivered a deed or conveyance for the same in due form of law, and the moneys received on such conveyance shall be paid to the person entitled thereto by law. Effect of such deed.

2. *And be it enacted*, That this act act shall be deemed a public act and take effect immediately.

Approved March 8, 1893.

CHAPTER LVIII.

A Supplement to an act entitled "An act for the preservation of clams and oysters," approved April fourteenth, anno domini one thousand eight hundred and forty-six.

1. BE IT ENACTED *by the Senate and General Assembly of the State of New Jersey*, That in order to better carry out and enforce the provisions of the act to which this act is a supplement, and the acts supplementary thereto, it shall be lawful for the directors of any association of oystermen duly incorporated under the laws of this state to appoint special officers, not exceeding three in number, Special officers, how appointed.

who shall be citizens of this state, and who shall be and hereby are empowered at all times while holding the office or position of such special officer, upon their own view, to arrest any person or persons who may be found violating or infringing any of the provisions of the act to which this act is a supplement or of any of the acts supplementary thereto, and to bring him or them before a magistrate for examination.

Special officers to have power to arrest all persons violating this act.

2. *And be it enacted*, That such special officers shall be paid for their services under this act by the association appointing them and not otherwise.

How special officers are paid.

3. *And be it enacted*, That this act shall be deemed a public act, and shall take effect immediately.

Approved March 8, 1893.

CHAPTER LIX.

An Act for extending the time for completing certain railroads.

Extending time for completion of certain railroad.

1. Be it enacted *by the Senate and General Assembly of the S'ate of New Jersey*, That whenever the time limited for the completion of any railroad authorized to be constructed within this state under any special or general act has expired or shall expire before the thirty-first day of December, one thousand eight hundred and ninety-four, such time shall be and the same is hereby extended for the further period of two years from the passage of this act; *provided, however*, that this act shall not apply unless money has actually been expended in surveys or location of route, or in acquisition of right of way or in construction since January first, one thousand eight hundred and eighty-six; *provided, further*, that this act shall not apply to any corporation unless such corporation shall first, and as the condition precedent to the exercise of any power granted by this act, file in the office of the

Proviso.

Proviso.

secretary of state an agreement, to be approved by the governor and attorney-general, waiving all right of exemption from taxation, and from privileges and advantages arising from any law or contract, if any there be, establishing any special mode of taxation of any such corporation and the further agreement to be bound by any general law of this state now in existence or that may be hereafter passed, taxing such corporations as are now authorized to be taxed by the legislature of the state under any general law, and further agreeing that the exercise of any power granted by this act shall not in any way affect the rights of this state, if any there exist, to take the property of such corporations under any existing law of this state, and agreeing, further, that all laws affecting such corporations shall be subject to alteration or repeal by the legislature.

2. *And be it enacted*, That this act shall be deemed a public act and shall take effect immediately.

Approved March 8, 1893.

CHAPTER LX.

An Act to amend an act entitled "An act to incorporate the chosen freeholders in the respective counties of the state" (Revision), approved April sixteenth, one thousand eight hundred and forty-six.

1. Be it enacted *by the Senate and General Assembly of the State of New Jersey*, That section twenty-eight of said act, which reads as follows: Section to be amended

"28. *And be it enacted*, That the county collectors of the several counties of this state shall be entitled to receive two cents, and no more, for each dollar of all taxes and other moneys which they shall receive and pay to the order of such corporation; but in case the board of chosen freeholders of any of the counties in this state are of opinion that the fees named in this section are too high, they are hereby authorized to fix the fees of the county collector for receiving and paying county money at a less rate; *provided*, the same shall be so fixed before the election of any county collector to be affected thereby," be and the same is hereby amended so as to read as follows:

County collectors' fees.

28. *And be it enacted*, That the county collectors of the several counties of this state shall be entitled to receive two cents, and no more, for each dollar of all taxes and other moneys which they shall receive and pay to the order of such corporation; but in case the board of chosen freeholders of any of the counties in this state are of the opinion that the fees named in this section are too high, they are hereby authorized to fix the fees of the county collector for receiving and paying county money at a less rate; *provided*, the same shall be so fixed before the election of any county collector to be affected thereby; *and provided, further*, that in all counties of the first class in this state the fees of the county collector so fixed, or hereafter to be fixed by the board of chosen freeholders of any such county of the first class, shall not be fixed at a less rate than shall give such county collector of any such county of the first class the sum of three thousand five hundred dollars per annum.

Proviso.

Proviso.

Repealer.

2. *And be it enacted*, That all acts and parts of acts inconsistent herewith be and the same are hereby repealed, and that this act shall take effect immediately.

Approved March 8, 1893.

CHAPTER LXI.

A Further Supplement to an act entitled "An act to incorporate the chosen freeholders in the respective counties of this state" (Revision), approved April sixteenth, one thousand eight hundred and forty-six.

1. BE IT ENACTED *by the Senate and General Assembly of the State of New Jersey*, That the auditor or other officer appointed by the board of chosen freeholders in any county of this state for the purpose of exercising supervision over the expenditure and receipt of moneys by the collector of said county shall hereafter be appointed and shall hold his office for the term of three years or until his successor shall have been elected and shall have qualified, unless he shall have been sooner removed in the manner provided by law. Term of office of county auditor.

2. *And be it enacted*, That this act shall take effect immediately.

Approved March 8, 1893.

CHAPTER LXII.

An Act enabling cities to construct connecting pipe lines or mains.

1. BE IT ENACTED *by the Senate and General Assembly of the State of New Jersey*, That it shall and may be lawful for the municipal board of any city having charge and control of the water works for the supply of the inhabitants thereof, whenever in its judgment it shall be expedient so to do, to cause to be constructed an additional The board having charge of water works authorized to have constructed an additional cast-iron pipe line.

suitable cast-iron pipe line or main to connect any reservoir or water supply of such city, located outside of the limits of such city, with any distributing reservoir within such city, or with the supply pipes or mains at any point within such city; *provided*, such pipe line shall be constructed by contract, after public bidding therefor in the manner prescribed in the laws now governing such city.

Proviso

Board authorized to issue water bonds.

2. *And be it enacted*, That in order to supply the funds required for such construction, it shall be the duty of the board having charge and control of the finances of such city, upon the request of the board having charge and control of the water supply therein, to issue the water bonds of the city to the amount so required, which bonds shall be sold at public sale for not less than par and accrued interest.

Bonds payable in thirty years.

To bear interest at five per cent. annually.

3. *And be it enacted*, That the bonds to be issued under the provisions of this act shall be payable in not more than thirty years from the date thereof; they shall bear interest at a rate not exceeding five per centum per annum, and be in such sums as said financial board shall determine; they shall be executed under the corporate seal of such city and the signature of the mayor, comptroller or other financial officer, and may be either registered or coupon bonds, as said financial board may direct; said financial board may, from time to time, at the request of the holders thereof, exchange coupon bonds for registered bonds; *provided, however*, that the total cost of such works and the bonds to be issued therefor shall not exceed in any city a sum equal to four dollars for each inhabitant thereof, as ascertained by the latest census, taken by the state or federal authorities, as the case may be.

Proviso.

Sinking fund shall be established

4. *And be it enacted*, That in order to redeem said bonds at maturity, there shall be established in such city a sinking fund, into which it shall be the duty of said water board to pay annually, in the month of July in each year, out of the income derived from such water supply, a sum equal to two percentum of the bonds issued under the provisions of this act, which sinking fund shall be under the charge and control of the sinking fund commissioners of such city, by whatsoever name they may be called.

5. *And be it enacted*, That the interest on said bonds shall be paid semi-annually, out of the collections for water rents in such city. Interest to be paid semi-annually.

6. *And be it enacted*, That this act shall take effect immediately.

Approved March 8, 1893.

CHAPTER LXIII.

An Act concerning the compensation of the city collector of any city of the first class in this state.

1. BE IT ENACTED *by the Senate and General Assembly of the State of New Jersey*, That the compensation of the city collector of any city of the first class in this state shall be fixed at such sum not exceeding five thousand dollars as the board of finance or board having control and custody of the finances of any such city shall determine. Compensation of collectors in cities of first class.

2. *And be it enacted*, That any deficiency in appropriation necessary to comply with the provisions of this act shall be provided by the board of finances or board having control and custody of the finances of any such city as aforesaid, who are hereby authorized to borrow the necessary amount and to pledge the faith of the city for payment thereof to be met by an appropriation in the tax levy next succeeding, and annually thereafter an appropriation shall be inserted in the tax levy sufficient to cover said expenditure. Board having control authorized to borrow necessary amount.

3. *And be it enacted*, That all acts and parts of acts inconsistent with the provisions of this act are hereby repealed, and this act shall take effect immediately. Repealer.

Approved March 8, 1893.

CHAPTER LXIV.

A Supplement to an act entitled "An act authorizing the inhabitants of townships to purchase or erect a building for township purposes," approved March first, one thousand eight hundred and eighty-six.

Township committee or governing body authorized to purchase lot and erect building for township purposes.

1. BE IT ENACTED *by the Senate and General Assembly of the State of New Jersey*, That in any township in this state in which the inhabitants thereof have authorized or may hereafter authorize the purchase or erection of a building for township purposes, in accordance with the provisions of the act to which this is a supplement, it shall be lawful for the township committee or other governing body of such township to purchase a lot and erect thereon a building, or to purchase a lot and building, taking title thereto in the corporate name of the inhabitants of said township; *provided*, that the total cost of such building, with the lot whereon the same shall stand, shall not exceed one per centum of the assessed valuation of the property in such township for the year next preceding the election at which the purchase of such lot and the erection of such building may have been authorized.

Proviso.

Powers herein conferred on township committees who have heretofore or may hereafter enter into contracts.

2. *And be it enacted*, That the provisions of this supplement and the powers herein conferred are hereby extended to and conferred on the township committees of the various townships of this state where they have heretofore entered into contracts, or may hereafter enter into contracts, for the purchase of a lot and the erection of a building under the authority of the act to which this is a supplement, or by virtue of authority granted for the erection of a building by the inhabitants of such township at an annual election or town meeting; and all acts done in connection therewith are hereby declared to be legal and valid and binding on such township or townships and the inhabitants thereof.

3. *And be it enacted,* That all acts and parts of acts inconsistent with the provisions of this act, be and the same are hereby repealed in so far as their operation may affect this act. Repealer.

4. *And be it enacted,* That this act shall take effect immediately.

Approved March 8, 1898.

CHAPTER LXV.

An Act to provide for the appointment of a collector of arrears of personal taxes in cities of the first class.

1. BE IT ENACTED *by the Senate and General Assembly of the State of New Jersey,* That it shall and may be lawful for the board having charge and control of the finances and the confirmation of the annual tax levy in any city of the first class in this state to appoint an officer to be known as "the collector of arrears of personal taxes" for such city; each appointment shall be for the term of three years from the date thereof, and said officer shall receive for his services a salary to be fixed by such board, not to exceed the sum of fifteen hundred dollars per annum, payable monthly. Board of finances in cities of first class authorized to appoint officer to be known as "the collector of personal taxes." Salary.

2. *And be enacted,* That all warrants and other processes for the collection of personal taxes in such city shall be directed to and executed by such collector, who shall have all the power in relation thereto now vested by law in any constable of the state of New Jersey. Powers of such collector.

3. *And be it enacted,* That this act shall take effect immediately.

Approved March 8, 1898.

CHAPTER LXVI.

An Act concerning the designation of official newspapers in cities of the first class in this state.

Municipal authorities of cities of the first class may designate an additional official newspaper.

1. Be it enacted *by the Senate and General Assembly of the State of New Jersey*, That it shall be lawful for the proper municipal authorities of any city of the first class in this state to designate as an official newspaper, in addition to the official newspapers authorized to be designated by the charter of such city, one daily newspaper which shall have been published in such city for a less period than one year.

Board of finance shall provide for payment of advertising or publishing done.

2. *And be it enacted*, That should there be no appropriation or fund applicable for the payment of any advertising or publishing done by any such city in such paper so designated as an official newspaper hereunder, that then and in such case the board or other authority having the charge and control of the finances in any such city shall make provision therefor in such manner as they may deem proper, and if money is borrowed for such purpose the amount so borrowed shall be placed in the next tax levy of such city.

Repealer.

3. *And be it enacted*, That all acts and parts of acts inconsistent with the provisions of this act be and the same are hereby repealed.

4. *And be it enacted*, That this act shall take effect immediately.

Approved March 8, 1893.

CHAPTER LXVII.

An Act to authorize corporations incorporated under the laws of this state to merge and consolidate their corporate franchises and other property.

Corporations incorporated under the laws of this state may merge and consolidate.

1. BE IT ENACTED *by the Senate and General Assembly of the State of New Jersey*, That any two or more corporations organized or to be organized under any law or laws of this state for the purpose of carrying on any kind of business of the same or a similar nature, may merge or consolidate such corporations into a single corporation, which may be either one of said merging or consolidating corporations, or a new corporation to be formed by means of such merger and consolidation.

How the consolidation or merger shall be made.

2. *And be it enacted*, That the said consolidation or merger shall be made under the conditions, provisions, restrictions, and with the powers hereafter mentioned and contained, that is to say:

Mode of proceeding for the merger and consolidation of corporations.

I. The directors of the several corporations proposing to merge or consolidate may enter into a joint agreement under the corporate seals of the respective corporations, for the merger or consolidation of said corporation, and prescribing the terms and conditions thereof, the mode of carrying the same into effect, the name of the new corporation (if one shall be so formed or created), or of the consolidated corporation, as the case may be; the number, names and places of residence of the first directors and officers of such new or consolidated corporation (who shall hold their offices until their successors shall be chosen or appointed, either according to law or according to the by-laws of the said corporation;) the number of shares of the capital stock, either common or preferred, and the amount or par value of each share of such new or consolidated corporation; and the manner of converting the capital stock of each of said merging or consolidating corporations into the stock or obligations of such new or consolidated corporation, and in case of the creation of a new corporation, how and when the directors and officers shall be chosen or appointed; together with all such other provisions and details as such first mentioned directors shall deem necessary to perfect the merger or consolidation of said corporation.

Agreement shall be submitted to the stockholders.

II. The said agreement shall be submitted to the stockholders of each of said merging or consolidating corporations, separately, at a meeting thereof, to be called for the purpose of taking the same into consideration; and twenty days' notice of the time, place and object of such meeting shall be mailed to the last known postoffice address of each of such stockholders respectively; and, at the said meetings of stockholders the said agreement of such directors shall be considered, and a vote of the stockholders of each corporation by ballot shall be taken separately, for the adoption or rejection of the same, each share of stock entitling the holder thereof to one vote, and said ballots shall be cast in person or by proxy; and if the votes of the holders of two-thirds of all the capital stock of each of the said merging or consolidating corporations shall be for the adoption of said agreement, then that fact shall be certified thereon by the secretary of each of the respective corporations, under the seal thereof, and the agreement, so adopted and so certified, shall be filed in the office of the secretary of state, and shall from thence be deemed and taken to be the agreement and act of merger or consolidation of the said corporations, and a copy of said agreement and act of merger or consolidation, duly certified by the secretary of state under the seal thereof, shall be evidence of the existence of such new or consolidated corporation.

Notice of the time, &c., of meeting.

Votes of the holders of two-thirds of all the capital stock required.

Agreement to be filed in office of secretary of state

Corporations merging or consolidating shall be taken to be one corporation.

3. *And be it enacted*, That upon the making and perfecting the said agreement and act of merger or consolidation, as provided in the preceding section, and filing the same in the office of the secretary of state, as aforesaid, the several corporations, parties thereto, shall be deemed and taken to be one corporation, by the name provided in said agreement (in case a new corporation shall be created thereby), or by the name of the consolidated corporation into which said other contracting corporation or corporations shall be so merged or consolidated, as the case may be, and possessing all the rights,

privileges, powers and franchises, as well of a public as of a private nature, and being subject to all the restrictions, disabilities and duties of each of such corporations so merged or consolidated, except as altered by the provisions of this act.

Upon merging or consolidating, as aforesaid, all the rights, privileges, property, &c., of each corporation shall be vested in the new or consolidated corporation.

4. *And be it enacted*, That upon the consummation of said act of merger or consolidation, as aforesaid, all and singular, the rights, privileges, powers and franchises of each of said corporations, parties to the same, and all property, real, personal and mixed, and all debts due on whatever account, as well for stock subscriptions as all other things in action or belonging to each of such corporations, shall be deemed and taken without further act or deed to be transferred to and vested in the corporation into which such merger or consolidation shall have been made; and all property rights, privileges, powers and franchises, and all and every other interest shall be thereafter as effectually the property of the said new or consolidated corporation as they were of the several and respective former corporations, parties to said agreement; and the title to any real estate, whether by deed or otherwise, under the laws of this state, vested in either of such corporations, shall not be deemed to revert or be in any way impaired by reason of this act; *provided, however*, that all rights of creditors and all liens upon the property of either of said former corporations shall be preserved unimpaired, and the respective former corporations may be deemed to continue in existence, in order to preserve the same; and all debts, liabilities and duties of either of said former corporations shall thenceforth attach to said new or consolidated corporation, and may be enforced against it to the same extent as if said debts, liabilities and duties had been incurred or contracted by it.

Proviso.

Any stockholder dissenting or refusing to convert his stock into the stock of the new or consolidated corporation may petition the court of common pleas for the appointment of appraisers.

5. *And be it enacted*, That where the corporation or corporations authorized to merge or consolidate by the first section of this act, shall have the right to exercise any franchise, for public use, then if any stockholder of any corporation hereby authorized to be merged or consolidated with any other or others, not voting in favor of such agreement, shall dissent therefrom and shall refuse or neglect to convert his or her stock into the stock of such new or consolidated corporation, or to dispose there-

of in the manner and on the terms specified in such agreement, such dissenting stockholder or such new or consolidated corporation may, at any time within thirty days after the adoption and filing of the said agreement of consolidation by the stockholders as in this act provided, apply by petition to the court of common pleas of the county in which the chief office of the corporation whose stockholders shall so dissent or neglect, was or is located, or to a judge of said court in vacation (if no such court sits within said period), on reasonable notice to be prescribed by said court or judge to said new or consolidated corporation, or to such dissenting stockholder, as the case may be, for the appointment of three disinterested appraisers to appraise the full market value of his or her stock, without regard to any depreciation or appreciation thereof in consequence of the said merger or consolidation, and whose award (or that of a majority of them), when confirmed by the said court, shall be final and conclusive on all parties, and said new or consolidated corporation shall pay to such stockholder the value of his or her stock as aforesaid; and on receiving such payment, or on a tender of such value, or in case of any legal disability or absence from the state, on the payment of such value into said court, said stockholder shall transfer his or her said stock to the said new or consolidated corporation, to be disposed of by the directors thereof, or to be retained for the benefit of the remaining stockholders thereof; and in case the value of said stock as aforesaid is not so paid or tendered within thirty days from the filing of said award and confirmation by said court, and notice thereof to be given in manner aforesaid unto said stockholder or said new or consolidated corporation, the amount of the value of said stock, so found and confirmed, shall be a judgment against said corporation, and may be collected as other judgments in said court are by law recoverable.

The award, when confirmed by said court, shall be final and conclusive on all parties.

The value of said stock, if not paid, shall be a judgment against said corporation.

6. *And be it enacted*, That in all cases of merger or consolidation of two or more corporations under and by virtue of the provisions of this act, the said new or consolidated corporation shall have power and authority to issue bonds or other obligations, negotiable or otherwise, and with or without coupons or interest certificates thereto attached, to an amount sufficient with its capital

New or consolidated corporation authorized to issue bonds, &c

stock to provide for all the payments it will be required to make or obligations it will be required to assume, in order to effect such merger or consolidation; to secure the payment of which bonds or obligations it shall be lawful to mortgage its corporate franchises, rights, privileges and property, real, personal and mixed; *provided*, such bonds shall not bear a greater rate of interest than six per centum per annum; and that it shall also be lawful for said new or consolidated corporation to purchase, acquire hold and dispose of the stocks of other corporations of this state or elsewhere, and to exercise in respect thereto all the powers of stockholders thereof; and that it shall also be lawful for said new or consolidated corporation to issue capital stock, either common or preferred or both, to such an amount as may be necessary, to the stockholders of such merging or consolidating corporations in exchange or payment for their original shares, in the manner and on the terms specified in said agreement of merger or consolidation; which agreement may also provide for the issue of preferred stock based on the property or stock of the merging or consolidating corporations conveyed to the new or consolidated corporation, as well as upon money capital paid in, and may fix the amount of such preferred stock. Proviso.

7. *And be it enacted*, That the provisions of this act shall not apply to any railroad company, insurance company (except companies for the insurance or guaranty of the title to lands or any estates or interests in lands), banking company, savings bank or other corporation intended to derive profit from the loan and use of money, turnpike company or canal company. Companies exempt from the provisions of this act.

8. *And be it enacted*, That all acts and parts of acts inconsistent herewith, be and the same are hereby repealed, and that this act shall take effect immediately. Repealer.

Approved March 8, 1893.

CHAPTER LXVIII.

An Act to authorize street railway companies, or companies owning railroads operated as street railways to lease their property and franchises to any other street railway company, or railroad company operated as a street railway, and to authorize the lessees to provide for the financial and other management of the property and franchises so leased.

Street railway companies authorized to lease their property and franchises.

1. *Be it enacted by the Senate and General Assembly of the State of New Jersey*, That it shall and may be lawful for any company owning any street railway or railways, or any company owning any railroad company operated as a street railway, whether such lessor company or companies are incorporated under any general or special act of this state, to lease their property and franchises to any other street railway company or railroad operated as a street railway created under the laws of this state and such other company or companies are hereby authorized to take such lease for such term or terms, upon such condition or conditions as to the use and operation of the property of the lessor corporation, the enjoyment of privileges of such lessor corporation according to the provisions and restrictions contained in any general act, or in the acts under which said lessor company was incorporated; and the amount of rent to be paid therefor, and the manner of making payment of said rent, and such other conditions, limitations and restrictions as said lessor and lessee corporations may agree upon; *provided*, that no greater tolls or charges shall be made or demanded by any lessee corporation than were or are authorized to be charged and collected for the same service by the corporation or corporations, lessor or lessors in said lease.

Proviso.

2. *And be it enacted*, That any stockholder of any company or companies whose property and franchises shall

be leased under the provisions of this act who shall not assent to such lease, or who shall resist or object to the making thereof, may at any time within thirty days after the making of such lease as in this act provided apply by petition to the circuit court of the county in which the chief office of the lessor corporation may be kept, or to a judge of said court in vacation, if no such court sits within such period, on reasonable notice to said company, to appoint three disinterested persons to estimate the damage, if any, done to such stockholder by said proposed lease; and whose award, or that of a majority of them, when confirmed by said court, shall be final and conclusive; and the persons so appointed shall also appraise said stock of such stockholder at the full market value thereof without regard to any depreciation or appreciation in consequence of the said lease; and the said lessor company may, at its election, either pay to the said stockholder the amount of damages so found and awarded, if any, or the value of the stock so ascertained and determined, and upon the payment of the value of the stock as aforesaid the said stockholder shall transfer the stock so held by him to said lessor company to be disposed of by the directors of said company or to be retained for the benefit of the remaining stockholders; and in case the value of said stock as aforesaid is not so paid within thirty days from the filing of said award and confirmation by said court, and notice to said lessor company, the damages so found and confirmed shall be a judgment against said company and collected as other judgments in said court are, by law, recoverable.

Any stockholder not assenting to such lease may petition the circuit court to appoint three disinterested persons to estimate the damage, whose award, when confirmed by the court, shall be final.

The value of said stock, if not paid, shall be a judgment against said corporations

3. *And be it enacted*, That it shall and may be lawful for any corporation or corporations which shall become lessee of any such railroad or railway, under the provisions of this act, to purchase, hold, sell, assign, transfer, mortgage, pledge, or otherwise dispose of the shares of the capital stock, securities, or other evidences of debt issued or created by any other corporation or corporations organized under the law of this state, and to exercise, while owners of such stock, securities, or other evidences of debt, all the rights, powers and privileges. including the right to vote on such stock, which natural

Lessee may purchase, sell, assign, transfer, mortgage or dispose of shares of capital stock, &c.

Lessee may increase its capital stock.

persons, being the owners of such stock, securities, or other evidences of debt, might, could or would exercise.

4. *And be it enacted*, That any corporation, so becoming a lessee corporation under and by virtue of the provisions of this act, may increase its capital stock to such amount as may be determined by its board of directors; *provided*, that such corporation shall, previous to issuing of any such stock, file in the office of the secretary of state a certificate, signed by its president and under its corporate seal attested by its secretary, setting forth the amount of the proposed increase of capital stock and the number of shares into which the same is to be divided, and also the assent in writing of stockholders owning at least two-thirds in value of the existing capital stock to said increase of capital stock.

Proviso.

Lessee may borrow money, issue bonds, &c.

5. *And be it enacted*, That any corporation so becoming a lessee corporation under and by virtue of the provisions of this act shall have the right to borrow from time to time such sum or sums of money as may be necessary for the financial and other management of the property, not exceeding at any one time the total amount of authorized capital stock of such lessee corporation, and for the repayment thereof may issue bonds registered or with coupons or interest certificates thereto attached or both, secured by a mortgage or mortgages, covering all the corporate franchises, rights, privileges, assets, real and personal, of such mortgagor corporation, including stock and securities of such corporation or in any other corporation whose stock or securities it owns, which mortgage may be recorded as mortgages of real estate are or hereafter may be by law required to be recorded, in the office of the clerk or register of deeds of the county or counties in which the railway or railways described in said mortgage may be located, and in the office of the clerk or register of deeds of the county in which the principal office of such corporation is situate, and such record or the lodgment of such mortgage in such clerk's or register's office for record shall have the same force, operation and effect as to all judgment creditors, purchasers or mortgagees in good faith, as the record or lodgment for that purpose of mortgages of real estate now

Mortgage may be recorded.

have, although such mortgage may not have been executed, proved or recorded as a chattel mortgage.

6. *And be it enacted*, That no corporation or corporations issuing bonds under the provisions of this act shall plead any statute or statutes against usury in any court of law or equity in any suit instituted to enforce the payment of such bonds or mortgages. Shall not plead statute against usury in any suit to enforce payment of bonds.

7. *And be it enacted*, That all acts and parts of acts inconsistent with this act, to the extent of such inconsistency, be and the same are hereby repealed, and that this act shall take effect immediately. Repealer.

Approved March 8, 1893.

CHAPTER LXIX.

An Act to amend an act entitled "An act to authorize street railway companies incorporated by or under the laws of this state to merge and consolidate their corporate franchises and other property," approved April sixteenth, one thousand eight hundred and ninety-one.

1. Be it enacted *by the Senate and General Assembly of the State of New Jersey*, That section one of the said act be amended to read as follows: Section to be amended

1. Be it enacted *by the Senate and General Assembly of the State of New Jersey*, That it shall be lawful for any horse or other street railway company or companies or any company or companies owning or operating a railroad operated as a street railway incorporated by or under the laws of this state, to merge and consolidate its corporate franchises and other property with the corporate franchises and other property of any other horse or other street railway company incorporated by or under the laws of this state, which merger and consolidation may be effected in the same manner provided by Horse or other street railway companies may merge and consolidate

the statutes of this state for the merger and consolidation of horse railroad companies.

Repealer.

2. *And be it enacted*, That all acts and parts of acts inconsistent with or repugnant to this act, to the extent of such inconsistency or repugnancy, be and the same are hereby repealed, and that this act shall take effect immediately.

Approved March 8, 1893.

CHAPTER LXX.

A Further Supplement to an act entitled "An act to increase the powers of township committees," approved March eleventh, one thousand eight hundred and eighty.

Additional powers given to township committees.

1. BE IT ENACTED *by the Senate and General Assembly of the State of New Jersey*, That the township committees of the several townships of this state shall hereafter have the following powers, in addition to the powers now vested by law in township committees; *provided, however*, that nothing in this act shall apply to or affect any street, avenue or highway under the charge or control of any county public road board in this state:

Proviso.

To order constructed any sewer or drain.

I. To order and cause to be constructed any sewer or drain, whether open or covered, for the drainage of any street, highway or public place; to order and cause any street, highway or alley already laid out or which may hereafter be laid out, or any part or parts thereof, to be straightened, altered or widened, and to take and appropriate for any such purposes any lands and real estate upon making compensation to the owner or owners thereof by the payment of damages;

To order any street, &c., to be straightened.

To take for such purpose lands upon compensating the owner.

To order street to be graded, paved, &c.

II. To order and cause any street, highway or alley, or any part or parts thereof, to be graded, graveled, paved, macadamized or otherwise improved, as to them may seem advisable;

III. To alter the grade of any sidewalk, street or highway, or of any part or parts thereof, and to ascertain and establish the boundaries of all streets, highways and alleys in said township, and to prevent and remove all obstructions and encroachments that may have been or may be made thereon;

To alter grade of sidewalks, &c.

To remove all obstructions.

IV. To regulate, clean, and keep in repair all sidewalks, streets, highways and alleys in said township; to direct and regulate the planting, rearing, trimming and preserving the shade trees in the same, and to authorize or to prohibit the removal or destruction of said trees; to enforce the removal of snow, ice or dirt from the sidewalks and gutters of said streets, highways or alleys by the owner or occupant of the premises fronting thereon, and also to prevent and forbid the removal of earth, gravel or any other road making materials from the highways by any person or persons not acting under the authority of the township committee, and also to abate and remove nuisances of every kind in any of the highways or public places of the township;

To regulate and repair sidewalks, &c.

To direct the planting of shade trees

To enforce removal of snow, &c., from sidewalks, &c.

To prevent removal of earth.

To abate and remove nuisances.

V. To prevent and punish immoderate driving or riding in any street or highway, driving over or upon any sidewalk, and any cruelty to animals, and to authorize the detaining without warrant, and the arrest of any person who may be guilty thereof;

To prevent immoderate driving

To authorize detaining without warrant

VI. To lay and regulate, or prohibit the laying of water or gas or sewer pipes in or under the streets and roads, or any part thereof, in said township, and to provide street lamps for, and to light the streets either with gas or other material;

To regulate laying of water, gas or sewer pipes.

To provide street lamps.

VII. To improve the streets, public roads and highways of the township by macadamizing, grading and paving the same, or otherwise, under the direction and control of the township committee, and also for the purpose of improving the sidewalks in said township, under the like direction and control, by curbing the same, or otherwise, and to determine in what manner any street, road or highway, or any part or parts thereof, shall be so improved;

To improve streets by macadamizing, &c., improve sidewalks by curbing, &c

To regulate erection of signs or awnings.

VIII. To regulate or prohibit the erection of signs or awnings over the streets or sidewalks.

Town committees may pass ordinances, prescribe penalties, prosecute offenders, &c

2 *And be it enacted*, That for the enforcement of the foregoing provisions of this act, the township committees of the several townships of this shall have power to pass, alter and repeal, from time to time, any and all such ordinances as they shall think proper, to carry into effect the powers conferred by any or all of the foregoing purposes; and shall have authority to prescribe a penalty or penalties for the violation of any ordinance or ordinances, passed for any purpose under the fifth subdivision above, by a fine not exceeding fifty dollars; and may, in the name of the clerk of the township, prosecute offenders against the said provisions or of the said ordinances, before any justice of the peace elected in the township; and that the book of records of the ordinances of the said township shall be taken and received in all courts or elsewhere, as evidence of the due passage of all the ordinances recorded therein.

Book of record of ordinances received in all courts

Notice to be served upon owners of lots before ordinance shall be passed.

3. *And be it enacted*, That when at any meeting of the township committee any ordinance shall be offered at said meeting by any member of said township committee, for any of the powers conferred on them by the first, second and third subdivisions hereof, such ordinance shall not be passed until the township committee shall have caused notice to be served upon the owners of lots or lands fronting or bordering upon the street affected by such ordinance, if such owners are known; such notice to contain a copy of the proposed ordinance, and stating the time and place when such ordinance will come before said township committee for final passage, which notice shall be served on such owner or owners, if known, at least five days prior to said time, by giving to each of them a copy thereof personally or left at their usual place of abode with a member of the family over the age of fourteen years, at which time and place all persons interested in said ordinance may appear and be heard by themselves, or their counsel, for or against the passage of such ordinance.

What such notice shall contain.

Ordinances shall be recorded by township clerk in book for that purpose, &c

4. *And be it enacted*, That all ordinances that shall hereafter be passed by any township committee shall be engrossed by the township clerk in a book to be provided

for that purpose, with a proper index, which book shall be deemed a public record of such ordinances, and shall be and remain in the custody of the township clerk, and that every such ordinance hereafter passed shall be signed in the said book of the record of ordinances by the chairman of the township committee and the township clerk.

5. *And be it enacted*, That every ordinance hereafter passed as aforesaid shall be published one issue in a newspaper printed and circulating in such township, or it none be printed in such township then in a newspaper printed in the county and circulating in such township, and until such ordinance shall have been so published as aforesaid, the same shall be of no effect.

Every ordinance shall be published in a newspaper or same shall be of no effect.

6. *And be it enacted*, That the said book of the record of ordinances shall be taken and received in all courts as evidence of said ordinances, and that copies of said ordinances, certified by the township clerk, under the corporate seal of the township, shall likewise be taken and received in all courts as evidence of said ordinances, and that the publication of said ordinances in a newspaper, as herein required, shall, in all cases, be presumed to have been made, until the contrary shall be proved.

The book of record of ordinances or copies certified by the township clerk, shall be received in all courts as evidence.

7. *And be it enacted*, That this act shall be deemed a public act, and shall take effect immediately.

Approved March 8, 1893.

CHAPTER LXXII.

An Act concerning the collection of arrears of taxes in cities of this state.

1. BE IT ENACTED *by the Senate and General Assembly of the State of New Jersey*, That in any city of this state in which the collection of arrears of taxes is now performed by deputy collectors of arrears of taxes, it shall and may be lawful for the receiver of taxes of such city, or other

The receiver of taxes authorized to appoint, with the consent of finance committee or board of finance, additional deputy collectors.

officer who has heretofore appointed the said deputy collectors in said city, to appoint, with the sanction and consent of the finance committee or board of finance of said city, such additional deputy collectors as may from time to time be necessary for the prompt and efficient collection of the arrears of taxes in said city; and said additional deputies shall have the same powers, perform the same duties and be subject to the same requirements as the said deputy collectors of arrears of taxes are now subject to in said city.

2. *And be it enacted*, That this act shall take effect immediately.

Approved March 9, 1898.

CHAPTER LXXIII.

A Further Supplement to an act entitled "An act to provide for sewage and drainage in incorporated townships in which there is a public water supply," approved April fourteenth, one thousand eight hundred and ninety.

Commissioners of assessment shall assess both for direct and prospective benefits all lands benefited or to be benefited.

1. BE IT ENACTED *by the Senate and General Assembly of the State of New Jersey*, That whenever in strict conformity with the provisions of section eight of the act to which this is a further supplement, commissioners of assessment so appointed by the circuit court shall determine that the sewage district or drainage area extends so as to include lands lying in adjacent cities, towns or townships, and that the drainage from such cities, towns or townships does or may discharge through the sewer or sewers which may have been constructed under the provisions of the act of which this is a further supplement; that the said commissioners shall assess both for direct and prospective benefits all such lands benefited or to be benefited within the said entire drainage area, and that

said assessments for benefits so assessed shall be a lien upon the lots, plots or parcels of land lying in the said adjacent cities, towns or townships respectively assessed.

Upon confirmation of the assessment the clerk of the township shall file with the clerks of adjacent cities, towns or townships a copy of report of said commissioners.

2. *And be it enacted*, That upon the confirmation of the assessment made in conformity with the act of which this is a further supplement the clerk of the township through which the said sewer or sewers have been constructed shall file with each of the clerks of the adjacent cities, towns or townships whose lands are included in the aforesaid assessment a copy of the report of the said commissioners; that it shall be the duty of each of the collectors in said adjacent cities, towns or townships to enter the said assessments, so far as it applies to his municipality, into a book to be kept in his office for the purpose, and he shall give notice for four weeks in some newspaper circulating in the said municipality that the said assessment report is on file and requiring payment of the several sums assessed against any owner of lands and real estate for such improvement within thirty days from and after the confirmation of said report by the circuit court of the said county; and in case said assessment shall remain unpaid at the expiration of the thirty days from and after the first publication of said notice, the said assessment shall draw interest thereupon from and after that time at a rate of one per centum per month, except the assessments for prospective benefits, which shall be governed as provided for in section two of the supplement of the act of which this is a further supplement, approved March twenty-fifth, one thousand eight hundred and ninety-one; and the governing bodies of said adjacent cities, towns or townships affected by said assessment shall have the same powers and rights to enforce the payments of said assessments as they have to enforce the collection of taxes or assessments by like proceedings.

Notice to be given by collectors, in newspaper, that said assessment report is on file and requiring payment of sums assessed.

Assessments unpaid after thirty days draw interest.

Moneys collected on account of aforesaid assessment kept in a separate fund.

3. *And be it enacted*, That all moneys collected on account of the aforesaid assessment by the respective adjacent cities, towns or townships shall be kept in a separate fund, which fund shall be applied to reimbursing the town through which the said sewer or sewers may have been constructed for such expenses, as said town may have incurred in the carrying out of said improvements; and it shall be the duty of the governing bodies of the

Governing bodies of adjacent cities, towns or townships to pay over such money whenever demanded.

said adjacent cities, towns or townships to pay over to the authorities of the aforesaid town, on demand, such sums of money as may have been collected whenever demand is made therefor.

Repealer

4. *And be it enacted*, That all acts and parts of acts whether general, public, local or special, inconsistent with this act be and the same are hereby repealed.

5. *And be it enacted*, That this act shall take effect immediately.

Approved March 9th, 1893.

CHAPTER LXXIV.

An Act to provide for the widening and constructing of roads or streets lying along or adjacent to the boundary lines of municipal corporations.

Governing body of incorporated town or township, upon presentation of petition, authorized to widen and improve road or streets.

1. Be it enacted *by the Senate and General Assembly of the State of New Jersey*, That in any incorporated town or township in this state in which there exists a public road or street having a width of thirty (30) feet or less and lying wholly within the corporate boundary of such town or township, it shall be lawful for the council or other governing body of said town or township, upon the presentation of a petition signed by property owners representing one-third of the total frontage on said road or street, to cause such road or street to be widened and improved, as hereinafter provided for.

Lawful to cause surveys, maps, &c., made by civil engineer, upon adoption of said maps, shall pass ordinance defining limit of said improvement.

2. *And be it enacted*, That upon the receipt and adoption of the said petition by the council or other governing body of the said town or township, it shall be lawful to cause to be made surveys, maps, profiles and grades by a competent civil engineer, sufficient to establish new lines for the widening of said road or street, and upon the adoption of said maps, profiles and grades the said council or other governing body shall pass an ordinance

defining the limit of the said improvement, which shall be advertised for two weeks in at least one newspaper circulating in said town or township and also in any adjacent or neighboring municipalities affected by the said improvement.

3. *And be it enacted*, That it shall be lawful for the circuit court of the count in which any lands or real estate which may be benefited by said improvement are situated, on application in writing made on behalf of said council or other governing body of said town or township, to appoint three disinterested commissioners, who shall make an estimate and assessment of the damages any owner or owners will sustain as well as for the taking of his, her or their lands or real estate with the appurtenances, as for the injury to the owner or owners by reason of the intended improvement; the said commissioners shall be sworn to make just and impartial awards and assessments of the costs, and shall present without delay to the said court a report in writing and accompanied by a map of such award and assessment, which shall be sufficient if signed by a majority of said commissioners; and that the said commissioners in making assessments for benefits for such widening shall take into careful consideration and shall assess all the lands benefited by the said improvement, both in the town or township through which the said road or street may be constructed, and also all lands lying in neighboring or adjacent munipalities; but no assessment shall be made against any land greater than the benefit received from such widening, and that said assessment for benefits so assessed shall be a lien upon the lots or plots or parcels of land lying in the said adjacent cities, towns or townships respectively assessed; that the said circuit court shall direct notice to be given by advertising in some newspaper circulating in said county for at least ten days, stating the time and place at which said court shall proceed to consider said report and any objections that may be made in writing thereto; and shall have power to consider the said report and objections thereto in a summary manner, and to revise and to confirm said report and accompanying map with or without alterations; said report, when confirmed by the court, and duly certified by the county clerk, shall at all times be

On application circuit court may appoint commissioners to make assessment of damages of land owners.

Commissioners shall be sworn and present a report in writing accompanied by a map of such award and assessment.

No assessment shall be greater than benefit received.

Notice to be given of time and place to consider objections.

Said report confirmed by court, certified by county clerk, shall be evidence of right of governing body to enter upon, take and use said land.

plenary evidence of the right of the said council or other governing body of said town or township to enter upon, take and use the said land and real estate with the appurtenances for the purpose of such road or street, and said council or other governing body of said town or township first sending to the owner or owners thereof, if resident of this state, the amount so awarded to them, and that if any owner is not a resident of this state or on due inquiry can not be found therein, or is a lunatic or idiot or under age, or is for any other cause incapacitated to receive the amount awarded, or will not receive the same, and sign a proper voucher or receipt therefor when tendered, an affidavit shall be made of the facts and filed in the office of the county clerk, and the amount of the award to any such owner shall be deposited in said circuit court before said council or other governing body of said town or township shall have the right to take or use said lands and real estate for the purposes herein stipulated; the court shall settle and determine the compensation to be paid said commissioners and the costs and expenses of the application and report, which shall be paid by the council or other governing body of said town or township on behalf of which the application is made; and in case any commissioner shall die or refuse to act as such, the court shall immediately make appointment of a proper person to fill any vacancy so created.

Compensation to be paid said commissioners.

Court shall fill vacancies.

Duties of town clerks.

4. *And be it enacted*, That upon the confirmation of the assessment as above provided for, the clerk of the town or township through which the said road or street lies shall file with each of the clerks of the adjacent cities, towns or townships whose lands are included in the aforesaid assessment a copy of the report of the said commissioners; that it shall be the duty of each of the collectors in said adjacent cities, towns or townships whose lands are assessed to enter the said assessment, so far as it applies to his municipality, into a book to be kept in his office for the purpose, and he shall give notice for two weeks in some newspaper circulating in his municipality, that the said assessment report is on file and requiring payment of the several sums assessed against any owner of lands and real estate for such improvement within thirty days from and after the confirmation of said report by the cir-

Duties of city or town collectors.

cuit court of the said county, and in case said assessment shall remain unpaid at the expiration of thirty days from and after the first publication of said notice, the said assessment shall draw interest thereupon from and after that time at the rate of one per centum per month; and the governing body of said adjacent city, town or township affected by said assessment shall have the same powers and rights to enforce the payments of said assessments as they have to enforce the collection of taxes or assessments by like proceedings.

Unpaid assessments draw interest.

Governing body have power to enforce collection of assessments.

5. *And be it enacted*, That all moneys collected on account of the aforesaid assessment by the respective adjacent cities, towns or townships whose lands are so assessed shall be kept in a separate fund, which fund shall be applied to reimbursing the town through which the road or street lies for such expenses as said town may have incurred in the carrying out of said improvements; and it shall be the duties of the governing bodies of the said adjacent cities, towns or townships to pay over to the governing bodies of the aforesaid town or townships in which the said road lies, on demand, such sums of money as may have been collected whenever demand is made therefor.

Moneys collected by adjacent cities and towns to be a separate fund.

Governing bodies shall pay over money when demanded.

6. *And be it enacted*, That in order to meet the necessary cost of said widening of such road or street and the proceeds relating thereto as mentioned in this act, the council or other governing body of the town or township through which said road or street lies may borrow the necessary money therefor temporarily upon the promissory notes of such corporation or may issue temporary improvement certificates in such form as said council or other governing body may prescribe; said notes and certificates shall bear interest at a rate not exceeding six per centum per annum, and shall be payable at the expiration of not more than two years from the date of issue, and all receipts from assessments made against property benefited as herein above provided shall be paid to the treasurer of said town or township, and shall be applied to the payment of such temporary indebtedness incurred by the said town or township therefor.

Governing body may borrow money temporarily.

Notes on improvement certificates draw interest not exceeding six per cent.

Receipts from assessment paid to the treasurer of said town.

7. *And be it enacted*, That upon the confirmation of the assessment for the widening, as provided for in section three of this act, the said council or other governing body of

Upon confirmation of assessment governing body, upon petition, may authorize construction of road or street.

said town or township may authorize, upon the receipt of a petition signed by property owners representing one-half the frontage on said road or street, asking for the improvement, by ordinance or ordinances passed and adopted by such council or other governing body, the construction of said road or street upon the lines, profiles and grades as described and laid down in the plans adopted as provided for in section two of the act; and shall employ a competent civil engineer to prepare specifications and details, and to supervise and direct such improvement.

Shall employ civil engineer.

Expenses incurred shall be assessed upon lands specially benefited.

8. *And be it enacted*, That the costs and expenses incurred for making any improvement or performing any work under and by virtue of the provisions of section seven of this act shall be assessed upon the lands and real estate specially benefited, in proportion to the benefits received thereby, but not exceeding the amount of such benefits; when such work is completed, the said common council or other governing body of such town or township shall apply to the circuit court of the county in which such township is situated; and on application, in writing, made by or on behalf of the council of said town or township or other governing body, and after notice of the time and place of making such application, published at least ten days previously in some newspaper circulating in said county, the circuit court shall appoint three disinterested commissioners, who shall make an estimate and assessment of the benefits that any lands and real estate may specially receive by the making of such improvements or public works; and if any of said commissioners die or refuse to act, the said court shall immediately make appointment of a proper person to fill any vacancy so created; the said commissioners shall be sworn to make a just and impartial estimate and assessment, and they shall assess upon the several lots or parcels of land benefited by such improvement a sum in proportion to the benefit received by each of said lots or parcels of lands, and no lot or parcel of land shall be assessed more than it is benefited; and the said commissioners shall, in making the assessment for such improvement, take into careful consideration, and shall assess all lands benefited by the said improvement, both

Circuit court, on application in writing, shall appoint commissioners, who shall make assessment of benefits specially received.

Court shall fill vacancies.

Commissioners shall be sworn

Duties of commissioners.

in the town or township through which the said road or street may be constructed, and also all lands lying in neighboring or adjacent municipalities, and that said assessment for benefits so assessed shall be a lien upon the lots or plots or parcels of land lying in the said adjacent cities, towns or townships respectfully assessed; that the said circuit court shall direct notice to be given, by advertisment in some newspaper circulating in said county, for at least ten days, stating the time and place at which said court shall proceed to consider said report and any objections that may be made in writing thereto, and shall have the power to consider the said report and objections thereto in a summary manner, and to revise and to confirm said report and accompanying map, with or without alterations; the court shall settle and determine the compensation to be paid said commissioners, and the cost and expenses of the application and report, which shall be paid by the council or other governing body of said town or township on behalf of which the application is made.

Notice to be given of time and place to consider report and any objections.

Court shall determine compensation of commissioners and cost and expenses.

9. *And be it enacted*, That upon the confirmation of the assessment as above provided for by section eight of this act, the clerk of the town or township through which the said road or street lies shall file with each of the clerks of the adjacent cities, towns or townships whose lands are included in the aforesaid assessment, a copy of the report of the said commissioners; that it shall be the duty of each of the collectors of said adjacent cities, towns or townships whose lands are assessed to enter the said assessment so far as it applies to his municipality, into a book to be kept in his office for the purpose, and he shall give notice for two weeks in some newspaper circulating in his municipality, that the said assessment report is on file and requiring payment of the several sums assessed against any owner of lands and real estate for such improvement, within thirty days from and after the confirmation of said report by the circuit court of the said county, and in case said assessment shall remain unpaid at the expiration of the thirty days from and after the first publication of said notice, the said assessment shall draw interest thereupon from and after that time at a rate of one per centum per month; and the governing

Clerk shall file report of assessment when confirmed.

Duties of collectors

Unpaid assessments shall draw interest

Governing body shall have power to enforce collection.

body of said adjacent cities, town or township affected by said assessment, shall have the same powers and rights to enforce the payments of said assessment as they have to enforce the collection of taxes or assessments by like proceedings.

Moneys collected kept in a separate fund and paid by governing bodies on demand

10. *And be it enacted*, That all moneys collected on account of the aforesaid assessment by the respective adjacent cities, towns or townships whose lands are so assessed shall be kept in a separate fund, which fund shall be applied to reimbursing the town through the road or street lies for such expenses as said town may have incurred in the carrying out of such improvements; and it shall be the duty of the governing bodies of the said adjacent cities, towns or townships to pay over to the governing bodies of the aforesaid town or township in which said road lies, on demand, such sums of money as may have been collected whenever demand is made therefor.

Governing body may borrow money on notes or certificates.

11. *And be it enacted*, That in order to meet the expenses for the construction of said street or road and of the proceedings in relation thereto, as mentioned in this act, the council of the said town or other governing body may borrow the money necessary therefor, temporarily, upon the promissory notes of such corporation, or may issue temporary improvement certificates from time to time as the work progresses in such form as the said council of said town or other governing body may prescribe; said notes and certificates shall bear interest at a rate not exceeding six per centum per annum, and shall be payable at the expiration of not more than two years from the date of issue; all receipts from assessments made against property benefited by such improvements shall be paid to the treasurer of the said town or township, and shall be applied to the payment for such improvements or to the payment of any temporary indebtedness incurred by the said town or township therefor.

Notes and certificates bear interest not exceeding six per cent.

Receipts from assessments to be paid to town treasurer.

Governing bodies may issue bonds, to run ten years, six per cent. interest.

12. *And be it enacted*, That in order to provide for so much of the cost of such improvements as may be required to be paid by any city, town or township, or for any notes or certificates of indebtedness issued therefor which may remain unpaid, it shall and may be lawful for such city or town or township to issue bonds to run for a period not to exceed ten years and to bear interest not

exceeding six per centum per annum, which said bonds shall be styled improvement bonds, shall be issued in such denomination as the governing bodies of the several municipalities may determine, and be executed under the corporate seal of the said municipality, signed by the proper official; coupons for every half year's interest shall be attached to each bond and numbered to correspond thereto, or the said bonds may be registered, at the option of the holder; they shall be sold for not less than their par value, and the proceeds thereof shall be used to pay the portion of the costs, damages and expenses of said improvements and public works required to be paid by such municipality as aforesaid, and to take up and pay off such temporary notes or certificates as have been given in payment of such costs and expenses that may be outstanding; *provided*, that in order to meet the interest on said bonds and redeem the same at maturity, it shall be the duty of the council or other governing bodies of such municipalities to order the interest thereon, together with a sinking fund of not less than five per centum of the total amount of said issue, to be raised in the annual tax levy.

Bonds not sold less than par value.

Proviso.

13. *And be it enacted*, That all acts and parts of acts, whether general, public, local or special, inconsistent with this act be and the same are hereby repealed. Repealer.

Approved March 9, 1893.

CHAPTER LXXV.

An Act to prohibit the laying or construction of any street or horse railroad along the streets of any municipality of this state without the consent of the governing body having the control of the streets in such municipality.

Unlawful to lay or construct street or horse railroad without consent of governing body having control of streets, &c.

1. BE IT ENACTED *by the Senate and General Assembly of the State of New Jersey*, That hereafter it shall be unlawful for any street or horse railroad company, organized under the act entitled "An act to provide for the incorporation of horse or street railway companies, and to regulate the same," approved April sixth, one thousand eight hundred and eighty-six; or any special or local act authorizing or incorporating any street or horse railroad company, to lay or construct any railroad track or tracks, or any extension of the same through or along any street of any municipality of this state without first obtaining the consent of the common council, board of aldermen, board of public works, or other governing body having the control of the public streets, avenues or roads of said municipality, or along the streets of which municipality said railroad company desires or intends to construct its said railroad.

On attempt to construct street railroad without consent of governing body the attorney-general, upon application, shall apply to court of chancery for order to forfeit the charter.

2. *And be it enacted*, That if any street or horse railroad company, incorporated under any general or special act, shall construct or attempt to construct any railroad through or upon any street, avenue or road of any municipality of this state without first obtaining the consent of the city council, board of aldermen, board of public works, or other governing body having the control of the streets, avenues or roads of said municipality, it shall be the duty of the attorney-general, upon the application of five residents of any municipality wherein said street or horse railroad company shall construct or attempt to construct said railroad, to apply to the court of chancery for an order to for-

feit the charter of said street or horse railroad company, which said court of chancery may upon the applications make an order declaring void and of no effect the charter or authority of said railroad company to construct, maintain and operate said railroad, and upon the making and filing of such order the rights of said street or horse railroad company shall be thereupon forfeited and of no force.

Repealer

3. *And be it enacted*, That all acts and parts of acts, general, special or local, inconsistent with the provisions of this act, be and the same are hereby repealed, and that this act shall take effect immediately.

Approved March 9, 1893.

LXXVI.

An Act to enable towns and townships in this state to construct water works for the extinguishment of fires and supplying the inhabitants thereof with pure and wholesome water.

Special election to be called upon petition by owners of real estate

1. Be it enacted *by the Senate and General Assembly of the State of New Jersey*, That the inhabitants of any town or township in this state, wherein it is desired to construct water works for the extinguishment of fires and supplying the inhabitants thereof with pure and wholesome water, may request the common council, township committee or other governing body of such town or township to call a special election for the purpose of obtaining the consent of a majority of the legal voters in said town or township to construct such water works in the manner hereinafter mentioned, and that such request shall be in the form of a petition in writing to the common council, township committee or other governing body of such town or township, signed by the owners of the majority of the real estate in such town or township, according to its assessed value in the year pre-

ceding the year at which such petition is presented to the common council, township committee or other governing body of such town or township, and shall be verified by the oath of the assessor of such town or township of the amount of the assessed value of the real estate owned by the signers to such petition, and that such amount is, at least, a majority of the real estate in such town or township, according to its assessed value in the year preceding.

Special election held within thirty days from filing petition.

2. *And be it enacted*, That upon the filing of such petition with the common council, township committee or other governing body of such town or township, the said common council, township committee or other governing body of such town or township, be and they are hereby authorized and required, within thirty days from the filing of such petition, to call a special election to be held in said town or township, at any time to be fixed by the common council, township committee or other governing body of such town or township, not less than thirty days from the filing of such petition, of which election the clerk of said town or township shall cause notice of the time and place or places of holding the same, to be given by advertisements signed by himself and set up in at least ten public places in said town or township, for at least ten days previous to the day of such election, and also published in one or more weekly newspapers printed therein, at least one issue before such election; and said clerk shall provide two printed ballots, one containing the words "for the adoption for this town (or township) of the provisions of an act entitled 'An act to enable towns and townships in this state to construct water works for the extinguishment of fires, and supplying the inhabitants thereof with pure and wholesome water;'" the other containing the words "against the adoption for this town (or township) of the provisions of an act entitled 'An act to enable towns and townships of this state to construct water works for the extinguishment of fires, and supplying the inhabitants thereof with pure and wholesome water;" and that each and every polling place in such town or township shall be provided by said clerk with a quantity of ballots of each kind above mentioned, equal to double the number of votes cast at such

Town clerk shall give notice by advertising and publishing same.

Clerk shall provide ballots.

Number of ballots to be provided.

polling place at the last election prior to the special election hereinbefore mentioned; that the polls of such election shall be held at the usual places of holding the annual town or township election in said town or township, and shall be opened at six o'clock in the morning and closed at seven o'clock in the evening, and such election shall be conducted by the proper election officers of said town or township for the time then being, and such officers shall return to the common council, township committee or other governing body of such town or township, a true and correct statement in writing, under their hands, of the result of said election, the same to be entered at large upon the minutes of said town or township by the clerk of such town or township.

Polls open at 6 close at 7 o'clock

3. *And be it enacted*, That if at such election a majority of the votes cast at such election shall be in favor of the adoption of the provisions of said act, the common council, township committee or other governing body of such town or township, shall be and hereby are authorized in the manner hereinafter provided, in the corporate name of such town or township, to take and convey from such source or sources as may be practicable, into and through said town or township, such quantity of pure and wholesome water as may be required for the extinguishment of fires and supplying the inhabitants thereof with pure and wholesome water, and other purposes, and to this end the said common council, township committee or other governing body of said town or township is hereby authorized and empowered in the corporate name of said town or township, to purchase, take, hold and enjoy, and convey and dispose of all real and personal estate, land and water rights, as may be necessary for the purposes of this act, and may construct and maintain canals, aqueducts, reservoirs, basins, stand pipes, buildings, machinery, and appurtenances, of every kind, that may be necessary and useful for such purposes, with full power and authority to lay and relay water pipes under any avenue, road, railroad, highway, street, or alley, within the said town or township, and to use the streets and roads of such town or township, to lay pipes in, and to put up fire hydrants, and to make alterations and additions to its said water works, and supply pumps, machinery, and lay pipes,

Common council, &c., authorized to supply pure water.

Common council, &c., authorized to purchase, &c., real estate, water rights, &c.

in any place, and to construct and acquire the necessary works, pumps, engines, boilers, and other requisite machinery, to be located in or out of the town or township, and to lay down mains and supply pipes, running in such direction throughout the town or township, as may be expedient, and as many fire hydrants as may be expedient, and that all work necessary to be done, or materials to be furnished to execute these powers may be done directly by the town or township, or through contractors, who after reasonable advertisement shall be deemed to afford the best security for completing the work, on the most advantageous terms, and who shall be the lowest bidder therefor, and who shall give bond with ample security for the faithful performance of the contract; all such bonds shall be executed to the town or township in its corporate name, and before being accepted shall be examined and approved by the attorney of such town or township.

Work may be done by contract.

Bond to be given.

Common council, &c, have all powers necessary to construct water works.

4. *And be it enacted*, That the said common council, township committee or other governing body of such town or township shall be and hereby are invested with all the powers necessary to enable them to construct, keep up and maintain such reservoirs, aqueducts and apparatus for elevating water as they may deem necessary from time to time, with such erections, works, establishments and fixtures as may be in their opinion required to effectuate the objects of this act, and to take and use such parts of the water of any stream, lake or pond necessary for the purposes contemplated by this act, and to lay all pipes under the streets or through private property that may be needed to conduct said water to the reservoirs, and from the reservoirs to such parts of the town or township and vicinity as the common council, township committee or other governing body of said town or township may from time to time deem expedient, and for these purposes said common council, township committee or other governing body of such town or township may make such contracts and employ all such engineers, surveyors, officers, agents, employes, workmen and laborers as they may deem necessary, subject, however, to the restrictions hereinafter provided.

5. *And be it enacted*, That if it should become necessary in the opinion of said common council, township com-

mittee or other governing body, to lay pipes through any private lands, or if any private lands shall be required for erecting reservoirs or other works thereon, or from which they may desire to take and use the water of any spring or springs, stream or streams of water or water rights, and no agreement can be made with the owner or owners thereof, as to the amount of compensation to be paid for the laying of said pipes through said lands, or the price of such lands or water rights as the case may be, by reason of the unwillingness of said owners, or any of them, to accept such compensation or price as said common council, township committee or other governing body may deem reasonable, or by reason of the absence or legal incapacity of said owners, or any of them, it shall be the duty of the justice of the supreme court of this state holding the circuit court in and for the county wherein said town or township is situated, upon application to him by said common council, township committee or other governing body, in the corporate name of such town or township, and after ten days previous notice in writing of such application to the persons interested, if known and in this state, or if unknown or out of the state, after publication thereof for any time, not less than two weeks in a newspaper published in such town or township, to appoint three disinterested appraisers, from the county wherein such town or township is situate, to determine the compensation to be paid for the laying of said pipes through said lands, or the price to be paid for said lands or water rights as the case may be; and it shall be the duty of said appraisers (after having taken an oath or affirmation faithfully and impartially to discharge the trusts herein reposed in them, and after having carefully viewed the premises) within twenty days after their appointment, to deliver to said common council, township committee or other governing body, a written appraisement under the hands and seals of them or a majority of them, of the award they have made, containing a full description of the lands or water rights, required as aforesaid, which appraisement the said common council, township committee or other governing body, shall cause to be recorded in the registry of deeds for the said county; and upon payment or tender by the

Appraisers appointed by justice of supreme court upon application.

Notice of application to be published.

Appraisers to take an oath.

Appraisement recorded in registry of deeds.

said common council, township committee or other governing body, to such owner or owners as aforesaid, or some one of them, of the sum awarded in such appraisement, if any, then the said common council, township committee or other governing body of said town or township, shall have power to enter upon and take possession of the said lands or water rights as the case may be, for the purposes aforesaid, and the said town or township shall be deemed seized in fee simple of the lands or water rights, required for the erection of the said reservoirs or other works as aforesaid, and the water supply aforesaid; and in case any owner or owners of such lands shall be feme covert, under age, non compos mentis, or out of the state, then and in that case it shall be sufficient for said common council, township committee or other governing body, to pay the amount which may have been appraised as aforesaid into court, to the clerk thereof, subject to the order of said court, for the use of the party or parties entitled to the same; the costs of all which proceedings shall be taxed by the said justice of the supreme court, and paid by the said common council, township committee or other governing body of said town or township.

Costs taxed by justice of supreme court.

The court have power to set aside award of appraisers.

6. *And be it enacted*, That in case the common council, township committee or other governing body of such town or township, or the owner or owners of the said land or water rights, shall be dissatisfied with the award of the appraisers named in the preceding section and shall apply to a justice of the supreme court of this state, holding the circuit court in and for the county wherein said town or township is situated, at the next term after filing of the said award; the court shall have power, upon good cause shown, to set the same aside, and thereupon to direct a proper issue for the trial of the said controversy, to be formed between the said parties, and to order a jury to be struck and a view of the premises to be had, and the said issue to be tried at the next circuit court to be holden in said county, upon the like notice and in the same manner as other issues in the said court are tried; and it shall be the duty of the said jury to assess the value of the said land, water rights or damages sustained, and if they shall find a greater sum

Trial by struck jury.

than the said appraisers shall have awarded in favor of the said owner or owners, then judgment therefor, with costs, shall be entered against said town or township and execution awarded therefor; but if the said jury shall be applied for by the said owner or owners, and shall find the same or a less sum than the common council, township committee or other governing body of said town or township shall have offered or the said appraisers awarded, then the said costs to be paid by said applicant or applicants, and either deducted out of the said sum found by the said jury or execution awarded therefor as the court shall direct; but such application shall not prevent the common council, township committee or other governing body of such town or township from taking or laying pipes through said lands upon the award of the appraisers, the value or damages being first paid, or upon a refusal to receive the same upon a tender thereof, or the owner or owners thereof being under any legal disability, the same being first paid into said court to the clerk thereof.

7. *And be it enacted*, That whenever it shall become necessary to make any repairs or alterations in any pipes which may have been laid through any private lands, either by virtue of the preceding section or by agreement with the owner or owners thereof, it shall be lawful for the said common council, township committee or other governing body with their workmen and agents and with necessary vehicles, tools and implements to enter upon said lands and make the necessary repairs and alterations, doing no unnecessary damage; *provided, always*, that nothing in this section contained shall be so construed as to protect the said common council, township committee or other governing body, or their workmen or agents from any action that may be brought against them individually by the owner or owners of said lands for any damage which they may have wilfully or unnecessarily done.

Lawful for common council, &c., to make necessary repairs, &c.

Proviso.

8. *And be it enacted*, That when said works shall have been sufficiently completed the said common council, township committee or other governing body shall have authority to furnish water to individuals and to establish such general rates of price and time of payment thereof

Common council, &c., prescribe rules and regulalions.

as they may deem proper, and to prescribe such rules, regulations, conditions and restrictions as to the use of water as may, in their opinion, be necessary to prevent abuse; the said common council, township committee or other governing body shall have power, and it shall be their duty, to stop off the water from any premises, the owner or occupants of which shall have neglected to pay such price at the time specified for the payment thereof, or shall have violated or permitted the violation of any of said rules, regulations, conditions or restrictions, and whenever the said common council, township committee or other governing body shall have caused the water to be stopped off from any premises for either of the causes aforesaid, they shall not permit the same to be restored until the applicant for such restoration shall have paid all arreages of water rent, together with the expenses incurred in stopping off the water; or in case said water shall have been stopped off by reason of any violation of the rules aforesaid, then they shall not permit the same to be restored until the expense of stopping off the same shall have been paid by the applicant for such restoration, and such applicant shall have given satisfactory security or assurance that such violation shall not again occur.

Powers of same when rules and regulations are violated.

Water rents draw interest.

9. *And be it enacted*, That the rents for the use of the water which said town or township may supply, as aforesaid, shall draw interest from the time they become due and shall be and remain, until paid, a lien upon the premises to which the same may be conducted and supplied; and said common council, township committee or other governing body shall have full power, in the corporate name of such town or township, to bring any suit or suits against any person or persons, corporation or corporations, for the collection of said water rents, with interest and costs, in any of the courts of this state, and it shall be the duty of said common council, township committee or other governing body of said town or township to enforce the collection in all cases where the water rents shall be in arrear.

Common council, &c., authorized to employ persons.

10. *And be it enacted*, That the said common council, township committee or other governing body of such town or township shall have power to employ proper persons in the management of the works aforesaid and in

the collection of the said water rents upon such terms as they may deem reasonable.

Common council, &c., to erect hydrants.

11. *And be it enacted*, That it shall be the duty of said common council, township committee or other governing body, to erect hydrants in the public streets of said town or township, through which pipes for the supply of water shall have been laid, in such number and locations as the common council, township committee or other governing body of said town or township, may from time to time direct, and supply the same with water from the aforesaid works.

Treasurer of town to prosecute persons who wilfully obstruct any water-pipes, &c.

12. *And be it enacted*, That if any person or persons shall wilfully do, or cause to be done, any act whatsoever whereby the said works, or any pipes, conduit, canal, plug, hydrant, cock, tank, cistern, reservoir, or any other thing appertaining to the same, shall be stopped, obstructed or injured, or who shall tap or make connection with any water pipe or main, for the purpose of obtaining a supply therefrom, without the knowledge or consent of the common council, township committee or other governing body of such town or township, the person or persons so offending shall, upon conviction thereof before a justice of the peace, forfeit and pay the sum of fifty dollars, with cost to be recovered by and in the name of the treasurer of said town or township, in an action of trespass in any court in this state having cognizance of the same, which sum shall be paid into the treasury of said town or township.

Persons who pollute any reservoir guilty of misdemeanor.

13. *And be it enacted*, That if any person or persons shall wilfully pollute or adulterate the waters in any reservoir, erected under the provisions of this act, any person so offending shall be deemed guilty of a misdemeanor, and on conviction thereof shall be punished by a fine not exceeding five hundred dollars, or by imprisonment at hard labor not exceeding three years, or both, at the discretion of the court before whom such conviction shall be had.

Common council, &c., authorized to borrow money.

14. *And be it enacted*, That the said common council, township committee or other governing body, are hereby authorized by, and in the corporate name of such town or township to borrow any sum not exceeding seventy-

five thousand dollars, for the purpose of defraying all the expenses and the cost of the purchase of real estate, water rights, works and appurtenances and of maintaining and extending the same, and for the purpose of defraying all the expenses and the cost of such other lands, buildings, or water privileges as shall be purchased or taken for the purposes of this act, and for the purchase of materials, the laying of pipes and mains in the said town or township, and constructing all works necessary to the full accomplishment thereof, and all expenses incidental thereto, and to secure the payment thereof, it shall be the duty of said common council, township committee or other governing body of said town or township, from time to time, to issue the bonds of said town or township for an amount not exceeding in the whole the sum of seventy-five thousand dollars, which bonds shall bear a rate of interest not exceeding five per centum per annum, payable semi-annually, the principal thereof to be payable at such time and in such manner as the said common council, township committee or other governing body of said town or township may deem expedient; *provided*, that a portion of said bonds shall be payable each year and that the last of said bonds shall be payable not more than thirty years from the date thereof, and it shall be the duty of the treasurer of said town or township to make public sale of the bonds so issued, as aforesaid, at not less than their par value, and to pay the proceeds of said sales into the treasury of said town or township, to be used by said common council, township committee or other governing body of said town or township to the discharge of the duties imposed upon them by this act; the loan hereby authorized shall be called the water loan of said town or township.

To issue bonds, interest not to exceed 5 per cent.

Proviso.

Bonds not taxable.

15. *And be it enacted*, That the bonds issued under the provisions of this act shall not be liable to any tax which ma hereafter be levied by order of the said town or township.

How money remaining after paying all expenses to be applied.

16. *And be it enacted*, That such portion of the moneys received from the water rents or prices paid for the use of water, and interest on arrears of water rents as may remain after paying all expenses for constructing and maintaining the works, and raising and distributing the water,

and salaries, wages, and incidental expenses and charges, shall be applied first to the payment of the interest upon the debt created for the construction of the works, and next to the payment of the principal of the bonds at maturity.

17. *And be it enacted*, That the said common council, township committee or other governing body of said town or township shall, on or before a certain day in each year, cause a careful estimate to be made of the interest on the water debt, and cost of managing and keeping in repair and operation of the works for the ensuing year, and of the amount to be received during the same year for the use of the water and water rents, and of the deficiency, if any, of such receipts for the payment of such expenditures, and said deficiency said town or township shall raise by tax, as other taxes are assessed, levied and collected, and said body shall in case of any estimated deficiency, furnish a copy of such report to the board or officer who by law is required to make assessments of taxes in said town or township.

If any deficiency, to be raised by tax.

18. *And be it enacted*, That the treasurer of said town or township shall keep accurate accounts of the receipts and disbursements in proper books, to be provided by said town or township for the purpose, and which shall always be open for the inspection of the common council, township committee or other governing body of said town or township; and which accounts shall be annually audited, and a short abstract thereof shall be published with the annual statement of the town or township finances, and at the expiration of his term of office said treasurer shall deliver to his successor, all books and papers which he may have in his possession or custody by virtue of his said office.

Treasurer shall keep accounts of receipts and disbursements.

Annual statement published.

19. *And be it enacted*, That it shall be lawful for the said common council, township committee or other governing body to elect or appoint any and all engineers, surveyors, officers, agents, or employees, that they may deem necessary or convenient for accomplishing the purposes contemplated by this act, to define their duties, regulate their compensation, and provide for their removal, and that the said engineers, surveyors, officers, agents, or employees so appointed or elected as aforesaid,

Common council, &c., define duties, regulate compensation, &c., of engineers, &c.

are hereby authorized and empowered to enter upon any land or water, for the purpose of making any and all surveys and examinations necessary under this act, and at all reasonable hours to enter any dwelling or other place, where the water so furnished is taken or used and where unnecessary waste thereof is known or suspected, and examine and inquire into the cause thereof, and the said engineers, surveyors, officers, agents, or employees, shall have full power to examine all service pipes, stop cocks, and other apparatus connected with the water supply, or drainage works, for the purpose of ascertaining whether the same are of the character and dimensions and fixed in the manner directed by the rules and regulations of said town or township, and if any person or persons shall refuse to permit such examinations, or oppose or obstruct any such engineers, surveyors, officers, agents, or employees in performance of such duty, he, she or they so offending shall have the supply of water shut off until the required examination is made and such alterations and repairs as may be found necessary shall be completed.

Common council, &c., authorized to make all ordinances necessary.

20. *And be it enacted*, That said common council, township committee or other governing body of said town or township, shall have power and they are hereby authorized to make, ordain and establish, all such ordinances, resolutions and regulations as said body may deem necessary and proper, for the distribution, supply, use, and protection of the said water, and the safety, security and protection of the buildings, machinery, canals, aqueducts, reservoirs, and other works and appurtenances thereto, and for fixing and collecting the water rents or prices for water, and for imposing penalties, in addition to cutting-off the water for the non-payment thereof, and that they may direct in what manner and for what purposes the publ c hydrants and fire plugs may be used.

Proviso

21. *And be it enacted*, That this act shall be deemed a public act, and shall take effect immediately; *provided, however*, that nothing in this act shall affect or apply to any street, avenue, or highway under the charge or control of any county public road board in this state.

Adproved March 9, 1893.

CHAPTER LXXVII.

A Supplement to an act entitled "An act to authorize any city of this state to enter into contracts with railroad companies whose roads enter their corporate limits, whereby said companies may re-locate, change or elevate their railroads and when necessary for that purpose to vacate, change the grade of or alter the lines of any streets or highways therein," approved March nineteenth, one thousand eight hundred and seventy-four.

Section to be amended.

1. BE IT ENACTED *by the Senate and General Assembly of the State of New Jersey,* That section one of the act to which this is a supplement be and the same is hereby amended so that the same shall read as follows:

Municipal authorities of cities authorized to contract with railroad companies.

1. BE IT ENACTED *by the Senate and General Assembly of the State of New Jersey,* That the proper municipal authorities respectively of any city of this state be and they are hereby authorized and empowered to enter into such contracts with any of the railroad companies whose roads now or hereafter may enter or lie within their cities respectively, or whose routes have been or may be located therein, as shall secure greater safety to persons and property therein, or facilitate the construction and maintenance of other than grade crossings of streets, highways, or other railroads therein, whereby the said railroad companies, or any of them, may locate, re-locate, change, alter grades of, depress or elevate their railroads within said cities, or either of them, as in the judgment of such municipal authorities respectively may be best adapted to secure the safety of lives and property, or to provide for other than grade crossings of streets or highways or of other railroads therein, or to promote the interests of said cities respectively, and for that purpose shall have power to open, vacate, alter the lines and change the grades of any streets or highways or any part thereof, within said cities or either of them, and to do all

such acts as may be necessary and proper to effectuall carry out such contracts; and any such contracts mad by any railroad company or companies, as aforesaid, wit said cities or either of them are hereby fully authorized ratified and confirmed.

2. *And be it enacted,* That this act shall take effect im mediately.

Approved March 9, 1898.

CHAPTER LXXVIII.

An Act supplemental to an act entitled "An act relativ to the supreme and circuit courts," approved Marc twenty-seventh, one thousand eight hundred and sev enty-four; and also for the appointment of three judge to hold said circuit courts and to define their powers

Circuit court judges to be appointed by the governor.

1. BE IT ENACTED *by the Senate and General Assembly of th State of New Jersey,* that there shall be nominated by the governor and appointed by him, by and with the advic and consent of the senate, three judges, each of whom shall be empowered to hold, in the absence of a justic of the supreme court, the respective circuit courts in every county of this state; and in like manner there shal be appointed successors to said judges respectively, when said offices or any of them shall become vacant by death expiration of the official term of the incumbents, or oth erwise; that each of said judges shall hold his office fo the term of seven years from the date of his commission and shall receive an annual salary of seven thousand five hundred dollars, payable monthly, in equal installments by the treasurer of the state.

Vacancy filled.

Term of office.

Salary.

Powers of said judges.

2. *And be it enacted,* That the said judges so to be ap pointed, and each of them, shall have the same authority power and jurisdiction, by virtue of their said office as is now vested by the common and statute law in the several

justices of the supreme court by reason of their being judges of said circuit courts.

3. *And be it enacted*, That the issues of the supreme court when sent down for trial, may be disposed of by consent of the parties in the manner following, to wit: a jury being waived, the justice of the supreme court may refer the matter for trial to the judge holding the county circuit court of the given county, who shall thereupon proceed to try the cause, either with or without a jury, as the said parties may agree; and the result of said trial having been reported to the said justice the same shall be received as conclusive evidence in the trial before him; and the supreme court shall be authorized to grant new trials in such procedures as in other cases.

Manner of disposing of supreme court issues

4. *And be it enacted*, That the supreme court may from time to time assign and appoint any of said circuit county court judges to hold such of such circuit courts as may be deemed expedient.

Supreme court may assign circuit court judges to hold court.

5. *And be it enacted*, That if it shall happen that any of said circuit court judges shall be prevented from attending any of said courts at any time or times, or from continuing the business therein transacting, the same proceedings, and the same results shall ensue as now obtain by law in case of a like default on the part of a justice of the supreme court.

Proceedings on failure of attendance of judges.

6. *And be it enacted*, That each of said judges shall, before he shall enter upon the duties of his said office, take and subscribe the following oath: I do solemnly promise and swear (or affirm) that I shall administer justice without respect to persons, and faithfully and impartially perform all the duties incumbent on me as a judge of the circuit courts of the counties of this state according to the best of my ability and understanding, agreeably to the constitution and laws of the state of New Jersey, so help me God.

Oath of judge.

7. *And be it enacted*, That this act shall take effect immediately.

Approved March 9, 1893.

CHAPTER LXXIX.

An Act concerning railroads.

Railroad corporations may purchase franchises of any other railroad sold by decree of court.

1. BE IT ENACTED *by the Senate and General Assembly of the State of New Jersey*, That whenever the railroad and franchises of any railroad corporation of this state or any part or parcel of the same has heretofore been or shall hereafter be sold in pursuance or by virtue of a decree, order or judgment of any court of competent jurisdiction it shall be lawful for any other railroad corporation of this state which owns, leases or operates a railroad having a physical connection therewith to purchase the said railroad and franchises so sold or to be sold, or any part or parcel of the same, either at the said sale or thereafter, from the purchaser or purchasers thereof, or from his, her or their heirs or assigns; and when such sale to the said purchasing railroad corporation shall be completed, the said railroad and franchises, or the part or parcel thereof so sold and purchased shall vest in and be merged with and become a component part of the railroad and franchises of the said railroad corporation so as aforesaid purchasing the same; *provided*, that the railroad corporation so purchasing shall file or cause to be filed a correct and accurate map and route of the railroad, or the part or parcel thereof so purchased, in the office of the secretary of state of this state.

Proviso

2. *And be it enacted*, That this act shall take effect immediately.

Approved March 9, 1893.

CHAPTER LXXX.

An Act concerning the taking of property for public use.

1. Be it enacted *by the Senate and General Assembly of the State of New Jersey*, That all reports of commissioners hereafter appointed by any court or by any justice of the supreme court to appraise the damages for the taking of lands or other property for public use shall be made or filed on or before a day to be fixed in the order of appointment, unless the court or justice shall by order extend the time, in which case the report shall be made on or before the day limited by said court or justice, and every appeal from such report shall be taken within five days after the day thus fixed.

Reports of commissioners appointed to appraise damages for taking lands for public use to be filed.

2. *And be it enacted*, That whenever an appeal shall be filed from an award of damages by commissioners heretofore or hereafter appointed in any proceeding for the taking of property for public use, notice in writing of such appeal shall be given by the party appealing to the other party within ten days after the filing of the petition of appeal, by service of such notice upon each person interested personally or by leaving at his residence if he resides in the state, or by service upon his attorney if any, who shall have appeared for him before the commissioners or any other attorney authorized to appear for him, and in case of a corporation, service may be made on such attorney or on any officer or agent upon whom a summons in an action at law against the company may be lawfully served; where it shall appear by affidavit that any person or corporation being a party to the proceedings is a non-resident of the state, or can not be found therein to be served, in such case notice shall be given in such manner as a judge of the court to which the appeal is taken may direct; the said notice of appeal shall set forth that an appeal has been taken from the award of the commissioners, and shall specify the time and place when and where the appellant will apply to the

Proceedings when appeal filed from award of damages by commissioners.

court to which such appeal is taken or any judge thereof to frame the issue and to fix a day for the striking of the jury, and a day for the trial of the appeal, which time named for said application shall be not less than five nor more than ten days from the date of service of the notice, but the court or judge may by order change the time or place on the application of either party and direct what notice of such change shall be given to the other party.

Court shall fix day for trial of appeal.

3. *And be it enacted*, That after an appeal to any court from the award of commissioners appointed to assess the damages for the taking of lands or other property for public use by condemnation shall have been filed, and notice thereof shall have been given as above provided, the court to which such appeal is taken or any judge thereof on application of either party shall fix a day for the trial of the appeal either during the term or vacation when such appeal shall be filed or during the following term or vacation, which day so fixed shall be not less than twenty nor more than forty days from the date of the order, and the court or judge shall also at the same time make an order framing the issue between the parties and directing a jury to be struck and a view of the premises and property to be had, and fixing a day and place for the striking of the jury for the trial of the appeal, which day shall be at least ten days before the day fixed for the trial of the appeal, and the filing of the order shall be notice to all parties of the day and place fixed thereby for the striking of the jury and of the trial, and the jury having been struck and the jurors summoned as required by law the cause shall be tried upon the day and at the place fixed unless for good cause shown the court shall adjourn the trial to another day which the court shall fix, in which case the court shall, in its discretion, either direct the same jurors to attend or order another jury to be struck and summoned in like manner, and all parties shall take notice of the day and place fixed for the adjourned trial.

Trial by struck jury

Trial may be adjourned.

Repealer, &c.

4. *And be it enacted*, That all acts or provisions inconsistent with the provisions of this act shall be and are hereby repealed, and the practice prescribed by this act shall supersede the existing practice in all condemnation cases before commissioners or on appeal, so far as the

provisions of this act shall extend, and the court shall make such further orders and take such further proceedings as may be requisite according to the practice of the court and the several statutes regulating appeals and the trials thereof in condemnation cases and may permit such amendments of the proceedings and plans as may be reasonable and proper for the fair trial of the case or for the promotion of the public purposes for which the power to condemn was conferred.

5. *And be it enacted*, That this act shall take effect immediately.

Approved March 9, 1893.

CHAPTER LXXXI.

A Supplement to an act entitled "An act for the formation and government of boroughs," approved March twelfth, one thousand eight hundred and ninety.

1. BE IT ENACTED *by the Senate and General Assembly of the State of New Jersey*, That no bonds heretofore issued by any borough under the act entitled "An act for the formation and government of boroughs," approved March twelfth, one thousand eight hundred and ninety, for the purpose of raising money to defray the expense of laying out, grading or improving any street or streets, sidewalk or sidewalks in said borough, shall be held invalid because the borough council has not passed an ordinance providing for such improvements, but that all such bonds heretofore issued pursuant to a resolution of the council of such borough, under the common seal and the signature of the mayor of such borough, and attested by the clerk thereof, shall have the same legal effect as though the act to which this is a supplement had been complied with in every particular; *provided, however*, that the work for the payment of which such bonds may

Bonds heretofore issued legalized.

Proviso

have been so issued shall have been actually done and performed in conformity with such resolution.

2. *And be it enacted*, That this act shall take effect immediately.

Approved March 9, 1893.

CHAPTER LXXXII.

A Supplement to an act entitled "An act concerning cities of the first class in this state and constituting municipal boards of street and water commissioners therein, and defining the powers and duties of such municipal boards and relating to the municipal affairs and departments of such cities, placed under the control and management of such boards, and providing for the maintenance of the same," approved March twenty-eighth, one thousand eight hundred and ninety-one.

Section to be amended.

1. BE IT ENACTED *by the Senate and General Assembly of the State of New Jersey*, That section six of the act to which this is a supplement, be amended so as to read as follows, viz.:

One-half of license fees to be set aside for repaving, &c.

6. *And be it enacted*, That it shall be lawful for that board of the city government having charge of the finances thereof, to instruct the city treasurer and city comptroller in any city of the first class to set aside and keep apart out of the license fees received in such city for licenses to sell spirituous or malt liquors, or to keep restaurants or hotels, one-half thereof for the repaving, repairing, and improving of paved streets and public places in such city, whenever in the judgment of such board there shall not be sufficient funds otherwise provided for that purpose, and said moneys when so set apart shall be disbursed, applied and expended for such purposes by said board of street and water commission-

ers, exclusive of any other board or authority whatever, and for no other purpose.

2. *And be it enacted*, That the provisions of this act shall apply to any moneys received from license fees in any city during the current year of the granting of such licenses, and the same shall be applied to the payment of any of said work or labor or materials furnished for such work already done or to be done, or that may be contracted for during the current year of the granting of such licenses. Applies to moneys received current year.

3. *And be it enacted*, That the said board of street and water commissioners may by a unanimous vote, at any time, out of said funds when so set aside, cause any part of a main thoroughfare in such city to be improved or paved or both, although the same may not have theretofore been paved. Said fund used to improve streets not heretofore paved.

4. *And be it enacted*, That all acts and parts of acts inconsistent with this act be and the same are hereby repealed, and that this act shall take effect immediately.

Approved March 9, 1898.

CHAPTER LXXXIII.

An Act authorizing cities of the first class to purchase land and erect buildings thereon for fire department purposes.

1. BE IT ENACTED *by the Senate and General Assembly of the State of New Jersey*, That in cities of the first class in this state, when the municipal board or authority having the control of the erection of buildings for fire department purposes shall certify to the municipal board of such city having the management and control of the finances of such city that the necessity exists for the purchase of ground and the erection thereon of a new building or buildings for fire department pur- Authorized to erect buildings for fire department purposes.

poses, that it shall be lawful for such municipal financial board or authority in such city and they are hereby authorized and empowered to issue bonds, either registered or coupon, to an amount not exceeding eight thousand dollars, to raise money to pay for the purchase of such plot and the erection and construction of said building or buildings; that said bonds shall be payable in eight years from the date thereof, and shall bear interest not exceeding four and one-half per centum per annum, to be sold not less than par, and that there shall be a sufficient sum appropriated and put in the tax levy of such city each year to pay the interest on such bonds, and also there shall in each year be appropriated and put in the tax levy of such city, the further sum of one thousand dollars towards the payment of said bonds, to be properly invested and deposited in the sinking fund of such city, to meet the payment of said bonds when they shall become due and payable.

Authorized to issue bonds

Rate of interest, shall not be sold for less than par value.

Special tax to be annually levied

Work done by contract.

2. *And be it enacted*, That all work and labor done and materials furnished for the erection of said building or buildings shall be done and finished by contract, awarded upon at least one week's advertisement in the official newspapers, to the lowest responsible bidder or bidders for the same.

Repealer.

3. *And be it enacted*, That all acts or parts of acts inconsistent herewith be and the same are hereby repealed, and this act shall take effect immediately.

Approved March 9, 1893.

CHAPTER LXXXIV.

A Further Supplement to an act entitled "An Act to enable cities in this state to furnish suitable accommodations for the transaction of public business" (title as amended), approved April fifteenth, one thousand eight hundred and eighty-seven.

1. BE IT ENACTED *by the Senate and General Assembly of the State of New Jersey*, That no bonds shall be issued under the provisions of said act and the supplements thereto, and acts amendatory thereof, beyond the amount of four hundred thousand dollars, except in cities of the first class, where bonds may be issued for the purposes of said acts to an amount not exceeding seven hundred and fifty thousand dollars; that said bonds shall be issued at a rate of interest not exceeding five per centum per annum; they shall be sold for not less than par and accrued interest; they shall be made payable in such manner that bonds to the amount of at least ten thousand dollars shall fall due each year from and after three years from the appointment of such commissioners; there shall be included in the tax levy and raised by taxation in such city each year, a sum equal to the interest upon the outstanding bonds and the principal of the bonds falling due within the year.

Authorized to issue bonds.

Rate of interest, &c.

Principal and interest on bonds, how paid

2. *And be it enacted*, That in cities of the first class the total cost for the purchase of lands, erection of building, furnishing and equipment thereof ready for occupancy by the various departments of the city, and all expenditures connected therewith, may equal but shall not exceed the sum of seven hundred and fifty thousand dollars, in addition to any amount derived from the sale of building and grounds, as provided in the acts in which this is a further supplement.

Expenditures not to exceed $750,000 in addition.

3. *And be it enacted*, That said city hall commissioners shall have power, in their discretion, to acquire on be

Commissioners authorized to purchase lands.

half of such city, from time to time, such lands as in their judgment may be required for such building for a city hall and the accommodation of the different offices and departments of the city government, which lands and all additions thereto shall be acquired in the method prescribed in the acts to which this is a further supplement.

Repealer. 4. *And be it enacted*, That all acts and parts of acts inconsistent with the provisions of this act be and the same are hereby repealed, and that this act shall take effect immediately.

Approved March 9, 1893.

CHAPTER LXXXV.

A Supplement to an act entitled "An act appropriating script for the public lands granted to the state of New Jersey by the act of Congress, approved July second, one thousand eight hundred and sixty-two," approved April fourth, one thousand eight hundred and sixty-four.

Board of visitors to agricultural college, how appointed. 1. BE IT ENACTED *by the Senate and General Assembly of the State of New Jersey*, That the board of visitors to the state agricultural college shall hereafter consist of two members from each congressional district in this state, to be appointed by the governor with the advice and consent of the senate.

Repealer. 2. *And be it enacted*, That all acts and parts of acts inconsistent herewith be and the same are hereby repealed, and that this act shall take effect immediately.

Approved March 10, 1893.

CHAPTER LXXXVI.

A Further Supplement to an act entitled "An act to incorporate societies for the promotion of learning" (Revision), approved April ninth, one thousand eight hundred and seventy-five.

1. Be it enacted *by the Senate and General Assembly of the State of New Jersey,* That the trustees of any seminary, institute or school now or hereafter organized under the act to which this is a supplement, or any other act now in force in this state, may consist of either ministers or laymen or both, in such proportion as the conference, synod, or other owners may determine, and may be classified into classes of one, two, three, or more years, as said conference or other owners may elect at the annual meeting or conference thereof, by the vote of a majority of the members present. Who to constitute trustees of seminaries, &c.

2. *And be it enacted,* That this act shall take effect immediately.

Approved March 10, 1898.

CHAPTER LXXXVII.

An Act respecting bills of costs in criminal cases.

1. Be it enacted *by the Senate and General Assembly of the State of New Jersey,* That all bills of costs which shall hereafter be taxed in the court of oyer and terminer or court of general quarter sessions of the peace, by the clerk of said courts, in any criminal case where sentence has been suspended, or a nolle prosequi or discontinu- When bills of costs hereafter taxed in criminal cases valid.

ance entered, or where there has been a non-conviction for any cause whatever, shall be as valid and effectual in law and shall be paid in the same manner, as bills of costs taxed in criminal cases in said courts upon conviction and sentence.

Repealer.

2. *And be it enacted*, That all acts and parts of acts, general or special, inconsistent with this act shall be and the same are hereby repealed, and that this act shall take effect immediately.

Approved March 10, 1893.

CHAPTER LXXXVIII.

An Act concerning bills of costs in criminal cases.

When bills of costs heretofore taxed in criminal cases valid.

1. BE IT ENACTED *by the Senate and General Assembly of the State of New Jersey*, That all bills of costs heretofore taxed and remaining unpaid, and which said costs have been taxed by the clerk of the court of oyer and terminer and the court of general quarter sessions of the peace in any criminal case in said courts of oyer and terminer or general quarter sessions of the peace where sentence has been suspended, a nolle prosequi or discontinuance entered, or where there has been a non conviction for any cause whatever, shall be as valid and effectual in law and shall be paid in the same manner as bills of costs taxed in criminal cases in said courts where there has been a conviction and sentence.

Repealer.

2. *And be it enacted*, That all acts or parts of acts inconsistent with this act be and the same are hereby repealed, and that this act shall take effect immediately.

Approved March 10, 1893.

CHAPTER LXXXIX.

An Act to regulate the running of steamboats upon the inland and private waters of this state for the conveying of passengers, and to provide for the inspection and licensing of steamboats and steamboat engineers.

1. Be it enacted *by the Senate and General Assembly of the State of New Jersey*, That it shall be the duty of the governor of this state to appoint such number of properly qualified persons, not less than one and not exceeding three, as to him shall seem necessary and advisable, to be official inspectors of steamboats and steamboat boilers in this state for the purposes hereinafter mentioned, and such inspectors shall be appointed to hold their office for one year from the date of their appointment respectively, and shall be commissioned by the governor, and any vacancy occurring may be filled from time to time by a like appointment by the governor at his discretion; and such inspectors shall, before they enter upon the discharge of the duties of their office, take and subscribe an oath well, faithfully and impartially to discharge the duties of their office according to law.

Governor to appoint inspectors of steamboats.

Term of office.

Vacancy, how filled.

Oath to be taken.

2. *And be it enacted*, That it shall be the duty of such inspector of steamboats and steamboat boilers respectively, whenever requested so to do by or in behalf of any owner or owners of any steamboat or boat propelled by steam power, navigating any of the inland or private waters of this state, and upon tender of the fees fixed by law for such service, to thoroughly and carefully inspect and examine such steamboat and to thoroughly and carefully inspect, examine and test the steam boiler or boilers thereof for the purpose of ascertaining whether such steamboat is so constructed and is in such safe and seaworthy condition and state of repair that passengers can be conveyed thereon in safety and the number of persons that can be carried thereon

Duties of inspectors.

with safety, and also for the purpose of ascertaining whether such steam boiler or boilers is or are safely constructed and in good repair and condition, and the number of pounds pressure per square inch which such boiler or boilers is or are capable of sustaining in safety, and forthwith to file in the office of the secretary of state a certificate certifying the result of such inspection, and it shall be the duty of the secretary of state to record such certificate in a book to be provided for that purpose, which record shall be a public record; and upon request by or in behalf of the owner or owners of such steamboat and upon payment of the fee therefor prescribed by law, in all cases where such certificate of the inspector shall show such steamboat or boat propelled by steam power to be seaworthy and safe for carrying passengers, and the number of persons who can safely be carried thereon at one time, and the boiler or boilers thereof to be in a safe and proper condition, to issue to the owner or owners of such steamboat a license under the great seal of the state, which license shall continue in force for one year from the date of such inspection and shall specify the name, description of the steamboat licensed, the name of the owner or owners thereof, the number of passengers it can safely carry at one time, and the number of pounds steam pressure per square inch the boiler or boilers thereof can safely carry and the date of such inspection and test and the name of the inspector and the fact that such steamboat and the boiler or boilers thereof were by such inspector at such date inspected and tested and found to be seaworthy and safe to the capacities stated.

Certificate filed in office of secretary of state.

License issued under great seal, for one year

Unlawful to carry passengers except boat been licensed.

3. *And be it enacted*, That it shall not be lawful to carry passengers upon boats propelled by steam power upon any of the inland or private waters of this state, except such boats have been licensed so to do according to law, and which license shall be publicly and conspicuously posted up upon such boat, and any person or corporation violating the provisions of this section of this act shall be deemed guilty of a misdemeanor and upon conviction thereof shall be liable to pay a fine of not less than fifty dollars and not more than five hundred dollars, at the discretion of the court, for each day they shall so offend.

Penalty for violation.

4. *And be it enacted*, That it shall not be lawful to carry at one time a greater number of persons upon any steamboat or boat propelled by steam, navigating the inland or private waters of this state, than the number specified in the license for such boat as the number of persons it can carry at one time in safety, and any person or corporation violating the provisions of this section of this act shall be deemed guilty of a misdemeanor and upon conviction thereof shall be liable to pay a fine of not less than twenty-five dollars or more than five hundred dollars, at the discretion of the court, for each offence.

Unlawful to carry more persons than number specified in license.

Penalty for violation.

5. *And be it enacted*, That it shall not be lawful to carry any greater number of pounds steam pressure per square inch in the boiler or boilers of any steamboat while carrying passengers over the inland or private waters of this state than the number of pounds steam pressure per square inch specified in such license as the limit of safety, and any person or corporation offending against this section of this act shall upon conviction thereof be liable to pay a fine of not less than twenty-five dollars or more than five hundred dollars for each offence, at the discretion of the court.

Unlawful to carry greater number pounds of steam than specified in license.

Penalty for violation.

6. *And be it enacted*, That it shall be the duty of each one of the persons appointed state inspector of steamboats and steamboat boilers to examine all such persons as shall apply to them for that purpose and as shall pay the examination fee established by law as to their scientific and mechanical knowledge, fitness and qualifications to follow the business or occupation of engineer upon boats propelled by steam power, and to issue to all persons so examined and found to be fit and qualified to follow such business or occupation a certificate of that fact under the signature of such inspector and stating the date of such examination, which certificate the person therein named and certified may file in the office of secretary of state, and thereupon it shall be the duty of the secretary of state to issue to such person a license reciting the fact that such person has been duly examined by such inspector and found duly qualified to follow the business or occupation of steamboat engineer, and a public record shall be kept of all such licenses issued in the secretary of state office.

Inspectors to examine persons as to fitness, &c., as engineers.

Certificate filed in office of secretary of state, and license issued by him.

Unlawful to carry passengers except boat has licensed engineer.

7. *And be it enacted*, That it shall not be lawful for any person or persons or corporation to run or navigate or cause or procure to be run or navigated upon any of the inland or private waters of this state any boat propelled by steam power for the purpose of carrying or conveying passengers, except the engine and boilers of such boat be under the charge, care and control of a licensed engineer within the meaning of this act, and any person or corporation violating this section of this act shall be deemed guilty of a misdemeanor and upon conviction thereof shall be liable to pay a fine of not less than twenty-five dollars or more than two hundred dollars, in the discretion of the court, for each day they shall so offend.

Penalty for violation

Compensation of inspectors.

8. *And be it enacted*, That for each inspection of a steamboat and its boiler or boilers under the provisions of this act the inspector performing such service shall be entitled to charge and receive the sum of fifteen dollars, and for each examination of an applicant for license as engineer under the provisions of this act the inspector who performs such service shall be entitled to charge and receive the sum of five dollars, and that for filing the certificate of inspection and issuing and recording a license to any steamboat under the provisions of this act the secretary of state shall be entitled to charge and receive a fee of three dollars, and that for filing a certificate of examination and issuing and recording a license to a steamboat engineer hereunder the secretary of state shall be entitled to charge and receive a fee of two dollars.

Compensation of secretary of state.

9. *And be it enacted*, That this act shall take effect on the first day of June, eighteen hundred and ninety-three.

Approved March 10, 1893.

CHAPTER XC.

An Act concerning railroad corporations.

1. BE IT ENACTED *by the Senate and General Assembly of the State of New Jersey*, That all railroad corporations of this state, whether created by a special law or incorporated under a general law, shall have full power and authority to lay out, construct, maintain and operate a branch line or branch lines of railroad extending from the main line of their respective railroads, or from any branch line thereof now existing or hereafter to be constructed, to any mill, factory or other manufacturing establishment or clay bed, whenever in the judgment of the board of directors of such corporation it shall be for the interest of such corporations to construct, maintain and operate such branch line or lines; and said corporations are hereby, for this purpose, again invested with all the powers, privileges and franchises given in their respective acts of incorporation, and in the various supplements thereto, for taking and acquiring title to lands required for their use; *provided, however*, that no such branch line shall be more than two miles in length; *and provided further*, that any railroad corporation which shall hereafter construct any branch line or lines in pursuance of the power and authority hereby conferred shall, before commencing the construction thereof file or cause to be filed a correct and accurate map and route of the same in the office of the secretary of state of this state; and also shall deposit with the treasurer of this state a sum of money amounting to at least two thousand dollars for every mile of road proposed to be constructed, which said sum shall be repaid to said corporation by said treasurer in sums of two thousand dollars for each mile of said road, upon the construction of which it shall be proved to his satisfaction that the said corporation have expended at least the sum of two thousand dollars; *and provided further*, that no railroad corporation shall con-

Railroad corporations authorized to construct, &c., branch lines.

Proviso.

Proviso.

Proviso.

struct any branch lines within the limits of any city or town of this state until it shall first obtain the consent of the municipal authorities of such city or town thereto.

Branch lines heretofore constructed legalized.

2. *And be it enacted*, That any railroad corporation of this state which has heretofore constructed any branch line or lines to any clay bed, mine or manufacturing establishment without authority of law, shall have as full power and authority to maintain and operate the same as if such branch line or lines had been constructed in pursuance of legislative authority conferred upon such corporation for that purpose; *provided, however*, that such corporation shall, within sixty days after the passage of this act, file or cause to be filed a correct and accurate map and route of such branch line or lines in the office of the secretary of state of this state.

Proviso

3. *And be it enacted*, That this act shall take effect immediately.

Approved March 10, 1898.

CHAPTER XCI.

An Act to fix the term of office of assessors of taxes in townships of this state.

Term of office

1. Be it enacted *by the Senate and General Assembly of the State of New Jersey*, That every assessor of taxes hereafter elected in any township in counties of the first class in this state shall hold his office for a term of three years, and until the qualification of his successor.

Repealer.

2. *And be it enacted*, That all acts or parts of acts inconsistent with this act be and the same are hereby repealed, and that this act shall take effect immediately.

Approved March 10, 1898.

CHAPTER XCII.

An Act concerning overseers of the poor in cities of the first class.

1. Be it enacted *by the Senate and General Assembly of the State of New Jersey*, That in all cities of the first class in this state it shall be lawful for the overseer of the poor to appoint and employ an assistant, by and with the consent of the board of aldermen who, shall receive a compensation of not exceeding one thousand dollars per annum, to be determined by the board having charge and control of the finances of such city.

Appointment and compensation of assistant overseer.

2. *And be it enacted*, That the money necessary for the purposes of this act shall be provided by the said board having charge and control of the finances as aforesaid, and shall be included in the tax levy of each year.

Money required included in tax levy.

3. *And be it enacted*, That this act shall take effect immediately.

Approved March 10, 1893.

CHAPTER XCIII.

An Act fixing the term of office of mayors in cities of the first class.

1. Be it enacted *by the Senate and General Assembly of the State of New Jersey*, That every mayor hereafter elected in any city of the first class shall hold his office for a term of two years and until the qualification of his successor.

Term of office.

2. *And be it enacted*, That all acts and parts of acts inconsistent with this act be and the same are hereby re- led, and this act shall take effect immediately.

Repealer.

Approved March 10, 1893.

CHAPTER XCIV.

An Act concerning the tenure of office of city collectors in cities of the third class.

Term of office.

1. BE IT ENACTED *by the Senate and General Assembly of the State of New Jersey*, That the term of office of the city collector or other officer charged with the collection of taxes and assessments in any city of the third class shall be three years.

Repealer.

2. *And be it enacted*, That all acts and parts of acts, either general or special, inconsistent with the provisions of this act be and the same are hereby repealed.

3. *And be it enacted*, That this act shall take effect immediately.

Approved March 10, 1893.

CHAPTER XCV.

An Act to regulate the pay of officers and employees of paid fire departments in cities of the second class in this state.

Compensation of officers and men of paid fire departments specified.

1. BE IT ENACTED *by the Senate and General Assembly of the State of New Jersey*, That in any city of the second class in this state having a paid fire department, the pay or salaries per annum of the following named officers and employees shall be as hereinafter specified, namely: to the chief engineer, the sum of two thousand dollars; to captain of companies, the sum of one thousand two hundred dollars each; to engineers of steamers, one thousand one hundred dollars each; to the privates, the sum

of one thousand dollars each; to the superintendent of electric fire alarm, one thousand dollars; to the veterinary surgeon, the sum of seven hundred and fifty dollars; in lieu of all other compensation whatsoever.

Acceptance or rejection of this act to be submitted by resolution to a vote of legal voters.

2. *And be it enacted*, That the provisions of this act shall remain inoperative in any such city until the same shall, by a resolution therefor of the board having control of the fire department of such city, be submitted to a vote of the legal voters of such city and be assented to by a majority of the legal votes cast for or against the acceptance or rejection of this act at any regular charter or general election to be hereafter held in such city or municipality next after the passage of such resolution; such submission shall not be made until notice of the adoption of said resolution by said board shall have been published every day for at least ten days next preceding the time when the official ballots must be ready for distribution for such election in such city, in the official daily newspaper in such city, by the clerk of such city; persons voting at any election at which this act shall be submitted as aforesaid, shall express their assent to or rejection of this act by depositing their ballots in the box provided for depositing ballots at such election in the election precincts, districts or wards of any such city; and those who are in favor of the acceptance of this act shall each deposit a ballot containing the words "for increase of pay of fire department," written or printed thereon, and those who are opposed thereto shall each deposit a ballot with the words "against increase of pay of fire department," written or printed thereon; but this acceptance or rejection may not be expressed upon the ballot on which are the names of the candidates for ward, city, county or state officers, but must be expressed upon a separate ballot, and the election officers in the several precincts, wards and districts of such city, and the board of canvassers of such city shall, in the canvassing, determining and returning the votes cast at such election, canvass, determine and return the votes, and the result of the votes at such election, upon the question of the acceptance or rejection of this act, in the same manner as for officers voted for at such election; and if a majority of the ballots on which there shall be the words "for increase of pay of fire de-

Notice to be given by said board

Form of ballots.

Separate ballot.

Election officers to count and canvass

Majority to decide

partment," or the words "against increase of pay of fire department," are in favor of the acceptance of this act, then this act shall take effect immediately.

When pay of officers goes into effect, and how provided for.

3. *And be it enacted*, That the increase of pay of officers, provided by this act, shall go into effect on the first day of the next calendar month after this act shall take effect as aforesaid, and the board or authority having control of the finances of such city shall make due provision for the payment of such additional expense and shall put such additional sum in the next and annual tax levy of such city thereafter as may be necessary for that purpose.

4. *And be it enacted*, That this act shall take effect immediately.

Approved March 10, 1893.

CHAPTER XCVI.

A Supplement to an act "An act respecting the prerogative court, and the power and authority of the ordinary," approved April sixteenth, one thousand eight hundred and forty-six.

Register authorized to receive commissions

1. Be it enacted *by the Senate and General Assembly of the State of New Jersey*, That the register of the prerogative court shall be entitled to charge and receive on all moneys and securities that are now or may be hereafter deposited with him under any law of this state or the rules of the prerogative court, the same commissions as are now allowed by law to the clerk in chancery for commissions on deposits.

Repealer.

2. *And be it enacted*, That all acts and parts of acts inconsistent with this act be and the same are hereby repealed, and that this act shall take effect immediately.

Approved March 10, 1893.

CHAPTER XCVII.

An Act to regulate the practice of courts of law.

Award a writ of attachment against lands, etc., how made.

1. BE IT ENACTED *by the Senate and General Assembly of the State of New Jersey*, That in all cases in which a capias ad respondendum may issue against the defendant or defendants in any action upon contract, the court, or a judge thereof, or a supreme court commissioner, may, at the request of the plaintiff, upon filing the affidavits required as a foundation for an order for bail, by an order made for that purpose, award a writ or writs of attachment against the lands and tenements, goods and chattels, rights and credits, moneys and effects of the defendant or defendants, in this state, whether such defendant or defendants, or either of them, be a resident or this state or not, and that the practice and procedure in relation to the issue, the levy, and the return of said writ or writs, and the vacation thereof when improperly issued, shall be the same as in the cases of attachment against non-resident debtors.

From time writ is delivered to sheriff, etc., the defendant's property bound.

2. *And be it enacted*, That every such writ of attachment shall bind the property of the defendant or defendants against whom the same shall be issued, from the time that such writ shall be delivered to the sheriff, under-sheriff, coroner, or other officer, to be executed; and for the better manifestation of the said time, such officer shall, upon the receipt of any such writ, endorse thereon, without fee for so doing, the day of the month and year when he received the same, and if two or more writs of attachment shall be delivered against the property of the same person on the same day, that which was first delivered shall be first executed; and the court out of which such attachment or attachments may issue shall have full power and authority to make inquiry and determine the priority of the said several writs.

Officer shall endorse date and year writ received.

First writ delivered, first to be executed.

3. *And be it enacted*, That the issuing of such writ of attachment shall be deemed the beginning of an action of

Issuing of writ the beginning of an action, no summons necessary.

law, and that no summons or other mesne process shall be necessary to bring the defendant into court, and that the plaintiff shall file his declaration within thirty days after the return day of said writ, and shall rule the defendant or defendants to plead thereto, which rule shall be served or published as the court may direct, and that the practice and procedure in the action shall be the same as if the action had been begun by summons, except as herein otherwise provided.

Special execution shall issue upon recovery of judgment.

4. *And be it enacted*, That the property of the defendant or defendants attached, shall remain during the pendency of the suit as security for any judgment which the plaintiff therein may ultimately recover, and upon the recovery of final judgment in the action, special execution shall issue against such of the attached property as may be liable to be levied upon and sold under the execution laws of this state, and the proceedings thereon shall be in conformity therewith; but in case the property attached, or any part thereof shall be such as is not liable to be levied upon and sold under the execution laws of this state, then and in such case the sheriff or other officer, to whom the said writ of execution shall have been issued, shall have authority, and it shall be his duty, in his own name as such sheriff, or other officer, to realize upon the said property and choses in action, by sale, collection, or otherwise, and to that end he shall have authority to bring suit in his name as such sheriff or other officer, for the recovery of any moneys due thereon, and he shall account therefor to the court out of which the the said execution issued.

When sheriff in his own name shall realize upon said property.

Upon giving bond the property may be released.

5. *And be it enacted*, That the property so attached may, by rule of court, be released from the lien of the said writ upon the defendant or defendants giving bond, with sufficient surety or sureties, to be approved by the court, or judge, or by the supreme court commissioner who awarded the said writ, and filed with the clerk, in double the amount of the plaintiff's claim or cause of action, or in double the value of the property so attached, conditioned for the payment of any judgment which may be ultimately recovered by the plaintiff or plaintiff's in that action.

6. *And be it enacted*, That the supreme court shall have power to make such rules and regulations concerning the practice to be had hereunder as may be necessary to carry out the provisions of this act, and that this act shall be construed in all courts of judicature in the most liberal manner for the detection of fraud, the advancement of justice and the benefit of creditors. Supreme Court authorized to make rules and regulations

7. *And be it enacted*, That this act shall take effect immediately.

Approved March 10, 1893.

CHAPTER XCVIII.

An Act to establish the rate of interest on arrears of taxes and assessments in cities of this state.

1. BE IT ENACTED *by the Senate and General Assembly of the State of New Jersey*, That the common council or other board having charge and control of the finances of any city in this state may by the same vote required to expend moneys, fix and change by resolution, the rate of interest on all past due taxes and assessments of all kinds which were due prior to January first, one thousand eight hundred and ninety-two, at and after a rate of not less than seven per centum per annum; *provided, however*, that such rate shall apply only to such taxes and assessments as are still due and unpaid to said city, and shall not apply to any taxes or assessments that have been or may be adjusted under the act of the legislature entitled "An act concerning the settlement and collection of arrearages of unpaid taxes, assessments and water rates or water rents in cities of this state, and imposing and levying a tax, assessment and lien in lieu and instead of such arrearages and to enforce the payment thereof, and to provide for the sale of lands subjected to further taxation and assessment," passed March thirtieth, one thousand eight hundred and eighty-six. Common council, etc., may fix rate of interest on past-due taxes. Proviso.

Repealer.

2. *And be it enacted*, That all acts or parts of acts so far as they conflict herewith be and the same are hereby repealed, and that this act shall take effect immediately.

Approved March 10, 1893.

CHAPTER XCIX.

A Further Supplement to an act entitled "An act to authorize the formation of railroad corporations and to regulate the same," approved April second, one thousand eight hundred and seventy-three.

Railroad corporations authorized to use motive power best adapted to its railway, etc.

1. BE IT ENACTED *by the Senate and General Assembly of the State of New Jersey*, That it shall and may be lawful for any railroad corporation in this state authorized to use steam as a motive power, or authorized to use steam or other motive power, to use, on any part of its railway, any motive power which shall in its judgment be best adapted to the economical operation of its railway; and to erect, construct, maintain, and use such machinery, engines, devices and appliances and such poles, wires, conduits, or other methods for conducting and distributing power as may be required; and for this purpose said railway corporation are hereby re-invested with all the powers originally conferred upon them and each of them by the acts under which they were created for the condemnation of lands; *provided*, that steam power shall not be used on any part of the road originally chartered as a horse car railroad.

Proviso.

Repealer

2. *And be it enacted*, That this act shall take effect immediately and that acts and parts of acts, inconsistent with this act, to the extent of such inconsistency, be and the same are hereby repealed.

Approved March 10, 1893.

CHAPTER C.

A Supplement to an act entitled "An act concerning evidence," approved March twenty-seventh, one thousand eight hundred and seventy-four.

1. **Be it enacted** *by the Senate and General Assembly of the State of New Jersey*, That the thirty-eighth section of the act to which this is a supplement be and the same is hereby amended so that the same shall read and be in the words following, to wit: Section to be amended.

38. *And be it enacted*, That any party in a civil cause desiring the testimony of any witness who resides out of this state may, instead of taking his testimony by commission take the testimony of such witness de bene esse before any judge of any supreme, circuit or district court, or court of common pleas, of the state where such witness is, or before any commissioner of deeds appointed by the governor of this state, resident in the state where such witness is, or before a commissioner specially appointed for that purpose by the court in which such action is pending, or any judge thereof, or before a master in chancery of this state; *provided*, that notice in writing of the time and place of such examination, and of the names of the witnesses to be examined shall be given to the adverse party, his attorney or solicitor, that he may be present and put interrogatories if he shall see fit, which notice shall be served, allowing time for attendance after service, not less than at the rate of one day (Sundays excluded), for every fifty miles of travel; *provided, also*, that in all cases at least ten days' notice, exclusive of Sundays, shall be given; *and provided further*, that in cases where such testimony is desired to be taken of witnesses residing in any foreign state or kingdom, or in any state or territory of the United States, situate upon the Pacific ocean, so many days' notice shall be given as shall be directed by the court in which said cause shall be pending, Testimony of witness residing out of state, how taken Proviso Proviso. Proviso.

or any judge thereof, at chambers; the officer taking such testimony shall first take an oath or affirmation fairly and impartially to take the same, before some person authorized to administer an oath in the state, territory or kingdom where he shall reside; the testimony of such witness shall be taken on oath or affirmation, administered according to the law of this state, upon interrogatories to be then and there put by the parties, or any of them, or any person authorized in their behalf, and such interrogatories and the answers thereto shall be reduced to writing by the officer taking such testimony, and shall be subscribed in his presence by the deponent; and thereupon the same shall be certified, sealed up, endorsed, directed and forwarded, as is required in case of depositions taken under the twenty-ninth section of this act, or if the testimony of such witness be taken before a master in chancery, such testimony may be certified and delivered by the master taking the same to the clerk of the court in which such action is pending, or to any judge thereof.

2. *And be it enacted*, That this act shall take effect immediately.

Approved March 10, 1898.

CHAPTER CI.

Supplement to an act entitled "An act respecting the orphans' court and relating to the powers and duties of the ordinary, and the orphans' court and surrogate," approved March twenty-seventh, one thousand eight hundred and seventy-four.

When foreign will may be recorded to make title to lands without letters testamentary.

1. Be it enacted *by the Senate and General Assembly of the State of New Jersey*, That an exemplified copy of any will or the record of any will, admitted to probate in any state or territory of the United States or the District of

Columbia, or in any foreign state or kingdom, and of the certificate of probate thereof, and of the letters testamentary, or of administration with the will annexed issued thereon, exemplified and authenticated according to the act of congress, heretofore or hereafter filed and recorded in the office of the surrogate of any county in this state, shall have the same force and effect in respect to all lands and real estate whereof the testator died seized as if said will had been admitted to probate and letters testamentary or of administration with the will annexed thereon had been issued in this state; and all conveyances of such real estate heretofore, or hereafter made by any executor or executors, or administrator or administrators with the will annexed, or the survivor or survivors of them, or by any devisee or devisees, shall be as valid as if said will had been admitted to probate and letters testamentary or of administration with the will annexed had been issued in this state; and such record or certified copies of said will, certificate and letters, or of the record thereof, shall be received in evidence in all courts of this state.

2. *And be it enacted*, That this act shall take effect immediately.

Approved March 10, 1898.

CHAPTER CII.

A Further Supplement to an act entitled "An act for the punishment of crimes," approved March twenty-seventh, one thousand eight hundred and seventy-four.

1. Be it enacted *by the Senate and General Assembly of the State of New Jersey*, That if any consignee, factor, bailee, clerk, employee, agent or servant, entrusted with the care or sale of any personal property, or entrusted with the collection or care of any moneys, shall fraud- The fraudulent conversion of the proceeds of the sale of personal property a misdemeanor.

ulently take and convert the same, or the proceeds of the sale of the same, or any part thereof, to his own use, or to the use of any person or persons whatsoever excepting the rightful owner thereof, he shall be deemed guilty of misdemeanor, and upon conviction thereof shall be punished by a fine not exceeding five hundred dollars or imprisonment not exceeding a term of two years, or both, at the discretion of the court before whom such conviction shall be had.

Penalty.

2. *And be it enacted*, That this act shall take effect immediately.

Approved March 10, 1898.

CHAPTER CIII.

An Act to further provide for the formation of a quorum in the boards of trustees of incorporated hospitals.

Board of trustees to determine.

1. BE IT ENACTED *by the Senate and General Assembly of the State of New Jersey*, That it shall be lawful for the board of trustees of any incorporated hospital in this state to determine by their by-laws from time to time what number of persons shall constitute a quorum, which shall not be less than seven persons, for the transaction of the business of said board.

Repealer.

2. *And be it enacted*, That so much of any act as is inconsistent with the provisions of this act be and the same is hereby repealed.

3. *And be it enacted*, That that this act shall take effect immediately.

Approved March 10, 1898.

CHAPTER CIV.

A Supplement to the act entitled "An act concerning sheriffs," approved March fifteenth, one thousand eight hundred and seventy-six.

1. BE IT ENACTED *by the Senate and General Assembly of the State of New Jersey*, That in case any sheriff before the expiration of his term of office hath heretofore died or removed out of the jurisdiction of the state or otherwise become disabled by law to execute the office, or shall hereafter die or remove out of the jurisdiction of the state, or otherwise become disabled by law to execute the office, it shall be the duty of the chief justice or any one of the associated justices of the supreme court, on being satisfied of the death, non-residence or disability of such sheriff, to designate by order under his hand and the seal of the circuit court of such county, one of the coroners of the said county to act as sheriff of said county and perform the duties of the office of sheriff of the said county in all respects provisionally until a new sheriff shall be appointed or elected and duly qualified; and when such new sheriff shall be appointed or elected and duly qualified the powers and duties of such coroner, so far as he shall have acted for the deceased, disqualified or disabled sheriff shall cease, and all writs, processes, papers, belonging or appertaining to the office of sheriff shall pass to and be vested in the said newly-appointed or elected sheriff as fully and as entirely as they were in the former sheriff when he ceased to act.

Providing for the filling of any vacancy occurring in the office of sheriff by death, removal or otherwise.

2. *And be it enacted*, That all writs and processes which had been delivered to such deceased, disqualified or disabled sheriff to be executed, remaining unexecuted or partially unexecuted in his hands at the time of his death, disqualification or disability shall be executed or the execution thereof completed by the said coroner so designated to act as sheriff, and by the said newly-appointed or elected sheriff; and all advertisements of sales of

When coroners shall perform the duties of the office of sheriff

goods and chattels, lands, tenements, hereditaments and real estate shall be continued, and adjournments of such sales may be made, of which all persons shall take notice without any other than the usual notice required by law for such advertisements, adjournments and sales; which said advertisements, adjournments and sales such coroner so designated to act as sheriff, or such newly-appointed or elected sheriff is hereby authorized and required to make in as full and ample manner to all intents and purposes as if the said writs and processes had been directed and delivered to such coroner or sheriff, without any scire facias or other order, and such coroner or sheriff shall be entitled to the same fees for their services, and be liable to all the penalties and consequences of law for neglect of duty, as if the said writs and processes had been originally directed and delivered to such coroner or sheriff.

Fees of such coroner.

Proceedings when writ of execution by fi. fa. has been levied and the party serving the same shall die, remove or become disabled by law, it shall be lawful for the party in whose favor the writ was issued, without any proceedings on scire facias, to sue out a writ of venditioni exponas

3. *And be it enacted*, That where any sheriff or coroner or other person to whom any writ of execution by fieri facias hath been heretofore directed, or shall hereafter be directed, hath levied, or shall levy the same execution on the goods and chattels, or on the lands, tenements, hereditaments and real estate of the party named therein, and such sheriff, coroner or other person hath died or shall die, or hath or shall become disabled by law to discharge the duties of their respective office or appointment, or hath removed or shall remove himself or themselves out of the jurisdiction of the state, and continue to reside thereout, without discharging the duties of their respective office or appointment by sale of the property or estate so levied on, then and in either of the said cases it shall and may be lawful for the party or parties in whose favor the said writ of execution shall have been issued, his, her or their legal representatives, without any proceedings on scire facias to sue out of the court out of which the said execution issued a writ of venditioni exponas, to be directed to the sheriff or coroner for the time being of the county where the levy was made, commanding the said sheriff or coroner to sell the property or estate so levied upon, or so much thereof as may be sufficient to satisfy the whole or the residue of the moneys due on said execution, which sale the said sheriff or coroner is hereby authorized and required to make in as full and ample

manner, to all intent and purposes, as if the said execution had been originally directed to such sheriff or coroner, and they shall be entitled to the same fees for services done, and be liable to all the penalties and consequences of law for neglect of duty, as if the said execution had been originally directed to such sheriff or coroner.

Fees for services.

4. *And be it enacted*, That all fees due for services rendered or expenses incurred by the deceased, disabled or disqualified sheriff shall be duly taxed and collected by the said coroner so acting as sheriff, or the said newly appointed or elected sheriff, for the benefit of the said former sheriff or his legal representatives.

Fees to be for benefit of former sheriff.

5. *And be it enacted*, That this act shall take effect immediately.

Approved March 10, 1898.

CHAPTER CV.

An Act concerning railroad companies which have merged and consolidated their corporate franchises and property.

1. BE IT ENACTED *by the Senate and General Assembly of the State of New Jersey*, That whenever any railroad companies in this state organized under the general law of this state shall have merged their corporate franchises and property by agreement made and entered into between their boards of directors and ratified by their stockholders and filed the same in the office of the secretary of state in accordance with the statutes of this state, that it shall and may be lawful for the new company created by such merger and consolidation, to make a survey and map of its line or lines of railroad and file the same in the office of the secretary of state, whereupon the railroad line or lines so described in said map and survey shall be deemed and taken to be the line or lines of railroad of said com-

Map of line of railroads merged and consolidated to be filed in office of secretary of state.

pany, and to the same extent and in the same manner as if it had been so described in the first location of the lines of railroad of said company, and all other routes, lines or locations shall be deemed and taken to be abandoned.

Rights and privileges of new company.

2. *And be it enacted*, That such new company or corporation shall be deemed and taken to have the same rights, powers and privileges as to condemnation of land for railroad purposes or otherwise as might or could have been enjoyed by it had it been newly organized under the laws providing for the organization of railroads in this state.

Repealer.

3. *And be it enacted*, That all acts or parts of acts inconsistent with the provisions of this act be and the same are hereby repealed, and that this act shall take effect immediately.

Approved March 10, 1893.

CHAPTER CVI.

An Act concerning police and fire commissioners in cities of this state.

Who are not eligible as aldermen, councilmen, etc.

1. BE IT ENACTED *by the Senate and General Assembly of the State of New Jersey*, That no member of any board having charge and control of the police or fire department in any city shall be eligible for election as a member of the board of aldermen, board of councilmen or other governing board in such city, but such police or fire commissioner may accept or hold any other place of public trust or emolument, appointive or elective, under state, county or municipal authority in this state.

Repealer.

2. *And be it enacted*, That all acts or parts of acts, general or special, inconsistent with this act, be and the same are hereby repealed, and that this act shall take effect immediately.

Approved March 10, 1893.

CHAPTER CVII.

A Further Supplement to the act entitled "An act for the punishment of crimes" (Revision), approved March twenty-seventh, one thousand eight hundred and seventy-four.

1. BE IT ENACTED *by the Senate and General Assembly of the State of New Jersey*, That it shall not be lawful hereafter to indict any person or persons for the offense of maintaining a common law nuisance or keeping a disorderly house under section one hundred and ninety-two of said act entitled "An act for the punishment of crimes, where the offense sought to be punished consists wholly in its unlawful sale of spirituous, vinous, malt or brewed liquors; but in all such cases the indictment shall be in form for the sale of intoxicating liquors contrary to law, and on conviction of such unlawful sale of any of said liquors the person or persons so convicted shall be punished as in and by said section one hundred and ninety-two of the said act entitled "An act for the punishment of crimes" is provided.

When not lawful to indict persons for keeping a disorderly house, etc.

Approved March 10, 1893.

CHAPTER CVIII.

An Act respecting elections for members of boards of commissioners or improvement commissions.

1. BE IT ENACTED *by the Senate and General Assembly of the State of New Jersey*, That it shall be lawful for any board of commissioners or improvement commission in any

Annual election for commissioners to be held.

town or village or within any townships in this state to hold the annual election for commissioners in the manner provided in the acts creating such boards of commissioners or improvement commissions and the supplements thereto, any act to the contrary notwithstanding; *and provided further*, that every citizen of this state entitled to vote at any general election for members of the legislature, and within the limits of the authority of such boards of commissioners, shall be entitled to vote at any such election for commissioners.

Proviso

Repealer.

2. *And be it enacted*, That all acts and parts of acts inconsistent with this act be and the same are hereby repealed, and that this act shall take effect immediately.

Approved March 10, 1893.

CHAPTER CIX.

An Act to amend an act entitled "An act to establish a system of public instruction" (Revision), approved March twenty-seventh, one thousand eight hundred and seventy-four.

Section to be amended.

1. Be it enacted *by the Senate and General Assembly of the State of New Jersey*, That section ninety-eight of an act entitled "An act to establish a system of public instruction" (Revision), approved March twenty-seventh, one thousand eight hundred and seventy-four, be and the same is hereby amended so as to read as follows:

No corporal punishment.

98. *And be it enacted*, That no principal, teacher or other person employed or engaged in any capacity in any school or educational institution within this state, whether public or private, shall be permitted to inflict, or direct, or cause to be inflicted, corporal punishment upon any child or pupil attending or that may attend the same.

2. *And be it enacted*, That any and every resolution, by-law, rule, ordinance or other act or authority heretofore or hereafter passed, adopted, approved, made or given, by any person or persons whomsoever, natural or artificial, permitting or authorizing corporal punishment to be inflicted upon any child or pupil attending or that may attend any school or educational institution in this state, is hereby made and shall be henceforth absolutely void and of no force or effect.

Resolutions, etc., authorizing corporal punishment void.

3. *And be it enacted*, That any and all acts and parts of acts, and any and all resolutions and parts of resolutions, enacted or passed by the legislature of this state, whether public or private, general or special, inconsistent with the provisions of this act, be and the same are hereby repealed.

Repealer.

4. *And be it enacted*, That this act shall be deemed and taken to be a public act and shall take effect immediately.

Approved March 10, 1898.

CHAPTER CX.

An Act authorizing the extension of the charters of literary, historical, genealogical, library and scientific societies, incorporated by or under any law of this state.

1. BE IT ENACTED *by the Senate and General Assembly of the State of New Jersey*, That it shall be lawful for any literary, historical, genealogical, library or scientific society heretofore or hereafter created under or by virtue of any law of this state, to adopt a resolution at the regular annual meeting of such society, declaring that it is the desire and purpose of such society to extend its charter beyond the time limited in the act or certificate of incorporation of such society, which resolution shall

Societies may extend charter by adopting a resolution at annual meeting.

also specify the term for which such society desires and proposes that its charter shall be extended, not exceeding fifty years from and beyond the time limited as aforesaid; and whenever a copy of such resolution, certified under the hand of its president, and under its common seal, attested by its recording secretary, shall be filed in the office of the secretary of state of this state, the charter of such society shall thereupon and thereby be extended for and during the term specified in such resolution.

Certified copy filed in office of secretary of state.

Approved March 10, 1898.

CHAPTER CXI.

An Act to amend an act entitled "A further supplement to an act entitled 'An act to regulate fees,' approved April fifteenth, one thousand eight hundred and forty-six," approved March twenty-second, one thousand eight hundred and ninety-two.

Section to be amended.

1. Be it enacted *by the Senate and General Assembly of the State of New Jersey*, That the first section of the act of which this act is amendatory be amended so as to read as follows:

Fees of master and special master.

1. Be it enacted *by the Senate and General Assembly of the State of New Jersey*, That for making every report in pursuance of any order or decree made, taken or entered in any suit, cause, matter or proceeding in the court of chancery of this state, after the passage of this act, every master in chancery and every special master in chancery shall be entitled to receive the sum of four dollars, and no more, and that for drawing every such report every such master in chancery and special master in chancery shall be entitled to receive thirty cents for every folio of one hundred words.

2. *And be it enacted*, That the third section of the act of which this act is amendatory be amended so as to read as follows:

3. *And be it enacted*, That every master in chancery, examiner in chancery, special master in chancery and supreme court commissioner shall be entitled to receive, upon taking the affidavits, depositions or examinations of witnesses upon or under any order or decree made in any cause, matter or proceeding by any of the courts of this state, or by any judge thereof, for his attendance at the taking of such affidavit or affidavits, deposition or depositions, or examination or examinations of a witness or witnesses, four dollars for every sitting, not exceeding two, under the same order or decree, to be paid by the party or person obtaining such decree or order, and included in his taxable cost. Fees of master, special master and supreme court commissioner

3. *And be it enacted*, That this act shall take effect immediately.

Approved March 10, 1893.

CHAPTER CXII.

A Further Supplement to an act entitled "An act providing for the adoption of children," approved March ninth, one thousand eight hundred and seventy-seven.

1. BE IT ENACTED *by the Senate and General Assembly of the State of New Jersey*, That section two of the act to which this act is a further supplement be and the said section hereby is amended to read as follows: Section to be amended

2. *And be it enacted*, That such petition shall specify the name, age and place of residence of the petitioner or petitioners and of the child or children, and the name or names by which the child or children shall be known; whether such child or children be possessed of any property, and the full description of the property if any; Form of petition

whether such child or children has or have either father or mother or both living; in case he, she or they are alive then the name or names and place of residence of such father and mother must be given, unless proven to be unknown to the petitioner or petitioners; the person or one of the persons petitioning as aforesaid shall be at least ten years older than the child or children sought to be adopted, and the petition shall be duly verified according to law; and no adoption heretofore granted in accordance with the provisions of the act to which this is a supplement shall be deemed in any way void or voided because the petitioners or either of them were not of the age required by said act; but such adoption shall be held in all respects valid and lawful; *provided, always*, that such adoption has been made agreeably to the provisions of this supplement.

Proviso.

Repealer

2. *And be it enacted*, That all acts or parts of acts inconsistent with this act be and the same are hereby repealed, and that this act shall take effect immediately.

Approved March 10, 1898.

CHAPTER CXIII.

An Amendment to the act entitled "An act relative to offices, commissions and resignations," approved April sixteenth, one thousand eight hundred and forty-six (Revision).

Section to be amended.

1. Be it enacted *by the Senate and General Assembly of the State of New Jersey*, That section four of the act to which this is an amendment be and the same is hereby amended to read as follows:

When a civil commission shall be void.

4. *And be it enacted*, That if any person holding a civil commission or an appointment to an office within this state, and under the authority thereof, shall hereafter be elected to represent this state in the senate or house of

representatives in the congress of the United States, and shall accept of the appointment or take his seat agreeably thereto, the commission or appointment of such person under the authority of this state, within the same, shall be and the same is hereby declared to be vacated and void; *provided*, that this section shall not apply to any person holding an office within this state and under the authority thereof, who was elected to represent this state in the house of representatives in the congress of the United States at the annual election held in this state on the eighth day of November, one thousand eight hundred and ninety-two. Proviso.

2. *And be it enacted*, That this act shall take effect immediately, and that all acts or parts of acts inconsistent with this act are hereby repealed. Repealer.

Approved March 10, 1893.

CHAPTER CXIV.

An Act to amend an act entitled "An act respecting the court of chancery" (Revision), approved March twenty-seventh, one thousand eight hundred and seventy-five.

1. BE IT ENACTED *by the Senate and General Assembly of the State of New Jersey*, That section eighteen of the act to which this is amendatory be and the same is hereby amended to read as follows: Section to be amended.

18. *And be it enacted*, That in case of a bill filed against any defendant against whom a subpœna or other process to appear shall issue, and such defendant shall not cause his appearance to be entered in such suit, as according to the practice of said court the same ought to be entered, in case such process has been duly served, and it shall be made to appear, by affidavit or otherwise, to the satisfaction of the chancellor, that such defendant is out of the state, or cannot, upon due inquiry, be found therein, Non-resident defendants, how notified.

or that he conceals himself within this state, every such defendant shall be deemed and taken to be an absent defendant, and thereupon the chancellor may, by order, direct such absent defendant to appear, plead, answer or demur to the complainant's bill, at a certain day therein to be named, not less than one nor more than three months from the date of such order; of which order such notice as the chancellor shall by rule direct shall, within ten days thereafter, be served personally on such defendant, by a delivery of a copy thereof to him, or be published in one or more of the public newspapers printed in this state and designated in such order, for four weeks successively, at least once in each week; and in case of such publication, a copy of such notice shall be mailed to such defendant, prepaid, directed to him at the post office nearest his residence or the post office at which he usually receives his letters, unless such residence or post office be unknown and cannot be ascertained upon making such inquiries as the chancellor may, by rule, prescribe in such case, which said notice shall also be published or served in any other manner that the chancellor may see proper in the same to direct; and in case such absent defendant shall not appear, plead, answer or demur within the time so limited, or within some further time to be allowed by the chancellor, if he shall think proper, and on proof of personal service, or the publication and the mailing of said notice, as aforesaid, and of the performance of the direction contained in said order, to the satisfaction of the chancellor, the chancellor may order and direct that the complainant's bill be taken as confessed against such absent defendant so failing to plead, answer or demur, or the chancellor may, at his discretion, order the complainant to procure documents, depositions, exhibits, or other evidence to substantiate and prove the allegations in the bill, or the chancellor may examine the complainant on oath or affirmation, touching or concerning the allegations in the bill, and thereupon such decree shall be made, in either case, as the chancellor shall think equitable and just; and that the provisions of this section shall apply to petitions and bills for divorce.

Decree pro confesso against, or proofs may be required.

2. *And be it enacted*, That the nineteenth section of the said act be amended to read as follows: Section to be amended.

19. *And be it enacted*, That any defendant upon whom such notice is served as herein directed shall be bound by the decree in such case as if he were served with process within the state; but in such cases where the same shall be published and sent by mail, if such defendant shall make oath that he did not receive the same, and that it did not in any way come to his knowledge, within ten days after the time within which it was directed to be served; or in cases where actual service is sworn to, if it shall be made to appear by satisfactory proof that such service was not made, the chancellor may, in his discretion, before executing such decree, proceed to take security in the manner provided in the twenty-first section of this act. Non-residents bound by the decree

3. *And be it enacted*, That the twenty-fourth section of the said act be amended to read as follows: Section to be amended.

24. *And be it enacted*, That when a subpœna to answer shall have been returned duly served by the proper officer, or the appearance of the defendant shall have been signed, or service of a subpœna acknowledged, as hereinbefore mentioned, the defendant shall file his plea or demurrer to the bill of complaint within thirty days from the return day of the subpœna, unless further time be granted, and the cause, within ten days thereafter, noticed and set down for argument for the next term, by the party demurring or pleading. Plea of demurrer, when to be filed.

4. *And be it enacted*, That the twenty-fifth section of the said act be amended to read as follows: Section to be amended.

25. *And be it enacted*, That the answer to any bill in chancery shall be filed within thirty days from the return day of the subpœna, in case no plea or demurrer be filed, unless further time be granted. Answer, when to be filed.

5. *And be it enacted*, That the thirty-first section of the said act be amended to read as follows: Section to be amended.

31. *And be it enacted*, That if the plea or demurrer be overruled, no other plea or demurrer shall be thereafter received; but in such case the defendant shall file his answer to the complainant's bill in twenty days after such overruling, and if he fail to do so, the said bill shall be If plea or demurrer overruled, answer must be filed

taken as confessed, and the said court shall thereupon proceed as directed in the twenty-eight section of this act.

Entering of appearance by defendant shall not stay execution.

6. *And be it enacted*, That in any suit hereafter commenced the entering of an appearance by a defendant shall not operate to stay the issuing of an execution therein.

When suits not affected.

Repealer.

7. *And be it enacted*, That this act shall take effect immediately, but shall not affect any suit heretofore commenced; and that all acts and parts of acts inconsistent herewith be and the same are hereby repealed.

Approved March 10, 1893.

CHAPTER CXV.

An Act to amend an act entitled "An act for the relief of creditors against absconding and absent debtors" (Revision), approved March twenty-seventh, one thousand eight hundred and seventy-four.

Section to be repealed.

1. Be it enacted *by the Senate and General Assembly of the State of New Jersey*, That section fifty-one of the act to which this is amendatory be and the same is hereby amended to read as follows:

Time of making sale of lands or goods or chattels.

51. *And be it enacted*, That where judgment, on the report of the said auditor, shall be entered against the said defendant by default, the said auditor may by virtue of an order of court for that purpose, make sale and assurance of the goods and chattels, lands and tenements, of the said defendant, which were attached and taken as aforesaid, and upon which the attachment remains a lien, or such part thereof as shall be necessary to satisfy the debts of the plaintiff, and the creditors who may have applied agreeably to the directions of this act; but notice of the sale of such goods and chattels shall be set up at five of the most public places in the county, and be advertised in some one of the newspapers circulating in

Must be advertised.

this state, for the space of thirty days prior to such sale; nor shall any sale of such lands and tenements be made in less than six months from the time of executing the writ of attachment, nor of any goods or chattels, till judgment be obtained against the defendant as aforesaid, unless the court in its discretion or a judge thereof shall, on the return of the said writ, or at any other time before judgment, order the said sheriff or auditor to sell such goods and chattels; in which case advertisements set up for the space of five days prior to the time of sale, in four of the most public places in the township, precinct or ward, shall be sufficient.

2. *And be it enacted*, That this act shall take effect immediately.

Approved March 10, 1898.

CHAPTER CXVI.

A Supplement to an act entitled "An act to secure to creditors an equal and just division of the estates of debtors who convey to assignees for the benefit of creditors" (Revision), approved March twenty-seventh, one thousand eight hundred and seventy-four.

Sales of land by assignees shall be confirmed by court.

1. Be it enacted *by the Senate and General Assembly of the State of New Jersey*, That it shall be lawful for the assignee or assignees of any debtor or debtors to make sale and conveyance of the real estate of such debtor or debtors at public or private sale in his or their discretion, but that such assignee or assignees shall not make any conveyance of such lands to any purchaser at a private sale thereof until such sale shall have been reported in writing to the orphans' court of the county in which such lands lie, and have been confirmed by the said court.

2. *And be it enacted*, That this act shall take effect immediately.

Approved March 10, 1898.

CHAPTER CXVII.

An Act to amend an act entitled "A supplement to an act entitled 'An act to provide for the purchase, construction and maintenance of public parks by the cities and other municipalities in this state,' approved March fourteenth, one thousand eight hundred and eighty-three," which supplement was approved May seventh, one thousand eight hundred and eighty-nine.

Section to be amended.

1. BE IT ENACTED *by the Senate and General Assembly of the State of New Jersey*, That section one, of which this is an amendment, shall be amended to read as follows:

Common council to levy tax for park purposes.

1. BE IT ENACTED *by the Senate and General Assembly of the State of New Jersey*, That in all cities of this state which have heretofore or may hereafter purchase a park or parks under the act to which this is a supplement, the common council of such city shall levy a tax of three-fifths of one mill on each dollar on all the taxable property in such city, such tax to be levied and collected in like manner as and with the other general taxes of said city, and to be known as "the park fund," and shall be used for the construction, improvement and maintenance of such parks.

2. *And be it enacted*, That this act shall take effect immediately.

Approved March 10, 1898.

CHAPTER CXVIII.

An Act amending an act supplementary to "An act concerning corporations," approved April seventh, one thousand eight hundred and seventy-five, supplement approved February twenty-seventh, one thousand eight hundred and eighty-nine.

1. Be it enacted *by the Senate and General Assembly of the State of New Jersey*, That the first section of the supplement to which this is amendatory be and the same is hereby amended to be in the following, to wit: Section to be amended.

1. Be it enacted *by the Senate and General Assembly of the State of New Jersey*, That it shall be lawful for any ten or more persons to associate themselves into a company to carry on any business which has for its object the selling, guaranteeing, indorsement, insurance of credit, or the limiting, insuring or guaranteeing of the losses of wholesale dealers, manufacturers, financial institutions and others, arising by reason of bad debts or inability to collect outstanding indebtedness or obligations, upon making and filing a certificate in writing of their organization in the manner hereafter mentioned; such certificates shall set forth, first, the name assumed to designate such company and to be used in its business and dealings; second, the place or places in this state where the central office of said company is to be located; third, the object for which said company shall be formed; fourth, the total amount of capital stock of such company, which shall not be less than fifty thousand dollars; the amount with which such company will commence business, which shall not be less than ten thousand dollars, paid into the said company in cash, and the number of shares into which the said capital stock is divided, and the par value of each share; fifth, the names and residences of the stockholders, the number of shares held by each; sixth, the period at which said company shall commence Purposes for which company may be formed.

Certificate, where recorded and filed.

and terminate, not exceeding fifty years; said certificate shall be approved or acknowledged and recorded, as required in deeds of real estate, in a book to be kept for that purpose, in the office of the clerk of the county where the principal office or place of business of such company in this state shall be located, and after being so recorded shall be filed in the office of the secretary of state; the said certificate, or a copy thereof, duly certified by such clerk or secretary, shall be evidence in all courts and places.

Deposit of securities with state comptroller.

2. *And be it enacted*, That said company, before it shall commence the transaction of any business, or the making of any contracts or other engagements, shall deposit with the comptroller of this state first bond and mortgage security, or other security, which shall be approved by the insurance commissioner of this state, to a not less amount than ten thousand dollars, and the said insurance commissioner shall be authorized, whenever, in his judgment, for the safety of the obligations of such company, it shall be necessary to so do, to call upon and direct the said company, within sixty days after the date of such notice, to deposit additional securities of like character to an additional amount not to exceed ten thousand dollars, which securities shall be and remain in the custody of said comptroller, subject to change or re-investment, with like approval of the said insurance commissioner, as a guarantee for the fulfillment of the obligations and undertakings of the said company.

Additional deposit of securities may be required.

Unlawful to perform or do certain acts.

3. *And be it enacted*, That it shall not be lawful for any company organized under the provisions of this act to require of any person, partnership or company, whose loss may have been limited or guaranteed by them, that they shall make final proof of any loss or losses sustained by them, to the company so guaranteeing or limiting, within a less period than ten days after the expiration of the end of the contract or ageement of guarantee.

Applies to corporations heretofore organized.

4. *And be it enacted*, That this act as amended shall apply to corporations heretofore organized under the act of which this is amendatory, in the same manner as if the certificate of organization had been filed under this act.

5. *And be it enacted*, That that all acts and parts of acts, general and special, inconsistent with the provisions of this act in regard to credit guaranteeing companies, be and the same are hereby repealed, and this act shall take effect immediately. Repealer.

Approved March 10, 1893.

CHAPTER CXIX.

An Act relative to the government and management of the insane asylums or hospitals owned by the state of New Jersey.

1. BE IT ENACTED *by the Senate and General Assembly of the State of New Jersey*, That "the state asylum for the insane at Morristown, New Jersey," shall hereafter be designated by the name, style and title of "The New Jersey State Hospital at Morris Plains," and that "the New Jersey state lunatic asylum" (located near Trenton), shall hereafter be designated by the name, style and title of "The New Jersey State Hospital at Trenton." Hereafter state asylums to be designated state hospitals.

2. *And be it enacted*, That the general management and control of both said hospitals shall be vested in one state board of managers, to be known and designated as "The Board of Managers of the State Hospitals," said board shall consist of seven persons, who shall respectively hold office for the period of five years; they shall be appointed by the governor, by and with the advice and consent of the senate; any vacancy occurring in the said board shall be filled for the unexpired term only. Board of managers, how appointed. How vacancy filled.

3. *And be it enacted*, That the board of managers now in office and appointed under and in pursuance of the act entitled "An act concerning the management of the lunatic asylums of this state," approved March seventeenth, one thousand eight hundred and ninety-one, shall continue in office as the board of managers under this Present board of managers continue in office.

act, and that their term of office shall expire pursuant to their appointment under said act approved March seventeenth, one thousand eight hundred and ninety-one.

Board of managers have the direction and control of said hospitals.

4. *And be it enacted*, That said board of managers shall have the general direction and control of all the property and concerns of said hospitals not otherwise provided for by law, and shall take charge of the general interests of said hospitals and see that the objects and designs thereof are carried into effect, and everything done faithfully according to the requirements of the legislature and the by-laws, rules and regulations of said hospitals.

Annual visit to be made.

5. *And be it enacted*, That it shall be the duty of the said board of managers to visit each county lunatic asylum in the state receiving state aid, at least once in each year, and to inspect such institutions and their management, and to make in their annual report such recommendations as they shall deem necessary concerning such local institutions.

Authorized to adopt rules and regulations.

6. *And be it enacted*, That the said board of managers be and they are hereby authorized, empowered and directed, by and with the consent of the governor of this state, and in the manner hereinafter provided, to make, adopt and enforce rules and regulations for the apportionment and distribution to and between the said hospitals of such patients as are now or may hereafter be sent to said hospitals, or either of them, by virtue of any law of this state, and for the removal of patients from either of the said hospitals to the other, and from time to alter and repeal such rules and regulations as the public interest may require; and all rules and regulations so made, adopted and altered, and all repealers, as aforesaid, shall have the force and effect of public statutes, and shall from time to time be published, as the said governor shall direct.

Rules and regulations to be published.

Each rule or regulation, &c., to be adopted by majority of board.

7. *And be it enacted*, That each rule or regulation, and each alteration or repeal of pre-existing rules or regulations, which shall be proposed to be made and adopted under the next preceding section of this act, shall be submitted in writing to the board of managers aforesaid, and if adopted by a majority of the whole number of such board shall then be submitted in writing to the governor of this state for his approval; and no rule or regu-

lation, nor alteration or repeal of pre-exisiting rules or regulations, shall take effect without the same is approved in writing by the governor; all rules, regulations, alterations and repeals aforesaid, approved by the governor as aforesaid, shall be deposited in the office of the secretary of state, and certified copies thereof, under the seal of said secretary, shall be plenary proof thereof in all the courts of this state.

Rules or regulations to be approved by governor and deposited in office of secretary of state.

8. *And be it enacted*, That each patient who shall be removed to either of said hospitals, by virtue of the rules and regulations aforesaid, shall be there continued and treated, and until discharged according to law shall be there supported by the same committee, relative, person, county or other corporation chargeable with such support at the time of such removal, in the same manner and to the same extent as if such patient had not been so removed; and the expense of removing any patient to either of said hospitals shall be paid by the party chargeable by law, as aforesaid, with his or her support, upon the order of the warden of the hospital to which such patient shall be removed, countersigned by the medical director thereof.

Expense of removing patient, by whom paid.

9. *And be it enacted*, That said board of managers may take and hold in trust for the state any grant or devise of land or any donation or bequest of money or other personality, to be applied to the maintenance of any inmate or inmates of said hospitals or the general use of said hospitals or either of them.

Board of managers to be trustees for state.

10. *And be it enacted*, That said board of managers is hereby authorized to establish such by-laws as they may deem necessary and expedient for the appointment of and regulating the appointment of the officers hereinafter mentioned, and for the appointment and regulating the appointment of executive officers, assistants, attendants and employes (including a secretary of said board of managers and a treasurer for each of said hospitals) as said board may determine to be necessary for said hospitals or either of them; for fixing the conditions of admission, support and discharge of patients and for conducting in a proper manner the affairs and business of said hospitals, and to ordain and enforce a suitable system of rules and regulations for the internal govern-

Executive officers, &c., how and by whom appointed.

ment thereof; the medical directors and assistant physicians and the wardens of said hospitals shall be designated resident officers of said hospitals, and the compensation of such resident officers and of the treasurers aforesaid and of the secretary of said board shall be fixed and determined by said board of managers, by and with the approval of the governor, which compensation shall be paid by the state treasurer on the warrant of the comptroller.

Compensation of officers.

Medical directors, by whom appointed.

11. *And be it enacted*, That said board of managers shall have power and it is hereby declared to be its duty to appoint a medical director of and for each of said hospitals, and so many assistant physicians for each of said hospitals as said board may deem necessary, all of whom shall be subject to the rules, regulations and by-laws prescribed from time to time by said board of managers for the control and good government of said hospitals.

Duties of medical directors.

12. *And be it enacted*, That the medical directors so appointed shall have charge, direction and control of all patients and of all persons engaged in the care of patients in said hospitals, with the powers and subject to the rules, regulations and by-laws prescribed, or hereafter to be prescribed and established, by the said managers; and they shall perform all such duties as shall be assigned to them by said managers; *provided*, they shall not assign to them any duty which does not relate to the care, management and treatment of patients, the direction and control of assistant physicians, nurses and attendants of patients.

Proviso.

Appointment and duties of wardens.

13. *And be it enacted*, That the said managers are empowered, and it is hereby declared to be their duty, to appoint a warden of each of said hospitals, who shall be the general manager of the buildings, grounds and farms, with the furniture, fixtures and stocks thereto belonging, and shall perform such other duties as shall be assigned to them by said managers, subject to the by-laws, rules and regulations prescribed, or hereafter to be prescribed by said managers; and before entering upon the duties of their offices said wardens shall execute a bond to the state of New Jersey with sufficient sureties to be approved by said managers, in such penal sum not less than three thousand dollars, as said managers may from

Bonds to be given.

time to time require, conditioned that they shall and will faithfully perform the duties of their office, and pay over and account for all moneys, goods and chattels belonging to said hospitals that shall come into their hands or custody, which bond shall be recorded in a book to be provided for that purpose and kept in the office of said wardens in said hospitals; and thereupon said bonds shall be filed in the office of the secretary of state, and recorded in the same manner as the official bonds of other state officers; *provided, nevertheless*, that the persons now acting as wardens of said hospitals or either of them shall continue to perform the duties of said office of warden under this act until removed, or a successor is appointed by said board of managers. Bonds to be filed and recorded

14. *And be it enacted*, That it shall also be the duty of said wardens annually to make an approximate estimate and detailed statement in writing of the amounts of money required for the support and maintenance of said hospitals and of the amount required from the state, including all salaries and supplies of every kind for the next ensuing fiscal year beginning on the first day of November next, and to submit the same to said managers, on or before the first Thursday of November of each year, and said managers shall annex the same to their annual report, with such comments thereon as they may deem advisable. Wardens annually make estimate of money required

15. *And be it enacted*, That it shall be the duty of said managers to appoint for each of said hospitals an expert accountant or bookkeeper, and such assistant accountants and bookkeepers as may be necessary to keep full and accurate accounts of all business transactions in any way connected with said hospitals. Bookkeepers, how appointed.

16. *And be it enacted*, That it shall be the duty of said managers to appoint a storekeeper for each of said hospitals, who shall receipt for and be charged with all supplies furnished to said hospitals, and take vouchers for all supplies by them distributed, and they shall perform such other duties as may be assigned to them by said managers, subject to such rules, regulations and by laws as said managers may from time to time prescribe. By whom storekeepers appointed. Duties of.

17. *And be it enacted*, That the by-laws prescribed, or which may hereafter be prescribed by said managers, By-laws prescribed obligatory on all officers, &c

shall be obligatory on all officers and agents of said hospitals, and such by-laws shall not be suspended, altered or repealed, except at a regular meeting of said board of managers, and by the consent of a majority of all the members of said board.

Exempt from jury duties, &c.

18. *And be it enacted*, That the resident officers of the said hospitals, and all attendants and assistants actually employed therein, during the time of such employment shall be exempt from serving on juries, and in time of peace from all service in the militia; and the certificate of the medical director or warden, for their respective departments, shall be evidence of the fact of such employment.

Books to be open for inspection

19. *And be it enacted*, That the board of managers shall keep, in bound books to be kept for that purpose, a fair and full record of all their doings, which shall be open at all times to the inspection of the governor of the state, and all persons whom he or either house of the legislature may appoint to examine the same.

How often managers shall visit the hospitals, &c

20. *And be it enacted*, That the managers shall maintain an effective inspection of the said hospitals, for which purpose one of them, or more, shall visit each of them at least once in every week; two or more, at least once in every month, a majority at least once in every three months, and the whole board once a year, at the time and in the manner prescribed in the by-laws; in a book to be kept for that purpose, the visiting manager or managers shall note the date of each visit, the condition of the patients, with remarks of commendation or censure, and all the managers present shall sign the same; the general results of these inspections, with suitable hints, shall be inserted in an annual report detailing the past year's operations and actual state of the hospitals, which the managers shall make to the governor, on or before the fifteenth day of November in each year, to be by him presented to the legislature, accompanied with an annual report of the medical director, warden and treasurer.

Annual report made to governor.

Officers shall exhibit books, papers, &c.

21. *And be it enacted*, That it shall be the duty of the resident officers to admit any of the managers into every part of the said hospitals, and to exhibit to him or them, on demand, all books, papers, accounts and writings belonging to the institution or pertaining to its business

management, discipline or government; also to furnish copies, abstracts and reports, whenever required by the managers.

Custodians of moneys, &c

22. *And be it enacted*, That the respective treasurers of said hospitals shall have the custody of all moneys, bonds, notes, mortgages, and other securities and obligations belonging thereto; they shall open an account at one or more banks, to be approved by the managers, in their own names, as treasurer of the hospital, and shall deposit therein all moneys, immediately on receipt thereof, and shall draw for the same only for the uses of the hospital, and in the manner prescribed in the by-laws, upon the written order of the warden, specifying the object of the payment; they shall keep full and accurate accounts of receipts and payments, in the manner directed in the by-laws, and such other accounts as the managers may prescribe; they shall balance all the accounts on their books annually, on the last day of October, and make a statement of the balances thereon and an abstract of the receipts and payments of the past year, which shall within two days thereafter be delivered to the auditing committee of the managers, who shall compare the same with the books and vouchers, and certify the correctness thereof, within the next ten days, to the managers; they shall, further, render a quarterly statement of their receipts and payments for the quarter ending on the last day of the month next preceding each regular quarterly meeting of the managers to the auditing committee, who shall compare and verify the same as aforesaid, and report the results thereof, duly certified, to the managers, who shall cause the same to be recorded in one of the books of the hospital; they shall, further, render an account of the state of their books, and of the funds and other property in their custody, whenever required so to do by the managers.

Where moneys deposited.

Treasurer shall balance accounts annually, and audited by committee

Quarterly statements to be made.

Vested with same powers as overseers of the poor

23. *And be it enacted*, That the said board of managers shall be vested with the same powers, rights and authority which are now given by law to the overseerers of the poor in any township or city of the state, so far as may be necessary for the indemnity and benefit of the said hospitals or either of them, and for the purpose of compelling a relative, or committee, or guardian, to defray the ex-

penses of a patient's support in the hospitals, and reimburse actual disbursements for his necessary clothing and traveling expenses, according to the by-laws of the institution; also for the purpose of coercing the payment of similar charges, when due, from any county that is liable for the support of any patient in said hospitals.

Authorized to recover sums due in an action brought.

24. *And be it enacted*, That said board of managers shall have authority to recover, for the use of said hospitals, any and all sums which may be due upon any note or bond in their hands belonging thereto; also, any and all sums which may be charged and due, according to the by-laws, for the support of any patient therein, or who may have been therein, or for actual disbursements made in his behalf for necessary clothing and traveling expenses, in an action to be brought by said managers by their official title of "The Board of Managers of the State Hospitals," against the individual county legally liable for the maintenance of said patient, and having neglected to pay the same, when demanded by the treasurer, in which action the declaration may be in a general indebitatus assumsit, and judgment shall be rendered for such sum as shall be found due, with interest from the time of the demand made as aforesaid; said board of managers may also, upon the receipt of the money due upon any mortgage belonging to said hospitals, execute and acknowledge, or cause to be executed and acknowledged, a release thereof, so that the same may be discharged of record.

Authorized to execute releases upon receipt of money due.

Wardens make all purchases, contracts, &c.

25. *And be it enacted*, That the respective wardens of said hospitals shall, under the direction of the board of managers or pursuant to the rules, by-laws and regulations established by said board, make all purchases for said hospitals and preserve the original receipts given on payment thereof, and keep full and accurate accounts of the same and copies of all orders drawn by them upon the treasurer; they shall also in like manner make contracts with all attendants, assistants and employees, and keep and settle their accounts; they shall also keep and render to the proper parties the accounts for the support of patients and expenses incurred in their behalf; they shall make quarterly abstracts of their accounts to the last days of January, April, July and October, for the

proper treasurer and the managers; they shall also be accountable for the careful keeping and economical use of all furniture, stores and other articles provided for said hospitals, and shall, annually, during the third week in October, make out and furnish the managers with a true and perfect inventory, verified by oath, of all the personal property belonging to the hospital and in and about the premises, with an appraisal thereof, made under oath or affirmation by the warden and two suitable persons whom the managers shall appoint for that purpose.

Make an inventory annually, verified by oath.

26. *And be it enacted*, That no person shall be admitted into said hospitals as a patient, except upon an order of some court or judge authorized to send patients, without lodging with the medical director—first, a request, under the hand of the person by whose direction he is sent, stating his age and place of nativity, if known, his christian name and surname, place of residence, occupation, and degree of relationship, or other circumstances of connection between him and the person requesting his admission; and second, a certificate dated within one month, under oath, signed by two reputable physicians, of the fact of his being insane; each person signing such request or certificate shall annex to his name his profession or occupation, and the township, county and state of his residence, unless these facts appear on the face of the document.

How and upon whose order patients admitted

27. *And be it enacted*, That the medical directors shall make, in books kept for the purpose, at the time of reception, a minute with date, of the name, residence, office and occupation of the person by whom and by whose authority each person is brought to said hospitals, and have all the orders, warrants, requests, certificates, and other papers accompanying him, carefully filed, and forthwith copied into said book.

Further duties of medical directors.

28. *And be it enacted*, That each county entitled to send patients to said hospitals, under said rules and regulations, may at all times keep such number of patients, in just proportion with other counties, as the hospitals can accommodate, which proportion shall be regulated by the managers; if any one or more of the counties should not send their full proportion, the vacancies may be allotted

Proportion of patients counties may have.

by the managers to other counties so entitled having patients whom they may desire to send.

How insane paupers are admitted, at expense of county

29. *And be it enacted*, That whenever any pauper, chargeable in the county entitled to send patients to said hospital under said rules and regulations, may be insane, it shall be the duty of the overseer of the poor in the township wherein he resides, to make application in his behalf to any judge of the court of common pleas of the county; and said judge shall call one reputable physician, and fully investigate the facts of the case, and if satisfied, after such examination, of the insanity of the pauper and that he is a proper subject to be admitted to either of said hospitals, he shall issue an order to such overseer, which shall be effectual when approved as hereinafter provided, requiring him without delay to take such insane pauper to the proper hospital, where he shall be kept and supported at the expense of the county in which is his residence until he shall be restored to soundness of mind, or removed or discharged therefrom according to law; the judge in such case shall have power to compel the attendance of witnesses, and shall present the certificate of the physician, taken under oath, and other papers relating thereto, and a statement of the proceedings and decision, to the chosen freeholders or freeholder, if there be but one by law, (or but one acting by reason of the death, sickness or other disability of the other,) of the township where such insane person is found, who shall examine the same, and if satisfied that said person has a legal settlement in their county as defined by the act entitled "An act for the settlement and relief of the poor," approved April tenth, one thousand eight hundred and forty-six, and is entitled to the relief afforded by this act, shall endorse the word "approved" upon said certificate and proceedings, and shall sign their official names thereto; which said certificate and proceedings shall be filed with the clerk of the county, who shall forward to the medical director of the hospital where such insane pauper is confined, copies of said proceedings and certificate authenticated by the clerk under seal of the court, and report the facts to the board of chosen freeholders, whose duty it shall be to raise the money requisite to meet the expenses of support, and, as soon thereafter as practicable

pay it to the treasurer of the proper hospital; but if said freeholders shall not be satisfied as aforesaid, they shall endorse on said certificate and proceedings the words "not approved" and shall sign their official names thereto, and the same shall then be filed with the clerk of the board of chosen freeholders, and said insane pauper shall not be admitted to the said hospital at the expense of the said county.

When not admitted at expense of county

30. *And be it enacted*, That when a person residing in this county entitled to send patients to said hospitals under said rules and regulations, and in indigent circumstances, not a pauper, becomes insane, application may be made in his behalf to any judge of the court of common pleas of the county where he resides; and said judge shall call a reputable physician and other credible witnesses, and fully investigate the facts of the case, and either with or without the verdict of a jury, at his discretion, decide the case as to his insanity and indigence; and if the said judge shall make a certificate that satisfactory proof has been adduced, showing him to be insane, and his estate insufficient to support him and his family (or if he has no family, himself), under the visitation of insanity, on such certificate, authenticated by the county clerk, under the seal of the court, he shall be admitted into the proper one of said hospitals, and supported there, at the expense of said county, until he shall be restored to soundness of mind, or removed or discharged therefrom according to law; the said judge in such case shall have requisite power to compel the attendance of witnesses and jurors and shall file the certificate of the physician, taken under oath, and other papers relating thereto, with a report of his proceedings and decision, with the clerk of the county, and report the fact to the board of chosen freeholders, whose duty it shall be to raise money requisite to meet the expenses of support, and, as soon thereafter as practicable, pay it to the treasurer of the proper hospital; *provided, however*, that if such investigation be made without summoning a jury therein, the said certificate and proceedings shall be presented to the freeholder or freeholders of the township where such indigent person is found, who shall examine and proceed thereon in all respects and with the same force and effect

How insane in indigent circumstances admitted at expense of county.

Proviso.

as is provided in that behalf in the last preceding section of this act; and the clerk of said county shall, if said freeholders approve said certificate and proceedings, report the facts to the board of freeholders, whose duty it shall then be to provide for the expenses of the support of said insane person, and pay the amount as soon as practicable to the treasurer of the proper hospital.

Authorized to make speciaal agreements.

31. *And be it enacted*, That the managers may authorize the medical directors to admit, under special agreements, whenever there are vacaucies in said hospitals, such cases as may seek admission.

Duties of town and county officers.

32. *And be it enacted*, That all town and county officers sending a patient to said hospitals shall, before sending him, see that he is in a state of perfect bodily cleanliness, and is comfortably clothed provided with suitable changes of raiment, as prescribed in the by-laws.

How persons acquitted upon trial upon plea of insanity admitted at expense of county.

33. *And be it enacted*, That when a person shall have escaped indictment, or have been acquitted of a criminal charge upon trial, on the ground of insanity, upon the plea pleaded of insanity, or otherwise, the court being certified by the jury or otherwise of the fact, shall carefully inquire and ascertain whether his insanity in any degree continues, and if it does, shall order him in safe custody, and to be sent to the hospital prescribed by the rules and regulations aforesaid; the county from which he is sent shall defray all his expenses while there, and of sending him back, if returned; but the county may recover the amount so paid from his own estate, if he has any, or from any relative or county that would have been bound to provide for and maintain him elsewhere.

How person confined under indictment, &c., appearing insane, admitted at expense of county.

34. *And be it enacted*, That if any person in confinement, under indictment or for want of bail for good behavior, or for keeping the peace, or appearing as a witness, or in consequence of any summary conviction, or by order of any justice, or under any other than civil process, shall appear to be insane, the judge of the circuit court of the county where he is confined shall institute a careful investigation, call a reputable physician and other credible witnesses, invite the prosecutor of the pleas to aid in the examination, and, if he shall deem it necessary, call a jury, and for that purpose is fully empowered to compel the attendance of witnesses and jurors, and if it

be satisfactorily proved that he is insane, said judge may discharge him from imprisonment, and order his safe custody and removal to one of said hospitals, prescribed by the rules and regulations aforesaid, where he shall remain until restored to his right mind; and then, if the said judge shall have so directed, the medical director shall inform the said judge and the county clerk and prosecutor of the pleas thereof, whereupon he shall be remanded to prison, and criminal proceedings be resumed, or otherwise discharged; the provisions of the last preceding section, requiring the county to defray the expenses of a patient sent to such hospital, shall be equally applicable to similar expenses arising under this section and the one next following.

35. *And be it enacted*, That persons charged with misdemeanors, and acquitted on the ground of insanity, may be kept in custody and sent to the hospital, prescribed by said rules and regulations, in the same way as persons charged with crime.

Persons charged with misdemeanors acquitted on insanity, sent to hospital

36. *And be it enacted*, That the price to be paid for keeping any person in indigent circumstances in the said hospitals, exclusive of clothing, shall be annually fixed by the managers, and shall not exceed three dollars per week.

Price indigent persons shall pay.

37. *And be it enacted*, That every insane person supported in said hospitals shall be personally liable for his maintenance therein and all necessary expenses incurred by the institution in his behalf; and the committee, relative, or county that would have been bound by law to provide for and support him, if he had not been sent to the hospital, shall be liable to pay the expenses of his clothing and maintenance therein, and actual necessary expenses to and from the same.

Personally liable for maintenance and expenses incurred.

38. *And be it enacted*, That the expenses of clothing and maintenance in said hospitals, of a patient who has been received upon the order of any court or judge, shall be paid by the county from which he was sent to such hospital; the county collector of said county is authorized and directed to pay to the treasurer of such hospital the bills for such clothing and maintenance, as they shall become due and payable, according to the by-laws thereof, upon the order of the warden; and the chosen free-

How money raised and by whom paid, to defray expenses of county patients.

holders of the said county shall annually levy and raise the amount of such bills, and such further sum as will probably cover all similar bills for one year in advance; said county, however, shall have the right to require every individual or county that is legally liable for the support of such patient, to reimburse the amount of said bills, with interest from the day of paying the same.

Expenses of removing county patients paid by the county.

39. *And be it enacted*, That whenever the managers shall order a patient removed from either of said hospitals to the county whence he came, the collector of said county shall audit and pay the actual and reasonable expenses of such removal, as part of the expenses of said county; but if any person be legally liable for the support of such patient, the amount of such expenses may be recovered, for the use of the county, by said collector; if such collector neglect or refuse to pay such expenses on demand, the treasurer of the proper hospital may pay the same, and charge the amount to said county, and the county collector shall pay the same with interest; and the chosen freeholders of said county shall levy and raise the amount, as other county charges.

Township or county authorized to recover amount of payments.

40. *And be it enacted*, That every township or county paying for the support of a patient in either of said hospitals, or for his expenses in going to or from the same, shall have the like rights and remedies to recover the amounts of such payments, with interest from the time of paying such bills, as if such expenses had been incurred for the support of the same, at other places under exisiting laws.

Authority of court of chancery not restrained.

41. *And be it enacted*, That none of the provisions of this act shall restrain or abridge the power and authority of the court of chancery over the persons and property of the insane.

When and by whom patients may be discharged

42. *And be it enacted*, That the said managers, upon the certificate of the medical director of a complete recovery, may discharge any patient, except those under a criminal charge, or liable to be removed to prison; and they may send back to the poorhouse of the county or township whence he came, any person admitted as "dangerous," who has been two years in either of said hospitals, upon the medical director's certificate that he is harmless and will probably continue so, and not likely to

be improved by further treatment in the said hospital; or when the hospital is full, upon a like certificate that he is manifestly incurable, and can probably be rendered comfortable at the poorhouse, they may also discharge and deliver any patient, except one under criminal charge as aforesaid, to the poorhouse of the township or county liable for his support, or to his relatives or friends, who will undertake, with good and approved sureties, for his peaceable behavior, safe custody and comfortable maintenance, without further public charge.

Justice of supreme court may order discharge of criminal patient

43. *And be it enacted*, That a patient of a criminal class may be discharged by order of one of the justices of the supreme court, if, upon due investigation, it shall appear safe, legal and right to make such order.

Money and clothing furnished.

44. *And be it enacted*, That no patient shall be discharged without suitable clothing, and if it cannot be otherwise obtained, the warden shall, upon the order of two managers, furnish it; also money, not exceeding ten dollars, to defray his necessary expenses, until he reaches home.

Traveling expenses paid, no compensation for services

45. *And be it enacted*, That said board of managers shall receive their actual traveling expenses, to be paid by the state treasurer, on the warrant of the comptroller, on the rendering of their accounts; no court, judge, clerk or other officer shall receive any compensation for any services performed under this act.

All purchases shall be for cash.

46. *And be it enacted*, That all purchases for the use of said hospitals shall be made for cash, and not on credit or time.

Meaning of term "lunatic" and "insane"

47. *And be it enacted*, The terms "lunatic" and "insane," as used in this act, include every species of insanity, and extend to all deranged persons and to all of unsound minds, other than idiots; a word denoting the singular number is to include one or many; and every word importing the masculine gender only, may extend to and include females.

Amount to be paid by state for each indigent patient.

48. *And be it enacted*, That there shall be paid from the state treasury, in quarterly payments, and upon the warrant of the comptroller, to the treasurers of the said hospitals, the sum of one dollar per week towards the maintenance and keep of each indigent patient in said hospitals.

How and when judge shall order insane pauper removed to a hospital.

49. *And be it enacted*, That if the judge to whom application shall be made on behalf of any insane pauper shall be satisfied upon the examination of the case made in the manner prescribed in section twenty-nine of this act, that such insane pauper cannot be provided for by the overseer of the poor of the township, or at the poorhouse of the township or county upon which he is chargeable, with comfort and without danger or prejudice to himself or others, the said judge shall order the said pauper to be removed to one of said hospitals, to be kept and supported in the manner and for the time in the said section mentioned.

Upon removing a patient from one hospital to the other, the official documents and papers must be delivered to medical directors.

50. *And be it enacted*, That when any patient shall be removed from one of the said hospitals to the other, under the rules and regulations hereinbefore authorized and directed, it shall be the duty of the medical director of the hospital from which he is removed, to deliver to the medical director of the hospital to which he is removed, the official documents and papers under the authority of which the said patient was received and under which he is retained, and the said documents and papers shall be as full and ample authority for detaining such patient in the hospital to which he is removed, as if such patient had not been so removed.

Repealer.

51. *And be it enacted*, That all acts and parts of acts inconsistent herewith or repugnant hereto, be and the same are hereby repealed, and that this act shall take effect immediately.

Approved March 11, 1893.

CHAPTER CXX.

A Supplement to an act entitled "An act respecting the orphans' court and relating to the powers and duties of the ordinary, and the orphans' courts and surrogates'," approved March twenty-seventh, one thousand eight hundred and seventy-four.

In case non-resident executor, administrator or guardian does not proceed to settle estate, any person interested may make complaint to orphans' court.

1. BE IT ENACTED *by the Senate and General Assembly of the State of New Jersey*, That in case any executor, administrator or guardian, heretofore or hereafter appointed by the orphans' court has removed or shall hereafter remove out of this state, or does not reside within the same, or shall be of unsound mind or mentally incapacitated from transacting business and does not proceed with the administration of the estate, the orphans' court of the county where such letters testamentary or administration or of guardianship have been granted, upon complaint being made by any person interested in such estate, may inquire into the matter in a summary manner, and revoke such letters testamentary or of administration or of guardianship granted to such executor, administrator or guardian, and may grant letters of administration de bonis non to such fit, responsible and discreet person or persons as such orphans' court shall see fit, or appoint such other guardian or guardians as such orphans' court shall see fit; *provided, however*, that before letters of administration de bonis non are issued, or such other guardian or guardians be appointed in pursuance of this act, such notice of such application shall be served upon or mailed to such executor, administrator or guardian, or served upon or mailed to such other person or persons as the court may direct, requiring such executor, administrator, guardian or other person, on a certain day to be named therein, to appear before said court and show cause why such letters testamentary or of administration or of guardianship shall not be revoked.

Proviso.

2. *And be it enacted*, That this act shall take effect immediately.

Approved March 11, 1893.

CHAPTER CXXI.

An Act concerning the appointment of municipal officers and boards in cities.

How and by whom the law officers of cities are appointed.

1. BE IT ENACTED *by the Senate and General Assembly of the State of New Jersey*, That the law officers of any city of the first class of corporation or city counsel, and corporation or city attorney, shall be appointed by the board in such city having charge of the financial affairs thereof and charged with the duty and power of confirming, by ordinance or otherwise, the annual tax levy or tax budget, by whatever name the same may be known in any city, by a vote of not less than two-thirds of all the members of any such board being recorded in favor of such appointment, in every case.

Appointment of municipal officers or members of boards by the mayor to be confirmed.

2. *And be it enacted*, That in every case in any city where the mayor thereof is now authorized by any law to appoint any municipal officer or member of any municipal board, the name of the person appointed shall be submitted to the board of such city government having the control and management of the financial affairs and the duty and power of confirming the annual tax levy or tax budget, by ordinance or otherwise, by whatever name the same may be known in such city, and no such appointment shall take effect until such board has confirmed the same by a vote in favor thereof of not less than two-thirds of all of the members of such board, duly recorded in the permanent minutes thereof; *provided*, that this act shall not apply to the appointment of any secretary to the mayor or any clerk in his office authorized by law, nor to any of the active members of any

Proviso.

police force or fire department in any city, other than the superintendents thereof.

3. *And be it enacted*, That if any section of this act shall, for any reason, be held to be unconstitutional or invalid, such holding shall not affect the other provisions of this act, or any of them. **When sections not invalidated.**

4. *And be it enacted*, That all acts or parts of acts inconsistent with this act be and the same are hereby repealed, and that this act shall take effect immediately. **Repealer.**

Passed March 11, 1893.

CHAPTER CXXII.

A Further Supplement to an act entitled "An act concerning taxes," approved April fourteenth, one thousand eight hundred and forty-six.

1. Be it enacted *by the Senate and General Assembly of the State of New Jersey*, That the dwelling house owned by any religious corporation, and the land upon which the same stands, while and during only the time actually used by the officiating clergyman of such religious corporation, shall be exempt from taxation to an amount not exceeding five thousand dollars, but not more than one dwelling actually used by any one religious corporation shall be so exempt. **Property exempt from taxation.**

2. *And be it enacted*, That all acts and parts of acts inconsistent herewith be and the same are hereby repealed. **Repealer.**

3. *And be it enacted*, That this act shall take effect immediately.

Approved March 11, 1893.

CHAPTER CXXIII.

An Act to authorize cities of the first class to provide for and pay amounts unpaid for lighting streets, public buildings and public places, arising from insufficient appropriations.

Authorized to borrow money to pay deficiency.

1. Be it enacted *by the Senate and General Assembly of the State of New Jersey*, That whenever in any city of the first class of this state, by reason of insufficient appropriations for lighting streets, public buildings and public places in such city, the persons or corporations which have furnished or shall hereafter furnish light to the streets, public buildings and public places, or either thereof, of such city, remain unpaid therefor in whole or in part, whether for one year or more, it shall be the duty of such city to borrow such sum or sums of money as shall be necessary to meet such deficiency, and to pay the same therewith.

Authorized to issue bonds.

2. *And be it enacted*, That in such case the board or authority of said city having charge of the lighting of said city, shall make its requisition for the sum needed for the purpose aforesaid, on the board or other authority having the management and control of the finances of said city, and that board or authority shall thereupon cause to be issued temporary bonds of such city for the amount named in such requisition, bearing interest at a rate not exceeding four and a half per centum per annum and to be sold at not less than par, and the proceeds thereof shall be applied to the payment of such unpaid amount.

Money to be raised by assessments and taxation.

3. *And be it enacted*, That the amount, principal and interest, of said bonds, shall be placed in the next annual tax levy and assessed and collected as other taxes.

4. *And be it enacted*, That this act shall take effect immediately.

Approved March 11, 1893.

CHAPTER CXXIV.

A Futher Supplement to an act entitled "An act for the formation of borough governments," approved April fifth, one thousand eight hundred and seventy-eight.

Sinking fund created for payment of municipal bonds, upon adoption of a resolution of mayor and council

1. Be it enacted *by the Senate and General Assembly of the State of New Jersey*, That it shall be lawful for any borough in this state organized under the provisions of the act entitled "An act for the formation of borough governments," approved April fifth, one thousand eight hundred and seventy-eight, and the several supplements thereto, and that has heretofore or shall hereafter issue its municipal bonds, creating a debt or obligation of such borough, to fall due at a future time, under or by virtue of the provisions of any law of this state authorizing the issuing of such bonds and the creation of such debt or obligation; by a resolution of the mayor and council of such borough to that effect duly passed and adopted, to provide for the creation and establishment of a sinking fund for the payment and cancellation of such bonds at their maturity, in the manner hereinafter provided.

Commissioners to be appointed.

2. *And be it enacted*, That it shall be lawful for the mayor and council of any such borough, after having passed and adopted a resolution to create and establish a sinking fund for the purpose specified in the first section of this act, to appoint three suitable persons, residents and freeholders within such borough, as commissioners to receive, take charge of, invest and pay over such sinking fund in the manner hereinafter provided; which commissioners, when so appointed shall be officially designated as commissioners of the sinking fund of the borough of (inserting the name of the borough), and of the three commissioners so to be appointed in the first instance, one shall be appointed to hold office for one year, one for two years and one for three years from the date of their appointment, and one such commissioner shall be appointed annually thereafter, to hold his office

Designated as commissioners of the sinking fund

Term of office.

Appointment at expiratirn of term. Vacancy. Bond.

for the term of three years and to take the place of the commissioner whose term then expires, any vacancy to be filled by appointment for the unexpired term only; and such commissioners, before entering upon the discharge of the duties of their appointment, shall severally enter into a bond to such borough, in such amount as the mayor and council of such borough shall, by resolution, fix and require, and with sureties to be approved by such mayor and council conditioned for the honest and faithful discharge of the duties of his office as commissioner of the sinking fund of such borough, which bond shall be renewed annually and shall be filed with the borough clerk.

Duties of commissioners of sinking fund.

3. *And be it enacted*, That such commissioners of the sinking fund when duly appointed and qualified shall be the lawful custodians of all such moneys as shall be levied and raised in such borough for the purpose of paying off and retiring the bonded indebtedness of such borough for which such sinking fund is to be raised, and it shall be the duty of such commissioners to loan and invest such funds and the interest accruing thereon from time to time, and keep the same loaned and invested at interest, upon such securities as the school fund of this state may be lawfully loaned and invested upon, but in the corporate name of such borough, and to pay the principal of such fund into the borough treasury when thereto required by resolution of the mayor and council of such borough for the purpose of paying off and retiring such bonded indebtedness of such borough; and it shall be the duty of such commissioners annually on the fifteenth day of February, and at such other time or times as they may be required so to do by resolution of the mayor and council, to furnish and report to the mayor and council of such borough a detailed statement of the condition ot such sinking fund in their hands and showing all receipts, disbursements and investments on that account by them during the twelve months next preceding such accounting and giving a description of such securities as may be in their hands for such funds as they may have loaned or invested; and all expenses necessarily and properly incurred by such commissioners in the discharge of their

Make annual statement of such sinking fund.

Expenses a legitimate debt

duties shall be a legitimate debt of such borough and be payable out of the sinking fund.

4. *And be it enacted*, That it shall be lawful to raise annually in such borough, by taxes levied, assessed and collected in the same manner as other taxes may be levied, assessed and collected in such borough, such sum in addition to the other moneys that may be lawfully raised in boroughs for general borough expenses as the mayor and council of such borough may by resolution determine to be necessary and proper to raise for the purpose of creating such sinking fund, which sum when collected by the borough collector shall be by him paid over to the commissioners of the sinking fund annually. Money required to create sinking fund to be raised by taxation

5. *And be it enacted*, That this act shall take effect immediately.

Approved March 11, 1893.

CHAPTER CXXV.

Supplement to the act entitled "An act for the preservation of the early records of the supreme court," approved April seventeenth, one thousand eight hundred and eighty-eight.

WHEREAS, Pursuant to the provisions of the act entitled "An act for the preservation of the early records of the supreme court," approved April seventeenth, one thousand eight hundred and eighty-eight, the clerk of the supreme court of the state has prosecuted the work thereby intrusted to him and has made large progress therein, and it is important to the interests of the state and the citizens thereof that the said work should continue to be prosecuted until the completion thereof; it appearing that the work already done has been prosecuted with the approval of the chief justice of the supreme court and that the appropriation heretofore Preamble made, to wit, the sum of two thousand dollars, has proved to be insufficient to defray the expenses of completing said record; therefore,

Clerk of supreme court to continue the duties imposed upon him.

1. Be it enacted *by the Senate and General Assembly of the State of New Jersey*, That the clerk of the supreme court be and he is hereby authorized and directed to continue and completely perform the work and duties imposed upon him by the act to which this is a supplement and that the expenses of continuing and completing said work shall be paid by the treasurer upon the warrant of the comptroller upon the approval of the chief justice; *provided*, that the expenses incurred under this supplemental act shall not exceed three thousand dollars, which sum is hereby appropriated for the purpose of continuing and completing the work authorized by this supplemental act.

Expenses, how paid

Proviso

2. *And be it enacted*, That this act shall take effect immediately.

Approved March 11, 1893.

CHAPTER CXXVI.

A Further Supplement to an act entitled "An act to authorize cities to construct sewers and drains, and to provide for the payment of the cost thereof," approved March eighth, one thousand eight hundred and eighty-two.

Preamble.

Whereas, after sewers are laid in the streets of cities, such streets are frequently opened and torn up for the purpose of making house connections with such sewers; therefore,

Common council, etc., authorized to make house connections with sewers

1. Be it enacted *by the Senate and General Assembly of the State of New Jersey*, That in all cities in this state where sewers are now being built or hereafter may be

built, under and by virtue of the act to which this is a supplement, the common council, board of aldermen or other municipal body charged by law with the construction of sewers in such cities, shall have power and authority to build and construct at the time of the building of such sewers house connections from such sewers proper to the curb line of the lots fronting on the street or streets through which such sewer or sewers shall or may be built.

2. *And be it enacted*, That the costs and expenses of making such house connections shall be charged to and borne by the lots and subdivisions of lots particularly benefited thereby, and shall be assessed against the same at the same time and by the same authority making the assessments for such sewers proper. By whom costs and expenses paid

3. *And be it enacted*, That all acts and parts of acts inconsistent with the provisions of this act be and the same are hereby repealed. Repealer.

4. *And be it enacted*, That this act shall take effect immediately.

Approved March 11, 1893.

CHAPTER CXXVII.

A Further Supplement to an act entitled "An act to incorporate societies for the promotion of learning" (Revision), approved April ninth, one thousand eight hundred and seventy-five.

1. BE IT ENACTED *by the Senate and General Assembly of the State of New Jersey*, That it shall and may be lawful for any corporation heretofore or hereafter to be incorporated under or by virtue and in pursuance of the act entitled "An act to incorporate societies for the promotion of learning" (Revision), approved April ninth, one Authorized to increase number of trustees or directors.

thousand eight hundred and seventy-five, or under or by virtue and in pursuance of any act supplementary thereto or amendatory thereof, to increase from time to time the number of trustees or directors of such corporation to any number not exceeding twenty-one in all, by filing or causing to be filed in the office of the secretary of state of this state a certificate, under the corporate seal of said corporation and signed by the president thereof, setting forth the number of trustees or directors who shall thereafter have the management of the affairs of such corporation, and the regulation and government thereof.

Certificate to be filed.

Trustees shall be residents of state.

2. *And be it enacted*, That a majority of the members so constituting the board of trustees or directors shall be residents or citizens of the state of New Jersey.

Repealer.

3. *And be it enacted*, That all acts or parts of acts inconsistent with or repugnant to this act, be and the same are hereby repealed, and that this act shall take effect immediately.

Approved March 11, 1893.

CHAPTER CXXVIII.

An Act regulating fraternal beneficiary societies, orders or associations.

Beneficiary associations exempt from provisions of insurance laws.

1. BE IT ENACTED *by the Senate and General Assembly of the State of New Jersey*, That a fraternal beneficiary association is hereby declared to be a corporation, society or voluntary association, organized and carried on for the sole benefit of its members and their beneficiaries, and not for profit, having a lodge system with a ritualistic form of work and a representative form of government, and making provision for the payment of benefits in case of sickness, disability or death, and also to provide for the payment, upon the expiration of a fixed period of not less than five years, to members whose beneficiaries or

distribution period may then expire, of such sum not exceeding the maximum amount named in the beneficiary certificate of its members, subject to their compliance with its constitution and laws, the fund from which the payment of such benefits shall be made and the fund from which the expenses of such association shall be defrayed being derived from assessments or dues collected from its members, and the payment of death benefits being made to the families, heirs, blood relatives, affianced husband or affianced wife of, or to persons dependent upon, the member; such associations shall be governed by this act and shall be exempt from the provisions of insurance laws of this state, and no law hereafter passed shall apply to them unless they be expressly designated therein.

Such associations now doing business may continue.

2. *And be it enacted*, That all such associations coming within the description as set forth in section one of this act, organized under the laws of this or any other state, province or territory, and now doing business in this state, may continue such business; *provided*, that they hereafter comply with the provisions of this act regulating annual reports and the designation of the commissioner of banking and insurance as the person upon whom process may be served as hereinafter provided.

Proviso

How such foreign associations not now doing business shall be admitted.

3. *And be it enacted*, That any such association coming within the description as set forth in section one of this act, organized under the laws of any other state, province or territory, and not now doing business in this state, shall be admitted to do business within this state when it shall have filed with the commissioner of banking and insurance a duly certified copy of its charter and articles of association, and a copy of its constitution or laws, certified to by its secretary or corresponding officer, together with an appointment of the commissioner of banking and insurance of this state as a person upon whom process may be served as hereinafter provided; *and provided*, that such association shall be shown by certificate to be authorized to do business in the state, province or territory in which it is incorporated or organized in case the laws of such state, province or territory shall provide for such authorization; and in case the laws of such state, province or territory do not provide for any formal authorization to do business on the part of any such association, then such

Proviso.

association shall be shown to be conducting its business in accordance with the provisions of this act, for which purpose the commissioner of banking and insurance of this state may personally, or by some person designated by him, examine into the condition, affairs, character and business methods, accounts, books and investments of such association at its home office, which examination shall be at the expense of such association, and shall be made within thirty days after demand therefor, and the expense of such examination shall be limited to the sum of fifty dollars.

Shall annually file report of its affairs.

4. *And be it enacted*, That every such association doing business in this state shall, on or before the first day of March of each year, make and file with the commissioner of banking and insurance of this state a report of its affairs and operations during the year ending on the thirty-first day of December immediately preceding, which annual report shall be in lieu of all other reports required by any other law; such reports shall be upon blank forms to be provided by the commissioner of banking and insurance, or may be printed in pamphlet form, and shall be verified under oath by the duly authorized officer of such association, and shall be published, or the substance thereof, in the annual report of the commissioner of banking and insurance under a separate part entitled, "Fraternal Beneficiary Associations," and shall contain answers to the following questions:

Blank forms provided for reports.

Questions to be answered.

I. Number of certificates issued during the year, or members admitted;

II. Amount of indemnity effected thereby;

III. Number of losses or benefit liabilities incurred;

IV. Number of losses or benefit liabilities paid;

V. The amount received from each assessment for the year;

VI. Total amount paid members, beneficiaries, legal representatives or heirs;

VII. Number and kinds of claims for which assessments have been made;

VIII. Number and kinds of claims compromised or resisted, and brief statement of reasons;

IX. Does association charge annual or other periodical dues or admission fees?

X. How much on each one thousand dollars annually or per capita, as the case may be?

XI. Total amount received, from what source, and the disposition thereof;

XII. Total amount of salaries paid to officers;

XIII. Does association guarantee in its certificates fixed amounts to be paid regardless of amount realized from assessments, dues, admission fees and donations?

XIV. If so, state the amount guaranteed, and the security of such guarantee;

XV. Has the association a reserve fund?

XVI. If so, how is it created and for what purpose, the amount thereof and how invested?

XVII. Has the association more than one class?

XVIII. If so, how many, and the amount of indemnity in each?

XIX. Number of members in each class;

XX. If voluntary, so state, and give date of organization;

XXI. If organized under the laws of this state under what law and at what time, giving chapter, and year and date of passage of the act;

XXII. If organized under the laws of any other state, province or territory, state such fact and the date of organization, giving chapter and year and date of passage of the act;

XXIII. Number of certificates of beneficiary membership elapsed during the year;

XXIV. Number in force at beginning and end of year; if more than one class, number in each class;

XXV. Name and address of its president, secretary and treasurer, or corresponding officers;

the commissioner of banking and insurance is empowered to address any additional inquiries to any such association in relation to its doings or condition, or any other matter connected with its transactions relative to the business contemplated by this act, and such officers of such association as the commissioner of banking and insurance may require shall promptly reply in writing, under oath, to all such inquiries.

5. *And be it enacted*, That each such association now doing or hereafter admitted to do business within this state

When and how the commissioner of banking and insurance shall be appointed lawful attorney.

and not having its principal office within the state, and not being organized under the laws of this state, shall appoint, in writing, the commissioner of banking and insurance or his successor in office to be its true and lawful attorney, upon whom all lawful process in any action or proceeding against it may be served, and in such writing shall agree that any lawful process against it which is served on said attorney shall be of the same legal force and validity as if served upon the association, and that the authority shall continue in force so long as any liability remains outstanding in this state; copies of such certificate, certified by said commissioner of banking and insurance, shall be deemed sufficient evidence thereof, and shall be admitted in evidence with the same force and effect as the original thereof might be admitted; service upon such attorney shall be deemed sufficient service upon such association; when legal process against any such association is served upon said commissioner of banking and insurance, he shall immediately notify the association of such service by letter, prepaid and directed to its secretary or corresponding officer, and shall within two days after such service forward in the same manner a copy of the process served on him to such officer; the plaintiff in such process so served shall pay to the commissioner of banking and insurance, at the time of such service, a fee of three dollars, which shall be recovered by him as part of the taxable costs if he prevails in the suit; the commissioner of banking and insurance shall keep a record of all processes served upon him, which record shall show the day and hour when such service was made.

Certified copies of certificate deemed sufficient evidence.

Proceedings when legal process is served.

Fee to be paid

6. *And be it enacted*, That the commissioner of banking and insurance shall, upon the application of any association having the right to do business within this state as provided by this act, issue to such association a permit in writing, authorizing such association to do business within this state, for which certificate and all proceedings in connection therewith such association shall pay to said commissioner the fee of five dollars.

Number of persons required to organize fraternal beneficiary organization.

7. *And be it enacted*, That hereafter nine or more persons may become an incorporated fraternal beneficiary association, within the descriptions set forth in section

one of this act, by filing in the office of the commissioner of banking and insurance a declaration executed and acknowledged by each of them, stating their intention to form such fraternal beneficiary association, the proposed name thereof (which shall not be the same as nor too closely resemble the name of any other fraternal beneficiary association doing business in this state); the mode in which its corporate powers are to be exercised and the names and official titles of the officers, trustees, directors, representatives or other persons, by whatsoever name or title designated, who are to have and exercise the general control and management of its affairs and funds, who shall be elected after the first year by representatives chosen by grand or subordinate lodges, councils or bodies, who shall be members of such association; there shall be endorsed upon such declaration, or annexed thereto, and forming a part thereof, the sworn statement of at least three subscribers thereto that two hundred persons, eligible under the proposed laws of such associations to membership therein, have, in good faith, made application in writing for beneficial membership, in the aggregate amount of at least four hundred thousand dollars, and have each paid in one full assessment in cash; if all the requirements of law be complied with, the commissioner shall thereupon file such declaration and cause it to be recorded, with the certificate of the attorney-general, that the same is in accordance with this act, and not inconsistent with the constitution and laws of this state, in a book to be kept for that purpose, and shall deliver to such association a certified copy of the papers so recorded in his office, together with the license or certificate of the commissioner to such association to carry on the work of a fraternal beneficiary association within the description set forth in section one of this act; for the filing of such declaration, and for all proceedings connected therewith, said commissioner of banking and insurance shall receive from such association a fee of ten dollars; any fraternal beneficiary association coming within the description as set forth in section one of this act, now doing business in this state, may become incorporated or re-incorporate under the provisions of this section, but nothing in this act shall be construed

A declaration executed by.

How officers, trustees, etc., elected.

Sworn statement endorsed on declaration.

Declaration to be filed.

Fees.

Associations now doing business not required to become incorporated.

as requiring any such association to become so incorporated or to so re-incorporate.

When paid agents may be employed.

8. *And be it enacted*, That such associations shall not employ paid agents in soliciting or procuring members, except in the organizing or building up of subordinate bodies or granting members inducements to procure new members.

When contract with association is invalid.

9. *And be it enacted*, That no contract with any such association shall be valid when there is a contract, agreement or understanding between the member and the beneficiary or any person for him shall pay such member's assessments and dues, or either of them.

Money or benefit, etc., not liable to attachment

10. *And be it enacted*, That the money or other benefit, charity, relief or aid to be paid, provided or rendered by any association authorized to do business under this act shall not be liable to attachment by trustee, garnishee or other process and shall not be seized, taken, appropriated or applied by any legal or equitable process, or by operation of law, to pay any debt or liability of a certificate holder or of any beneficiary named in a certificate, or of any person who may have any right thereunder.

Provision for meetings in other states.

11. *And be it enacted*, That any such association organized under the laws of this state may provide for the meetings of its legislative or governing body in any other state, province or territory wherein such association shall have subordinate bodies; and all business transacted at such meetings shall be valid in all respects as if such meetings were held in this state; and where the laws of any such association provide for the election of its officers by vote to be cast in its subordinate bodies, the votes so cast in its subordinate bodies, in any other state, province or territory, shall be valid as if cast within this state.

When election of officers in other states valid.

When persons or physician guilty of misdemeanor.

12. *And be it enacted*, That any person, officer, member or examining physician, who shall knowingly or willfully make any false or fraudulent statement or representation, in or with reference to any application for membership, or for the purpose of obtaining any money or benefit in any association transacting business under this act, shall be guilty of misdemeanor and upon conviction shall be punished by a fine of not less than one hundred dollars, nor more than five hundred dollars, or imprisonment in the county jail for not less than thirty days nor more

Penalty.

than one year, or both, in the discretion of the court; and any person who shall willfully make a false statement of any material fact or thing in a sworn statement as to the death or disability of a certificate holder in any such association, for the purpose of procuring payment of a benefit named in a certificate of such holder, and any person who shall willfully make any false statement in any verified report or declaration under oath required or authorized by this act, shall be guilty of perjury and shall be proceeded against and punished as provided by the statutes of this state in relation to the crime of perjury.

When persons are guilty of perjury

13. *And be it enacted*, That whenever said commissioner of banking and insurance shall become satisfied that any such association doing business within this state is exceeding its power, or conducting its business fraudulently, he may personally, or by some person to be designated by him, examine into the condition, affairs, character and business methods, accounts, books and investments of such association at its home office, which examination shall be at the expense of such association, and such expense shall be limited to the sum of fifty dollars.

When and by whom examination made and expenses paid.

14. *And be it enacted*, That any such association refusing or neglecting to make the report as provided in this act shall be excluded from doing business within this state; said commissioner of banking and insurance must within sixty days after failure to make such report, or in case any such association shall exceed its powers, or shall conduct its business fraudulently, or shall fail to comply with any of the provisions of this act, or shall refuse to submit its accounts, books, papers and vouchers for examination by said commissioner or person designated by him, shall give notice in writing to the attorney-general, who shall immediately commence an action against such association to enjoin the same from carrying on any business; and no injunction against any such association shall be granted by any court, except on application by the attorney-general, at the request of the commissioner of banking and insurance; no association so enjoined shall have authority to continue business until such report shall be made, or overt act or violations complained of shall have been corrected; nor until the costs of such action be paid by it;

Failure to make report excludes from doing business.

When the attorney-general shall proceed against associations.

Proviso

provided, the court shall find that such association was in default as charged, whereupon the commissioner of banking and insurance shall re-instate such association, and not until then shall such association be allowed to again do business in this state; any officer, agent or person acting for any association or subordinate body thereof, within this state, while such association shall be so enjoined or prohibited from doing business pursuant to this act, shall be deemed guilty of a misdemeanor, and on conviction thereof shall be punished by a fine not less than twenty-five dollars nor more than two hundred dollars, or by imprisonment in the county jail not less than thirty days nor more than one year, or by both such fine and imprisonment, in the discretion of the court.

Penalty when officer or agent violates this act.

15. *And be it enacted*, That any person who shall act within this state as an officer, agent or otherwise, for any association which shall have failed, neglected or refused to comply with, or shall have violated any of the provisions of this act, or shall have failed or neglected to procure from the commissioner of banking and insurance proper certificates of authority to transact business, as provided for by this act, shall be subject to the penalty provided in the last preceding section for the misdemeanor therein specified.

Applies to fraternal beneficiary associations only.

16. *And be it enacted*, That this act shall not apply to any corporation, society or association carrying on the business of life, health, casualty or accident insurance for profit or gain, but it shall apply to fraternal beneficiary associations only, as defined in section one of this act; this act shall not affect or apply to any grand or subordinate lodges of the ancient order of free and accepted masons, independent order of odd fellows, improved order of red men, junior order of American mechanics, as they now exist, nor of the knights of Pythias (exclusive of the endowment rank), nor to similar orders, nor to any association not working on the lodge system, or which limits its certificate holders to a particular class, or to the employees of a particular town or city, designated firm, business house or corporation.

Lodges not affected.

Fees, and to whom paid.

17. *And be it enacted*, That every association to which this act shall be applicable shall pay the following fees to the commissioner of banking and insurance, for defraying the expenses of this act, viz.:

For filing the declaration or a certified copy of charter required by this act, ten dollars;

For filing the annual report therein provided, five dollars;

For every copy of any paper filed or recorded in his office, eight cents per folio;

For affixing his official seal on such copy, and certifying same, one dollar.

18. *And be it enacted*, That all acts or parts of acts inconsistent with the provisions of this act are hereby repealed, and that this act shall take effect immediately. Repealer

Approved March 11, 1893.

CHAPTER CXXIX.

A Supplement to an act entitled "An act concerning street railroad companies," approved March sixth, one thousand eight hundred and eighty-six.

1. BE IT ENACTED *by the Senate and General Assembly of the State of New Jersey*, That section two of the act entitled "An act concerning street railroad companies," approved March sixth, one thousand eight hundred and eighty-six, be and the same is hereby amended so that said section shall read as follows: Section to be amended.

2. *And be it enacted*, That any street or horse railway company in this state may use electric or chemical motors, or grip cables, as the propelling power of its cars, instead of horses; *provided*, it shall have first obtained the consent of the township committee, or the municipal authorities having charge of the public streets or highways on which it is proposed to use such motors or grip cables, which consent may be granted by ordinance. Authorized to use electric motors or grip cables. Proviso.

2. *And be it enacted*, That the municipal board, or any county public road board, or other authorities having the charge or control of any streets, highways or avenues in Municipal board, &c., by ordinance, may authorize use of poles in public streets.

any city, county, town or township of this state may, when they deem it proper, authorize the use of poles located or to be located in the public streets or highways with wires strung thereon for the purpose of supplying the motors with electricity, and when a board grants such authority it may in such case prescribe the manner in which, and the places where such poles shall be located, and the manner in which the wires shall be strung thereon, and the same may be authorized and prescribed by ordinance.

Consent heretofore granted valid.

3. *And be it enacted*, That any consent heretofore granted, contingent or otherwise, whether by resolution or in any other way by any municipality to any street or horse railway company to use electric or chemical motors or grip cables as the propelling power of its cars, of the construction and character in such ordinance or resolution specified, or of which the plan of construction has been or may be in any way assented to or approved by such municipal authorities, shall be as valid and effectual as if the same had been granted pursuant to the provisions of this act to the extent authorized by this act; *provided, however*, that no such consent heretofore granted shall be validated by virtue of anything in this act contained, without the assent and approval of the state board of commissioners of electrical subways first had and obtained.

Proviso.

Duties of commissioners of electrical subways not curtailed.

4. *And be it enacted*, That nothing in this act contained shall curtail, abridge or otherwise interfere with any of the powers and duties of the state board of commissioners of electrical subways.

Repealer

5. *And be it enacted*, That all acts and parts of acts, inconsistent with this act be and the same are hereby repealed, and this act shall take effect immediately.

Approved March 11, 1893.

CHAPTER CXXX.

A Supplement to an act entitled "A further supplement to an act entitled 'An act to regulate elections,'" approved April eighteenth, one thousand eight hundred and seventy-six, which supplemental act was approved May twenty eighth, one thousand eight hundred and ninety.

1. BE IT ENACTED *by the Senate and General Assembly of the State of New Jersey*, That section nineteen of said supplemental act be and is hereby amended, so that henceforth said section nineteen shall be and read as follows, to wit: That the boards of registry and election and said registry or poll clerks appointed as hereinbefore provided for, shall, in their respective election districts, hold and conduct the next and all succeeding annual elections to be held on the first Tuesday after the first Monday in November in any year, and also the annual "town meetings" or township elections hereafter to be held throughout this state under and in pursuance of the act entitled "An act incorporating the inhabitants of townships, designating their powers and regulating their meetings," approved April fourteenth, one thousand eight hundred and forty-six, and the act entitled "An act concerning townships and township officers," approved April twenty-first, one thousand eight hundred and seventy-six, and the several supplements to said two acts, or either of them, and the foregoing provisions of this act shall apply to said town meetings or township elections so far as the same may be applicable; there shall be no new registration for said town meetings or township elections, but the said boards of registry and elections shall procure and use at such town meetings or township elections the certified copy of the register of voters filed with the township or other clerk pursuant to section seven of this act; said board of registry and election and

Section to be amended.

Boards to conduct general elections and town meetings.

Certified copy of register to be used at town meetings.

When boards to meet and revise register.

said poll clerks shall meet to revise and correct said register in the manner hereinbefore provided on the Tuesday next preceding the town meeting or township election, and each of said registry or poll clerks of each election district shall cause at least three notices of the time and place of such meeting to revise and correct said register to be conspicuously posted in public places within their respective election districts at least one week before such meeting; no copy of such revised and corrected registry need be posted, but a copy shall be filed with the county clerk within one day thereafter, and on the Thursday next preceding the said annual town meeting, and any charter election in said county, and from day to day thereafter, as may be necessary, the court of common pleas of the several counties of the state shall be in session at the court house in their respective counties, for the purpose of revising and correcting the register of voters, so as aforesaid, to be filed with the county clerk; and the clerk shall produce such of said registers as may be required at the sessions of the court; and the said court of common pleas shall proceed in the same manner as is provided in section eighteen of the act to which this is a supplement.

Clerks to give notice of meeting.

Copy of revised registry not posted, but filed.

When court holds session for revising and correcting register.

Clerk produces registers at court.

2. *And be it enacted*, That this act shall take effect immediately.

Approved March 13, 1893.

CHAPTER CXXXI.

An Act for the protection of shad fishermen in the Delaware bay eastward of the ships channel.

When unlawful to anchor in dredging oysters.

1. BE IT ENACTED *by the Senate and General Assembly of the State of New Jersey*, That hereafter it shall be unlawful for any vessel engaged in dredging oysters to anchor, or leave their buoys on the flats between Arnold's point

buoy and Stony point in the Delaware bay, between sunset or sunrise of each day previous to the twenty-fifth of May in any year.

2. *And be it enacted*, That it shall be unlawful for any person or persons to throw any dredge or other appliances from the deck of any boat or vessel into any gill net; any person or persons violating this section shall be deemed guilty of a misdemeanor. A misdemeanor to throw any dredge into any gill-net.

3. *And be it enacted*, That it shall be lawful for any fish warden or the sheriff of any county in which this act is violated, to arrest any person or persons guilty of violating any of the provisions of this act; and any person or persons so offending shall upon conviction before any justice of the peace be punished by a fine not less than fifty dollars, and not more than two hundred dollars and imprisonment in the county jail for a term not to exceed six months. Fish warden or sheriff authorized to arrest. Penalty.

4. *And be it enacted*, That this act shall take effect immediately.

Approved March 18, 1893.

CHAPTER CXXXII.

A Supplement to an act entitled "An act to authorize the partition of lands, in cases where particular undivided shares therein are limited over," approved March sixth, eighteen hundred and fifty-two.

1. BE IT ENACTED *by the Senate and General Assembly of the State of New Jersey*, That whenever it shall be made to appear to the court of chancery that any land in this state, or any estate therein, hereafter sold in any partition proceeding by the order or decree of any court of this state, has been devised by any last will or testament of any person or persons, a citizen or resident of any other state at the time of the making of such last will and tes- Chancellor to direct payment of proceeds when portion made through lands limited over.

tament, upon any trust, or subject to any limitation over by way of expectancy or otherwise, it shall be the duty of the chancellor to direct the payment of the proceeds of such sale to such devisee or devisees, being trustees as aforesaid, as are, by the provisions of such last will and testament, under said trust, entitled to have and hold the land sold as aforesaid, notwithstanding the estate of such devisee or devisees, trustees as aforesaid, created or passed by said last will and testament, be subject to a limitation over or be less than estate in fee simple; which proceeds of sale shall be held, accounted for and disposed of by such devisee or devisees, trustees as aforesaid, in all respects as directed by the provisions of such last will and testament and not otherwise; *provided*, that nothing herein contained shall relieve such devisee or devisees, trustees as aforesaid, from the duty to give security, in the state of which such testator was a citizen or resident at the time of his death, for the faithful execution of such trust in respect to such proceeds of said sale, when required so to do either by the provisions of such last will and testament or by the order of any court of competent jurisdiction in said state.

Proceeds of sale, how disposed of.

Proviso.

Repealer.

2. *And be it enacted*, That all acts and parts of acts inconsistent with the provisions this act, to the extent of such inconsistency, be and the same are hereby repealed and that this act shall take effect immediately.

Approved March 13, 1898.

CHAPTER CXXXIII.

A Farther Supplement to an act entitled "An act to authorize the appointment of a board of commissioners to represent the state of New Jersey at the world's Columbian exposition, to be held in Chicago, in the year one thousand eight hundred and ninety-three," approved March eighteenth, one thousand eight hundred and ninety-one.

Further appropriation for expenses

1. BE IT ENACTED *by the Senate and General Assembly of the State of New Jersey*, That in order to further the work of the board of commissioners appointed under the act to which this is a further supplement, and to enable the state board of agriculture, the state board of education and the geological survey to make a full and proper exhibit in their respective departments, and to maintain a proper building for the use of the citizens of this state in attendance at such exposition, there be and is hereby appropriated the sum of sixty thousand dollars, in excess of the sums heretofore appropriated, and that said sum, together with the unexpended balance of the previous appropriation of seventy thousand dollars, except such part thereof as may be needed by the governor to properly perform the duties devolved on him by said original act, shall be paid by the treasurer of the state, upon the warrant of the comptroller, to the treasurer of the commission, in such sums as may from time to time be required and requested by a resolution of the commissioners, duly certified by the president of said commission, with the approval of the governor; and said sums so paid by the treasurer of the state to the treasurer of the board of commissioners shall be expended only by resolution of said board, upon the approval of the president of said board; and the treasurer of the commission shall report to the comptroller of the treasury once in each month the amount and direction of said expenditure; *provided*,

To be paid by treasurer on warrant of comptroller.

Proviso.

that upon resolution of the legislative joint committee, duly certified by the chairman of said committee, with the approval of the governor, such part or parts of the sum so appropriated shall be paid by the treasurer of the state, upon the warrant of the comptroller of the state, to the chairman of such joint committee, as may be necessary to defray the expenses of said joint committee incurred or to be incurred in the discharge of their duties as such committee under the concurrent resolution of the legislature introduced in the general assembly, February twenty-eighth, one thousand eight hundred and ninety-three, which resolution directs said committee to visit Chicago and co-operate with said board of commissioners, and to employ a secretary to said committee; and that said part or parts of said appropriation so paid to such chairman shall be expended only by resolution of said committee, and the chairman of said committee shall report to the comptroller the amount of such expenditures.

Section to be amended.

2. *And be it enacted*, That section five of the act to which this is a supplement shall be amended so as to read as follows:

Receive no compensation, except the secretary.

5. *And be it enacted*, That the members of said New Jersey commission shall not receive any compensation for their services, except the secretary, whose compensation shall be fixed by the commission, with the approval of the governor.

3. *And be it enacted*, That this act shall take effect immediately.

Approved March 18, 1893.

CHAPTER CXXXIV.

A Supplement to an act entitled "An act concerning evidence," approved March twenty-seventh, one thousand eight hundred and seventy-four.

Deposition of non-resident party to any action taken by commission.

1. Be it enacted *by the Senate and General Assembly of the State of New Jersey*, That the deposition of any party to any action in any of the courts of this state, who reside out of the state while such action is pending, may be taken by commission or upon notice in the same manner and upon the same terms as provided in case of witnesses residing out of the state; and that such deposition may be read and used upon the trial of such cause; it being the intention of this amendment to give the parties to actions who reside out of the state the same privilege to have their depositions taken out of the state as to other witnesses in such actions residing out of the state.

2. *And be it enacted*, That this act shall take effect immediately.

Approved March 13, 1893.

CHAPTER CXXXV.

An Act to amend an act entitled "A supplement to an act entitled 'An act constituting "district courts" in certain cities of this state,'" approved March ninth, one thousand eight hundred and seventy-seven, which supplement was approved April fifth, one thousand eight hundred and seventy-eight.

Section to be amended.

1. BE IT ENACTED *by the Senate and General Assembly of the State of New Jersey*, That section seven of the said supplement be amended so as to read as follows:

What constitutes lawful service of summons in action for removal of tenants.

7. *And be it enacted*, That in all actions brought under said act for the removal of tenants, where admission to the dwelling or premises occupied by the tenant is denied to the officer attempting to serve a notice of demand for the payment of rent or surrender of premises or a summons, or where such tenant resides out of the county in which the demised premises are located, and there is no person in actual occupation thereof, it shall be a lawful service of such notice or such summons if the said officer shall post or affix a copy of the same upon the door or other conspicuous part of such dwelling or premises, and the said officer shall make a return of such service accordingly; *provided*, that in case the tenant shall not be a resident of the county in which said demised premises are situated and the same shall be in the occupation of any other person, then said notice of said summons may be served either personally upon such person or by leaving the same with a member of his family above the age of fourteen years.

Proviso.

2. *And be it enacted*, That this act shall be deemed a public act, and shall take effect immediately.

Approved March 13, 1893.

CHAPTER CXXXVI.

An Act in relation to the practice in the court of chancery on bills of interpleader.

1. Be it enacted *by the Senate and General Assembly of the State of New Jersey,* That in all cases in which the court of chancery shall decree an interpleader as between the defendants to a bill of interpleader, the said court shall award to the complainant a counsel fee commensurate with the service of his counsel in the cause, to be taxed in the bill of costs and collected therewith. Counsel fee awarded to complainant

2. *And be it enacted,* That this act shall take effect immediately.

Approved March 13, 1893.

CHAPTER CXXXVII.

A Supplement to an act entitled "An act concerning clerks of grand juries," approved March ninth, one thousand eight hundred and seventy-seven.

1. Be it enacted *by the Senate and General Assembly of the State of New Jersey,* That the clerk of the grand jury of each of the juries in all counties of this state having, by the state census of one thousand eight hundred and eighty-five, a population of two hundred thousand or more inhabitants shall also act as clerk to the procecutor of the pleas of such county and for such service as clerk of the grand jury and as clerk to the prosecutor of the pleas, shall receive a salary of eighteen hundred dollars per year and no Shall act as clerk to the prosecutor of pleas. Salary.

more, and said salary shall be payable monthly, by collector of the county.

Repealer. 2. *And be it enacted,* That all acts or parts of acts inco sistent with the terms of this act be and the same a hereby repealed, and this act shall be a public act an take effect immediately.

Approved March 13, 1893.

CHAPTER CXXXVIII.

A Supplement to an act entitled "An act to amend an act concerning corporations," approved April seventh, one thousand eight hundred and seventy-five, which amendatory act was approved March twentieth, one thousand eight hundred and ninety-one.

Attorney-general to proceed in court of chancery for appointment of a receiver.

1. Be it enacted *by the Senate and General Assembly of the State of New Jersey,* That after any corporation of this state has failed and neglected for the space of two consecutive years to pay the taxes imposed upon it by law, and the comptroller of this state shall have reported such corporation to the governor of this state, as provided in said amendatory act, then it shall be lawful for the attorney general of this state to proceed against said corporation in the court of chancery of this state for the appointment of a receiver, or otherwise, and the said court in such proceeding shall ascertain the amount of the taxes remaining due and unpaid by such corporation to the state of New Jersey, and shall enter a final decree for the amount so ascertained, and thereupon a fieri facias or other process shall issue for the collection of the same as other debts are collected, and if no property which may be seized and sold on fieri facias shall be found within the said state of New Jersey, sufficient to pay such decree, the said court shall further order and decree that the said corporation,

Final decree to be entered and fieri facias issue.

within ten days from and after the service of notice of such decree upon any officer of said corporation upon whom service of process may be lawfully made, or such notice as the court shall direct, shall assign and transfer to the trustee or receiver appointed by the court, any chose in action, or any patent or patents, or any assignment of, or license under any patented invention or inventions owned by, leased or licensed to or controlled in whole or in part by said corporation, to be sold by said receiver or trustee for the satisfaction of such decree, and no injunction theretofore issued nor any forfeiture of the charter of any such corporation shall be held to exempt such corporation from compliance with such order of the court; and if the said corporation shall neglect or refuse within ten days from and after the service of notice of such decree to assign and transfer the same to such receiver or trustee for sale as aforesaid, it shall be the duty of said court to appoint a trustee to make the assignment of the same, in the name and on behalf of such corporation, to the receiver or trustee appointed to make such sale, and the said receiver or trustee shall thereupon, after such notice and in such manner as required for the sale under fieri facias of personal property, sell the same to the highest bidder, and the said receiver or trustee, upon the payment of the purchase money, shall execute and deliver to such purchaser an assignment and transfer of all the patents and interests of the corporation so sold, which assignment or transfer shall vest in the purchaser a valid title to all the right, title and interest whatsoever of the said corporation therein, and the proceeds of such sale shall be applied to the payment of such unpaid taxes, together with the costs of said proceedings.

Court shall order assignment of any chose in action, &c., to receiver appointed, to be sold to satisfy amount due.

No injunction theretofore issued shall exempt from compliance with such order.

When trustee to be appointed to make assignment.

Sell to highest bidder

Proceeds of sale, how applied

2. *And be it enacted*, That whenever it is established to the satisfaction of the governor that any corporation named in said proclamation has not neglected or refused to pay said tax within two consecutive years, or has been inadvertently reported to the governor by the comptroller as refusing or neglecting to pay the same as aforesaid, that the governor be and he is hereby authorized to correct such mistake, and to make the same known by filing his proclamation to that effect in the office of the secretary of state.

When and by whom mistakes corrected.

3. *And be it enacted,* That that this act shall take effect immediately.

Approved March 18, 1898.

CHAPTER CXXXIX.

An Act to amend an act entitled "An act concerning roads" (Revision), approved March twenty-seventh, one thousand eight hundred and seventy-four.

Section to be amended.

1. BE IT ENACTED *by the Senate and General Assembly of the State of New Jersey,* That section seventy-nine of the act of which this is amendatory be amended to read as follows:

Effect of act with respect to cities.

79. *And be it enacted,* That nothing in this act shall be construed to extend to narrowing, widening or altering any street in any of the cities, towns or villages in this state, or to pulling down or removing any dwelling house, market house or other public building heretofore erected and which may encroach on any highway; *provided, however,* that the grade of any street may be altered or any street therein may be narrowed, widened or altered; *provided,* that three-fourths of the owners in interest of the lots fronting on the part of said road or street so proposed to be narrowed, widened or altered, or the grade thereof to be changed, shall consent in witing thereto; *and provided, further,* that nothing in this act shall be construed to deprive any person not so consenting, of damages, as heretofore.

Proviso.

Proviso.

Proviso.

2. *And be it enacted,* That this act shall take effect immediately.

Approved March 18, 1898.

CHAPTER CXL.

An Act to repeal the act entitled "A further supplement to 'An act for the suppressing of vice and immorality'" (Revision), approved March twenty-seventh, one thousand eight hundred and seventy-four, which said further supplement was approved March twenty-fourth, one thousand eight hundred and ninety-two.

1. BE IT ENACTED *by the Senate and General Assembly of the State of New Jersey*, That the said act, entitled "A further supplement to 'An act for the suppressing of vice and immorality'" (Revision), approved March twenty-seventh, one thousand eight hundred and seventy-four, which said supplement was approved March twenty-fourth, one thousand eight hundred and ninety-two, be and the same is hereby repealed. Repealer.

2. *And be it enacted*, That this act shall take effect immediately.

Approved March 13, 1893.

CHAPTER CXLI.

A Supplement to an act entitled "An act for the formation and government of boroughs," approved April second, one thousand eight hundred and ninety-one.

1. BE IT ENACTED *by the Senate and General Assembly of the State of New Jersey*, That it shall be lawful for the mayor and council of any borough incorporated under this act to make and establish ordinances for the following purposes, viz.: to license and regulate the owners and drivers of express wagons, trucks, hacks, cars, omnibuses, stages and all other carriages and vehicles used

Mayor and council authorized to make ordinances to license and regulate owners and drivers of express wagons, &c.

for the transportation of passengers, baggage, merchandise and goods and chattels of every kind; also to license and regulate the owners and drivers of all vehicles used in connection with any business for the purpose of soliciting orders or delivering goods within the limits of the municipality; also to license and regulate all auctioneers, common criers, hawkers, peddlers, pawn brokers, junk wagons, news stands, sweeps, scavengers, traveling and other street shows, street exhibitions, street parades, circuses, concerts, theatres, skating rinks, merry-go-rounds, observation roundabouts, razzle dazzles, or circular swings, organ grinders, itinerant venders of merchandise, medicines and remedies, and to fix the license fee to be paid therefor, which may be imposed for the purpose of revenue; and also to designate and locate stands and places which hackmen, cartmen, and all other persons engaged in carrying passengers, baggage and merchandise shall be privileged to occupy when soliciting business, and to prevent the occupying of other places for such purposes, and to fix and prescribe penalties for the violation of any such ordinance or ordinances, or section thereof, either in the nature of a fine or imprisonment, under the authority of the act to which this is a supplement.

Prescribe penalties for violation of such ordinance.

Repealer.

2. *And be it enacted*, That all acts and parts of acts inconsistent herewith be and the same are hereby repealed, and that this act shall take effect immediately.

Approved March 18, 1898.

CHAPTER CXLII.

A Supplement to an act entitled "An act respecting the court of chancery," approved March twenty-seventh, in the year one thousand eight hundred and seventy-five.

1. Be it enacted *by the Senate and General Assembly of the State of New Jersey*, That in all actions hereafter com-

menced in the court of chancery of New Jersey, by bill, petition, or otherwise, whenever it shall appear by the allegations of said bill or petition, duly verified by the affidavit of the complainant or petitioner, or by one of them, if there shall be more than one complainant or petitioner, or his or their agent or solicitor, thereto annexed, that any person mentioned in said bill or petition, or his heirs, devisees or personal representatives, are proper parties defendant to said bill of complaint or said petition; and that the complainant, after diligent and careful inquiry therefor, made as in case of absent defendants, has been unable to ascertain whether such person is still alive, or, if he is known or believed to be dead, has been unable to ascertain the names and residences of his heirs, devisees or personal reprepsentatives, or such of them as may be proper parties defendant as aforesaid, such action may proceed against such person by name, and his heirs, devisees and personal representatives, as in the case of absent defendants whose names are known; *provided, nevertheless*, that such notice as is now required by law to be published against absent defendants in default of personal service, addressed to such person by name, and to "heirs, devisees and personal representatives," and containing such further statements and giving such further time as the chancellor may, by his order direct be first published and mailed in such manner as the chancellor may, by his order in said action, direct; and in case such person, or his heirs, devisees or personal representatives, shall not appear, plead, answer or demur within the time limited in said notice, or further allowed by the chancellor, if he shall think proper, on proof to the satisfaction of the chancellor of mailing and publication of said notice as directed; such action may proceed in all respects as if such person, or his heirs, devisees or personal representatives had been duly named and described and served with process of subpœna in said action, and had failed to plead, answer or demur to the complainant's bill of complaint, or petitioner's petition within the time thereto allowed by law.

Proceedings absent persons defendants when unable to ascertain name and residence of heirs, devisees or personal representatives.

Proviso.

2. *And be it enacted*, That all such defendants, and all persons falling within the description of "heirs, devisees

When heirs, devisees or personal representatives bound by orders and decrees.

or personal representatives" of the defendant supposed to be dead as aforesaid, shall thereupon be bound by all orders and decrees in said cause as if they had been duly named and described and served with process in this state.

How proofs made, costs allowed, &c., may be had.

3. *And be it enacted*, That proofs may be made, costs allowed, security ordered and proceedings for restitution or other relief from said decrees and orders had in like manner as the same are now allowed by law in the case of absent defendants.

Repealer.

4. *And be it enacted*, That all acts or parts of acts inconsistent with the provisions of this act be and the same are hereby repealed, and that this act shall take effect immediately.

Approved March 13, 1893.

CHAPTER CXLIII.

A Further Supplement to an act entitled "An act to reorganize the board of chosen freeholders in counties of the first class in this state," approved April third, one thousand eight hundred and eighty-nine, and the supplements thereto.

Term of office.

1. BE IT ENACTED *by the Senate and General Assembly of the State of New Jersey*, That the term of office of the members of the board of chosen freeholders, in counties of the first class in this state, except the director-at-large, shall begin on the second Wednesday of May next after every election of such members, and shall continue for three years and until others shall be chosen and legally qualified in their stead; and the term of office of such director-at-large shall begin as heretofore and continue for three years and until another shall be chosen and legally qualified in his stead; the term of office of the present director-at-large, in counties of the first class in

Term of office of director-at-large.

this state, shall continue until the first day of December, one thousand eight hundred and ninety-four, and until his successor shall be elected and qualified; and the first election of such director shall be held on the first Tuesday after the first Monday in November, of the year one thousand eight hundred and ninety-four, from and after the passage of this act the director-at-large shall be entitled to vote at all meetings of the board in the same manner as any other member thereof; which power he shall possess in addition to that which he now possesses of approving or refusing to approve the resolutions and acts of said board; and said last mentioned act shall be held and construed to include all appointments to or dismissals from any office or place under the jurisdiction or control of said board.

When director elected

Duties of director-at-large

2. *And be it enacted*, That the election for chosen freeholders, other than the director-at-large, shall be conducted pursuant to the provisions of an act entitled "A further supplement to an act entitled 'An act to regulate elections,'" approved April eighteenth, one thousand eight hundred and seventy-six, which supplement was approved May twenty-eighth, one thousand eight hundred and ninety, and the supplements thereto; candidates may be nominated, and such nominations shall be certified and filed as therein provided, and it shall be the duty of the clerks of the respective counties, at least eight days before any election of chosen freeholders other than director whereat any candidate nominated in any certificate or petition filed with him is to be voted for, to make and certify under his hand and seal of office and forward to the clerks of the respective cities, towns, villages, townships or other municipalities in their respective counties a statement of all the candidates nominated by certificate or petition filed in their office, for whom voters within any such municipality may be by law entitled to vote at such election; such certificate shall include the names and residences of the candidates, the officers for which they are nominated, and the names of the parties by which or the political appellation under which, they are respectively nominated; candidates nominated by petition, without distinctive political appellations, shall be certified as independent candidates; the names of the candidates

How election conducted.

Duty of clerks

Certificate shall include

Ballots contain.

shall be printed as far as possible, upon the ballots containing the names of the other candidates, to be voted for at the municipal elections; the ballots containing the names so certified shall, in all respects, conform to the requirements of law and shall be placed in envelopes and voted accordingly.

Register of voters used, and mode of receiving, counting and certifying votes.

3. *And be it enacted*, That the register of voters used for the election of chosen freeholders, other than the director, shall be the same and shall be used with the same effect and in the same manner, as that corrected, revised and used in and for the municipal election held at the same time, and that all provisions of law regulating the manner of voting, the conduct of the elections, the mode of receiving, counting and certifying the votes in the case of municipal elections, shall apply to the case of elections of chosen freeholders.

How director-at-large nominated

4. *And be it enacted*, That the nominations for director-at-large shall be made and certified as by law other nominations for county officers are made and certified, and the provisions of law relative to the registry of voters, the manner of voting, the conduct of elections, and all proceedings thereafter taken, and all other requirements of of law concerning elections shall apply to the election of directors-at-large.

Board of canvassers meet

5. *And be it enacted*, That the meeting of the board of canvassers shall be held as now required by the supplements to the act to which this is a supplement.

Costs and expenses, how paid.

6. *And be it enacted*, That one-third of the costs and expenses of any election whereat members of the board are elected, other than the director, including the revision of the registry, shall be paid out of the county funds and two-thirds by the respective municipalities.

7. *And be it enacted*, That this act shall take effect immediately.

Approved March 13, 1893.

CHAPTER CXLIV.

An Act to appropriate three thousand dollars for the purchase of a burial plot for the home of disabled soldiers, at Kearney, New Jersey.

1. Be it enacted *by the Senate and General Assembly of the State of New Jersey*, That the sum of three thousand dollars be and is hereby appropriated for the purchase of a burial plot for the home of disabled soldiers, at Kearney, New Jersey, and the state treasurer is hereby directed to pay the same on the warrant of the comptroller, to the treasurer of the home for disabled soldiers at Kearney, New Jersey, out of any moneys not heretofore appropriated by law. Treasurer to pay same on warrant of comptroller.

2. *And be it enacted*, That this act shall take effect immediately.

Approved March 14, 1893.

CHAPTER CXLV.

An Act to enable cities to purchase lands, erect, furnish and fit up a building or buildings for public school purposes.

1. Be it enacted *by the Senate and General Assembly of the State of New Jersey*, That the common council or other legislative body of any city of the second class of this state shall have power to borrow any sum or sums of money, not exceeding in the aggregate the sum of fifty thousand dollars, to be used for the purchase of lands and the erecting, furnishing and fitting up of a building or build- In cities of second class common council authorized to borrow money and issue bonds

ings for public school purposes in said city; and that the said common council or other legislative body of said city may secure the repayment of the said sum or sums so borrowed, together with interest thereon at a rate not to exceed five per centum per annum, in such manner and upon such terms as to the said common council or other legislative body may seem proper, by the issuing of bonds in the corporate name of said city, to be signed by the mayor or other chief executive officer of said city and countersigned by the city clerk or other person performing the duties of recording officer for the said common council or other legislative body, as the case may be, and sealed with the common seal of said city; *provided*, that in cities having a board of education or other board having control of the public schools than the common council, the purchase of land, erecting, furnishing and fitting up of a school house or school houses with the money so borrowed shall be made in the same manner as heretofore provided by law for the city borrowing money by virtue of this act.

Proviso.

2. *And be it enacted*, That this act shall take effect immediately.

Approved March 14, 1893.

CHAPTER CXLVI.

An Act act to authorize the inferior courts of common pleas of the various counties of this state to transfer any license granted by them to sell spirituous, vinous, malt and brewed liquors, in quantities from one quart to five gallons, not to be drunk on or about the premises where sold.

Courts of common pleas authorized to transfer licenses, good only for unexpired term thereof.

1. Be it enacted *by the Senate and General Assembly of the State of New Jersey*, That the inferior courts of common pleas of the various counties of this state are hereby authorized and empowered in their discretion to transfer

any license granted by them to sell spirituous, vinous, malt and brewed liquors, in quantities from one quart to five gallons not to be drunk on or about the premises where sold, to any person or persons or to any place within such county, and in case of transfer the license so transferred shall only be good or effective for the unexpired term thereof, at either the place or premises mentioned in the original license or else at the place or premises to which the same shall be transferred within said county, and in case of revocation of any license aforesaid any person selling or offering for sale thereunder shall be liable to all the penalties provided by law for selling without a license; *provided*, that before any transfer shall be made by any of said courts as aforesaid, there shall be paid a fee for such transfer by said court of not less than three dollars and fifty cents.

Penalties liable to in case of revocation of license.

Proviso.

2. *And be it enacted*, That this act shall take effect immediately.

Approved March 14, 1893.

CHAPTER CXLVII.

An Act to repeal the act entitled "A further supplement to an act entitled 'An act to prescribe the notice to be given of applications to the legislature for laws when notice is required by the constitution,'" approved January twenty-sixth, one thousand eight hundred and seventy-six, the further supplement approved March twenty-ninth, one thousand eight hundred and ninety-two.

Repealer.

1. Be it enacted *by the Senate and General Assembly of the State of New Jersey*, That the act entitled "A further supplement to an act entitled 'An act to prescribe the notice to be given of applications to the legislature for

laws when notice is required by the constitution,'" approved January twenty-sixth, one thousand eight hundred and seventy six, which further supplement was approved March twenty-ninth, one thousand eight hundred and ninety-two, be and the same is hereby repealed.

2. *And be it enacted*, That this act shall take effect immediately.

Approved March 14, 1893.

CHAPTER CXLVIII.

An Act to amend an act entitled "A further supplement to an act entitled 'An act to enable incorporated towns to construct water works for the extinguishment of fires, and supplying the inhabitants thereof with pure and wholesome water,'" passed March fifth, one thousand eight hundred and eighty-four, which said supplement was approved March seventeenth, one thousand eight hundred and eighty-seven.

Section to be amended

1. BE IT ENACTED *by the Senate and General Assembly of the State of New Jersey*, That section one of the act of which this is amendatory be and the same is hereby amended so as to read as follows:

When certain sum is insufficient to construct or complete water works, election to be had to determine whether additional sum shall be raised, &c

1. BE IT ENACTED *by the Senate and General Assembly of the State of New Jersey*, That whenever the board of water commissioners of any town, incorporated borough, camp meeting association, or other municipal commission of this state shall find that said sum of sixty thousand dollars, provided for in the act of which this is a supplement, is insufficient for the purpose of constructing and fully completing said water works, or that the water works and reservoirs, aqueducts, apparatus, erections, works, establishments and fixtures for supplying water of any such town, incorporated borough, camp meeting

association, or other municipal commission are inadequate to furnish a sufficient amount of pure and wholesome water for the purpose designated in and contemplated by said act, that then the said board of water commissioners shall report said fact to the board of commissioners, or other governing body of such town, incorporated borough, camp meeting association, or other municipal commission, and it shall thereupon be the duty of such board of commissioners or other board or body to order and appoint an election of the legal electors thereof, to be held in such town, incorporated borough. camp meeting association, or other municipal commission, to determine whether an additional sum shall be raised for said purpose, and if so, what sum, not exceeding, with the sum already appropriated, in the whole three hundred thousand dollars; of which election the clerk of such town, incorporated borough, camp meeting association, or other municipal commission shall cause public notice of the time and place of holding the same to be given by advertisements, signed by himself, and set up in at least five public places in such town, incorporated borough, camp meeting association, or other municipal commission, and published in one or more newspapers printed therein at least six days previous to the day of said election, and said clerk shall provide for each elector voting at such election, ballots to be printed or written, or partly printed and partly written, on which shall be either the words, "For an additional appropriation for water supply under the provisions of the act entitled 'An act to enable incorporated towns to construct water works for the extinguishment of fire, and supplying the inhabitants thereof with pure and wholesome water,' and the supplements thereto $," or "Against an additional appropriation for water supply under the provisions of the act entitled 'An act to enable incorporated towns to construct water works for the extinguishment of fire, and supplying the inhabitants thereof with pure and wholesome water,' and the supplements thereto;" and that the polls for such election shall be held at the same places, and shall be opened and closed at the same hours, and such election shall be conducted by the same officers, and in the same manner, and such officers shall return a statement of the

Sum not to exceed certain amount.

Notice of election to be given.

Form of ballots

Election, by whom and how held.

result of such election, which shall be entered in the same manner as is prescribed and provided for in the twentieth section of the act of which this is a supplement.

2. *And be it enacted*, That this act shall take effect immediately.

Approved March 14, 1893.

CHAPTER CXLIX.

An Act concerning the rate of interest on certain municipal bonds.

Common council, &c., authorized to fix rate of interest.

1. Be it enacted *by the Senate and General Assembly of the State of New Jersey*, That wherever by any act of the legislature any of the cities in this state are authorized to issue bonds for public improvements, and in and by such act or acts the rate of interest on such bonds is fixed at six per centum per annum or any other fixed rate or sum, that hereafter it shall be lawful for any such cities to issue such bonds at a rate of interest to be fixed by the common council, board of aldermen or other governing body, such rate not to exceed the sum of five per centum per annum.

Repealer.

2. *And be it enacted*, That all acts and parts of acts inconsistent with the provisions of this act be and the same are hereby repealed.

3. *And be it enacted*, That this act shall take effect immediately.

Approved March 14, 1893.

CHAPTER CL.

An Act to amend an act entitled "An act for the formation and government of boroughs," approved April second, one thousand eight hundred and ninety-one.

1. BE IT ENACTED *by the Senate and General Assembly of the State of New Jersey*, That section thirty-six of said act be and the same is hereby amended so as to read as follows: Section to be amended

36. *And be it enacted*, That the inhabitants of any district in this state adjacent to and adjoining any borough heretofore created, or hereafter to be created, under any general law of this state, may become a part of such borough with all the powers and liabilities conferred upon the original corporation, and with the same rights and duties as it it had been included within the boundaries of the borough of which it seeks to become a part when the same was incorporated; *provided*, that the district to be added shall not increase the area of the whole borough beyond the size provided for in the act under which such borough was incorporated; *and provided further*, that the proceedings to annex any district to an existing borough shall be the same as is provided by this act for the incorporation of a borough, and the result of the election in the territory to be annexed shall be submitted to the mayor of the existing borough who shall at the next ensuing annual election submit the question of annexation to the legal voters in the existing borough, and if a majority of the said legal voters shall vote "against annexation" the result of the election shall be certified by the election officers, and all papers relating to the proceedings shall be filed in the clerk's office, as provided by this act, and the question of annexing the same territory shall not be again acted upon for five years; but if a majority of the legal voters in the existing borough shall vote "for annexation," then as soon as the result of the election is certified and filed in the clerk's

District adjacent to borough may become a part thereof.

Proviso.

Proviso

office as provided by this act, the annex district shall become a part of the original borough; *and provided further*, that nothing in this act shall apply to, affect or include any street, road or highway that is now or may hereafter be under charge, direction, management or control of any county public road board in this state, whether created or organized under or by virtue of any special or general act of the legislature.

Proviso.

2. *And be it enacted*, That this act shall take effect immediately.

Approved March 14, 1893.

CHAPTER CLI.

Supplement to an act respecting the orphans' court, and relating to the powers and duties of the ordinary, and the orphans' court and surrogates" (Revision), approved March twenty-seventh, one thousand eight hundred and seventy-four.

How time may be extended to present claims against insolvent decedent.

1. Be it enacted *by the Senate and General Assembly of the State of New Jersey*, That upon the application of any creditor of any insolvent decedent, the orphans' court of the proper county may extend the time within which claims may be presented by creditors of such decedent upon such terms as the court may deem just; *provided*, distribution shall not have been made; *and provided further*, that such notice of such application as the court may deem proper shall be given to the executor or administrator of such deceased insolvent.

Proviso.

Proviso.

2. *And be it enacted*, That this act shall take effect immediately.

Approved March 14, 1893.

CHAPTER CLII.

Supplement to an act entitled "An act respecting conveyances" (Revision), approved March twenty-seventh, one thousand eight hundred and seventy-four.

1. BE IT ENACTED *by the Senate and General Assembly of the State of New Jersey*, That the acknowledgment or proof of any deed or conveyance of lands, tenements or hereditaments, lying and being in this state, heretofore made or that hereafter shall be made before any master in chancery of this state in any foreign kingdom, state, nation or colony in which said party acknowledging or witness proving the said deed or conveyance happen to be, in the manner such acknowledgment or proof of deeds is now taken by a master in chancery in this state, shall be as good and effectual as if such acknowledgment or proof had been made in this state before and certified by one of the justices of the supreme court of this state.

Any master in chancery authorized to take acknowledgment or proof of deeds in any foreign kingdom state, &c.

2. *And be it enacted*, That this act shall take effect immediately.

Approved March 14, 1898.

CHAPTER CLIII.

An Act for the incorporation of bond and indemnity companies.

1. BE IT ENACTED *by the Senate and General Assembly of the State of New Jersey*, That it shall be lawful for any number of persons, not less than seven, to associate themselves into a company to guarantee the faithful performance of

Authorizes organization of companies to guarantee and indemnify, &c.

duty by public officials and of individuals or corporations, and to guarantee and indemnify individuals, firms or corporations against the wrongful act or default of any of their officers, agents or employees, and to indemnify and hold harmless any person or persons, private or public corporations, municipal or otherwise, against loss or damage by the misfeasance or malfeasance of any officer, agent or employee, and to become surety for the faithful discharge of duty in any station of employment or trust.

What certificate shall specify.

2. *And be it enacted*, That the persons associating shall under their hands and seals make a certificate which shall specify the following matters:

I. The name assumed to conduct the business;

II. The amount of capital stock which shall be fixed by them and the number and par value of the shares thereof;

III. The names and residences of the shareholders and the number of shares held by each;

IV. The place of the home office of the company;

Certificate to be acknowledged and recorded.

which certificate shall be acknowledged before a master of the court of chancery of this state and recorded in the office of the secretary of state, and upon the same being so recorded said association shall be a body corporate and entitled to all the rights and privileges as such under the laws of this state.

Amount of authorized capital stock required.

3. *And be it enacted*, That before any such corporation shall be authorized to do business under their certificate of organization they shall satisfy the banking and insurance commissioner that they have a well invested or cash capital of not less than twenty-five thousand dollars, actually paid in, and an authorized capital stock of not less than one hundred thousand dollars fully subscribed for by bona fide subscriptions, upon which at least twenty-five per centum has been paid in in cash, and the said company, before it shall be authorized to commence business, shall secure from and file in its office a certificate of the commissioner to that effect.

Who shall conduct the business.

4. *And be it enacted*, That upon compliance with the foregoing provisions of this act such company shall have all the powers mentioned in the first section of this act, with the right to have and reserve such rates of premium for its guarantee, and risk incurred as may be provided

by its by-laws, and shall conduct its business by a board of directors, of not less than seven in number, who shall be stockholders and shall be elected annually at a stockholders' meeting to be provided for in the by-laws of the association; said board of directors shall elect from their number a president, and shall provide for the election and appointment of such other officers and agents as may be necessary.

How president elected.

5. *And be it enacted*, That this act shall take effect immediately.

Approved March 14, 1893.

CHAPTER CLIV.

A Further Supplement to an act entitled "An act for the formation of borough governments," approved April fifth, one thousand eighteen hundred and seventy-eight.

1. BE IT ENACTED *by the Senate and General Assembly of the State of New Jersey*, That it shall be lawful for any borough organized under the act to which this is a supplement, to order and cause, by contract or otherwise, sewers and drains to be constructed in any part of such borough, and to provide, maintain and alter a general system of sewerage and drainage for such borough, or any part thereof, conformably to which all sewers and drains shall be constructed, and to establish and maintain one or more outlets or places of deposit, within or without such borough, for sewerage and drainage from such borough, and to repair and cleanse such sewers and drains.

Authorized to provide, &c., system of sewerage, establish outlets or places of deposit, &c.

2. *And be it enacted*, That whenever a petition in writing of any owners of property interested, not less than ten, shall be presented to the mayor and council of such borough, asking for the construction of a sewer or drain in the whole or any particular section of such borough,

When the mayor or council shall adopt resolution declaring intention.

it shall be lawful for such mayor or council to adopt a resolution declaring its intention to cause such sewers or drains to be constructed; and the said council shall forthwith cause public notice of such intention to be given by its mayor in two or more newspapers printed or circulating in such borough, for the space of ten days, briefly describing the proposed work, and the section or part of such borough to be affected, and requesting such persons as may object thereto to present their objections in writing at or before the expiration of ten days from date of such notice, to the officers signing the same; and if persons owning or representing more than one-half of the whole lineal frontage of land along the streets through which it is proposed to construct any sewer or drain, shall so present their objections in writing, then such proceedings shall cease, but not otherwise; and after the expiration of said ten days, it shall be lawful for such mayor and council to adopt an ordinance for the construction of such sewers or drains, to award contracts for the same, or for any part or section thereof, and to take all necessary steps for properly carrying into effect the desired improvement.

Notice to be published.

When proceedings shall cease

Appointment of commissioners

3. *And be it enacted*, That if, in the judgement of the said mayor and council, the construction of such sewer or drain is likely to benefit and increase the value of lands and any real estate in the vicinity thereof, the said council shall apply to the judge of the circuit court of the county wherein such borough is situate, for the appointment of commissioners to estimate and assess such benefits, of the time and place of which application notice shall be given by ten days' publication in two newspapers printed within the county and circulating within such borough, at which time and place, or at such other time and place as the said judge shall designate, said judge shall, without unnecessary delay, appoint three commissioners, who shall be freeholders of such borough making the application, to estimate and assess the said benefits; the said judge shall have power to remove any commissioner and appoint another in his place, and also to fill any vacancy that may occur in the office of any commissioner from any cause; the said commissioners before entering upon the execution of the duties required

Notice to be given.

Removal of commissioners.

of them by this act, shall take and subscribe, before some person duly authorized to administer the same, an oath or affirmation that they will make all estimates and assessments required of them fairly, legally and equitably, according to the best of their skill and understanding, which oath or affirmation shall be attached to the report that they are hereinafter required to make. Oath of commissioners.

4. *And be it enacted*, That the said commissioners, having thus qualified, shall give notice, under the direction of the said judge, of the time and place when and where they will hear any persons in interest who may present themselves to be heard, and at such time and place, and at such other times and places to which they may adjourn for that purpose, the said commissioners shall attend, and shall give a public hearing to those persons in interest who may desire to be heard; the said commissioners shall have power to examine witnesses under oath, to be administered by any one of them, and to enter upon and view any premises that they may deem necessary, and to adjourn from time to time in their discretion, or as directed by the judge of said court; they shall use diligent effort to ascertain the names of the owners of the lands and real estate benefited by the construction of such sewer or drain as aforesaid, and shall state the same in the report hereinafter mentioned, but the failure to ascertain the name of any such owner or to state the same correctly, or the omission of any such name from the said report, shall not be deemed to invalidate the said assessment, nor to be a bar to the collection of the same. Notice of meeting. Power to examine witnesses. To ascertain name of owners. Failure to ascertain not to invalidate assessment.

5. *And be it enacted*, That after having given opportunity as aforesaid for a public hearing of the persons in interest, and having viewed the premises likely, in their judgment, to be benefited by the construction of such sewer or drain, the said commissioners shall make a report in writing of their estimates and assessments to the judge of said court, accompanied by a survey and map to be prepared under their direction by a civil engineer, to be appointed by the mayor and council of such borough, showing the lots or parcels of land and real estate peculiarly benefited by such sewer or drain; the said report shall state the cost of the whole work, including in such cost all necessary expenditure for engineers, plans, Make report. To state cost, and names, and amount of assessment.

salaries, legal fees and charges, and such other incidental expenses as in the proper prosecution of the work may be necessarily incurred, the portion, if any, assessed upon the borough at large, and shall give the names, so far as ascertained, of the owners of said lots or parcels of land and real estate, and the amount of the assessment to each owner for each of such lots or parcels of land and real estate for the said benefits; which assessment shall, in each case, be in proportion, as near as may be, to the advantage which each of such owners shall be deemed to have acquired by the construction of such sewer or drain; in case the costs and expenses of such work shall exceed the amount of benefits, the expense thereof shall be paid by the borough at large, and raised by general tax; in no case shall any property or owner thereof to be assessed beyond the amount of benefit actually derived from the construction of such sewer or drain.

Costs and expenses, how paid.

Objections to assessments

6. *And be it enacted*, That upon the coming in of any such report, signed by the said commissioners, or any two of them, the judge of said court shall cause such notice to be given as it shall deem proper of the time and place of hearing any objections that may be made to such assessment, and after hearing any matter that may be alleged against the same, the judge of said court, either by rule or order, shall confirm the said report, or shall refer the same to the same commissioners for revision and correction, or to new commissioners to be appointed by him, forthwith to reconsider the subject-matter thereof; and the said commissioners to whom such report shall be referred by the court shall return the same, corrected and revised, or a new report to be made by them in the premises, to the said court, without unnecessary delay, and the same being so returned, shall be confirmed, or again referred by the judge of said court in the manner aforesaid, as right and justice shall require, and so from time to time until a report shall be made or returned in the premises which the said court shall confirm; such report, when so confirmed, shall be final and conclusive, as well upon the said borough as upon the owners of any lands and real estate affected thereby; the said court shall thereupon cause a certified copy of such report, and the accompanying map, to be filed in the office

Report to be final and conclusive.

of the clerk of the county in which said borough shall be located, and said clerk shall transmit a certified copy of the report, and rule or order of said court confirming the same, and also a certified copy of the map accompanying the same, to the treasurer of such borough.

And filed with the clerk.

7. *And be it enacted*, That no certiorari shall be allowed by any court to review any of the proceedings in relation to such improvement, nor to in any way affect any assessments made by such commissioners, after the lapse of thirty days from the making of the order of the court confirming such assessments; the court shall designate what notice, if any, shall be given, by publication or otherwise, of the confirmation of the report of said commissioners.

Limit of certiorari

Confirmation of report.

8. *And be it enacted*, That all assessments made under the provisions of this act shall be and remain a first lien upon the lands and real estate affected thereby, notwithstanding any error or omission in stating the name or names of the owner or owners of such lands and real estate, to the same extent as taxes and assessments are now a lien under the general laws of this state, and shall bear interest at the rate of six per centum per annum.

Assessment a first lien

Rate of interest.

9. *And be it enacted*, That the mayor and council may pay the expenses of any such improvement by the issue of temporary improvement certificates from time to time as the work progresses, in such form as the council may prescribe; said certificates shall bear interest at a rate not exceeding six per centum per annum, to be fixed by the council, and shall be payable at the expiration of not more than three years from the date of their issue.

May issue improvement certificates.

When payable.

10. *And be it enacted*, That it shall be the duty of the mayor and council of any such borough to incorporate in the annual tax levy, in each year, such amount as shall be required to be paid by such borough at large, or on account of any such improvement made, in the next preceding fiscal year, over and above the total amount of the assessment made against the lands and real estate peculiarly benefited; and the same shall be raised by general taxes, and the moneys received for assessments, and the moneys so raised by the general tax for the purpose aforesaid, shall be raised for and exclusively applied to the payment for such improvement, or to the payment of any temporary indebtedness incurred by the said

Amount required put in annual tax levy

Money raised by general taxes applied to payment of bonds or certificates issued

borough therefor, or for any bonds or certificates that may be issued as in this act provided.

Time and object of election.

11. *And be it enacted*, That the mayor and council of such borough shall order an election to determine whether bonds shall be issued to procure money for the payment of the cost and expenses of the proposed improvement, and shall designate the time and place for holding the same, and appoint judges and inspectors thereof; the polls shall be open from ten o'clock in the forenoon until three o'clock in the afternoon, and every person who is now authorized to vote at the corporate election in such borough, may vote at such election; on the tickets voted at such election shall be printed or written "for the issue of bonds," or "against the issue of bonds," and the judge and inspectors shall certifiy the result of said election to the clerk of the county in which borough is situated.

Election officers.

Opening and closing of polls.

Form of ballots.

Bonds issued if majority vote in favor of.

12. *And be it enacted*, That if there shall be a majority of votes cast in favor of the issue of bonds it shall then be lawful for the mayor and council of such borough to issue registered or coupon bonds of said borough, such issue being hereby expressly authorized for the purpose of providing funds to pay for such improvements; the bonds may be made payable at times to be therein specified, not more than twenty years after date, but so that an equal amount shall fall due each year after the first, the rate of interest not to exceed six per centum, and the denominations to be fixed by the mayor and council issuing the same; the bonds shall be of two classes, namely, "assessment bonds," which shall be paid out of the assessments for benefits, made by the commissioners appointed for that purpose, against lands benefited, and "sewer bonds," which shall represent the cost of the improvement above the amount assessed for benefits.

Bonds payable, rate of interest, denominations and classes

How lands may be released from assessment.

13. *And be it enacted*, That any land owner whose lands may be subject to an assessment for benefits derived from the construction of such sewer may have his lands released at any time by paying to the treasurer of the borough the full amount assessed against his property with interest at six per centum; it shall be the duty of the county clerk to file in his office the receipt of the treasurer for any such payment and also to enter upon the assessment list and map a short memorandum show-

Duty of county clerk.

ing that the assessment against such land owners and lands has been paid, and thereafter such lands shall be free from the lien of such assessment and shall not be liable to any assessment or tax to raise money to provide for the payment of assessments against any other property or the bonds mentioned in this act as "assessment bonds," but shall remain liable for any tax that shall be levied to provide for the payment of that part of the costs which is charged to the borough at large, or for the payment of any certificates or bonds issued therefor.

14. *And be it enacted*, That if a majority shall at such election vote against the issue of bonds, then the said mayor and council shall have power to issue certificates to pay for the cost of such work; such certificates shall bind the land assessed for benefits, and be a lien upon the same to the extent that each lot or parcel may be assessed as hereinbefore provided; and the same shall be a paramount lien upon said lands respectively, until the amounts due from each of the respective owners shall be paid, and the record of the assessment cancelled as herein provided; in issuing such certificates the mayor and council may also include the amount of any damages assessed against the borough at large, but such certificates shall be distinguished from those issued to represent the amount assessed for benefits; and the whole issue of certificates shall be divided into three classes, one-third to mature in one year, one-third in two years and one-third in three years; and to provide for their payment it shall be the duty of the borough assessor to assess and levy the tax for the same in the manner herein provided for the payment of bonds, certificates or other indebtedness incurred for such improvement.

Certificates issued if majority vote against issue of bonds

Certificates divided in classes.

Assessors levy tax for payment.

15. *And be it enacted*, That there shall be paid to each commissioner of assessment three dollars for every day he shall be actually engaged in the performance of the duties herein required of him; and they shall also have authority to employ a secretary at a cost of not over two dollars for each day he may be employed.

Compensation.

May employ a secretary.

16. *And be it enacted*, That the mayor and council of any borough in this state shall by resolution submit the question of the acceptance or rejection of this act to the vote of any such borough at a special election to be held

Special election may be held

for that purpose, whereof at least ten days' previous notice shall be given by public advertisement in at least two of the newspapers published and circulated in said borough if there be so many; the resolution shall fix the time and place for holding such election, and the said mayor and council shall appoint inspectors of the election, who shall hold the same as provided by said resolution, and return the result thereof to the said council; each ballot deposited by those who favor the acceptance of this act shall contain the words "the sewer accepted," written or printed thereon, and those opposed shall each deposit a ballot with the words "the sewer act rejected" written or printed thereon, and if a majority of the ballots so cast shall be found to be for the acceptance of this act, it shall then (but not otherwise) go into effect and be binding upon said borough; those persons who are qualified to vote at the annual municipal borough election for the election of the officers of any such borough shall be qualified to vote at the election provided for in this section.

Time of holding.

Election officers.

Form of ballots.

Entitled to vote.

Authorized to raise additional money.

17. *And be it enacted*, That any borough accepting the provisions of this act is authorized to raise such additional amount of money each year as may be necessary to carry out the provisions of this act, over and above what they are now allowed by law.

Repealer.

18. *And be it enacted*, That all acts, general and special, so far as they conflict herewith, be and the same are hereby repealed, and that this act shall take effect immediately.

Approved March 14, 1893.

CHAPTER CLV.

An Act providing for the making of assessments, in certain cases, of benefits conferred by local improvements in cities of this state.

1. BE IT ENACTED *by the Senate and General Assembly of the State of New Jersey*, That where, in any city of this state, a trunk or intercepting sewer has been or shall be constructed, or any local improvement has been or shall be made by such city, which sewer or improvement drains, covers, affects or benefits such a large area that, in the opinion of the common council or other governing body of such city, an estimate and assessment of the benefits conferred by such sewer or improvement ought to be made by freeholders residing outside of said city, not owning or interested in any real estate therein, upon the passage of a resolution by such governing body declaring such to be its opinion, the proper law officer of such city shall thereupon make application, upon ten days' public notice, to the justice of the supreme court holding the circuit in which said city is situate, for the appointment of three commissioners to make such estimate and assessment, and the said justice is hereby authorized and empowered to thereupon appoint as such commisioners three freeholders residing outside of such city, but in the state of New Jersey, who do not own and are not in any way interested in any real estate in said city. Justices of supreme court authorized to appoint commissioners

2. *And be it enacted*, That all such commissioners, when so appointed shall, in all respects, be governed in making such assessments by the laws now or hereafter in force relating to and regulating the making and confirmation of assessments for local improvements it such city. Commissioners to be governed by laws in force.

3. *And be it enacted*, That this act shall take effect immediately.

Approved March 14, 1893.

CHAPTER CLVI.

A Supplement to the act entitled "An act concerning taxes," approved April fourteenth, one thousand eight hundred and forty-six.

Assessors or commissioners of appeal authorized to deduct debt due upon mortgage to the chancellor, &c.

1. Be it enacted *by the Senate and General Assembly of the State of New Jersey*, That it shall be lawful for the assessor, or for the commissioners of appeal in cases of taxation, to deduct from the valuation of the taxable property for which any person shall be assessed, any debt or debts due and owing from such person upon any mortgage made to the chancellor, in his official capacity, or to the state of New Jersey, for the investment of money in the court of chancery, or upon any mortgage made to commissioners appointed by an order of the supreme court of this state, or by an order of any circuit court, inferior court of common pleas or orphans' court of any of the counties of this state, upon claim for such deduction being made according to law.

How taxes on mortgages are assessed and collected

2. *And be it enacted*, That such mortgages or the debts secured thereby shall be assessed for taxation by the assessor or commissioners of appeal, making the deduction on account thereof, and the tax thereon shall be collected by the collector of taxes in and for the city or township wherein the lands in the mortgage described are situated.

To whom assessment made.

3. *And be it enacted*, That such assessment shall be made to the person or persons having the beneficial interest in the said mortgage and mortgages, or who may be entitled to have the income or interest thereof at the time of such assessment, whether such person or persons reside in this state or not.

Unpaid taxes, how collected

4. *And be it enacted*, That where the person or persons assessed as aforesaid is or are resident or residents of the state of New Jersey, and such taxes remain unpaid for the space of sixty days after the expiration of the time appointed for the payment of taxes, then it shall be the duty

of the collector to proceed to collect such delinquent taxes in the manner provided for by the act entitled "A further supplement to the act entitled 'An act concerning taxes'" (Revision), approved April fourteenth, one thousand eight hundred and forty-six, approved April seventeenth, one thousand eight hundred seventy-six.

5. *And be it enacted*, That where the person or persons assessed as aforesaid, is or are a non-resident or non-residents of the state of New Jersey, it shall be the duty of the person claiming deductions to pay the taxes so assessed, and payment of the same may be enforced by like means and processes as if the same had been originally assessed to such person, and any taxes which such person may pay or satisfy as aforesaid, shall be deemed and taken to be a payment, so far as such payment will extend, on the interest or income due or to grow due on or secured by the said mortgage. When person claiming deduction pays the taxes.

6. *And be it enacted*, That this act shall take effect immediately, and that all acts and parts of acts inconsistent herewith be and the same are hereby repealed. Repealer.

Approved March 14, 1893.

CHAPTER CLVII.

An Act to amend chapter fifty-two of the laws one thousand eight hundred and eighty, entitled "A supplement to an act entitled 'An act to prevent the willful pollution of the waters of any of the creeks, ponds or brooks of this state'" (Supplement Revision), approved February twenty-seventh, one thousand eight hundred and eighty.

1. BE IT ENACTED *by the Senate and General Assembly of the State of New Jersey*, That the first section of the said act be amended so as to read as follows: Section to be amended.

Punishment for polluting waters.

1. Be it enacted *by the Senate and General Assembly of the State of New Jersey*, That if any person or persons shall throw, cause or permit to be thrown into any reservoir, or into the waters of any creek, pond or brook of this state which runs through or along the border of any city, town or borough of this state, or the waters of which are used to supply any aqueduct or reservoir for distribution for public use, any carcass of any dead animal, or any offal or offensive matter whatsoever calculated to render said waters impure, or to create noxious or offensive smells, or shall connect any water closet with any sewer, or other means whereby the contents thereof may be conveyed to and into any such creek, pond or brook, or shall so deposit or cause or permit to be deposited any such carcass, offal or other offensive matter that the washing or waste therefrom shall or may be conveyed to and into any such creek, pond, brook or reservoir, such person or persons shall be deemed guilty of a misdemeanor, and, on conviction thereof shall be punished by a fine not exceeding one thousand dollars, or by imprisonment not exceeding two years, or both.

Penalty

Repealer.

2. *And be it enacted*, That all acts and parts of acts inconsistent with this act in as far as they are inconsistent herewith be and the same are hereby repealed, and that this shall take effect immediately.

Approved March 14, 1893.

CHAPTER CLVIII.

A Supplement to an act entitled "An act for the formation and government of boroughs," approved March twelfth, one thousand eight hundred and ninety.

Period to redeem lands sold for taxes.

1. Be it enacted *by the Senate and General Assembly of the State of New Jersey*, That whenever, in any of the boroughs of this state heretofore incorporated under the

provisions of the act to which this is a supplement, any real estate shall be sold for taxes under the provisions of section twenty-three of the said act, then and in every such case the owner of such lands shall have the period of two years in which to redeem the said lands, as now provided by law, and failing so to do within such time the same shall vest in the purchaser in fee simple; *provided*, that the said owner shall have been notified of the sale of said lands and of his right to redeem the same, as now provided by law, by payment of arrears of taxes, interest and costs; which notice shall be in writing, signed by the purchaser or his agent and served personally on him if resident in the borough, or mailed to his last known address if nonresident, at least sixty days prior to the expiration of said period of two years. Proviso.

2. *And be it enacted*, That this act shall take effect immediately.

Approved March 14, 1898.

CHAPTER CLIX.

An act to regulate the practice of pharmacy in New Jersey.

1. Be it enacted *by the Senate and General Assembly of the State of New Jersey*, That from and after the passage of this act it shall and may be lawful for any duly registered or licensed physician, authorized by the laws of this state to practice medicine and surgery therein, and located as a practitioner of medicine and surgery in any city, town, borough or village of this state, not exceeding one thousand in population, to engage in the practice of pharmacy in such city, town, borough, or village, and he shall be deemed and taken to be and shall possess all the rights, powers and privileges of a registered pharmacist, When a registered or licensed physician may practice pharmacy.

subject, however, to all the regulations and restrictions imposed by law upon a registered pharmacist.

Repealer.

2. *And be it enacted*, That all acts and parts of acts inconsistent with this act be and the same are hereby repealed.

3. *And be it enacted*, That this act shall take effect immediately.

Approved March 14, 1898.

CHAPTER CLX.

A Further Supplement to an act entitled "An act relative to sale of lands under a public statute, or by virtue of any judicial proceedings" (Revision), approved March twenty-seventh, one thousand eight hundred and seventy-four.

Preamble.

WHEREAS, The provisions in force relative to the sales of lands, and the advertisement and adjournment of the same, have not been in all respects known or complied with, whereby the titles to certain lands are alleged to be defective and uncertain.

When title to lands not invalidated.

1. BE IT ENACTED *by the Senate and General Assembly of the State of New Jersey*, That no sale of lands heretofore made by any executors or administrators shall be invalidated by reason of such sale having been adjourned for a time or times exceeding two months in the whole, or by reason of the omission to advertise adjournments; but that the purchaser or purchasers of any lands at such sale who shall have paid the price thereof, and received a deed therefor, such sale having been duly reported to and confirmed by the proper court, shall have as good and complete a title thereto as if said sale had been adjourned from time to time, not exceeding two months in the whole, and the adjournments thereof duly advertised.

2. *And be it enacted*, That this act shall take effect immediately.

Approved March 14, 1893.

CHAPTER CLXI.

A Supplement to an act entitled "An act to provide for the appointment of commissioners for the promotion of uniformity of legislation in the United States," approved April fourteenth, one thousand eight hundred and ninety-one.

1. BE IT ENACTED *by the Senate and General Assembly of the State of New Jersey*, That the term of office of the commissioners heretofore appointed under the act to which this a supplement be and the same is hereby extended for three years from the expiration of said term. Term of office extended.

2. *And be it enacted*, That this act shall take effect immediately.

Approved March 14, 1893.

CHAPTER CLXII.

An Act authorizing religious corporations, incorporated by general or special acts of the legislature, to change their names and modify their terms of incorporation.

1. BE IT ENACTED *by the Senate and General Assembly of the State of New Jersey*, That whenever any religious corporation, incorporated by general or special act of the leg- Proceedings to change name.

islature, shall desire to change its corporate name it shall and may be lawful for said corporation, by a two-thirds vote at any regular meeting, to change the corporate name of the said corporation, specifying by such vote what the new corporate name shall be; and thereafter the said corporation shall be known by such new name so adopted, and shall, by such new name, have, hold and retain all its property, and shall enjoy the same rights, privileges and powers and be subject to the same liabilities as it would have enjoyed and been subject to had said name not been changed.

Change of officers, &c., and terms therof.

2. *And be it enacted*, That it shall be lawful for any such religious corporation, by a majority vote at any regular meeting, to make such change or changes in the number of officers and managers or trustees of said corporation, and the terms of their office, as shall be considered expedient for the interests of the corporation.

May establish new departments.

3. *And be it enacted*, That it shall be lawful for any such religious corporation, at any regular meeting, by a majority vote, to establish any new department or departments of religious work not specified in the act of incorporation, and to maintain the same.

Certificate to be filed.

4. *And be it enacted*, Whenever any or all of the changes provided for in this act are made, a certificate of such change or changes, over the hand of the presiding officer of the corporation, attested by the secretary thereof, shall be filed with the secretary of state within thirty days after

Fee for filing

such change is made; and one dollar shall be the established fee for such filing.

5. *And be it enacted*, That this act shall take effect immediately.

Approved March 14, 1893.

CHAPTER CLXIII.

An Act concerning the improvement of public roads in this state.

Contracts heretofore made by chosen freeholders, &c., not invalidated.

1. BE IT ENACTED *by the Senate and General Assembly of the State of New Jersey*, That contracts for the improvement of any road heretofore made by the board of chosen freeholders of any county, or the township committee of any township in this state, in good faith, under which public roads or any portion of a public road has been completed, and public money appropriated for that purpose has been expended, shall not be invalidated or set aside as illegal, as to the work completed, by reason of any irregularity in or want of conformity of the petition asking for said improvement, to the provisions of the act under which said improvements were to be made; *provided*, said act was designated in said petition and the requisite number of property owners along the line of the proposed improvement had signed the same; *and provided further*, that the said board of chosen freeholders or township committee were authorized by said act to order said improvement to be made, without the presentation of said petition.

Proviso

Proviso.

2. *And be it enacted*, That this act is a public act, and shall take effect immediately.

Approved March 14, 1893.

CHAPTER CLXIV.

A Further Supplement to an act entitled "An act for the incorporation of safe deposit and trust companies," approved April twentieth, one thousand eight hundred and eighty-five.

Section to be amended.

1. BE IT ENACTED *by the Senate and General Assembly of the State of New Jersey*, That section one of the act to which this is a further supplement be amended so as to read as follows:

When authorized to discount bills, &c., buy and sell gold, &c., buy and sell bills of exchange, &c.

1. BE IT ENACTED *by the Senate and General Assembly of the State of New Jersey*, That in addition to the provisions of the act to which this is a supplement, and the powers and authority therein and thereby giveu, it shall and may be lawful for any trust company, incorporated or organized under said act or any special law, and doing business in any city or village in this state where now there is no national or state bank of discount and deposit, to discount bills, notes and other evidences of debt, to buy and sell gold and silver bullion and foreign coins and money, and to buy and sell bills of exchange and commercial paper and to use so much of their capital, deposits and funds for such purposes as their respective directors shall, from time to time, designate; *provided, however*, that the assent in writing be first obtained of two-thirds of the stockholders of such company or companies as may decide by a unanimous vote of its or their board of directors to avail themselves of the privileges of this act.

Proviso.

2. *And be it enacted*, That this act shall take effect immediately.

Approved March 14, 1898.

CHAPTER CLXV.

A Further Supplement to an act entitled "An act for the formation and government of boroughs," approved April second, one thousand eight hundred and ninety-one.

Council authorized to provide music for public parks, &c., by assessment.

1. BE IT ENACTED *by the Senate and General Assembly of the State of New Jersey*, That it shall be lawful to assess and collect in any borough incorporated under this act, whenever the council shall deem it to the best interest of and for the good of the borough, one mill, or any portion thereof on each dollar of the assessed valuation of the property therein, for the purpose of providing music for the public parks, and other public places to which the people resort for pleasure, recreation and amusement.

Mayor and council direct assessment made.

2. *And be it enacted*, That whenever the mayor and council of any such borough shall deem it to the public interests, and for the good of the borough, that an assessment should be made for the purpose aforesaid, they may, by resolution, regularly adopted, direct the assessor of said borough to raise such sum of money as they shall deem necessary for the purpose aforesaid, which shall not, however, exceed one mill on the dollar as aforesaid.

Assessor to assess amount called for.

3. *And be it enacted*, That the assessor, on receipt of a resolution, such as is provided for in the preceding section, shall, at the time when the annual taxes are assessed, assess the amount called for in said resolution, against all property in said borough, and said assessment shall be collected at the same time that the annual taxes are collected, and by the same officer, and said borough shall have the same remedies for the collection thereof that are provided for the collection of the regular borough tax.

How collected.

4. *And be it enacted*, That this act shall take effect immediately.

Approved March 14, 1893.

CHAPTER CLXVI.

A Supplement to an act entitled "An act to regulate the practice of courts of law," approved March twenty-seventh, one thousand eight hundred and seventy-four.

How to revive and re-instate action or suit when failure to file pleadings caused by neglect, &c., of attorney.

4-13 9

1. Be it enacted *by the Senate and General Assembly of the State of New Jersey*, That where any action or suit has heretofore been commenced in either the supreme or circuit courts of this state, either under or by virtue of any statute or at common law, and said action or suit has been dismissed, abated and judgment of non prosequi entered by reason of the failure of any attorney to file any pleading within the time limited by law, it shall be lawful for either of said courts or any justice thereof to revive and re-instate said case upon such terms as may seem to him equitable and just, if in the opinion of said court or justice the facts in said cause show that the failure to file said pleadings was on account of the neglect, fault, error or mistake of said attorney, and that great injury and wrong would result either to the plaintiff or defendant.

2. *And be it enacted*, That this act shall take effect immediately.

Approved March 14, 1893.

CHAPTER CLXVII.

A Further Supplement to "An act concerning roads" (Revision), approved March twenty-seventh, one thousand eight hundred and seventy-four.

WHEREAS, By reason of the opening and grading of streets and avenues in new towns and colonies in various portions of this state, parts of old laid out roads running through the wild lands thereof have become useless and practically abandoned, the said new streets and avenues affording better access to the same points than by the said parts of old roads; *and whereas*, for small changes or vacations, proceedings under the present act to which this is a supplement, are both expensive and troublesome, and attended with much delay, so much so that few persons are willing for the public good to incur the expenses of such proceedings; for remedy whereof, Preamble

1. BE IT ENACTED *by the Senate and General Assembly of the State of New Jersey*, That whenever ten or more persons, being freeholders, shall think the vacation of a part of any public road necessary in any part of the county wherein they reside, they may make application in writing to the inferior court of common pleas of such county, or to one of the judges thereof, setting forth in writing the road or portion thereof, which it is proposed to have vacated, describing the same by courses and distances, to which description there shall be attached a map showing the location of the road, or portion thereof to be vacated, and if within ten days after such application shall have been made, as aforesaid, or if at the time of making such application, there shall be presented to said court or judge the consent in writing of the owners of all the lands by such old road or portion thereof proposed to be vacated, and also the written consent of the township committee of the township wherein such lands do lie, that such applica- Application to vacate part of any public road Map showing location

tion shall be granted, then it shall be lawful for said court or judge to cause said application, with the accompanying survey, map and return, and the written consents of the owners of lands as aforesaid, and of the township committee, to be filed with the clerk of the county, to be by him recorded in the book of roads for said county, and when said application and papers have been so filed, such portion of such old road shall thereupon and thereby be deemed to be vacated; *provided*, that no portion of any old road proposed to be vacated under this act, shall exceed one thousand yards in length.

Consent of owners, &c

Map, return, consents, &c, to be filed.

Proviso.

2. *And be it enacted*, That this act shall take effect immediately.

Approved March 14, 1893.

CHAPTER CLXVIII.

An Act to enable street railway companies, or companies owning railroads operated as street railways, to unite and consolidate their corporate franchises and other property with those of traction companies and to prescribe a method therefor.

Authorized to merge and consolidate.

1. Be it enacted *by the Senate and General Assembly of the State of New Jersey*, That it shall and may be lawful for any street railway company or other company owning a railroad operated as a street railway, incorporated under any law of this state, to merge and consolidate its property and franchises with those of any motor power company created under any law of this state.

Consolidation made under conditions, provisions, &c.

2. *And be it enacted*, That said consolidation shall be made under the conditions, provisions, restrictions and with the powers hereafter in this act mentioned and contained, that is to say:

Directors prescribe terms and conditions, &c.

I. The directors of the several corporations proposing to consolidate may enter into a joint agreement, under the corporate seal of the company, for the consolidation of said companies and railways, and prescribing the terms and conditions thereof, the mode of carrying the same into effect, the name of the new corporation, the number and names of the directors and other officers thereof, who shall be the first directors and officers, and their places of residence, the number of shares of the capital stock, the amount or par value of each share and the manner of converting the capital stock of each of the said companies into the new corporation, and how and when directors and officers shall be chosen, with such other details as they shall deem necessary to perfect such new organization and the consolidation of said companies or railways;

Agreement submitted to stockholders

II. Said agreement shall be submitted to the stockholders of each of said companies or corporations at a meeting thereof, called separately, for the purpose of taking the same into consideration; due notice of the time and place of holding such meeting, and the object thereof, shall be delivered to such persons respectively, or sent to them by mail, when their post office address is known to the company; and, also, by a general notice published in some newspaper in the city, town or county where such company has its principal office or place of business; and at said meeting of stockholders the agreement of the said directors shall be considered, and a vote, by ballot, taken by each company separately, for the adoption or rejection of the same, each share entitling the holder thereof to one vote; and said ballots shall be cast in person or by proxy, and if two-thirds of all the votes of all the stockholders, voting separately, shall be for adoption of said agreement, then that the fact shall be certified thereon by the secretary of the respective companies, under the seal thereof; and the agreement so adopted, or a certified copy thereof, shall be filed in the office of the secretary of state, and shall, from thence, be deemed and taken to be the agreement and act of consolidation of the said companies; and a copy of said agreement and act of consolidation, duly certified by the secretary of state, under the seal of his office, shall be evidence of the existence of said new corporation.

Notice of meeting.

Notice published in newspapers.

Vote taken by ballot.

Vote for adoption certified by secretaries, and copy filed

Evidence of existence of new corporation

Upon filing agreement with secretary of state, deemed one corporation

3. *And be it enacted*, That upon the making and perfecting the agreement and act of consolidation, as provided in the preceding section, and filing the same, or copy, with the secretary of state as aforesaid, the several corporations, parties thereto, shall be deemed and taken to be one corporation, by the name provided in said agreement and act, possessing within this state all rights, privileges and franchises, and subject to all the restrictions, disabilities and duties of each of such corporations so consolidated.

When rights, &c., of each corporation deemed to be transferred, &c.

4. *And be it enacted*, That upon the consummation of said act of consolidation as aforesaid, all and singular the rights, privileges and franchises of each of said corporations, parties to the same, and all property, real, personal and mixed, and all debts, due on whatever account, as well as stock subscriptions and other things in action belonging to each of such corporations, shall be taken and deemed to be transferred to and vested in such new corporation without further act or deed; and all property, all rights of way, and all and every other interests shall be effectually the property of the new corporation as they were of the former corporations, parties to said agreement; and the title to real estate, either by deed or otherwise, under the laws of this state vested in either of such corporations shall not be deemed to revert or be in any way impaired by reason of this act; *provided, however*, that all rights of creditors and all liens upon the property of either of said corporations shall be preserved unimpaired, and the respective corporations may be deemed to continue in existence to preserve the same; and all debts, liabilities and duties of either of said companies shall thenceforth attach to said new corporation and be enforced against it to the same extent as if said debts, liabilities and duties had been incurred or contracted by it.

Title to real estate not impaired.

Proviso.

How suits brought.

5. *And be it enacted*, That suits may be brought and maintained against such new company in any of the courts of this state in the same manner as against other railway companies therein.

6. *And be it enacted*, That any stockholder of any company hereby authorized to consolidate with any other, who shall refuse to convert his stock into the stock of

the consolidated company, may, at any time within thirty days after the adoption of the said agreement of consolidation by the stockholders, as in this act provided, apply, by petition, to the circuit court of the county in which the chief office of said company may be kept, or to a judge of said court in vacation, if no such court sits within said period, on reasonable notice to said company, to appoint three disinterested persons to estimate the damage, if any, done to such stockholder by said proposed consolidation, and whose award, or that of a majority of them, when confirmed by the said court, shall be final and conclusive, and the persons so appointed shall also appraise said stock of such stockholder at the full market value thereof, without regard of any depreciation or appreciation in consequence of the said consolidation, and the said company may, at its election, either pay to the said stockholder the amount of damages so found and awarded, if any, or the value of the stock so ascertained and determined, and upon the payment of the value of the stock as aforesaid, the said stockholder shall transfer the stock so held by him to said company, to be disposed of by the directors of said company, or be retained for the benefit of the remaining stockholders; and in case the value of said stock as aforesaid is not so paid within thirty days from the filing of the said award and confirmation by said court, and notice to said company, the damages so found and confirmed shall be a judgment against said company and collected as other judgments in said court are, by law, recoverable.

Disinterested persons appointed to estimate damage to stockholder refusing to convert his stock.

Confirmation of award by court final.

Company may pay stockholder damages awarded or value of stock ascertained

When damages so confirmed shall be judgment against company.

7. *And be it enacted*, That in all cases of consolidation of two or more railway companies under and by virtue of the provisions of this act, the said consolidated company shall have power and authority to issue bonds registered, or with coupons or interest certificates thereto attached, or both, to an amount sufficient to cover all the indebtedness of the company so merged and consolidated, and to aid in the completion and equipment of said railway, to secure the payment of which it shall be lawful for them to create a mortgage, covering their corporate franchises, rights, privileges and property, real and personal; *provided*, that the bonds shall not bear a greater rate of interest than six per centum per annum;

Authorized to issue bonds and create a mortgage.

Proviso.

the bonds so issued may be given in lieu, exchange and satisfaction of and for all bonds or other debts against the companies thus merged and consolidated, upon such terms as may be agreed upon by and between the holders of said debts or claims; *provided*, that such company shall not plead any statute or statutes against usury, in any court of law or equity, in any suit instituted to enforce the payment of any bond or mortgage executed under any of the provisions of this act.

Proviso.

Repealer.

8. *And be it enacted*, That all acts and parts of acts inconsistent with this act, to the extent of such inconsistency, be and the same are hereby repealed, and that this act shall take effect immediately.

Approved March 14, 1898.

CHAPTER CLXIX.

An Act to authorize street railway companies, or companies owning railroads operated as street railways, to lease their property and franchises to traction companies, and to prescribe a method therefor.

Authorized to lease upon such conditions as may be agreed upon.

1. BE IT ENACTED *by the Senate and General Assembly of the State of New Jersey*, That it shall and may be lawful for any company owning any street railway or railways or any company owning any railroad operated as a street railway, whether such lessor company or companies are incorporated under any general or special act of this state, to lease their property and franchises to any traction company created under the laws of this state for such term or terms, upon such condition or conditions as to the use and operation of the property of the corporation, the enjoyment of privileges or immunities of such lessor corporation and the amount of rent to be paid therefor, and the manner of making payment of said rent, and such

other conditions, limitations and restrictions as said lessor and lessee corporations may agree upon.

How disinterested person may be appointed to estimate damages.

2. *And be it enacted*, That any stockholder of any company or companies whose property and franchises shall be leased under the provisions of this act, who shall not not assent to such lease, or who shall resist or object to the making thereof, may at any time within thirty days after the making of such lease as in this act provided, apply by petition to the circuit court of the county in which the chief office of the lessor corporation may be kept, or to a judge of said court in vacation if no such court sits within such period, on reasonable notice to said company, to appoint three disinterested persons to estimate the damage, if any, done to such stockholder by said proposed lease, and whose award, or that of a majority of them, when confirmed by the said court shall be final and conclusive; and the persons so appointed shall also appraise said stock of such stockholder at the full market value thereof, without regard to any depreciation or appreciation in consequence of the said lease; and the said lessor company may, at its election, either pay to the said stockholder the amount of damages so found and awarded, if any, or the value of the stock so ascertained and determined, and upon the payment of the value of the stock as aforesaid, the said stockholder shall transfer the stock so held by him to said lessor company, to be disposed of by the directors of said company or to be retained for the benefit of the remaining stockholders; and in case the value of said stock as aforesaid is not so paid within thirty days from the filing of the said award and confirmation by said court, and notice to said lessor company, the damages so found and confirmed shall be a judgment against said company and collected as other judgments in said court are, by law, recoverable.

Stock shall be appraised.

When upon filing said award and confirmation of same shall be a judgment.

Repealer

3. *And be it enacted*, That all acts and parts of acts inconsistent with this act, to the extent of such inconsistency, be and the same are hereby repealed, and that this act shall take effect immediately.

Approved March 14, 1893.

CHAPTER CLXX.

An Act to amend an act entitled "An act to amend an act entitled 'A further supplement to an act entitled "An act concerning roads"'" (Revision), approved April sixteenth, one thousand eight hundred and forty-six, which supplement was approved March twenty-seventh, one thousand eight hundred and seventy-four, and which amending act was approved March fourth, one thousand eight hundred and eighty.

Section to be amended

1. BE IT ENACTED *by the Senate and General Assembly of the State of New Jersey*, That the said act of which this is amendatory, entitled "An act to amend an act entitled 'A further supplement to an act entitled "An act concerning roads"'" (Revision), approved April sixteenth, one thousand eight hundred and forty-six, which supplement was approved March twenty-seventh, one thousand eight hundred and seventy-four, which amending act was approved March fourth, one thousand eight hundred and eighty, be so amended that section one of said act, which is as follows:

Application to court for appointment of surveyors to alter short section of road.

"1. BE IT ENACTED *by the Senate and General Assembly of the State of New Jersey*, That whenever six or more persons, being freeholders residing in the township, shall think any alteration of any public road necessary in any part of the county wherein they reside, by having a portion of such road vacated, not exceeding in length six hundred yards, and said road changed by relaying it in another place (the road so relaid not to exceed in length six hundred yards), they may make application in writing to one of the judges of the court of common pleas of the county wherein said portion of said road lies, at his chambers, for the appointment of three surveyors of the highways, one of which shall be from the township in which that portion of the road to be vacated lies; of which application to said judge, the said applicants shall give at least ten days' notice of the time and place when, and the name and residence of the judge before whom said application is to be made by putting up written notices thereof, signed by themselves, and put up in three of the most public places in the said township, in which the said road to be vacated lies; which notice shall contain a description of the portion of the road proposed to be vacated and a general description of the road proposed to be laid out, in lieu of the one so vacated, and upon proof being made to said judge of the putting up of said notices, he shall thereupon appoint three surveyors of the highways, as aforesaid, by an order in writing under his hand, and shall, in and by said order, fix the time and place of meeting of said surveyors, and for so doing he shall receive the sum of one dollar; *provided nevertheless*, and it is hereby further enacted, in order to save the expenses necessarily attendant both to applicants and townships, upon the vacation of roads, that whenever any road which has heretofore been laid out by the surveyors of the highways according to law, or any portion of such road shall have been unused for public travel for a period of not less than five years, then and in such case the said road or such portion thereof as shall have been unused for public travel for the term aforesaid, shall be and hereby is declared to be vacated; *provided*, the owners of the lands on both sides of said road, or of said portion thereof, unused as aforesaid, shall file in the office of the clerk of the county where such road or such portion of road lies, their assent in writing to said vacation," be and the same is hereby amended so as to read as follows:

Notice of application to be given.

Notice to contain what.

Appointment of surveyors.

Proviso.

Proviso

1. Be it enacted *by the Senate and General Assembly of the State of New Jersey*, That whenever six or more persons, being freeholders residing in the township, shall think any alteration of any public road, or the vacation of a portion of any public road necessary in any part of the county wherein they reside, either by having a portion of such road, not exceeding in length six hundred yards, vacated, or by changing such road by vacating a portion thereof, not exceeding in length six hundred yards, and by relaying it in another place (the road so relaid not to exceed in length six hundred yards), they may

Application to court for appointment of surveyors to vacate portion thereof make application in writing to one of the judges of the court of common pleas of the county wherein said portion of such road lies, at his chambers, for the appointment of three surveyors of the highways, one of which shall be from the township in which that portion of road to be vacated or changed lies; of which application to said judge the said applicants shall give at least ten days' notice of the time and place when and the name and residence of the judge before whom said application is to be made, by putting up written notice thereof, signed by themselves, and put up in three of the most public places in the said township in which the said road to be vacated or changed lies; which notice shall contain a description of the portion of the road proposed to be vacated or changed, and in case of a change of such road, as is herein defined, a general description of the road proposed to be laid out in lieu of the one so vacated, and upon proof being made to the said judge of the putting up of said notices, he shall thereupon appoint three surveyors of the highways, as aforesaid, by an order in writing under his hand, and shall, in and by said order, fix the time and place of meeting of said surveyors, and for so doing he shall receive the sum of one dollar; *provided, nevertheless*, and it is hereby further enacted, in order to save the expenses necessarily attendant both to applicants and townships, upon the vacation of roads, that whenever any road which has heretofore been laid out by the surveyors of the highways according to law, or any portion of such road shall have been unused for public travel for a period of not less than five years, then and in such case the said road, or such portion thereof as shall have been unused for public travel for the term aforesaid, shall be and hereby is declared to be vacated; *provided*, the owners of the lands on both sides of said road, or of said portion thereof unused as aforesaid, shall file in the office of the clerk of the county where such road or such portion of road lies, their assent in writing to said vacation.

Notice of application to be given.

Notice to contain.

Appointment of surveyors.

Proviso.

Proviso.

Repealer.

2. *And be it enacted*, That all acts and parts of acts inconsistent with the provisions of this act be and the same are hereby repealed, and that this act shall take effect immediately.

Approved March 14, 1893.

CHAPTER CLXXI.

A Further Supplement to an act entitled "An act concerning corporations" (Revision), approved April seventh, one thousand eight hundred and seventy-five.

1. BE IT ENACTED *by the Senate and General Assembly of the State of New Jersey*, That it shall and may be lawful for any corporation or corporations created under the provisions of the act to which this is a further supplement to purchase, hold, sell, assign, transfer, mortgage, pledge or otherwise dispose of the shares of the capital stock of any other corporation or corporations created under the law of this or any other state, and to exercise while owners of such stock all the rights, powers and privileges, including the right to vote thereon, which natural persons, being the owners of such stock, might, could or would exercise. Authorized to purchase, hold, sell, &c., shares of capital stock of other corporations.

2. *And be it enacted*, That it shall and may be lawful for any corporation described in the preceding section of this act to purchase, hold, sell, assign, transfer, mortgage, pledge, or otherwise dispose of any securities or evidences of debt created by other corporation or corporations of this or any other state, in the same manner and to the same extent as natural persons, being the owners thereof, might, could or would do. Lawful to do same, in manner as natural persons, being owners, could do.

3. *And be it enacted*, That all acts and parts of acts inconsistent with this act, to the extent of such inconsistency, be and the same are hereby repealed, and that this act shall take effect immediately. Repealer.

Approved March 14, 1893.

CHAPTER CLXXII.

An Act to authorize the formation of traction companies for the construction and operation of street railways, or railroads operated as street railways, and to regulate the same.

Authorized to organize corporation to construct machinery, &c., for supplying motive power to street railways.

1. BE IT ENACTED *by the Senate and General Assembly of the State of New Jersey*, That it shall and may be lawful for three or more persons, one of whom shall be a resident of the state of New Jersey, to associate themselves into a corporation for the construction and operation of motors, cables and other machinery for supplying motive power to street railways, or other railroads operated as street railways, and the necessary apparatus for applying the same; and such corporation when formed in accordance with the provisions of this act shall have power to enter upon any street, road, lane, alley or other highway upon which any street railway, or other railroad operated as a street railway, is now or may hereafter be constructed (with the consent of the owner or owners, lessee or lessees of such railway or of the person or persons operating the same), and make, construct, apply, maintain and operate such railway, motors, cables, electrical or other devices and appliances, with power to erect, construct, apply, maintain and use such tunnels, subways, for cables, poles, wire, conduits or other devices for transmitting and using electrical or other forces, as will provide for the traction of cars on street railways, or other railroads operated as street railways, and to construct lines of street or passenger railway, and all necessary turnouts, sidings and bridges on, along, through or over any street, road, lane, alley, stream or highway, either by extension of existing railways or by the building of new lines thereon, either wholly within or partly within, or wholly between or partly within and between cities, towns, boroughs, villages, townships and counties,

Powers of corporation, &c.

and the same when constructed to equip, maintain, use and operate for the carriage of persons and property for compensation to be made such corporation, and to contract with any other person or persons, natural or artificial, for such construction, equipment, maintenance, use or operation, and to purchase, hold, sell, pledge, mortgage or otherwise dispose of any capital stock or securities of any other corporations owning, using, leasing or operating any street railway or other railroad operated as a street railway, turnpike or plank road, or engaged in the construction or equipment thereof, or in creating or supplying power of any kind for the operation thereof, and to exercise all the rights, powers and privileges in respect to such capital stock and securities, incidental to the use and ownership thereof, which any natural person or persons might, could or would do, and to purchase, hold, sell or otherwise dispose of such real or personal property as may be convenient or necessary for the use of the corporations created under this act, and to pledge or mortgage the same with the franchises of such corporations; *provided*, that no corporation created under this act shall enter upon or use any street, road, lane, alley, or other highway, under color or by virtue of this act, for the extension or construction of new lines of railway, or for the operation thereof, without the consent of the board of aldermen, common council or body having control of streets or highways, or other governing body of the city, town, borough, village, township or county, into or within the limits of which such new line of railways is proposed to be extended, constructed or operated, nor shall any corporation created under this act possess the power to use on any of its railways, within the limits of any street and in the surface thereof, any locomotive or other engine moving on its rails, which is propelled by steam; *provided, further*, that the adoption of any motor or motive power herein authorized to be used, shall not be deemed to preclude change to any other motor or motive power herein authorized, when and as often as the business of such corporation may from time to time in its judgment so require.

Proviso.

Proviso.

2. *And be it enacted*, That all corporations created under this act shall, in addition to the preceding, possess

Other powers conferred. the following powers, and such other powers as are now, or hereafter may be, conferred upon corporations created under the laws of this state which do not possess the general power of condemning lands, or engaging in the business of insurance or banking or deriving profit from the loan or use of money:

Limit of existence, &c. I. To have perpetual succession, by its corporate name, for the period limited in its certificate of incorporation, and to make and use a common seal and alter the same at pleasure.

To sue and be sued, to mortgage or pledge, &c. II. To sue and be sued in any court of law or equity;

III. To mortgage or pledge by way of mortgage, any or all of its property or franchises, or both;

To appoint officers, &c. IV. To appoint such officers and agents as the business of such corporation shall require, upon such suitable compensation as may be agreed;

To make by-laws, &c. V. To make by-laws, not inconsistent with the consitution and laws of this state, or of the United States, for the regulation of the election of its directors, the government of its affairs, the transfer of its stock, and to prescribe and enforce penalties for the breach thereof, not exceeding twenty dollars;

To have other powers. VI. To have all other powers necessary to the performance of its duties and the exercise of its privileges imposed or conferred by this act.

To make and file certificate 8. *And be it enacted*, That whenever three or more persons shall desire to create themselves and their associates into a corporation under this act, they shall make and file a certificate in writing, to be executed and acknowledged as deeds for the conveyance of lands in this state now are or hereafter may be required to be executed and acknowledged, which certificate shall set forth:

Name assumed to designate company. I. The name assumed to designate such company and to be used in its business and dealings;

Place of principal office. II. The place in this state where the principal office of such company is to be located;

Amount of capital stock, &c. III. The total amount of capital stock of such company, which shall not be less than one hundred thousand dollars; the amount with which they shall commence business, which shall not be less than twenty-five thousand

Paid to state treasurer. dollars; the number of shares into which the said capital stock is divided, and the par value of each share, which last mentioned sum shall be paid to the treasurer of the state of New Jersey upon filing said certificate, and withdrawn from the treasury as hereinafter provided;

IV. The names and residences of the stockholders and the number of shares held by each; Names and residences of stockholders.

V. The period at which such corporation shall commence and terminate, which shall not exceed one hundred years; Period of existence.

VI. Such provisions relating to common or preferred stock, or limitations upon the exercise of the powers of the corporation, the directors and stockholders, that the parties signing the same desire; *provided*, such limitation shall not attempt to exempt the corporation, its directors or stockholders from the performance of any duty imposed by law; which certificate, when executed and acknowledged as aforesaid, shall be recorded in the office of the clerk of the county where the principal office of such corporation is to be located, and after being so recorded shall be filed in the office of the secretary of state; the said certificate, or a copy thereof, duly certified by said clerk or secretary, shall be evidence in all courts and places, and upon the execution, acknowledgment, record and the filing thereof, as aforesaid, and the payment of said money to the treasurer of the state as aforesaid, the said persons so associated, their successors and assigns shall be, from the time of the commencent fixed in the said certificate and until the expiration of the time therein expressed, incorporated into a company by the name mentioned in the said certificate; *provided*, that the legislature may at any time dissolve any corporation created by this act, or change, alter, modify, repeal or suspend this act at its discretion. Common or preferred stock. Proviso Proviso

4. *And be it enacted*, That upon filing with the secretary of state of this state any certificate of organization or incorporation of any corporation created under this act there shall be paid by the corporation named in such certificate to the secretary of state for the use of the state the sum of twenty-five dollars for all corporations having an authorized capital not exceeding one hundred thousand dollars, and the sum of one-fifth of one dollar per thousand upon the largest amount of capital authorized by its certificate of organization or incorporation by any such corporation Fees upon filing certificate

having an authorized capital exceeding one hundred thousand dollars.

Limit of time for filing certificates.

5. *And be it enacted*, That if any corporation created under this act shall, in the exercise of powers conferred by this act, enter upon any railway for the purpose of operating the same, it shall within ten days thereafter file in the office of the secretary of state a certificate under its corporate seal, attested by its president or other head officer, setting forth the name of the corporation under which such entry shall have been made, the date of such entry and the period of time during which the possession and operation of such railway is to continue, together with a description and map of the route of the railway so entered upon, and in default of the filing of such certificate, description and map as aforesaid, such corporation shall forfeit and pay to the state of New Jersey the sum of one hundred dollars for each day after the expiration of said ten days during which such default shall continue, which sum may be recovered in an action of debt, prosecuted in the name of the state by the attorney-general in any court of competent jurisdiction, and the judgment recovered therein shall be a first and paramount lien on all property and assets of such corporation.

Penalty for violation.

Upon making extension or new line shall file description and map thereof.

6. *And be it enacted*, That whenever any corporation created under this act desires to extend any existing railway or to build any new line of railway, in the exercise of powers conferred by this act, such corporation shall, before beginning the construction of such extension or new line, file in the office of the secretary of state a description of the route of such extension or new line showing the termini of such extension or new line, together with a map exhibiting the same with the courses and distances thereof, and upon filing such description and map such corporation shall thereby secure the exclusive right to build such extension or new line for a period of six months, and thereafter for the additional period of two years, if within said six months such corporation shall have begun in good faith, to construct such extension or new line, and shall have diligently pursued such construction to the completion of such extension or new line within the period of the two years and six months aforesaid, to be computed from the day of the filing of such descrip-

Time for building same.

tion and map; *provided, however*, that such corporation shall have obtained the consent of the board of alderman, common council, or the body having control of streets and highways other or governing body of any city, town, village, township or county as to the location of the route of such extension or new line. Proviso

7. *And be it enacted*, That the board of alderman, common council, or the body having control of streets or highways, or other governing body of any city, town, borough, village, township or county, upon the petition of the directors of any company incorporated under this act, or a majority thereof, for a location of the tracks of any extension or new line of its railway conformably to the route designated in description of the route of such extension or new line, and the map exhibiting the same filed as aforesaid in the office of the secretary of state shall give notice to all parties interested by publication in one or more newspapers published and circulated in said municipality, or if none be published there, then by posting in five of the most public places in such municipality or township, at least fourteen days before their meeting, of the time and place at which they will consider such application for location, and after hearing they shall either pass a resolution refusing such location or pass a resolution or ordinance, as may be necessary or proper, granting the said location or any part thereof, under such lawful restrictions as they deem the interests of the public may require, and the location thus granted shall be deemed and taken to be the true location of the tracks of the railway, if an acceptance thereof in writing by said directors shall be filed with the secretary of state within thirty days after receiving notice thereof, and a copy thereof delivered to the clerk or other equivalent officer of the municipality or township. Directors to petition board of aldermen, &c., for location of tracks. Notice to be given of time and place of meeting. Pass resolution or ordinance. Acceptance to be filed.

8. *And be it enacted*, That whenever any corporation organized under this act shall fail to acquire from the board of aldermen, the common council, or the body having control of the streets and highways, or other governing body of any city, town, borough, village, township or county within the limits of which it shall seek to construct its road, the right to locate its track or any satisfactory operative portion thereof, it may file Upon failure to acquire right to locate tracks, file an amended description.

with the secretary of state an amended description of the route of such extension or new line, showing the termini of such extention or new line, together with a map exhibiting the same with the courses and distances thereof, and upon filing such amended description and maps such corporation shall thereby secure the exclusive right to build such extension or new line for a period of six months from the day of the filing of such amended description and map; *provided, however*, that such corporation shall have obtained the consent of the board of alderman, common council, or body having control of streets and highways, or other governing body of any city, town, borough, village, township or county, as to location of the route of such amended description of the route of such extension or new line.

Proviso.

Directors to petition board of aldermen, &c., upon filing amended description of route.

9. *And be it enacted*, That the board of alderman, common council, or the body having control of streets, highways or other governing body of any city, town, borough, village, township or county, upon the petition of the directors of any company incorporated under this act, or a majority thereof, for a location of the tracks of any extension or new line of its railway conformably to the route designated in the amended description of the route of such extension or new line, and the map exhibiting the same filed as aforesaid in the office of the secretary of state, shall give notice to all parties interested by publication in one or more newspapers published and circulated in said municipality, or if none be published there, then by posting in five of the most public places in such municipality or township at least fourteen days before the meeting, of the time and place at which they will consider such application for location in accordance with such amended description, and after hearing they shall either pass a resolution refusing such amended location or pass a resolution or ordinance, as may be necessary or proper, granting the said amended location or any part thereof, under such lawful restrictions as they deem the interests of the public may require, and the location thus granted shall be deemed and taken to be the true location of the tracks of the railway if any acceptance thereof in writing by said directors shall be filed with the secretary of state within thirty days after

Notice to be given of time and place of meeting

Pass resolution or ordinance.

Acceptance to be filed

receiving notice thereof and a copy thereof delivered to the clerk or other equivalent officer of the municipality or township.

10. *And be it enacted*, That when the location of the route of the extension of any railway or of any new line shall have been made, under the provisions of this act, it shall and may be lawful for the corporation so locating the same, at any time before such extension or new line shall have been completely constructed, to relocate the same or any part thereof, in accordance with the provisions of this act, applicable to the original location thereof, in the same manner and under the same conditions as though the extension or new line, or the part of such extension or new line to be relocated, had never been located.

When lawful to relocate line

11. *And be it enacted*, That it shall and may be lawful for any corporation created under this act, to use, for the purpose of locating, constructing, maintaining and operating any extension of any railway, or any new line of railway, and for the purpose of erecting, maintaining and using poles, wires, conduits or other devices and appliances for the transmission or application of any motive power, so much of the area of any highway, along which any turnpike or plank road shall be built and in use as shall be necessary for such purposes; *provided*, that the consent of the corporation owning such turnpike or plank road, or if it be an ordinary highway, that of the board of alderman, the common council, or the body having control of streets or highways, or other governing body of any city, town, borough, village, township, or county within the limits of which such highway may be situate, shall have been first had or obtained.

Lawful to use as much of highway as necessary.

Proviso.

12. *And be it enacted*, That the treasurer of state of New Jersey, shall hold the said sum of twenty-five thousand dollars, with which any corporation organized under this act shall commence business, and so paid to said treasurer as hereinbefore provided, subject to be repaid to the directors or treasurer of the said company, when it shall be proven to his satisfaction, that the said corporation has expended an amount equal to or in excess of twenty-five thousand dollars in the accomplishment of

When state treasurer shall repay money.

the aims and purposes named in the certificate of incorporation of such corporation.

When lawful to take more lands.

18. *And be it enacted*, That it shall and may be lawful for any company organized under this act to take so much land or material as may be necessary for the construction of any railway built under the provisions of this act, either as an extension of the line of an existing railway or a new line, not exceeding sixty feet in width, except where a greater amount shall be required for the slopes of cuts and embankments, and such easements in lands lying within or without the limits of any street, road, lane, alley or other highway as may be necessary for the accomplishment of the objects of said company, or such lands or materials as may be required for the purpose of locating and constructing all necessary works, buildings, conveniences, and equipments for the construction and operation of such machinery, engines, boilers or appliances, including the erection of poles for the support of wires and conduits or the making of tunnels or subways for the production or supply of any of the motive power authorized to be used under this act, and for any of the said purposes to enter at all times upon all lands lying within or without the limits of any street, road, lane, alley or other highway for the purpose of exploring and surveying the same and of locating the right of way thereon and the necessary easements, works, buildings, conveniences, equipments and appliances aforesaid or any of them, doing no unnecessary injury to private or other property; and when the location or locations of such right of way, easements, works, conveniences, equipments and appliances shall have been determined upon and a survey of such location or locations deposited in the office of the secretary of state, then it shall be lawful for every corporation formed under this act, upon payment or tender of such compensation as is hereafter provided by its officers, agents, engineers, superintendents, workmen and other persons in their employ, to enter upon, take possession of, hold, have, use and occupy any lands or materials so surveyed, and to do all other things which may be suitable or necessary for use of such land or materials and the enjoyment of said easements or the construction of such right of way, works, buildings, con-

May enter upon lands within or without the limits.

Where survey deposited.

When may enter and take possession of lands.

veniences, equipments and appliances aforesaid, and each and every of them, and for the maintenance, repair or operation thereof, and of every part thereof; *provided, always*, that the payment or tender of the payment of all damages for the occupancy of all lands upon which the said right of way, easements, works, buildings, conveniences, equipments and appliances of such company may be located or the use of materials shall be made before the said company, or any person under their direction or employ shall enter upon or break ground in the premises, except for the purpose of surveying and laying out said works, right of way, easements, buildings, conveniences, equipments and appliances and of locating the same, unless the consent of the owner or owners of such lands be first had and obtained. Proviso.

14. *And be it enacted*, That when any company incorporated under this act, or its agents, cannot agree with the owner or owners of lands or materials required for any of the purposes aforesaid, or for the use or purchase thereof, or when by the legal incapacity or absence of such owner or owners no such agreement can be made, a particular description of the land or materials so required for the use of such company incorporated under this act for any of the purposes aforesaid, shall be given in writing under oath or affirmation of some engineer or proper agent of the company, and also the name or names of the occupant or occupants, if any there be, and of the owner or owners, if known, and their residence, if the same can be ascertained, to one of the justices of the supreme court of this state, who shall cause any company incorporated under this act to give notice thereof to the persons interested, if known and in this state, or if unknown and out of this state to make publication thereof, as he shall direct, for any term not less than ten days, and to assign a particular time and place for the appointment of the commissioners hereinafter named, at which time, upon satisfactory evidence to him of the service or publication of such notice aforesaid, he shall appoint, under his hand and seal, three disinterested, impartial and judicious freeholders, residents in the county in which the land in controversy lies or the owners reside, commissioners to examine and appraise the said land required for any of the puposes afore- When and how commissioners are appointed. Notice to be given.

said or materials and to assess the damages, upon such notice to be given to the persons interested, as shall be directed by the justice making such appointment, to be expressed therein, not less than ten days; and it shall be the duty of said commissioners (having first taken and subscribed an oath or affirmation before some person duly authorized to administer an oath, faithfully and impartially to examine the matter in question and to make a true report according to the best of their skill and understandstanding), to meet at the time and place appointed and to proceed to view and examine the said land or materials, and to make a just and equitable estimate or appraisement of the value of the same, and an assessment of damages to be paid by the company for such lands or materials and damages aforesaid, which report shall be made in writing under the hands and seals of the said commissioners, or any two of them, and filed within ten days thereafter, together with the aforesaid description of the lands or materials and the appointment and oaths or affirmations aforesaid, in the clerk's office of the county in which the land or materials are situate, and after filing said report said commissioners, within not less than fifteen days nor more than thirty days, shall meet at a convenient place in said county to hear and consider objections to said report, and said commissioners shall cause notice of the filing of said report, and of the time and place of said meeting to hear objections to said report, by advertisements under their hands, to be set up in ten public places in said county at least ten days before the time appointed for said meeting, which advertisement shall also be published in at least three newspapers published and circulated in said county at least once a week for two weeks successively; the first publication of said notice shall be made at least ten days before the time appointed for said meeting; and thereupon said commissioners shall have power to alter and amend their report in any respect they may deem necessary, or as equity and justice may require; and after said commissioners shall have filed their certificate that they do not desire to make any alteration or amendment to their said report, the said company shall apply to a justice of the supreme court to appoint a time and place when and where he will sit to hear a motion

Oath to be taken

Report to be filed.

Notice of meeting to consider objections to be given and published.

By whom report of commissioners confirmed.

to confirm the report of said commissioners, and said justice shall order at least ten days' notice to be given to the time and place appointed for the hearing said motion, which notice shall be posted and published in the same manner as hereinbefore directed for the posting and publishing of the notice of the meeting of said commissioners to hear objections to said report; all objections to the confirmation of said report shall be made in writing and filed in the county clerk's office at least two days before the time appointed to hear said motion; and the said justice having heard the parties interested on such report and the objections thereto, may confirm the said report in all things, or refer the same back to said commissioners to be reformed, corrected or amended in such respects as said justice may deem equitable and just, and if the said report of said commissioners be confirmed by said justice, or if, pursuant to the direction of said justice, the same be reformed, corrected or amended as by said commissioners upon filing of said report reformed, corrected or amended as aforesaid, the same shall be taken and considered as confirmed, and remain of record in said clerk's office; and thereupon and on payment or tender of payment of the respective amounts assessed and awarded as herein provided, the said company is hereby empowered to take possession of the lands and easements in said report mentioned required for any of the purposes aforesaid, and to have, hold, use, occupy, possess and enjoy the same for any or all of said purposes; but in case the party or parties entitled to receive any of the respective amounts so awarded shall refuse, upon tender thereof being made, to receive the same, or shall be out of the state, or under any legal disability, or in case there be any doubt as to who is legally entitled to receive any of the respective sums so awarded, then the payment of the respective amounts awarded as aforesaid into the circuit court of the county wherein said report is filed shall be deemed valid and legal payment, and the said report or a copy thereof, certified by the clerk of said county, and proof of the payment or tender of the several amounts so awarded or payment of the same into court as aforesaid, shall at all times be considered as plenary evidence of the

Objections to confirmation of report to be filed.

When report considered as confirmed.

When empowered to take possession of lands, &c.

When amount awarded to be paid into court.

right of such company to have, hold, use, occupy, possess and enjoy the said lands for the purposes aforesaid or any of them; and said justice of the supreme court shall, upon application of any party interested, and on such reasonable notice to the others as he may direct, tax and allow such fees and expenses to the justice of the supreme court, commissioners, clerks, and other persons as he shall think equitable and right, which shall be paid by the company.

By whom fees and expenses are to be taxed.

When not liable to pay amount awarded.

15. *And be it enacted*, That in case said company shall within six months after the confirmation of said report, determine not to proceed with the construction of such railway, or shall decide not to use said lands or any part thereof for any of the purposes aforesaid, and file a notice to that effect in the clerk's office of said county, then, and in that case, said company shall not be liable to pay the money awarded to said owner or owners, but only such costs, expenses and reasonable counsel fees as are hereinbefore provided for in the preceding section of this act.

Authorized to lease property, &c., of other corporations.

16. *And be it enacted*, That any corporation created under this act may lease the property and franchises of any other corporation owning or operating any street railway or other railroad operated as a street railway, or any turnpike or plank road, or any motor power or traction company, and such other corporation and corporations are hereby authorized to make such lease and after such lease the corporation created under this act may use and operate the franchises and property of such corporation or corporations so leased upon such compensation to be made to the lessee company as such respective lessor corporation may have been entitled to demand from persons using or traveling in or upon the property of such lessor corporation; *provided*, that all rights of creditors and all liens upon the property of the corporation lessor, and all privileges and immunities of such lessor corporation shall be preserved unimpaired to the same extent as if such lease had not been made; and all debts, liabilities and duties of such lessor corporation shall thenceforth attach to the lessee corporation, and be enforced against or be enjoyed by it to the same extent and in the same manner as they were enforceable against

Proviso.

or enjoyed by the lessor corporation; *and provided further*, that no greater tolls or charges shall be made or demanded by any corporation created under this act than were or are authorized to be charged and collected for the same service by the corporation or corporations, lessor or lessors in said lease. Proviso.

17. *And be it enacted*, That any stockholder of any company whose property and franchises shall have been leased to a corporation created under this act who shall not assent to lease, or who shall resist or object to the making thereof, may at any time within thirty days after the making of such lease as in this act provided apply by petition to the circuit court of the county in which the chief office of the lessor corporation may be kept or to a judge of said court in vacation, if no such court sits within such period, on reasonable notice to said company, to appoint three disinterested persons to estimate the damage, if any, done to such stockholder by said proposed lease; and whose award, or that of a majority of them, when confirmed by the said court, shall be final and conclusive; and the persons so appointed shall also appraise said stock of such stockholder at the full market value thereof without regard to any depreciation or appreciation in consequence of the said lease; and the lessor company may at its election either pay to the said stockholder the amount of damages so found and awarded, if any, or the value of the stock so ascertained and determined, and upon the payment of the value of the stock as aforesaid the said stockholder shall transfer the stock so held by him to said lessor company to be disposed of by the directors of said company or to be retained for the benefit of the remaining stockholders; and in case the value of said stock as aforesaid is not so paid within thirty days from the filing of the said award and confirmation by said court, and notice to said lessor company, the damages so found and confirmed shall be a judgment against said company, and collected as other judgments in said court are, by law, recoverable.

How and when persons appointed to estimate damages.

Stock to be appraised

When award shall be a judgment.

18. *And be it enacted*, That any corporation created under this act may unite and consolidate its stock, property, franchises and railway with those of any other corporation owning or operating any street railway, or railroad

Authorized to consolidate

operated as a street railway, or any turnpike or plank road, and such consolidated company may continue from time to time to unite and consolidate its stock, property, franchises and railway with those of any other corporation or corporations of this state owning or operating any street railway or railroad operated as a street railway, turnpike or plank road.

Conditions, &c., of consolidation

19. *And be it enacted*, That such consolidation or consolidations shall be made under the conditions, provisions, restrictions and with the powers hereafter in this act mentioned and contained, that is to say:

Directors to enter into joint agreement.

I. The directors of the several corporations proposing to consolidate may enter into a joint agreement under the corporate seal of the respective companies for the consolidation of said companies and railways, and prescribing the terms and conditions thereof, the mode of carrying the same into effect, the name of the new corporation, the number and names of the directors and other officers thereof, and who shall be the first directors and officers, and their places of residence, the amount and number of shares of the capital stock, the par value of each share and the manner of converting the capital stock of each of the said companies into the new corporation, and how and when directors and officers shall be chosen, with such other details as they shall deem necesary to perfect such new organization and the consolidation of said companies and railways;

Agreement to be submitted to stockholders.

Notice to be given.

Vote by ballot.

II. Said agreement shall be submitted to the stockholders of each of the said companies or corporations at a meeting thereof, called separately, for the purpose of taking the same into consideration; due notice of the time and place of holding such meetings, and the object thereof, shall be delivered to such persons respectively, or sent to them by mail, when their postoffice address is known to the company, and also, by a general notice published in some newspaper in the city, town or county where such company has its principal office or place of business; and at said meeting of stockholders the agreement of the said directors shall be considered and a vote, by ballot, taken by each company separately, for the adoption or rejection of the same, each share entitling the holder thereof to one vote; and said ballot shall be cast in person or by proxy, and if two-thirds of all the votes of all the stockholders, voting separately, shall be for adoption of said agreement, then that fact shall be certified thereon by the secretary of the respective companies under the seal thereof and a certificate under the seal of the company signed by the secretary and president certifying to the fact of consolidation, the name to be used by such consolidated company under and by virtue of the provisions of this act, and the amount of the authorized capital stock of such consolidated company shall be filed in the office of the secretary of state, and shall from thence be deemed and taken to be the evidence of the agreement and act of consolidation of the said companies; and a copy of said certificate duly certified by the secretary of state, under the seal of his office, shall be evidence of the existence of said new corporation.

Certificate of result, &c., to be filed.

20. *And be it enacted*, That upon the making and perfecting the agreement and act of consolidation as aforesaid and filing the said certificate or a copy with the secretary of state as aforesaid, the several corporations parties thereto, with the amount of capital stock set out in said certificate, shall be deemed and taken to be one corporation by the name provided in said agreement and act, possessing within this state all rights, privileges and franchises and subject to all the restrictions, disabilities and duties of each of such corporations so consolidated.

When deemed to be one corporation.

21. *And be it enacted*, That upon the consummation of said act of consolidation as aforesaid, all and singular the rights, privileges and franchises of each of said corporations parties to the same, and all property, real, personal and mixed, and all debts due on whatever account, as well as stock subscriptions and other things in action belonging to each of such corporations, shall be taken and deemed to be transferred to and vested in such new corporation without further act or deed; and all property, all rights of way and all and every other interest shall be as effectually the property of the new corporation as they were of the former corporations, parties to said agreement; and the title to real estate, either by deed or otherwise, under the laws of this state vested in either of such corporations shall not be deemed to revert or be in any way impaired by reason of this act; *provided, however*, that

When the rights, privileges, &c., deemed to be transferred.

Proviso.

all rights of creditors and all liens upon the property of either of said corporations shall be preserved unimpaired, and the respective corporations may be deemed to continue in existence to preserve the same; and all debts, liabilities and duties of either of said companies shall thenceforth attach to said new corporation and be enforced against it to the same extent as if said debts, liabilities and duties had been incurred or contracted by it.

How suits may be brought.

22. *And be it enacted*, That suits may be brought and maintained against such company in any of the courts of this state in the same manner as against other railroad companies therein.

Persons to be appointed to estimate damages when stockholder refuses to convert his stock.

23. *And be it enacted*, That any stockholder of any company hereby authorized to consolidate with any other, who shall refuse to convert his stock into the stock of the consolidated company, may at any time within thirty days after the adoption of the said agreement of consolidation by the stockholders, as is in this act provided, apply, by petition, to the circuit court of the county in which the chief office of said company may be kept, or to a judge of said court in vacation, if no such court sits within the said period, on reasonable notice to said company, to appoint three disinterested persons to estimate the damage, if any, done to such stockholder by said proposed consolidation, and whose award, or that of a majority of them, when confirmed by the said court, shall be final and conclusive, and the persons so appointed shall also appraise said stock of such stockholder at the full market value thereof, without regard to any depreciation or appreciation in consequence of the said consolidation, and the said company may, at its election, either pay to the said stockholder the amount of damages so found and awarded, if any, or the value of the stock so ascertained and determined, and upon the payment of the value of the stock as aforesaid, the said stockholder shall transfer the stock so held by him to said company, to be disposed of by the directors of said company, or to be retained for the benefit of the remaining stockholders, and in case the value of said stock as aforesaid is not so paid within thirty days from the filing of the said award and confirmation by said court and notice to said company the damages so found and confirmed shall be a judgment against said

Award final and conclusive when confirmed.

When the award shall be a judgment.

company, and collected as other judgments in said court are, by law, recoverable.

How capital stock may be increased.

24. *And be it enacted*, That the corporation created or consolidated under this act may increase its capital stock to such amount as may be determined by its board of directors; *provided*, that such corporation shall, previous to the issuing of any such stock, file in the office of the secretary of state of this state a certificate, signed by its president and under its corporate seal, attested by its secretary, setting forth the amount of the proposed increase of capital stock and the number of shares into which the same is to be divided, and also the assent in writing of stockholders owning at least two-thirds in value of the existing capital stock to said proposed increase of capital stock.

Proviso.

Authorized to issue bonds, and create a mortgage.

25. *And be it enacted*, That in all cases of consolidation of two or more railway companies under and by virtue of the provisions of this act, the said consolidated company shall have power and authority to issue bonds, registered or with coupons or interest certificates thereto attached, or both, to an amount sufficient to cover all indebtedness of the company so consolidated, and to aid in the completion and equipment of said railway, to secure the payment of which it shall be lawful for them to create a mortgage covering their corporate franchises, rights, privileges, property, assets, real and personal; *provided*, that the bonds shall not bear a greater rate of interest than six per centum per annum; the bonds so issued may be given in lieu, exchange and satisfaction of and for all bonds or other debts against the companies thus consolidated, upon such terms as may be agreed upon by and between the holders of said debts or claims.

Proviso.

Authorized to borrow money, and issue bonds and mortgages.

26. *And be it enacted*, That in all cases of such consolidation under and by virtue of the provisions of this act the said companies shall have the right to borrow from time to time such sum or sums of money as may be necessary for the accomplishment of the objects of such corporation not exceeding at any one time the total amount of the authorized capital stock of such corporation, and for the repayment thereof may issue bonds registered or with coupons or interest certificates thereto attached, or both, secured by a mortgage or mortgages

covering all the corporate franchises, rights, privileges, immunities, assets, real and personal, of such mortgagor corporation.

Authorized to borrow money, and issue bonds and mortgages.

27. *And be it enacted*, That any corporation created under this act may borrow from time to time such sum or sums of money as may be necessary for the accomplishment of the objects of such corporation not exceeding at any one time the total amount of the authorized capital stock of such corporation, or any increase thereof, and to secure the repayment thereof, or of any part or portion thereof, may issue bonds registered or with coupons or interest certificates thereto attached, or both, secured by a mortgage of any or all of its franchises, real estate or personal property, including stocks and securities of such corporation or of any other corporation whose stocks or securities it owns, which mortgage may be recorded as mortgages of real estate are or hereafter may be by law required to be recorded in the office of the clerk or register of deeds of the county or counties in which the railway or railways described in said mortgage may be located, and in the office of the clerk or register of deeds of the county in which the principal office of such corporation is situate, and such record or the lodgment of such mortgage in such clerk's or registers's office for record shall have the same force, operation and effect as to all judgment creditors, purchasers or mortgagees in good faith, as the record of lodgment for that purpose of mortgages of real estate now have, although such mortgage may not have been executed, proved or recorded as a chattel mortgage.

Mortgages to be recorded.

Cannot plead any statute against usury.

28. *And be it enacted*, That no corporation or corporations issuing bonds under the provisions of this act shall plead any statute or statutes against usury in any court of law or equity in any suit instituted to enforce the payment of such bonds or mortgages.

Stock issued upon purchase of real estate, &c.

29. *And be it enacted*, That the directors of any company incorporated under this act may purchase and hold real and personal property necessary and convenient for the business of such company, and also the stocks and securities of other corporations, and issue stock to the amount of the value thereof, in payment therefor, and the stock so issued shall be declared and be taken to be full paid stock, and shall not be liable to any further

call, neither shall the holder thereof be liable for any further payments or assessments upon such stock; and such stocks shall have legibly stamped upon the face thereof, "issued for property purchased," and in all statements and reports of the company to be published, such stock shall not be reported or stated as being issued for cash paid into the company, but shall be reported according to the fact.

How stocks stamped.

30. *And be it enacted*, That whenever any company incorporated under this act, shall have a duty imposed upon it, or a privilege which it is authorized to exercise, and there is a limited time within which such duty is to be discharged or such privilege exercised, and such company may be restrained by the decree, order or writ of any court from the discharge of such duty, or prevented by the ommission of any board of alderman, common council or body having control of streets, or highways or other governing body of any city, town, borough, village, township or county to give any consent required by this act; for the exercise of any privilege conferred by this act, then so much of the time aforesaid during which such restraint exists, or such omission continued, shall not be computed, as any portion of the time limited for the discharge of such duty or the exercise of such privilege.

When limit of time to perform certain duties shall not be computed.

31. *And be it enacted*, That any corporation created under this act, whether by consolidation or otherwise, may change the gauge or width of track of any railway consolidated therewith or leased thereto.

May change gauge or width of track.

32. *And be it enacted*, That any consent required by this act to be given by any public body may be given by a resolution or ordinance of such body, which consent, when accepted by any corporation created under this act in a writing under its corporate seal, filed with the clerk of such body, or in the office of the clerk of the county in which such body exists shall have the force and effect of a contract.

Any consent required given by resolution or ordinance.

33. *And be it enacted*, That all acts and parts of acts inconsistent with this act, to the extent of such inconsistency, be and the same are hereby repealed, and that this act shall take effect immediately.

Repealer

Approved March 14, 1893.

CHAPTER CLXXIII.

An Act to amend an act entitled "A supplement to an act entitled 'An act to regulate elections,'" approved April eighteenth, one thousand eight hundred and seventy-six, respecting election districts, which supplement was approved April twenty-eighth, one thousand eight hundred and eighty-five.

Section to be amended.

1. BE IT ENACTED *by the Senate and General Assembly of the State of New Jersey*, That section one of an act entitled "A supplement to an act entitled 'An act to regulate elections,'" approved April eighteenth, one thousand eight hundred and seventy-six, respecting election districts, which supplement was approved April twenty-eighth, one thousand eight hundred and eighty-five, be amended so as to read as follows:

When and by whom election district shall be divided, &c.

That when, at any township, ward, city, county, state, congressional or national election, more than six hundred votes shall be or shall have been cast in any township or ward in any city not divided into election districts, or when in any election district, in any township or ward in any city more than six hundred votes shall be or shall have been cast at any such election, such township, ward in any city or election district shall forthwith be divided by the mayor and common council or township committee into two or more election districts, or, in lieu thereof, the boundary lines of any existing election district or districts may be changed, or such districts readjusted; *provided, however*, that each of such districts, after such division, change or readjustment, shall not contain more than six hundred, nor less than one hundred and fifty voters; and in such division, change or readjustment, the geographical compactness of such district and the convenience of the voters shall be first considered.

Proviso.

2. *And be it enacted,* That all acts or parts of acts, inconsistent herewith, are hereby repealed, and that this act shall take effect immediately. Repealer

Approved March 14, 1893.

CHAPTER CLXXIV.

A Supplement to an act entitled an "Act to fix the minimum of salary of the prosecutors of the pleas in the counties of the third class in this state," approved April twentieth, one thousand eight hundred and eighty-five.

1. Be it enacted *by the Senate and General Assembly of the State of New Jersey,* That in all counties of the third class in this state in which the prosecuters of the pleas now receive an annual salary, each of the prosecutors of the pleas of such counties shall receive an annual salary of at least twelve hundred dollars, to be paid to him in quarterly annual payments by the county collector of such county. Salary of prosecutors, $1,200

2. *And be it enacted,* That this act shall only apply to those prosecutors of the pleas whose term of office shall hereafter commence, or to those now in office whose term does not expire during the present year, who may file their assent in writing under their hands to the provisions of this act in the office of the clerk of the county of which he is prosecutor; *provided, however,* that nothing in this act contained shall in any ways be considered or held as reducing the salary of any of the prosecutors of the pleas in any of the counties of the third class of this state. Assent to be filed. Proviso.

3. *And be it enacted,* That all acts and parts of acts inconsistent with the provisions of this act be and the same are hereby repealed, and that this act shall be a public act and take effect immediately. Repealer

Approved March 14, 1893.

CHAPTER CLXXV.

A Further Supplement to "An act for the punishment of crimes" (Revision), approved March twenty-seventh, one thousand eight hundred and seventy-four.

When unlawful to permit racing, &c., of horses, &c.

1. BE IT ENACTED *by the Senate and General Assembly of the State of New Jersey*, That it shall be unlawful to permit the racing, running, trotting or pacing of horses, mares or geldings on any race track in this state for a purse, prize or other consideration or for any other purpose whatsoever between the first day of December in any year and the first day of March of the succeeding year.

Upon violation, guilty of misdemeanor.

2. *And be it enacted*, That any person or persons or corporation or corporations violating the provisions of this act, or aiding, abetting or assisting in the violation of the provisions of this act shall be deemed guilty of a misdemeanor, and on conviction thereof shall be punished by a fine of not less than one thousand dollars nor more than ten thousand dollars or by imprisonment for not less than six months nor more than two years, or both, in the discretion of the court.

Penalty.

How and when to apply to the governor.

3. *And be it enacted*, That when it shall come to the knowledge of the governor of this state that any person or persons or corporation or corporations is or are violating the provisions of this act or when an application shall be made to him signed by one hundred or more of the residents of any county in this state setting forth that the provisions of this act are being violated in such county, it shall be the duty of the governor forthwith to order the chief of the state police to enforce the provisions of this act in such county and to place under arrest all persons found violating the same or aiding or abetting in the violation thereof and the governor shall designate to assist the said chief of the state police in the performance of his duties under this act, such portion of the police force of any city or municipality of this state as the governor

When state police ordered by governor to act.

shall deem necessary to effectively carry out its provisions.

4. *And be it enacted*, That it shall be the duty of the chief of the state police when discharging the duties imposed upon him under the third section of this act to maintain a sufficient portion of the police officers that have been designated to assist him in his duties at every such race track to prevent a violation of the provisions of this act. Duty of chief of police.

5. *And be it enacted*, That in case the police force so designated is unable to prevent the violation of the provisions of this act it shall be the duty of the governor to call upon the state militia to aid in enforcing the provisions thereof upon any race track or race tracks whereon they are being violated. When and by whom state militia called.

6. *And be it enacted*, That all acts and parts of acts inconsistent with the provisions of this act be and the same are hereby repealed, and that this act shall take effect immediately. Repealer.

Approved March 14, 1898.

CHAPTER CLXXVI.

An Act to amend an act entitled "An act to establish a system of public instruction" (Revision), approved March twenty-seventh, one thousand eight hundred and seventy-four.

1. BE IT ENACTED *by the Senate and General Assembly of the State of New Jersey*, That section forty-nine of an act entitled "An Act to establish a system of public instruction" (Revision), approved March twenty-seventh, one thousand eight hundred and seventy-four, be and the same is hereby amended so as to read as follows: Section to be amended.

49. *And be it enacted*, That there shall be in each county a county board of examiners, which shall be composed of

Constitution and duties of county board of examiners.

the county superintendent, who shall, ex-officio, be chairman, and of a number of teachers, not to exceed three, to be appointed by him, who shall hold office for one year from the time of their respective appointments; but no person shall be appointed as a county examiner unless he holds either a state or a first grade county certificate; the county superintendent shall fill vacancies that occur from absence or other cause, but if he cannot find any teacher in his county qualified under the provisions of this section willing to serve, he shall conduct the examination himself; the board shall meet at such places as may be designated by the chairman, and shall hold at least three regular sessions each year; each member of the county board of examiners, except the county superintendent, shall receive for his services, in addition to traveling expenses, such compensation as may be fixed by the state board of education, not exceeding ten dollars for each regular examination, to be paid by the county collector on the order of the county superintendent; *provided*, that whenever said board shall hold sessions at any other time than as appointed by the state board of education, no compensation shall be allowed from the county; but in case of special examinations said board may charge each applicant an examination fee not exceeding two dollars; the county board of examiners shall have power to conduct examinations and to grant certificates of different grades, in accordance with the general regulations on the subject prescribed by the state board of education.

Compensation of board.

Proviso.

Section to be amended.

2. *And be it enacted*, That section sixty-four of said act shall be amended to read as follows:

School year.

64. *And be it enacted*, That the school year shall begin on the first day of July, and end on the last day of June.

3. *And be it enacted*, That this act shall take effect immediately.

Approved March 15, 1893.

CHAPTER CLXXVII.

An Act to amend an act entitled "An act for the instruction and maintenance of indigent deaf and dumb, blind and feeble-minded persons, inhabitants of this state" (Revision), approved March twelfth, one thousand eight hundred and seventy-three.

WHEREAS, The act to which this is an amendment does not confer upon the governor any power to send to the institutions therein named, worthy blind persons who shall lose their sight at an adult age, and thus enable them to learn a trade by which they may earn a livelihood; therefore, Preamble

1. BE IT ENACTED *by the Senate and General Assembly of the State of New Jersey*, That section eight of an act entitled "An act for the instruction and maintenance of indigent deaf and dumb, blind and feeble-minded persons, inhabitants of this state" (Revision), approved March twelfth, one thousand eight hundred and seventy-three, which section reads as follows:

"8. *And be it enacted*, That any person not under five years nor more than twenty-one years of age may be entitled to the benefits of this act," Section to be amended.

be and the same is hereby amended so as to read as follows:

8. *And be it enacted*, That any deaf and dumb, blind or feeble-minded person not under five years of age, of a suitable age and capacity for instruction, may be entitled to the benefits of this act. Who entitled to benefit of act.

2. *And be it enacted*, That this act shall take effect immediately.

Approved March 15, 1898.

CHAPTER CLXXVIII.

An Act providing for the licensing of dogs.

License fee provided for by resolution.

1. BE IT ENACTED *by the Senate and General Assembly of the State of New Jersey*, That it shall and may be lawful for the board of aldermen, common council, township committee, or other governing body of any city, town, borough, township and other municipality of this state, on or before the first day of May in each and every year, to provide by resolution the amount of a license fee for the ensuing year to be paid by the owner of every dog within such city, town, borough or other municipality; and the harboring of a dog or dogs shall be evidence of ownership for the purposes of such license.

boring evidence of ownership.

How license fees assessed and collected.

2. *And be it enacted*, That the amount of such license fee, when so fixed, shall be assessed and collected at the same time and in the same manner that other taxes are assessed and collected; and the assessment for such license fees shall be in addition to the amount which such common council, township committee, or other governing body are or may be authorized to raise by taxation for other purposes.

How license fees appropriated.

3. *And be it enacted*, That the amount of such license fees, when collected, shall be appropriated and applied by the board of aldermen, common council, township committee, or other governing body of the municipality wherein the same shall be collected, towards the payment of the general expenses of such municipality.

What constitutes district municipality.

4. *And be it enacted*, That for the purposes of this act any portion of any township incorporated as a city, town, borough or village be considered as a distinct municipality from the rest of such township.

Repealer, &c

5. *And be it enacted*, That all acts and parts of acts inconsistent with the provisions of this act be and the same are hereby repealed; and that this act shall not be construed to limit, or in any manner abridge any other or greater power that may be possessed by the governing

body of any city, town, borough, township, or other municipality of this state, respecting the licensing of dogs.

6. *And be it enacted*, That this act shall take effect immediately.

Approved March 15, 1893.

CHAPTER CLXXIX.

A Supplement to an act entitled "An act to establish a state industrial school for girls," approved April fourth, one thousand eight hundred and seventy-one.

1. BE IT ENACTED *by the Senate and General Assembly of the State of New Jersey*, That from and after the passage of this act the sheriff, constable or other officer executing the order or warrant of the court committing a girl to the state industrial school, shall be entitled to the fees for transportation and no others as are now allowed the several sheriff's and their deputies for the transportation of prisoners to the state prison. Fees allowed.

2. *And be it enacted*, That this act shall be deemed a public act and shall take effect immediately.

Approved March 15, 1893.

CHAPTER CLXXX.

A Further Supplement to an act entitled "An act to provide for the more permanent improvement of the public roads of this state," approved April fourteenth, one thousand eight hundred and ninty-one.

When contract not invalidated.

1. Be it enacted *by the Senate and General Assembly of the State of New Jersey*, That no contract heretofore made and awarded by the board of chosen freeholders of any county in this state under the provisions of an act entitled "An act to provide for the more permanent improvement of the public roads of this state," approved April fourteenth, one thousand eight hundred and ninety-one, and the supplement thereto, shall be invalidated by reason of the omission to publish the advertisement for bids in two daily newspapers printed and circulated in the county for the period of two weeks provided for in the act to which this is a supplement, or any other act supplementary thereto; *provided*, that all other provisions of said act shall have been complied with.

Proviso

2. *And be it enacted*, That this act shall take effect immediately.

Approved March 15, 1898.

CHAPTER CLXXXI.

An Act concerning cities.

1. Be it enacted *by the Senate and General Assembly of the State of New Jersey*, That whenever objections or remonstrances in writing to the paving of any public

street or alley shall be received in answer to the public notice of intention of the common council, board of aldermen or other governing body of any city to cause any public street or alley, or section of such street or alley, to be paved pursuant to the determination of said common council or other governing body, and such objections are from the owners of one-half in running feet of lots fronting or bordering upon said street or alley, or section of a street or alley, the common council or other governing body of any such city may, notwithstanding any such objections, proceed to adopt an ordinance for the paving of said public street or alley, or section of such street or alley, and to award contracts for the doing of said work; *provided, however*, that any such ordinance for the paving of any such public street or alley shall require for its final passage a vote of not less than four-fifths of the whole number of such common council or other governing body. Common council, &c., authorized to adopt ordinance for paving street, &c., notwithstanding objections thereto. Proviso.

2. *And be it enacted*, That all acts or parts of acts inconsistent herewith be and the same are hereby repealed, and that this act shall take effect immediately. Repealer

Approved March 15, 1898.

CHAPTER CLXXXII.

An Act to repeal an act entitled "A supplement to an act entitled 'An act for the preservation of clams and oysters,'" approved March tenth, anno domini one thousand eight hundred and eighty.

1. Be it enacted *by the Senate and General Assembly of the State of New Jersey*, That the act entitled "A supplement to an act entitled 'An act for the preservation of clams and oysters,'" approved March tenth, anno domini one thousand eight hundred and eighty, be and the same is hereby repealed. Repealer.

2. *And be it enacted*, That this act shall take effect immediately.

Approved March 15, 1893.

CHAPTER CLXXXIII.

A Supplement to an act entitled "An act to establish a system of public instruction" (Revision), approved March twenty-seventh, one thousand eight hundred and seventy-four.

School trustees, board of education, &c., authorized to borrow money.

1. BE IT ENACTED *by the Senate and General Assembly of the State of New Jersey*, That the board of education, board of school trustees or other body having charge and control of the public schools in any school district in this state acting under a special charter or under the provisions contained in the charter of any city, town, borough, or other municipality may after the first day of September and before the thirty-first day of December in any year, borrow a sum of money not exceeding four-tenths of the amount apportioned to such district from the state school moneys for such year for the purpose of paying teachers' salaries falling due within said year; and that the said district may pay the amount so borrowed, together with interest thereon at a rate not exceeding six per centum per annum, out of the state school moneys apportioned to said district for the then current school year as soon as the same have been received by the city treasurer or other person designated by law as the custodian of the school moneys belonging to such district.

Repealer

2. *And be it enacted*, That all acts and parts of acts inconsistent with the provisions of this act be and the same are hereby repealed, and that this act shall take effect immediately.

Approved March 15, 1893.

CHAPTER CLXXXIV.

An Act relative to the salaries of mayors of certain cities.

1. BE IT ENACTED *by the Senate and General Assembly of the State of New Jersey,* That the annual salary of any mayor of any city having a population of from seventy-five thousand to one hundred thousand inhabitants shall be and the same is hereby fixed and determined at the sum of two thousand dollars; *provided, however,* that this act shall not apply to any such city wherein such officer now receives a greater sum.

Salary

Proviso

2. *And be it enacted,* That this act shall take effect immediately.

Approved March 15, 1893.

CHAPTER CLXXXV.

An Act concerning streets and avenues in towns and townships in this state.

1. BE IT ENACTED *by the Senate and General Assembly of the State of New Jersey,* That in any case where any person or corporation owns a tract of land bounded on three of its four sides by streets or avenues already opened along the full length of such three sides, in any town or township of this state, and occupies and uses such tract of land and the buildings thereon erected for charitable, educational or religious purposes; and where such town or township has taken proceedings to open a street or avenue through such tract of land, and has also taken proceedings to widen one of such three streets or avenues bounding three of the sides of such tract by taking the land

When town council, township committee, &c., authorized to accept land donated for streets, &c., and enter into contract

from such tract along its full length for such widening; and where it is desired by any such person or corporation, except as to the land to be taken for such opening and for such widening, to preserve such tract entire for any of the purposes aforesaid; and where such person or corporation in consideration of no other street or avenue being hereafter opened or extended through any part of such tract shall offer to donate and dedicate to such town or township the land necessary for such street or avenue to be opened through such tract, and also for the widening of such street or avenue along such tract, in such case it shall be lawful for such town or township, through its town council or township committee or other governing body, and such council, committee or body is hereby empowered and authorized to by resolution accept such offer upon such condition and to enter into and execute a contract with such person or corporation, in consideration of such donation and dedication, not to open or extend through such tract or any part thereof, any street or avenue other than such street or avenue for the opening of which and such street or avenue for the widening of which the land shall be donated and dedicated as aforesaid.

Deed to be filed. 2. *And be it enacted*, That when a deed of donation or dedication as aforesaid has been executed and acknowledged by such person or corporation and filed with the clerk of such town or township, which deed it shall be the duty of said clerk to file when presented to him for filing, and shall be accepted by such council or committee by resolution, then it shall not be lawful at any time thereafter unless with the consent of the owner of such tract to open or extend through any part of such tract any street or avenue other than that for the opening of which and that for the widening of which the land shall be donated or dedicated as aforesaid.

When unlawful to open or extend street.

Repealer. 3. *And be it enacted*, That all parts of all acts inconsistent with this act be and the same are hereby repealed, and this act shall take effect immediately.

Approved March 15, 1893.

CHAPTER CLXXXVI.

An Act providing for the payment of claims incurred in repairing public buildings in any city.

1. BE IT ENACTED *by the Senate and General Assembly of the State of New Jersey*, That in any city in this state where the board having charge and control of repairing public buildings shall have heretofore made any necessary or required repairs to any public building or buildings in excess of any appropriation or provision made or transferred to any such board for such purpose, then in such case, and upon the board of such city having charge and control of the finances therein being satisfied that such repairs have been made, said financial board shall make a sufficient appropriation for that purpose to said board having charge and control of such repairs, and the claims for the same shall thereupon be paid; that said financial board shall have power to borrow such additional appropriation by the issue of temporary loan bonds and to provide for the re-payment thereof in the tax levy next thereafter to be made; *provided*, that such additional appropriation shall not exceed the sum of thirty-three hundred dollars.

When finance board shall make appropriation.

Authorized to issue loan bonds

Proviso.

2. *And be it enacted*, That this act shall take effect immediately.

Approved March 15, 1898.

CHAPTER CLXXXVII.

An Act to amend an act entitled "A further supplement to an act entitled 'An act concerning roads,' approved March twenty-seventh, one thousand eight hundred and seventy-four" (Revision), which supplemental act was approved March twenty-eighth, one thousand eight hundred and ninety-two.

Section to be amended.

1. BE IT ENACTED *by the Senate and General Assembly of the State of New Jersey*, That section two of said supplemental act be and the same is hereby amended so that henceforth said section shall be and read as follows, to wit:

Other portion of road.

2. *And be it enacted*, That the portion of said road other than that which shall be used by reason of any alteration or change which shall be made respecting the original course of the said road, or portion thereof, shall, irrespective of use, be declared finally vacated, without the notice and application and any other proceedings specified in the act to which this is a supplement, or any act supplementary thereto, and not subject to an appeal or certiorari after two days from the date and time of the filing of the map as aforesaid.

Section to be amended.

2. *And be it enacted*, That section four of said supplemental act be and the same is hereby amended so that henceforth said section four shall be and read as follows, to wit:

4. *And be it enacted*, That this act shall be deemed a public act and shall take effect immediately.

3. *And be it enacted*, That this act shall take effect immediately.

Approved March 16, 1893.

CHAPTER CLXXXVIII.

An Act authorizing cities to renew maturing bonds.

1. Be it enacted *by the Senate and General Assembly of the State of New Jersey*, That whenever any bonds heretofore legally issued by any incorporated city in this state under authority of law shall at any time or times hereafter become due, the board of aldermen, common council or other board having charge and control of the finances of such city, with the approval of the mayor of such city, may renew said indebtedness or any part thereof by the issuing of the bonds of said city for that purpose; *provided, however*, that no such bonds shall be renewed in cases where there are moneys or securities in any sinking fund of such city specifically appropriated for the redemption of said maturing bonds until after the moneys and securities of said sinking fund so specifically appropriated shall have been exhausted in the payment of maturing bonds.

Authorized to issue bonds to renew indebtedness.

Proviso.

2. *And be it enacted*, That the bonds to be issued under the provisions of this act shall be exempt from taxation, and made payable at periods not exceeding thirty years from the date of issuing the same, and shall draw such rate of interest not exceeding five per centum per annum, and be in such sums as the board having charge and control of the finances of said city shall determine, which bonds shall be executed under the corporate seal of said city, and the signature of the mayor, comptroller or other proper financial officer thereto, and may be either registered or coupon bonds, as said board may direct; *provided*, that in order to redeem the bonds issued under the provisions of this act at maturity, it shall be the duty of the board having charge and control of the finances of such city to establish a sinking fund, which shall be created by a special tax of not less than two per centum on the issues herein provided for, to be raised in each annual tax levy, or from the collection of water rents in cases where the bonds hereby authorized

Exempt from taxation

Interest.

Proviso.

to be re-issued were originally issued for the water department of such city.

Interest to be collected by special tax annually.

3. *And be it enacted*, That the interest on the bonds hereby authorized to be issued from time to time shall be raised and paid by a special tax or appropriation, to be annually levied and collected as other taxes in such city are now or may hereafter be levied and collected, and the whole of each year's interest shall be so raised, levied, collected and paid within each year; *provided*, that the interest on all bonds re-issued in place of maturing water bonds shall be paid out of the collections for water rents in such city for said year.

Proviso.

Sold at public or private sale.

4. *And be it enacted*, That the board or authority having charge and control of the finances of such city may dispose of the bonds hereby authorized at a public sale or private sale in case a more favorable bid can be obtained than shall have been bid publicly therefor, but in no case for less than par, which issues and sales may be made in anticipation of the retirement of said maturing bonds, and all of the moneys received from the sale of said bonds shall be applied and used for the purposes of this act, and for no other purpose; *provided*, that no increase in the bonded indebtedness of any such city shall be made under this act.

Not less than par value.

How applied.

Proviso.

5. *And be it enacted*, That this act shall take effect immediately.

Approved March 16, 1893.

CHAPTER CLXXXIX.

A Supplement to an act entitled "An act to incorporate societies for the promotion of learning" (Revision), approved April ninth, one thousand eight hundred and seventy-five.

1. BE IT ENACTED *by the Senate and General Assembly of the State of New Jersey*, That the trustees of any semi-

nary, college, school or other institution now or hereafter organized under the act to which this is the supplement, or any other act now in force in this state, may purchase, take, hold, receive and enjoy all lands, tenements and hereditaments, in fee simple or otherwise, and also all goods, chattels, legacies and donations, in money or otherwise, of what kind or nature soever, that may be granted and conveyed or given and devised to the seminary or other institution of which they shall be trustees as aforesaid, by the grant, gift, alienation or devise of any person or persons able to grant, give or devise the same for the support, endowment or otherwise, of said seminary or school, whether in general or for particular chairs or departments thereof, or for special objects or subjects taught therein; and also that the said trustees and their successors shall and may grant, assign and sell, or otherwise dispose of all or any of their said lands, tenements or hereditaments, goods, chattels and personal estate whatsoever, received and held by them as aforesaid, as to them shall seem meet for the best interests of their said seminary or other institution, unless otherwise provided and limited by the deeds, wills, or other instruments in writing by which they received and hold the same; *provided, nevertheless*, that the proceeds of the sale or other disposition of any real or personal estate so received and held by such trustees for said endowment objects or purposes shall be duly re-invested in other good real or personal estate, as soon thereafter as practicable, and the annual income therefrom only used for such endowment and educational purposes.

Trustees authorized to purchase, &c., lands, also receive goods, &c., granted, devised, &c.

Trustees authorized to dispose of lands, goods, &c., unless otherwise provided, &c.

Proviso.

2. *And be it enacted*, That this act shall take effect immediately.

Approved March 16, 1893.

CHAPTER CXC.

A Further Supplement to an act entitled "An act for the preservation of clams and oysters," approved April fourteenth, one thousand eight hundred and forty-six, and of the supplements thereto.

When and where unlawful to dredge.

1. Be it enacted *by the Senate and General Assembly of the State of New Jersey*, That from and after the passage of this act it shall be unlawful to dredge for oysters in any of the creeks on the east side of Delaware river, of Delaware bay and Maurice river cove south of Cohansey creek at any time, and in Cohansey creek and in all creeks north of said Cohansey creek, in Delaware river and Delaware bay it shall be unlawful to dredge for oysters except during the time from the first day of April to the fifteenth day of June, both days inclusive, and any person offending against the provisions of this act shall be deemed guilty of a misdemeanor and on conviction thereof shall be punished by a fine not exceeding two hundred dollars or by imprisonment at hard labor for a period not exceeding one year, or both, at the discretion of the court, and any boat or vessel employed in the commission of any offense against the provisions of this act, with all her tackle, apparel and furniture shall be forfeited and the same seized, secured and disposed of in the manner prescribed in the eighth, ninth and tenth sections of the act entitled "An act for the preservation of clams and oysters," approved April fourteenth, one thousand eight hundred and forty-six.

Offenders guilty of misdemeanor.

Penalty, &c

Repealer.

2. *And be it enacted*, That all acts and parts of acts inconsistent herewith be and the same are hereby repealed, and that this act shall be deemed a public act and take effect immediately.

Approved March 16, 1898.

CHAPTER CXCI.

A Further Supplement to an act entitled "An act to provide for a commission to revise and consolidate the general statutes of this state relating to villages, towns and townships," approved March ninth, one thousand eight hundred and ninety-one.

WHEREAS, The commissioners appointed under the provisions of the act to which this is a further supplement, after giving their entire time and individual attention and study to the prosecution of the work in said act directed, a partial report of which has been made to the legislature at this session, find the time limited by said act and the supplement thereto approved March twenty-second, one thousand eight hundred and ninety-two, inadequate to complete the work assigned to them in a substantial and thorough manner; therefore, Preamble.

1. BE IT ENACTED *by the Senate and General Assembly of the State of New Jersey*, That the said commission be and is hereby continued with the same duties and powers imposed and conferred upon the members thereof by the act to which this is a further supplement, and that the said commissioners shall lay before the next legislature a complete report of the work of said commission. Commission continued, and to report.

2. *And be it enacted*, That the commissioners appointed under the provisions of said act shall receive such compensation on account of the work heretofore done by them, and for which they have not heretofore been compensated, as the governor, comptroller and treasurer shall deem just and proper, together with such necessary expenses as they may have incurred in carrying out the provisions of the act to which this is a further supplement, which shall be paid by the treasurer on the warrant of the comptroller. Compensation

3. *And be it enacted*, That in the further pursuance of their work, they shall receive from time to time their necessary Further compensation, by whom paid.

expenses incurred in carrying out the provisions of this act, and at the completion of the same shall receive such further compensation as the governor, comptroller and treasurer shall deem just and proper, which said expenses and further compensation shall be paid by the treasurer on the warrant of the comptroller.

4. *And be it enacted*, That this act shall take effect immediately.

Approved March 16, 1893.

CHAPTER CXCII.

An Act to authorize and regulate the construction of street railways upon turnpikes.

Authorized to construct street railways in counties of second class.

1. Be it enacted *by the Senate and General Assembly of the State of New Jersey*, That any duly incorporated street railway company of this state may construct and operate a street railway upon and along the roadbed of any turnpike company located within counties of the second class in this state, which shall have granted or conveyed such right or privilege to such street railway company.

Board of commissioners, &c., by resolution or ordinance locate track.

2. *And be it enacted*, That the board of commissioners, common council, township committee or other governing body or bodies of any city, incorporated town, borough or township within or through the limits whereof such turnpike shall lie or extend shall, upon the petition of such street railway company and proof of the granting of such permission or right of way by the turnpike company, by resolution or ordinance locate the track or tracks of such street railway company upon the roadbed of such turnpike company; *provided*, such governing body may require the surrender by said turnpike company of its toll and other turnpike franchises as a condition upon which such location shall be made.

Proviso.

3. *And be it enacted*, That in case said turnpike lies within the boundaries of any incorporated city, town,

borough or borough commission in whole or in part, it shall be necessary for such company to be first authorized by ordinance or resolution of the governing body of such city, town, borough or borough commission before the construction of such street railroad within the corporate limits of such city, town, borough or borough commission. When necessary to be authorized by ordinance or resolution of governing body.

4. *And be it enacted*, That after such location shall have been made as herein provided, such street railway company shall in other respects conform to the law concerning horse and street railways. Must conform to the law.

5. *And be it enacted*, That all acts or parts of acts inconsistent herewith be and the same are hereby repealed, and that this act shall take effect immediately. Repealer.

Approved March 16, 1898.

CHAPTER CXCIII.

A Further Supplement to an act entitled "An act for the better enforcement in Maurice river cove and Delaware bay of an act entitled 'An act for the preservation of clams and oysters,'" approved April fourteenth, one thousand eight hundred and forty-six, and of the supplements thereto.

1. BE IT ENACTED *by the Senate and General Assembly of the State of New Jersey*, That the first section of the supplement to said act, approved April sixteenth, one thousand eight hundred and ninety-one, be and is hereby amended so as to read as follows: Section to be amended.

1. BE IT ENACTED *by the Senate and General Assembly of the State of New Jersey*, That hereafter it shall be unlawful to take oysters by dredging from the natural oyster beds in Maurice river cove and Delaware bay, known severally as the East Points beds, the Pepper beds, the Ballast beds, the beds at the mouth of Dividing creek and Oranoke Unlawful to dredge.

creek, and in the creeks where there is a natural growth of oysters, and the beds that fall bare, for any purpose whatever, and any person offending against the provisions of this act shall be deemed guilty of a misdemeanor, and on conviction thereof shall for every such offense be punished by a fine not exceeding one hundred dollars and by imprisonment at hard labor for a period not exceeding one year, or both, at the discretion of the court.

Guilty of misdemeanor.

Penalty.

Repealer.

2. *And be it enacted*, That all acts and parts of acts inconsistent herewith be and the same are hereby repealed, and that this act shall take effect immediately.

Approved March 16, 1893.

CHAPTER CXCIV.

An Act relating to sales of lands for taxes or assessments.

By whom, when tax deed is annulled or set aside, money shall be refunded.

1. Be it enacted *by the Senate and General Assembly of the State of New Jersey*, That whenever any tax deed heretofore or hereafter given by any city, town or township or by the public body or public officer authorized by law to make conveyance of lands sold for taxes shall be annulled or set aside on account of any defect in the levying of the tax for which said property is sold, or in the proceedings for the collection of said tax or the sale of said lands, or for any defect in the giving of notice to redeem, where such defect results from the fault or omission of said city, town or township or of any of its officers or representatives, it shall be the duty of such city, town or township to refund to the person or persons who shall have purchased said land at said tax sale, or who shall have purchased the right of said city, town or township to said lands under such tax sale, his or their heirs or assigns, any and all sums of money received by said city, town or township as consideration of said tax deed, and for other taxes upon said lands in arrears when said pur-

chase was made or deed taken, together with interest thereon from the date of such payment by the grantee in said deed named.

When money has been refunded all taxes are re-established as a lien upon said lands.

2. *And be it enacted*, That whenever any tax deed or sale of lands for taxes or assessments shall be set aside for any omission, fault or defect in the proceedings for such sale or in the giving of notice to redeem or otherwise, and the said city, town or township shall have refunded to the purchaser of said tax title the amount so paid the said tax or assessment shall not thereby become discharged as against the lands originally lawfully chargeable therewith, but the said tax or assessment and all other taxes thereon paid contemporaneously therewith shall thereupon be re-established as a lien or incumbrance upon said lands to the same extent and with the same force and effect as said lien existed before proceedings for sale of lands for such taxes or assessments were taken; and such city, town or township may re-advertise said lands for sale and sell the same in the same manner and execute certificate of sale and deed for the same in the same manner and with the same force and effect as if such defective sale or proceedings had not been taken.

Lands re-advertised for sale.

3. *And be it enacted*, That this act take effect immediately.

Approved March 16, 1898.

CHAPTER CXCV.

An Act to amend an act entitled "An act to amend an act entitled 'A supplement to an act entitled "An act for the support of the New Jersey state reform school for boys,"'" approved March thirty-first, eighteen hundred and eighty-two, which last amending act was approved March thirty-first, eighteen hundred and eighty-five.

Section to be amended.

1. Be it enacted *by the Senate and General Assembly of the State of New Jersey*, That section one of the act of which this is amendatory, which said act was approved March thirty-first, eighteen hundred and eighty-five, be and the same is hereby amended so as to read as follows:

To whom trustees submit quarterly report.

1. Be it enacted *by the Senate and General Assembly of the State of New Jersey*, That it shall be the duty of the trustees of the New Jersey state reform school to make and submit a report to the governor of the state at the expiration of every three months, dating from January first, anno domini one thousand eight hundred and ninety-three, showing the average number of boys maintained in the school during such period, which said report shall be duly certified by the president and attested by the secretary of the board; and in order to support the said school the treasurer of this state shall pay out of any moneys in the treasury not otherwise appropriated, to the treasurer of the New Jersey state reform school, such a sum as shall be considered necessary by the trustees and approved by the governor of this state for the maintenance of said school for the succeeding three months, such sum not to exceed the maximum sum of forty dollars for each boy maintained in said school, which said sum shall be based on the average number of inmates for the last preceding quarter, such sum to be paid upon a warrant of the comptroller.

State treasurer to pay money necessary to maintain school.

Maximum sum to be paid.

2. *And be it enacted*, That all acts or parts of acts inconsistent with this act be and the same are hereby repealed. Repealer

3. *And be it enacted*, That this act shall take effect immediately.

Approved March 16, 1898.

CHAPTER CXCVI.

An Act to fix the minimum salary of the prosecutor of the pleas in counties of the fourth class in this state.

1. BE IT ENACTED *by the Senate and General Assembly of the State of New Jersey*, That in all counties of the fourth class, the prosecutors of the pleas shall receive an annual salary in lieu of all fees and costs now received by them; and all such fees and costs shall be taxed in all bills of costs the same as now taxed, and shall be collected by the sheriffs of the several counties and be by them paid over to the county collectors for the use of the said counties. Shall receive salary in lieu of fees, &c.

2. *And be it enacted*, That each of the prosecutors of the pleas of such counties shall receive an annual salary of four hundred dollars, to be paid to him in quarterly annual payments by the county collector of such county. Salary, how and by whom paid.

3. *And be it enacted*, That this act shall only apply to those prosecutors of the pleas whose term of office shall hereafter commence, or to those now in office who may file their assent in writing, under their hands, to the provisions of this act, in the office of the clerk of the county of which he is such prosecutor; *provided, however*, that nothing in this act contained shall in anywise be construed or held as reducing the salary of any of the prosecutors of the pleas in any of the counties of the fourth class in this state. Shall file assent. Proviso

4. *And be it enacted*, That this act shall be a public act, and take effect immediately.

Approved March 16, 1898.

to be re-issued were originally issued for the water department of such city.

Interest to be collected by special tax annually.

3. *And be it enacted*, That the interest on the bonds hereby authorized to be issued from time to time shall be raised and paid by a special tax or appropriation, to be annually levied and collected as other taxes in such city are now or may hereafter be levied and collected, and the whole of each year's interest shall be so raised, levied, collected and paid within each year; *provided*, that the interest on all bonds re-issued in place of maturing water bonds shall be paid out of the collections for water rents in such city for said year.

Proviso.

Sold at public or private sale.

4. *And be it enacted*, That the board or authority having charge and control of the finances of such city may dispose of the bonds hereby authorized at a public sale or private sale in case a more favorable bid can be obtained than shall have been bid publicly therefor, but in no case for less than par, which issues and sales may be made in anticipation of the retirement of said maturing bonds, and all of the moneys received from the sale of said bonds shall be applied and used for the purposes of this act, and for no other purpose; *provided*, that no increase in the bonded indebtedness of any such city shall be made under this act.

Not less than par value.

How applied.

Proviso.

5. *And be it enacted*, That this act shall take effect immediately.

Approved March 16, 1898.

CHAPTER CLXXXIX.

A Supplement to an act entitled "An act to incorporate societies for the promotion of learning" (Revision), approved April ninth, one thousand eight hundred and seventy-five.

1. Be it enacted *by the Senate and General Assembly of the State of New Jersey*, That the trustees of any semi-

nary, college, school or other institution now or hereafter organized under the act to which this is the supplement, or any other act now in force in this state, may purchase, take, hold, receive and enjoy all lands, tenements and hereditaments, in fee simple or otherwise, and also all goods, chattels, legacies and donations, in money or otherwise, of what kind or nature soever, that may be granted and conveyed or given and devised to the seminary or other institution of which they shall be trustees as aforesaid, by the grant, gift, alienation or devise of any person or persons able to grant, give or devise the same for the support, endowment or otherwise, of said seminary or school, whether in general or for particular chairs or departments thereof, or for special objects or subjects taught therein; and also that the said trustees and their successors shall and may grant, assign and sell, or otherwise dispose of all or any of their said lands, tenements or hereditaments, goods, chattels and personal estate whatsoever, received and held by them as aforesaid, as to them shall seem meet for the best interests of their said seminary or other institution, unless otherwise provided and limited by the deeds, wills, or other instruments in writing by which they received and hold the same; *provided, nevertheless*, that the proceeds of the sale or other disposition of any real or personal estate so received and held by such trustees for said endowment objects or purposes shall be duly re-invested in other good real or personal estate, as soon thereafter as practicable, and the annual income therefrom only used for such endowment and educational purposes.

Trustees authorized to purchase, &c., lands, also receive goods, &c., granted, devised, &c.

Trustees authorized to dispose of lands, goods, &c., unless otherwise provided, &c.

Proviso.

2. *And be it enacted*, That this act shall take effect immediately.

Approved March 16, 1893.

CHAPTER CXC.

A Further Supplement to an act entitled "An act for the preservation of clams and oysters," approved April fourteenth, one thousand eight hundred and forty-six, and of the supplements thereto.

When and where unlawful to dredge.

1. BE IT ENACTED *by the Senate and General Assembly of the State of New Jersey*, That from and after the passage of this act it shall be unlawful to dredge for oysters in any of the creeks on the east side of Delaware river, of Delaware bay and Maurice river cove south of Cohansey creek at any time, and in Cohansey creek and in all creeks north of said Cohansey creek, in Delaware river and Delaware bay it shall be unlawful to dredge for oysters except during the time from the first day of April to the fifteenth day of June, both days inclusive, and any person offending against the provisions of this act shall be deemed guilty of a misdemeanor and on conviction thereof shall be punished by a fine not exceeding two hundred dollars or by imprisonment at hard labor for a period not exceeding one year, or both, at the discretion of the court, and any boat or vessel employed in the commission of any offense against the provisions of this act, with all her tackle, apparel and furniture shall be forfeited and the same seized, secured and disposed of in the manner prescribed in the eighth, ninth and tenth sections of the act entitled "An act for the preservation of clams and oysters," approved April fourteenth, one thousand eight hundred and forty-six.

Offenders guilty of misdemeanor.

Penalty, &c

Repealer.

2. *And be it enacted*, That all acts and parts of acts, inconsistent herewith be and the same are hereby repealed, and that this act shall be deemed a public act and take effect immediately.

Approved March 16, 1898.

CHAPTER CXCI.

A Further Supplement to an act entitled "An act to provide for a commission to revise and consolidate the general statutes of this state relating to villages, towns and townships," approved March ninth, one thousand eight hundred and ninety-one.

WHEREAS, The commissioners appointed under the provisions of the act to which this is a further supplement, after giving their entire time and individual attention and study to the prosecution of the work in said act directed, a partial report of which has been made to the legislature at this session, find the time limited by said act and the supplement thereto approved March twenty-second, one thousand eight hundred and ninety-two, inadequate to complete the work assigned to them in a substantial and thorough manner; therefore, Preamble.

1. BE IT ENACTED *by the Senate and General Assembly of the State of New Jersey*, That the said commission be and is hereby continued with the same duties and powers imposed and conferred upon the members thereof by the act to which this is a further supplement, and that the said commissioners shall lay before the next legislature a complete report of the work of said commission. Commission continued, and to report

2. *And be it enacted*, That the commissioners appointed under the provisions of said act shall receive such compensation on account of the work heretofore done by them, and for which they have not heretofore been compensated, as the governor, comptroller and treasurer shall deem just and proper, together with such necessary expenses as they may have incurred in carrying out the provisions of the act to which this is a further supplement, which shall be paid by the treasurer on the warrant of the comptroller. Compensation

3. *And be it enacted*, That in the further pursuance of their work, they shall receive from time to time their necessary Further compensation, by whom paid.

expenses incurred in carrying out the provisions of this act, and at the completion of the same shall receive such further compensation as the governor, comptroller and treasurer shall deem just and proper, which said expenses and further compensation shall be paid by the treasurer on the warrant of the comptroller.

4. *And be it enacted,* That this act shall take effect immediately.

Approved March 16, 1898.

CHAPTER CXCII.

An Act to authorize and regulate the construction of street railways upon turnpikes.

Authorized to construct street railways in counties of second class.

1. BE IT ENACTED *by the Senate and General Assembly of the State of New Jersey,* That any duly incorporated street railway company of this state may construct and operate a street railway upon and along the roadbed of any turnpike company located within counties of the second class in this state, which shall have granted or conveyed such right or privilege to such street railway company.

Board of commissioners, &c., by resolution or ordinance locate track.

2. *And be it enacted,* That the board of commissioners, common council, township committee or other governing body or bodies of any city, incorporated town, borough or township within or through the limits whereof such turnpike shall lie or extend shall, upon the petition of such street railway company and proof of the granting of such permission or right of way by the turnpike company, by resolution or ordinance locate the track or tracks of such street railway company upon the roadbed of such turnpike company; *provided,* such governing body may require the surrender by said turnpike company of its toll and other turnpike franchises as a condition upon which such location shall be made.

Proviso.

3. *And be it enacted,* That in case said turnpike lies within the boundaries of any incorporated city, town,

the highest bidder, in the manner prescribed by this act, which warrant shall include all lots and parcels of land and real estate subject to liens for taxes or assessments, or both, at the time of the passage of this act which shall not then have been fully paid or discharged; *provided, however*, that no lot or parcel of land shall be sold for less than the amount due thereon, and interest, penalties and costs of sale. Sale to be public. Proviso.

2. *And be it enacted*, That all lands and real estate which have been heretofore sold for a term of years, for, or on account of, the non-payment of any tax or assessment to any board or officer of such town for the use or benefit thereof, and which shall not have been redeemed therefrom at the time of issuing said warrant, shall be deemed and taken to be lands and real estate upon which taxes or assessments, as the case may be, are unpaid and in arrears, within the meaning of the first section of this act. Lands sold to town and not redeemed, how held.

3. *And be it enacted*, That where, in any town of this state, taxes or assessments hereafter levied or imposed upon any lands or real estate therein, shall remain unpaid and in arrears for the period of three years after the time limited or appointed by law for the payment thereof, it shall be lawful for the town council or other governing body of such town, at any time after the expiration of said period, to issue its warrant under the corporate seal of the town, signed by the chairman thereof and attested by the town clerk, directed to the treasurer of the town, commanding him to sell at public auction, to the highest bidder, in the manner provided by this act, each and every lot and parcel of land and real estate upon which such taxes or assessments shall remain unpaid and in such warrant mentioned and described; which said warrant shall include all lots and parcels of lands in arrears for the same taxes or assessments; *provided, however*, that no lot or parcel of land shall be sold for less than the amount of the tax or assessment due thereon, and interest, penalties and costs of sale. Warrant may be issued after the expiration of three years for collection of unpaid taxes. Sale to be public. Proviso

4. *And be it enacted*, That the warrants provided to be issued by the first and third section of this act shall contain a brief description of each lot or parcel of land directed to be sold, adding thereto the lot and block What warrant shall contain.

23

number thereof on the official map of the town, if any, and shall set forth, in connection with each lot or parcel of land, the amount of each tax and assessment due thereon.

Notice of sale to be given, and contain.

5. *And be it enacted*, That on receiving said warrant, it shall be the duty of the town treasurer to give notice of such intended sale by advertisements published in two newspapers published in the county in which such town is situated and circulating in such town for four weeks successively, at least once in each week, next preceding the time appointed for such sale; said advertisements shall specify and set forth the time and place of sale, and shall briefly describe the property affected, adding the lot and block number of the same on the official map of the town, if any, and shall specify and set forth the amount due for taxes and assessments upon each lot or parcel so advertised to be sold.

Sale to be public.

6. *And be it enacted*, That it shall be the duty of said town treasurer to attend at the time and place specified in the notice of sale, and to expose for sale at public auction, separately, all the lots and parcels of land and real estate described and set forth in the notice of sale, and shall sell to the highest bidder, but not for less than the amount due on each lot or parcel as aforesaid; *provided, however*, that in case any of the lots or parcels advertised to be sold shall remain unsold for want of purchasers, the said treasurer shall adjourn the sale of the unsold lots or parcels for a period not less than three weeks nor more than six weeks; notice of such adjournment shall be published in the newspapers in which the notice of sale shall have been published, at least once in each week next preceding the adjourned day of said sale; affidavits of the publication of the notice of sale, and, in case of adjournment, of the notice thereof in the manner above provided, made by the publishers of the newspapers, or by some person or persons in their employ having cognizance of such publication, shall be filed in the office of the town clerk, and shall constitute prima facie evidence of the matters stated therein in all courts and places.

Proviso.

When and by whom deed executed.

7. *And be it enacted*, That on receipt of the purchase money on any sale the said treasurer shall deliver to the

purchaser a certificate of such sale; upon surrendering such certificate of sale and filing proof with said treasurer of the publication of the notice thereof and proof of the service or mailing thereof, or of due inquiry, as hereinafter provided, the said treasurer shall at the expiration of six months from the date of the last publication of such notice execute and deliver to the purchaser, his heirs, devisees or assigns a deed for the lot or parcel purchased by him; which deed shall be signed by said officer, be sealed with the corporate seal of the town and attested by the town clerk, and be proved or acknowledged in the usual manner; which deed shall convey, and said purchaser, his heirs, legal representatives or assigns shall take and hold thereunder a good and sufficient title to the lands and real estate sold in fee simple absolute, free of all incumbrances, except taxes and assessments levied subsequently to the taxes or assessments mentioned and set forth in the notice of sale, of which the said deed shall be presumptive evidence in all courts and places and in any proceeding or action to be by such purchaser, his heirs, legal representatives or assigns taken, prosecuted or defended for the recovery of the possession of the property sold as aforesaid, or in the establishment or defense of his title shown as aforesaid by such deed, the title shall not fail or be defeated by reason of any irregularity or formal defect in the procedure taken under this act; from and after the delivery of the deed to him as aforesaid, the said purchaser shall be entitled to the possession of the premises described therein.

What the deed conveys.

8. *And be it enacted*, That when any lots or parcels of land so advertised as aforesaid shall be exposed for sale on any adjourned day, and the same shall then remain unsold for want of purchasers, it shall be lawful for such town, acting by the chairman of its town council or other governing body, to purchase such unsold lots or parcels with the same right, title and effect as any other purchaser, and the certificate of such sale shall be delivered to said chairman of the town council or other governing body of such town, who shall, in behalf of the town, cause notice of the sale to be published and given as hereinafter provided, and upon filing with the town treasurer proof thereof as hereinafter provided; and at the expira-

When council or governing body may purchase.

tion of six months from the date of the last publication of such notice the town, by its corporate name, shall be entitled to a deed the same as any other purchaser; the town council or other governing body of such town, at any time before the delivery of the deed, are hereby authorized and empowered to sell and assign the certificate of sale, and at any time after the delivery of the deed said town council or governing body are hereby authorized and empowered to grant, sell and convey by good and sufficient deed, either by private sale or by public auction to any person or persons any lot or parcel of land so purchased by it; *provided, however*, that no such sale, assignment or conveyance shall be made for less consideration than the amount of the taxes or assessments or both, on account of which the lot or parcel was sold, with interest and costs.

Authorized to sell or assign certificate of sale.

Proviso.

When owner may redeem.

9. *And be it enacted*, That the owner, or any incumbrancer, of any lot or parcel of land or real estate sold by virtue of the provisions of this act, may, at any time before the expiration of six months from the date of the last publication of the notice hereinafter provided for, or before a deed for the same shall have been delivered, redeem such lot or parcel by paying to the town treasurer of such town, for the use of the purchaser, his heirs, legal representatives, or assigns, the sum paid by him at such sale, with interest at the rate of ten per centum per annum from the date of the sale, together with the cost of publishing the notice of the sale, and one dollar for each copy thereof served as hereinafter provided; and upon such redemption, the town treasurer shall pay to the purchaser, his legal representatives or assigns, the amount received from the person redeeming; such notice shall be advertised in a newspaper published in the county in which such town is situated for the period of six weeks, at least once in each week, and, in addition to other appropriate particulars, shall specify the date of sale, the name of the purchaser, the place where redemption from the sale may be made, and shall describe the lot or parcel of land sold, by metes and bounds, and also by reference to the lot and block numbers of the same on the official map of the town (if any); within thirty days after the first publication of such notice a copy

Duty of town treasurer upon redemption.

thereof shall be served personally on the owner or owners and all mortgagees and incumbrancers of record, if resident in the county in which the town is situated, and in case any owner, mortgagee or incumbrancer shall be non-resident of the county, a written or printed copy of such notice shall, within the same period, be deposited in a post office enclosed in a wrapper, postage prepaid, directed to such owner, mortgagee or incumbrancer at his last known post office address; and in case the post office address of any such owner, mortgagee or incumbrancer is unknown, or cannot, upon due inquiry, be ascertained, or in case any such owner, mortgagee or incumbrancer, his or her heirs, devisees or legal representatives shall be unknown, then the publication of the notice, above provided for, shall be continued for the further period of six weeks so that such notice shall be published for twelve weeks successively instead of six weeks as herein above provided; inquiry for the name, residence, or post office address of any owner, mortgagee or incumbrancer as aforesaid, shall be made upon the lands purchased at the sale, if the same are occupied, and wherever else in the town the same may be likely to be ascertained, and also by examination of the record of the deed, mortgage or incumbrance on account of which such notice is given; an affidavit shall be made by the purchaser or his agent, setting forth the manner and particulars of the service of the notice and what inquiry was made to ascertain the name, residence and post office address of the owner, mortgagee or incumbrancer, and how and where and to whom such notice was mailed, and an affidavit of the publication of such notice shall be made by the publisher of the newspaper or some one in his employ having cognizance of such publication; all of said affidavits shall be filed in the office of the town treasurer within one month after the date of the last publication of the notice, and shall be prima facie evidence in all courts and places of the matters stated therein; any mortgagee or incumbrancer redeeming from such sale shall have a lien on the property so redeemed for the amount paid by him prior to all other liens and incumbrances whatsoever, and on any sale of such property to satisfy any lien or

Mortgagee or incumbrancer redeeming shall have lien on property.

incumbrance thereon, shall be entitled to be first paid out of the proceeds of sale the amount paid by him, with legal interest.

Surplus money to be held.

10. *And be it enacted*, That any surplus of the purchase money paid for any lot or parcel of land sold under the provisions of this act, shall be held for the use of, and be paid over to the person legally entitled thereto, upon his establishing his right to the same, but no interest shall be recoverable from the town; *provided, however*, that in case any mortgagee or other incumbrancer shall, in writing, notify the town council of the nature and extent of his lien or incumbrance at any time before the deed is delivered, the town shall, immediately after the delivery of the deed, pay such surplus into the circuit court of the county, which court, on application of any party interested, may make such order in relation to the disposition and distribution of the same as shall be just and equitable.

Proviso

Clerk to keep record of redemption.

11. *And be it enacted*, That the town clerk shall keep a record in a book to be provided for that purpose, which shall be a public record, of all sales made under this act and of the names and residences of the purchasers, and in case of redemption, the time of redemption and the name and residence of the person redeeming.

Form of deed

12. *And be it enacted*, That in any deed given under this act, it shall not be necessary to set out at length the proceedings taken under this act, but it shall be sufficient to state generally therein that such deed is made and executed upon proceedings taken under authority of this act.

Repealer.

13. *And be it enacted*, That all acts and parts of acts, local, general or special, inconsistent with the provisions of this act be and the same are hereby repealed, and that this act shall take effect immediately.

Approved March 16, 1893.

CHAPTER CCIII.

An Act to enable township committees to encourage the use of broad tires on wagons and carts by a rebatement of taxes.

1. Be it enacted *by the Senate and General Assembly of the State of New Jersey*, That township committees be and they are hereby authorized, when in their judgment it is for the public good, to pass an ordinance allowing a rebate of taxes for township or road purposes to all owners or possessors of wagons and carts used in said township for transportation of goods, wares, merchandise, produce, passengers and for general farm, freight and express purposes, having tires of not less than four inches in width; *provided*, the said rebate shall not exceed fifty cents for each wheel in use in any one year. Authorized to pass ordinance allowing rebate. Proviso

4. *And be it enacted*, That this act shall take effect immediately.

Approved March 16, 1893.

CHAPTER CCIV.

An Act to amend an act entitled "An act concerning taxes," approved April fourteenth, one thousand eight hundred and forty-six.

1. Be it enacted *by the Senate and General Assembly of the State of New Jersey*, That section eleven of an act entitled "An act concerning taxes," approved April fourteenth, one thousand eight hundred and forty-six, which reads as follows: Section to be amended.

"11. *And be it enacted*, That the township collector, within sixty days after the receipt of the transcript or duplicate of the said assessment, shall demand payment of the tax or sum assessed on each individual in his township, in person or by notice left at his or her place of residence, and also give notice of the time and place of the meeting of the said commissioners of appeal, and the said collector shall pay the taxes by him collected, and the fine and forfeitures by him received, by virtue of any law of this state, to the collector of the county, by the twenty-second day of December in every year,"
be and the same is hereby amended so as to read as follows:

To demand tax.

11. *And be it enacted*, That the township collector, within sixty days after the receipt of the transcript or duplicate of the said assessment, shall demand payment of the tax or sum assessed on each individual in his township, in person or by notice left at his or her place of residence, or where the residence and post office address is precisely known to said collector, by mailing such notice to the post office address of such person or persons, with the postage prepaid thereon, and also give notice of the time and place of the meeting of the said commissioners of appeal; and the said collector shall pay the taxes by him collected, and the fines and forfeitures by him received, by virtue of any law of this state, to the collector of the county, by the twenty-second day of December in every year.

Time for payment to county collector.

2. *And be it enacted*, That this act shall take effect immediately.

Approved March 16, 1893.

CHAPTER CCV.

A Supplement to an act entitled "An act for the relief of creditors against absconding and absent debtors," approved March twenty-seventh, one thousand eight hundred and seventy-four.

1. BE IT ENACTED *by the Senate and General Assembly of the State of New Jersey*, That if any order for the sale of goods and chattels by an auditor shall hereafter be made by the court under the provisions of the act to which this act is a supplement, it shall be sufficient, unless the court shall provide otherwise in said order, to advertise the said sale in the same manner as sales of goods and chattels by the sheriff under an execution are now advertised. Manner of advertising sales.

2. *And be it enacted*, That this act shall take effect immediately.

Approved March 16, 1893.

CHAPTER CCVI.

An Act to amend an act entitled "An act for the prevention of cruelty to animals," approved March eleventh, one thousand eight hundred and eighty.

1. BE IT ENACTED *by the Senate and General Assembly of the State of New Jersey*, That section sixteen of the act to which this is amendatory shall read as follows: Section to be amended.

16. *And be it enacted*, That any member, officer or agent of the New Jersey society for the prevention of cruelty to animals, or any sheriff, under sheriff, constable

Acknowledgments and proofs of deeds made by commissioners after expiration of term of office confirmed and made legal.

certificates thereof, heretofore taken or made before or by any commissioner of deeds in and for this state, whose term of office had expired or whose office had been vacated, or whose commission was void at the time of taking such acknowledgment or proof, and the record of such deeds, mortgages and other writings are hereby confirmed and made valid and legal and effectual to the extent that the same would have been valid, legal and effectual if the term of office of the commissioner taking such acknowledgment or proof had not expired, nor his office been vacated, nor his commission become void as aforesaid.

2. *And be it enacted*, That this act shall be deemed a public act and shall take effect immediately.

Approved March 16, 1893.

CHAPTER CCII.

An Act providing for the sale of lands for unpaid taxes and assessments heretofore levied or imposed, or which may be hereafter levied or imposed, in towns of this state.

Warrant may be issued after expiration of one year for collection of unpaid taxes for public improvements.

1. Be it enacted *by the Senate and General Assembly of the State of New Jersey*, That where in any town of this state taxes or assessments for public improvements heretofore levied or imposed upon any lands or real estate therein which now remain due and in arrears shall remain due and unpaid for the period of one year after the passage of this act it shall be lawful for the town council or other governing body of such town at any time after the expiration of said period to issue its warrant under the corporate seal of the town, signed by the chairman thereof and attested by the town clerk, directed to the treasurer of the town, therein and thereby commanding him to sell such lands and real estate at public auction to

the highest bidder, in the manner prescribed by this act, which warrant shall include all lots and parcels of land and real estate subject to liens for taxes or assessments, or both, at the time of the passage of this act which shall not then have been fully paid or discharged; *provided, however*, that no lot or parcel of land shall be sold for less than the amount due thereon, and interest, penalties and costs of sale.

Sale to be public.

Proviso.

2. *And be it enacted*, That all lands and real estate which have been heretofore sold for a term of years, for, or on account of, the non-payment of any tax or assessment to any board or officer of such town for the use or benefit thereof, and which shall not have been redeemed therefrom at the time of issuing said warrant, shall be deemed and taken to be lands and real estate upon which taxes or assessments, as the case may be, are unpaid and in arrears, within the meaning of the first section of this act.

Lands sold to town and not redeemed, how held.

3. *And be it enacted*, That where, in any town of this state, taxes or assessments hereafter levied or imposed upon any lands or real estate therein, shall remain unpaid and in arrears for the period of three years after the time limited or appointed by law for the payment thereof, it shall be lawful for the town council or other governing body of such town, at any time after the expiration of said period, to issue its warrant under the corporate seal of the town, signed by the chairman thereof and attested by the town clerk, directed to the treasurer of the town, commanding him to sell at public auction, to the highest bidder, in the manner provided by this act, each and every lot and parcel of land and real estate upon which such taxes or assessments shall remain unpaid and in such warrant mentioned and described; which said warrant shall include all lots and parcels of lands in arrears for the same taxes or assessments; *provided, however*, that no lot or parcel of land shall be sold for less than the amount of the tax or assessment due thereon, and interest, penalties and costs of sale.

Warrant may be issued after the expiration of three years for collection of unpaid taxes.

Sale to be public.

Proviso

4. *And be it enacted*, That the warrants provided to be issued by the first and third section of this act shall contain a brief description of each lot or parcel of land directed to be sold, adding thereto the lot and block

What warrant shall contain.

number thereof on the official map of the town, if any, and shall set forth, in connection with each lot or parcel of land, the amount of each tax and assessment due thereon.

Notice of sale to be given, and contain.

5. *And be it enacted*, That on receiving said warrant, it shall be the duty of the town treasurer to give notice of such intended sale by advertisements published in two newspapers published in the county in which such town is situated and circulating in such town for four weeks successively, at least once in each week, next preceding the time appointed for such sale; said advertisements shall specify and set forth the time and place of sale, and shall briefly describe the property affected, adding the lot and block number of the same on the official map of the town, if any, and shall specify and set forth the amount due for taxes and assessments upon each lot or parcel so advertised to be sold.

Sale to be public.

6. *And be it enacted*, That it shall be the duty of said town treasurer to attend at the time and place specified in the notice of sale, and to expose for sale at public auction, separately, all the lots and parcels of land and real estate described and set forth in the notice of sale, and shall sell to the highest bidder, but not for less than the amount due on each lot or parcel as aforesaid; *provided, however*, that in case any of the lots or parcels advertised to be sold shall remain unsold for want of purchasers, the said treasurer shall adjourn the sale of the unsold lots or parcels for a period not less than three weeks nor more than six weeks; notice of such adjournment shall be published in the newspapers in which the notice of sale shall have been published, at least once in each week next preceding the adjourned day of said sale; affidavits of the publication of the notice of sale, and, in case of adjournment, of the notice thereof in the manner above provided, made by the publishers of the newspapers, or by some person or persons in their employ having cognizance of such publication, shall be filed in the office of the town clerk, and shall constitute prima facie evidence of the matters stated therein in all courts and places.

Proviso.

When and by whom deed executed.

7. *And be it enacted*, That on receipt of the purchase money on any sale the said treasurer shall deliver to the

purchaser a certificate of such sale; upon surrendering such certificate of sale and filing proof with said treasurer of the publication of the notice thereof and proof of the service or mailing thereof, or of due inquiry, as hereinafter provided, the said treasurer shall at the expiration of six months from the date of the last publication of such notice execute and deliver to the purchaser, his heirs, devisees or assigns a deed for the lot or parcel purchased by him; which deed shall be signed by said officer, be sealed with the corporate seal of the town and attested by the town clerk, and be proved or acknowledged in the usual manner; which deed shall convey, and said purchaser, his heirs, legal representatives or assigns shall take and hold thereunder a good and sufficient title to the lands and real estate sold in fee simple absolute, free of all incumbrances, except taxes and assessments levied subsequently to the taxes or assessments mentioned and set forth in the notice of sale, of which the said deed shall be presumptive evidence in all courts and places and in any proceeding or action to be by such purchaser, his heirs, legal representatives or assigns taken, prosecuted or defended for the recovery of the possession of the property sold as aforesaid, or in the establishment or defense of his title shown as aforesaid by such deed, the title shall not fail or be defeated by reason of any irregularity or formal defect in the procedure taken under this act; from and after the delivery of the deed to him as aforesaid, the said purchaser shall be entitled to the possession of the premises described therein.

What the deed conveys.

8. *And be it enacted*, That when any lots or parcels of land so advertised as aforesaid shall be exposed for sale on any adjourned day, and the same shall then remain unsold for want of purchasers, it shall be lawful for such town, acting by the chairman of its town council or other governing body, to purchase such unsold lots or parcels with the same right, title and effect as any other purchaser, and the certificate of such sale shall be delivered to said chairman of the town council or other governing body of such town, who shall, in behalf of the town, cause notice of the sale to be published and given as hereinafter provided, and upon filing with the town treasurer proof thereof as hereinafter provided; and at the expira-

When council or governing body may purchase.

tion of six months from the date of the last publication of such notice the town, by its corporate name, shall be entitled to a deed the same as any other purchaser; the town council or other governing body of such town, at any time before the delivery of the deed, are hereby authorized and empowered to sell and assign the certificate of sale, and at any time after the delivery of the deed said town council or governing body are hereby authorized and empowered to grant, sell and convey by good and sufficient deed, either by private sale or by public auction to any person or persons any lot or parcel of land so purchased by it; *provided, however*, that no such sale, assignment or conveyance shall be made for less consideration than the amount of the taxes or assessments or both, on account of which the lot or parcel was sold, with interest and costs.

Authorized to sell or assign certificate of sale.

Proviso.

When owner may redeem.

9. *And be it enacted*, That the owner, or any incumbrancer, of any lot or parcel of land or real estate sold by virtue of the provisions of this act, may, at any time before the expiration of six months from the date of the last publication of the notice hereinafter provided for, or before a deed for the same shall have been delivered, redeem such lot or parcel by paying to the town treasurer of such town, for the use of the purchaser, his heirs, legal representatives, or assigns, the sum paid by him at such sale, with interest at the rate of ten per centum per annum from the date of the sale, together with the cost of publishing the notice of the sale, and one dollar for each copy thereof served as hereinafter provided; and upon such redemption, the town treasurer shall pay to the purchaser, his legal representatives or assigns, the amount received from the person redeeming; such notice shall be advertised in a newspaper published in the county in which such town is situated for the period of six weeks, at least once in each week, and, in addition to other appropriate particulars, shall specify the date of sale, the name of the purchaser, the place where redemption from the sale may be made, and shall describe the lot or parcel of land sold, by metes and bounds, and also by reference to the lot and block numbers of the same on the official map of the town (if any); within thirty days after the first publication of such notice a copy

Duty of town treasurer upon redemption.

thereof shall be served personally on the owner or owners and all mortgagees and incumbrancers of record, if resident in the county in which the town is situated, and in case any owner, mortgagee or incumbrancer shall be non-resident of the county, a written or printed copy of such notice shall, within the same period, be deposited in a post office enclosed in a wrapper, postage prepaid, directed to such owner, mortgagee or incumbrancer at his last known post office address; and in case the post office address of any such owner, mortgagee or incumbrancer is unknown, or cannot, upon due inquiry, be ascertained, or in case any such owner, mortgagee or incumbrancer, his or her heirs, devisees or legal representatives shall be unknown, then the publication of the notice, above provided for, shall be continued for the further period of six weeks so that such notice shall be published for twelve weeks successively instead of six weeks as herein above provided; inquiry for the name, residence, or post office address of any owner, mortgagee or incumbrancer as aforesaid, shall be made upon the lands purchased at the sale, if the same are occupied, and wherever else in the town the same may be likely to be ascertained, and also by examination of the record of the deed, mortgage or incumbrance on account of which such notice is given; an affidavit shall be made by the purchaser or his agent, setting forth the manner and particulars of the service of the notice and what inquiry was made to ascertain the name, residence and post office address of the owner, mortgagee or incumbrancer, and how and where and to whom such notice was mailed, and an affidavit of the publication of such notice shall be made by the publisher of the newspaper or some one in his employ having cognizance of such publication; all of said affidavits shall be filed in the office of the town treasurer within one month after the date of the last publication of the notice, and shall be prima facie evidence in all courts and places of the matters stated therein; any mortgagee or incumbrancer redeeming from such sale shall have a lien on the property so redeemed for the amount paid by him prior to all other liens and incumbrances whatsoever, and on any sale of such property to satisfy any lien or

Mortgagee or incumbrancer redeeming shall have lien on property.

incumbrance thereon, shall be entitled to be first paid out of the proceeds of sale the amount paid by him, with legal interest.

Surplus money to be held.

10. *And be it enacted*, That any surplus of the purchase money paid for any lot or parcel of land sold under the provisions of this act, shall be held for the use of, and be paid over to the person legally entitled thereto, upon his establishing his right to the same, but no interest shall be recoverable from the town; *provided, however*, that in case any mortgagee or other incumbrancer shall, in writing, notify the town council of the nature and extent of his lien or incumbrance at any time before the deed is delivered, the town shall, immediately after the delivery of the deed, pay such surplus into the circuit court of the county, which court, on application of any party interested, may make such order in relation to the disposition and distribution of the same as shall be just and equitable.

Proviso.

Clerk to keep record of redemption.

11. *And be it enacted*, That the town clerk shall keep a record in a book to be provided for that purpose, which shall be a public record, of all sales made under this act and of the names and residences of the purchasers, and in case of redemption, the time of redemption and the name and residence of the person redeeming.

Form of deed

12. *And be it enacted*, That in any deed given under this act, it shall not be necessary to set out at length the proceedings taken under this act, but it shall be sufficient to state generally therein that such deed is made and executed upon proceedings taken under authority of this act.

Repealer.

13. *And be it enacted*, That all acts and parts of acts, local, general or special, inconsistent with the provisions of this act be and the same are hereby repealed, and that this act shall take effect immediately.

Approved March 16, 1893.

CHAPTER CCIII.

An Act to enable township committees to encourage the use of broad tires on wagons and carts by a rebatement of taxes.

1. Be it enacted *by the Senate and General Assembly of the State of New Jersey*, That township committees be and they are hereby authorized, when in their judgment it is for the public good, to pass an ordinance allowing a rebate of taxes for township or road purposes to all owners or possessors of wagons and carts used in said township for transportation of goods, wares, merchandise, produce, passengers and for general farm, freight and express purposes, having tires of not less than four inches in width; *provided*, the said rebate shall not exceed fifty cents for each wheel in use in any one year. Authorized to pass ordinance allowing rebate. Proviso

4. *And be it enacted*, That this act shall take effect immediately.

Approved March 16, 1893.

CHAPTER CCIV.

An Act to amend an act entitled "An act concerning taxes," approved April fourteenth, one thousand eight hundred and forty-six.

1. Be it enacted *by the Senate and General Assembly of the State of New Jersey*, That section eleven of an act entitled "An act concerning taxes," approved April fourteenth, one thousand eight hundred and forty-six, which reads as follows: Section to be amended.

"11. *And be it enacted*, That the township collector, within sixty days after the receipt of the transcript or duplicate of the said assessment, shall demand payment of the tax or sum assessed on each individual in his township, in person or by notice left at his or her place of residence, and also give notice of the time and place of the meeting of the said commissioners of appeal, and the said collector shall pay the taxes by him collected, and the fine and forfeitures by him received, by virtue of any law of this state, to the collector of the county, by the twenty-second day of December in every year,"
be and the same is hereby amended so as to read as follows:

To demand tax.

11. *And be it enacted*, That the township collector, within sixty days after the receipt of the transcript or duplicate of the said assessment, shall demand payment of the tax or sum assessed on each individual in his township, in person or by notice left at his or her place of residence, or where the residence and post office address is precisely known to said collector, by mailing such notice to the post office address of such person or persons, with the postage prepaid thereon, and also give notice of the time and place of the meeting of the said commissioners of appeal; and the said collector shall pay the taxes by him collected, and the fines and forfeitures by him received, by virtue of any law of this state, to the collector of the county, by the twenty-second day of December in every year.

Time for payment to county collector.

2. *And be it enacted*, That this act shall take effect immediately.

Approved March 16, 1893.

CHAPTER CCV.

A Supplement to an act entitled "An act for the relief of creditors against absconding and absent debtors," approved March twenty-seventh, one thousand eight hundred and seventy-four.

1. Be it enacted *by the Senate and General Assembly of the State of New Jersey*, That if any order for the sale of goods and chattels by an auditor shall hereafter be made by the court under the provisions of the act to which this act is a supplement, it shall be sufficient, unless the court shall provide otherwise in said order, to advertise the said sale in the same manner as sales of goods and chattels by the sheriff under an execution are now advertised. Manner of advertising sales.

2. *And be it enacted*, That this act shall take effect immediately.

Approved March 16, 1893.

CHAPTER CCVI.

An Act to amend an act entitled "An act for the prevention of cruelty to animals," approved March eleventh, one thousand eight hundred and eighty.

1. Be it enacted *by the Senate and General Assembly of the State of New Jersey*, That section sixteen of the act to which this is amendatory shall read as follows: Section to be amended.

16. *And be it enacted*, That any member, officer or agent of the New Jersey society for the prevention of cruelty to animals, or any sheriff, under sheriff, constable

Any member, officer or agent of society, sheriffs, &c., may make arrests without warrant, and take before nearest magistrate.

or police officer shall have power to arrest, without warrant, any person or persons found violating the provisions of this act in the presence of said member, officer, agent, sheriff, under sheriff, constable or police officer, and to take the same before the nearest magistrate or justice of the peace or court as aforesaid, there to be proceeded against as provided for in section eleven of said act.

Approved March 16, 1893.

CHAPTER CCVII.

Supplement to an act entitled "An act concerning contagious and infectious diseases among animals, and to repeal certain acts relating thereto," approved May fourth, one thousand eight hundred and eighty-six.

Registry of cattle to be kept in cities.

1. BE IT ENACTED *by the Senate and General Assembly of the State of New Jersey*, That the local board of health of any city of this state shall by ordinance require, from time to time, a registry of all cattle kept within the limits of said city, which registry shall state the place of keeping the number in each case kept, and the number of these intended, or used, as milch cows; and it shall be the

Duty of owners of cattle.

duty of the owner of any such cattle to make registry thereof at the time, place and in the manner that the

Penalty.

board of health of said city may direct, under a penalty

Proviso.

not exceeding fifty dollars for any neglect of the same; *provided*, that no such registry shall be made by any board of health until after the examination of the stables and place in which said cattle are kept, and until it is known to the satisfaction of said board that they are in good sanitary condition.

When inspection shall be ordered.

2. *And be it enacted*, That whenever any local board of health of any city shall have reason to suspect the existence of any contagious disease among cattle, or such as may be a risk or danger to the food or milk supply,

or whenever they may deem it necessary, in order to prevent the occurrence of such risk or danger, they shall order the inspection of all cattle that are kept or intended for meat or milk production, by a competent veterinarian chosen by them, and may for such inspection require so much payment for such service as may be necessary for the expenses attending such inspection; *it being, however, provided*, that in no case shall the amount charged exceed fifty cents a head per year for dairies of ten cows or under, and for all dairies above ten cows, twenty-five cents per head per year; *provided, further*, that no charge shall be made against any one keeping a single cow for family use.

Payment of expenses.

Proviso.

Proviso.

3. *And be it enacted*, That whenever any local board of health, or any veterinary inspector appointed by said board shall find or suspect any disease in any cow, or in any herd of milk-producing cattle, which may prove harmful to the meat or milk supply, the state board of health and the state dairy commissioner shall be notified, and it shall be the duty of the dairy commissioner to investigate the same, and he shall prohibit the sale or use of the milk from any such milch cow, but he, or the owner of said milch cow, may ask, through the state board of health, a report from some veterinarian appointed by the state board of health as to whether, or how long, it will be necessary to continue the prohibiton of the use of said milk, and the dairy commissioner or the state board of health may prohibit the use of said milk or of meat of any animal declared by a veterinarian of the state board to be unfit for use.

When state dairy commissioner shall be notified, and their duties.

4. *And be it enacted*, That this act shall take effect immediately.

Approved March 16, 1893.

CHAPTER CCVIII.

A Further Supplement to an act entitled "An act to provide for the more permanent improvement of the public roads of this state," approved April fourteenth, one thousand eight hundred and ninety-one.

When public road or section thereof may be improved.

1. BE IT ENACTED *by the Senate and General Assembly of the State of New Jersey*, That where any public road or section thereof in any township of this state shall lie between and extend to and connect with any street or avenue in any city, borough or incorporated town or village in this state, and any such street or avenue shall furnish a continuation of said public road or section thereof, or where the public road lies between any city, borough or incorporated town or village and a county line, the said public road or section thereof may be improved under and by virtue of the act to which this is a supplement, though the said public road or section thereof be less than one mile in length.

How improvements shall be assessed.

2. *And be it enacted*, That where the line between any city, borough or incorporated town or village, and any township in this state shall run along the middle of any such public road or section thereof, the lands within such city fronting on said road or section shall be assessed for the improvement thereof in the same manner as the lands in such township.

3. *And be it enacted*, That this act shall take effect immediately.

Approved March 16, 1898.

CHAPTER CCIX.

An Act for the better protection of manufacturers of malt liquors, using and owning butts, hogsheads, barrels, casks, kegs or other packages in the sale and delivery of the same.

Unlawful to use butts, hogsheads, barrels, &c., without permission of original owner.

1. BE IT ENACTED *by the Senate and General Assembly of the State of New Jersey,* That it shall be unlawful for any person or persons hereafter, other than the lawful owner or owners, to fill with malt liquor or liquors or other substance, for any purpose whatever, or to use, traffic in, purchase, sell, dispose of, detain, convert, mutilate or destroy; or to willfully or unreasonably refuse to return or deliver to such owner, upon demand being made for the same, any butt, hogshead, barrel, half-barrel, cask, half-cask, quarter-cask or keg or other packages which may be branded or stamped with the name of such lawful owner, or from which such brand or stamp has been removed, cut off, defaced or obliterated; or to remove, cut off, deface or obliterate the name stamped thereon; or to brand or stamp other brands or stamps on the same without the written permission of the original or lawful owner or owners thereof, unless there shall have been a sale in express terms of any such package, exclusive of the malt liquor contained therein, to such person or persons by the original or lawful owner or owners thereof.

Penalty.

2. *And be it enacted,* That any person or persons who shall violate any of the provisions of section one of this act shall be liable to the penalty of fifty dollars, to be recovered in an action of debt with costs in any court of this state having cognizance thereof; said action to be brought by the owners of such packages, and execution against the goods and chattels and the person of the defendant shall issue for the penalty and costs so recovered.

3. *And be it enacted,* That one-half of all the penalties

Distribution of penalties.

recovered under this act shall be for the use of the poor of the city, borough, town, township wherein such violation shall have been committed, and the other half shall be for the use of the owner in whose name the complaint is made; and the officer collecting the same shall immediately upon receipt thereof pay over the same, as aforesaid, to the officer of such city, borough, town or township, who is by law charged with the care of the poor, and to the said owner.

Violators guilty of misdemeanor.

Penalty.

4. *And be it enacted*, That any person who shall violate any of the provisions of section one of this act shall also be deemed guilty of a misdemeanor, and on conviction thereof shall be punished by a fine not exceeding one hundred dollars or by imprisonment not exceeding six months or both, at the discretion of the court.

When search warrant shall issue.

By whom search warrant served.

5. *And be it enacted*, That on probable cause shown on oath or affirmation of the owner of any such butts, hogsheads, barrels, casks or other packages upon which said owner's name is branded or stamped, or of his agent thereunto specially authorized, that any person has in his possession any such packages in violation of the provisions of section one of this act, or with intent to violate the same, a search warrant shall issue to discover and obtain the said packages; and said search warrant shall be issued and served or executed by any of the several officers now authorized under the laws of this state to issue, serve or execute search warrants, and the same proceedings shall be had thereon as is now required by law in cases where search warrants are issued.

6. *And be it enacted*, That this act shall take effect immediately.

Approved March 16, 1898.

CHAPTER CCX.

An Act to revise and amend "An act to tax intestates' estates, gifts, legacies and collateral inheritance in certain cases," approved March twenty-third, one thousand eight hundred and ninety-two.

Gifts, legacies and collateral inheritance subject to a tax of $5 on every $100, except churches, hospitals and orphan asylums.

1. BE IT ENACTED *by the Senate and General Assembly of the State of New Jersey*, That after the passage of this act all property which shall pass by will or by the intestate laws of this state from any person who may die seized or possessed of the same while being a resident of the state, and all property which shall be within this state, and any part of such property, and any interest therein or income therefrom, which shall be transferred by inheritance, distribution, bequest, devise, deed, grant, sale or gift aforesaid, made or intended to take effect in possession or enjoyment after the death of the intestate, testator, grantor or bargainor, to any person or persons, or to a body politic or corporate, excepting churches, hospitals and orphan asylums, in trust or otherwise, or by reason whereof any person or body politic or corporate shall become beneficially entitled, in possession or expectancy, to such property, or to the income thereof, other than to or for the use of a father, mother, husband, wife, children, brother or sister, or lineal descendants born in lawful wedlock, or the wife or widow of a son, or the husband of a daughter, shall be subject to a tax of five dollars on every hundred dollars of the clear market value of such property, to be paid to the treasurer of the state of New Jersey for the use of the state, and all administrators, executors and trustees shall be liable for any and all such taxes until the same shall have been paid as hereinafter directed; *provided*, that an estate which may be valued at a less sum than five hundred dollars shall not be subject to said duty or tax.

Proviso.

2. *And be it enacted*, That when any person shall bequeath or devise, convey, grant, sell or give as afore-

Property to be appraised and tax due immediately.

said any property, or interest therein, or income therefrom, to a father, mother, husband, wife, children, brother or sister, the widow of a son, or a lineal descendant, during life or for a term of years, and the remainder to a collateral heir of the decedent, or to a stranger in blood, or to a body politic or corporate, the property so passing shall be appraised immediately after the death of said testator or grantor, as the case may be, at what shall then be the fair market value thereof, in the manner hereinafter provided, and after deducting therefrom the value of said life estate, or term of years, the tax prescribed by this act on the remainder shall be immediately due and payable to the treasurer of the state of New Jersey, and, together with the interest thereon, shall be and remain a lien on said property until the same is paid; *provided*, that the person or persons, or body politic or corporate beneficially interested in the property chargeable with said tax, may elect not to pay the same until they shall come into the actual possession or enjoyment of such property, or, and in that case, such person or persons, or body politic or corporate, shall give a bond to the state of New Jersey in a penalty three times the amount of the tax arising upon personal estate, with such sureties as the chancellor may approve, conditioned for the payment of said tax and interest thereon, at such time or period as they or their representatives may come into the actual possession or enjoyment of such property, which bond shall be filed in the office of the clerk in chancery; *provided further*, that such person shall make a full verified return of such property to the chancellor of the state and file the same in the office of the clerk in chancery within one year from the death of the decedent, and within that period enter into such security and renew the same every five years.

Proviso.

Proviso.

Bequests to executors or trustees exceeding reasonable compensation, excess to be taxed.

8. *And be it enacted*, That whenever a decedent appoints or names one or more executors or trustees, and makes a bequest or devise of property to them in lieu of their commissions or allowances, which otherwise would be liable to said tax, or appoints them his residuary legatees, and said bequest, devises or residuary legacies exceed what would be a reasonable compensation for their services, such excess shall be liable to said tax, and the chancellor

or the orphans' court having jurisdiction in the case shall fix such compensation.

4. *And be it enacted*, That all taxes imposed by this act, unless otherwise herein provided for, shall be due and payable at the death of the testator, grantor or intestate, as the case may be, and if the same are paid within one year, interest at the rate of six per centum per annum shall be charged and collected thereon, but if not so paid, interest at the rate of ten per centum per annum shall be charged and collected from the time said tax accrued; *provided*, that if said tax is paid within six months from the accruing thereof, interest shall not be charged or collected thereon, but a discount of five per centum shall be allowed and deducted from said tax; and in all cases where the executors, administrators or trustees do not pay such tax within one year from the death of the decedent they shall be required to give a bond, in the form and to the effect prescribed in section two of this act, for the payment of said tax, together with interest.

Interest on tax

Proviso

5. *And be it enacted*, That the penalty of ten per centum per annum imposed by section four hereof for the non-payment of said tax shall not be charged, where in cases by reason of claims made upon the estate, necessary litigation or other unavoidable cause of delay, the estate of any decedent, or a part thereof, cannot be settled at the end of a year from the death of the decedent, and in such cases only six per centum per annum shall be charged upon the said tax from the expiration of such year until the cause of such delay is removed.

Part of penalty remitted where necessary litigation occurs.

6. *And be it enacted*, That any administrator, executor or trustee having in charge or trust any legacy or property for distribution, subject to said tax, shall deduct the tax therefrom, or if the legacy or property be not money, he shall collect the tax thereon upon the appraised value thereof from the legatee or person entitled to such property, and he shall not deliver or be compelled to deliver any specific legacy or property subject to tax to any person until he shall have collected the tax thereon; and whenever any such legacy shall be charged upon or payable out of real estate, the heir or devisee, before paying the same, shall deduct said tax therefrom and pay the same to the executor, administrator or trustee, and the same shall

Executors, &c., not to deliver legacies until tax is paid or deducted.

remain a charge on such real estate until paid, and the payment thereof shall be enforced by the executor, administrator or trustee in the same manner that the payment of such legacy might be enforced; if, however, such legacy be given in money to any person for a limited period, he shall retain the tax upon the whole amount, but if it be not in money, he shall make application to the court having jurisdiction of his accounts to make an apportionment, if the case require it, of the sum to be paid into his hands by such legatees, and for such further order relative thereto as the case may require.

Executors, &c., authorized to sell property.

7. *And be it enacted*, That all executors, administrators and trustees shall have full power to sell so much of the property of the decedent as will enable them to pay said tax, in the same manner as they may be enabled by law to do for the payment of debts of their testators and intestates, and the amount of said tax shall be paid as hereinafter directed.

Executors, &c., to pay tax to state treasurer, take his receipt, countersigned by the comptroller.

8. *And be it enacted*, That any sum of money retained by any executor, administrator or trustee, or paid into his hands for any tax or any property, shall be paid by him, within thirty days thereafter, to the treasurer of the state of New Jersey; and the said treasurer shall deliver a receipt of such payment to the comptroller of the state, whose duty it shall be to countersign the same and return it to the executor, administrator or trustee, whereupon it shall be a proper voucher in the settlement of his accounts, but an executor, administrator or trustee, shall not be entitled to credit in his accounts, nor to be discharged from liability for such tax unless he shall produce a receipt so countersigned by the comptroller, or a copy thereof certified by him.

Executors, &c., to give information in writing to the comptroller.

9. *And be it enacted*, That whenever any of the real estate of which any decedent may die seized, shall pass to any body, politic or corporate, or to any person other than the father, mother, husband, wife, lawful issue, brother or sister, wife or widow of a son, or husband of a daughter, or in trust for them, or some of them, it shall be the duty of the executors, administrators or trustees of such decedent to give information thereof in writing to the comptroller of the state within six months after they undertake the execution of their respective duties,

or if the fact be not known to them within that period, then within one month after the same shall have come to their knowledge.

When proportion of tax may be refunded.

10. *And be it enacted*, That whenever any debts shall be proven against the estate of a decedent, after the payment of legacies or distribution of property from which the said tax has been deducted, or upon which it has been paid, and a refund is made by the legatee, devisee, heir or next of kin, a proportion of the tax so paid shall be repaid to him by the executor, administrator or trustee, if the said tax has not been paid to the state treasurer, or by them if it has been so paid.

When foreign executors, &c., assign and transfer stocks, &c.

11. *And be it enacted*, That whenever any foreign executor or administrator shall assign or transfer any stocks or loans in this state, standing in the name of a decedent, or in trust for a decedent, which shall be liable to the said tax, such tax shall be paid to the state treasurer on the transfer thereof, otherwise the corporation permitting such transfer shall become liable to pay such tax; *provided*, that such corporation has knowledge before such transfer that said stocks or loans are liable to said tax.

Proviso.

How tax paid erroneously refunded.

12. *And be it enacted*, That when any amount of said tax shall have been paid erroneously to the state treasurer, it shall be lawful for the comptroller of the treasury, on satisfactory proof rendered to him of such erroneous payments, to draw his warrant on the state treasurer, in favor of the executor, administrator, person or persons who have paid any such tax in error, or who may be lawfully entitled to receive the same, for the amount of such tax so paid in error; *provided*, that all such applications for the re-payment of such tax, shall be made within two years from the date of such payment.

Proviso

Surrogate or register of prerogative court to appoint appraisers

13. *And be it enacted*, That in order to fix the value of property of persons whose estates shall be subject to the payment of said tax, the surrogate or register of the prerogative court, on the application of any interested party, or upon his own motion, shall appoint some competent person as appraiser as often as, and whenever occasion may require, whose duty it shall be forthwith to give such notice by mail, and to such persons as the surrogate or register of the prerogative court may by order direct, of the time and place he will appraise such prop-

erty, and at such time and place to appraise the same at its fair market value, and make a report thereof in writing to said surrogate or register of the prerogative court, together with such other facts in relation thereto as said surrogate or register of the prerogative court may by order require, to be filed in the office of such surrogate or register of the prerogative court, and from this report the said surrogate or register of the prerogative court shall forthwith assess and fix the then cash value of all estates, annuities and life estates, or term of years growing out of said estates, and the tax to which the same is liable, and shall immediately give notice thereof by mail to the state comptroller and to all parties known to be interested therein; any person or persons dissatisfied with said appraisement or assessment may appeal therefrom to the ordinary or orphans' court of the proper county, within sixty days after the making and filing of such assessment, on paying or giving security, approved by the ordinary or orphans' court, to pay all costs, together with whatever tax shall be fixed by said court; the said appraiser shall be paid by the state treasurer on the warrant of the comptroller, on the certificate of the ordinary or surrogate, duly filed with the comptroller, at the rate of three dollars per day for every day actually and necessarily employed in said appraisement, together with his actual and necessary traveling expenses.

Appeal from appraisement.

Compensation of appraisers.

Penalty for taking fee or reward.

14. *And be it enacted*, That any appraiser appointed by virtue of this act who shall take any fee or reward from any executor, administrator, trustee, legatee, next of kin or heir of any decedent, or from any other person liable to pay said tax or any portion thereof, shall be guilty of a misdemeanor, and upon conviction in any court having jurisdiction of misdemeanors he shall be fined not less than two hundred and fifty dollars nor more than five hundred dollars, and imprisoned not exceeding ninety days, and in addition thereto the register of the prerogative court or surrogate shall dismiss him from such service.

Jurisdiction of ordinary or the orphans' court

15. *And be it enacted*, That the ordinary or the orphans' court in the county in which the real property is situate of a decedent who was not a resident of the state, or in the county of which the decedent was a resident at the

time of his death, shall have jurisdiction to hear and determine all questions in relation to the tax arising under the provisions of this act.

Proceedings when tax is not paid.

16. *And be it enacted*, That if it shall appear to the register of the prerogative court or surrogate that any tax accruing under this act has not been paid according to law, such officer shall issue a citation citing the persons interested in the property liable to the tax to appear before the ordinary or orphans' court on a day certain, not more than three months after the date of such citation, and show cause why said tax should not be paid; the service of such citation and the time, manner and proof thereof, and fees therefor, and the hearing and determination thereon, and the enforcement of the determination or decree shall conform to the provisions of the law for the service of citations now issued by the ordinary or orphans' court, and the hearing and determination thereon and its enforcement; and the register of the prerogative court or surrogate shall, upon the request of any prosecutor of the pleas or the state comptroller, furnish one or more transcripts of such decree, and the same may be by them docketed and filed by the county clerk of any county in the state, and the same shall have the same effect as a lien by judgment.

State comptroller to notify prosecutors of pleas when tax is not paid,

17. *And be it enacted*, That whenever the state comptroller shall have reason to believe that any tax is due and unpaid under this act, after the refusal or neglect of the persons interested in the property liable to said tax to pay the same, he shall notify the prosecutor of the pleas of the proper county in writing, of such failure to pay such tax, and the prosecutor of the pleas so notified, if he have probable cause to believe a tax is due and unpaid, shall prosecute the proceeding before the ordinary of the orphans' court in the proper county, as provided in section sixteen of this act, for the enforcement and collection of such tax; all costs awarded by such decree to such prosecutor, that may be collected after the collection and payment of the tax to the state treasurer, may be retained by the prosecutor of the pleas for his own use.

18. *And be it enacted*, That the register of the prerogative court, the surrogate and the register of deeds or

Quarterly reports of register of prerogative court, surrogate and register of deeds or county clerk.

county clerk of each county shall every three months make a statement in writing, to the state comptroller, of the property from which or the party from whom he has reason to believe a tax under this act has become due since his last report.

Expenses paid by state treasurer.

19. *And be it enacted*, That whenever the surrogate of any county, or the register of the prerogative court, shall certify to the state comptroller, that there was probable cause for issuing a citation and taking the proceedings specified in section sixteen of this act, the state treasurer shall pay upon the warrant of the comptroller, to the proper officials all expenses incurred for the issuing and services of the citation and all other lawful disbursements that have not otherwise been paid.

Books to be furnished by comptroller.

20. *An be it enacted*, That the comptroller of the state shall furnish to the register of the prerogative court and to each surrogate a book in which he shall enter, or cause to be entered, the returns made by appraisers, the cash value of annuities, life estates and term of years and other property fixed by him, and the tax assessed thereon, and the amounts of any receipts for payments thereon filed with him, which books shall be kept in the office of the register of the prerogative court of the surrogate as a public record, and shall furnish all other forms and blanks necessary for use in the proper enforcement of this law.

Surrogates' fees paid by state treasurer upon warrant of comptroller.

21. *And be it enacted*, That in addition to the fees above mentioned the fees of the surrogates for each county for the duties heretofore or hereafter to be performed by them in each estate under this act and the act entitled "An act to tax intestates' estates, gifts, legacies and collateral inheritance in certain cases," approved March twenty-third, one thousand eight hundred and ninety-two, shall be paid by the state treasurer upon the warrant of the comptroller, and shall not exceed the following rates: on all sums paid to the state treasurer, not exceeding three thousand dollars, five per centum; if over three thousand dollars three per centum on such excess.

Persons entitled to a receipt from treasurer.

22. *And be it enacted*, That any person, or body politic or corporate, shall be entitled to a receipt from the state treasurer, countersigned by the state comptroller, for the

payment of any tax paid under this act, which receipt shall designate on what real property, if any, of which any decedent may have died seized, said tax has been paid, and by whom paid, and whether or not it is in full of said tax, and said receipt may be recorded in the clerk's office of the county in which said property is situate, in a book to be kept by said clerk for such purpose, which shall be labeled "collateral tax." Collateral tax book.

23. *And be it enacted*, That the "Act to tax intestates' estates, gifts, legacies and collateral inheritance in certain cases," approved March twenty-third, one thousand eight hundred and ninety-two, and all other acts inconsistent with the provisions of this act, are hereby repealed, except so far as herein re-enacted; but nothing in this repealer shall affect or impair the lien of any taxes heretofore assessed, or due and payable, or any remedies for the collection of the same, or to surrender any remedies, powers, rights or privileges acquired by the state under said act hereby revised, or to relieve any person or corporation from any penalty imposed by said act. Repealer, &c.

24. *And be it enacted*, That this act shall take effect immediately.

Approved March 16, 1893.

CHAPTER CCXI.

A Supplement to an act entitled "An act concerning the settlement and collection of arrearages of unpaid taxes, assessments and water rates or water rents in cities of this state, and imposing and levying a tax, assessment and lien in lieu and instead of such arrearages, and to enforce the payment thereof, and to provide for the sale of lands subjected to further taxation and assessment," passed March thirtieth, one thousand eight hundred and eighty-six.

Section to be amended.

1. BE IT ENACTED *by the Senate and General Assembly of the State of New Jersey*, That section one of the supplement to said act, which supplement was approved April fifth, one thousand eight hundred and ninety-two, shall be and the same is hereby amended so as to read as follows:

By whom costs and expenses to be paid on redeeming lands sold.

1. BE IT ENACTED *by the Senate and General Assembly of the State of New Jersey*, That whenever any person shall desire to redeem any lands and real estate sold under and by virtue of the provisions of the act to which this is a supplement, and the acts supplementary thereto and amendatory thereof, every such person shall, in addition to the sum or sums of money required to be paid as now provided by law, pay to the purchaser of such lands and premises, or to his assignee, in case of assignment, or to the city for the use of said purchaser, or his assignee, all the costs and expenses necessarily incurred in proceedings taken for the purpose of perfecting title thereto, including fees for searching, at the rates allowed by law to the county clerks or registers of deeds for like services, but not including counsel fees; *provided, however*, that no purchaser or assignee shall be allowed for such search or notice fees upon the redemption of said property unless he shall have filed with the city clerk of said city before such redemption a statement of such fees, costs and expenses

Proviso.

incurred in serving notices and searching as above provided.

2. *And be it enacted*, That section three of the supplement to the act of which this is a supplement, approved April eight, one thousand eight hundred and ninety-two, be and the same is hereby amended so as to read as follows: Section to be amended.

3. *And be it enacted*, That the assignee of the certificate or certificates of sale given pursuant to the provisions of said act and supplements, may give notice, in his or their names, of such sale to the owners, mortgagees and other persons interested as required by said act and supplements, and to acquire title to the lands and receive the deed or deeds thereof, in the same manner and to the same effect and extent as if such assignee or assignees were the original purchaser or purchasers at the tax sale, and such notice or notices heretofore given by such assignee or assignees are declared to be valid and effectual and to have the same force and effect as if given pursuant to this act, and any notice of sale heretofore or hereafter given by the purchaser at a tax sale, including a city if it be the purchaser, under said acts and supplements and before assignment of the tax certificate, shall enure to and be for the benefit of the assignee of such tax certificate, and such assignee shall be entitled to receive a deed for the lands in such certificate named, which shall convey the same as fully and to the same effect and extent as if such assignee had given notice of sale in his own name and as if the said deed had been made and delivered to the original purchaser and the certificate of sale had not been assigned, and any such deed heretofore made, executed and delivered to any such assignee shall have such force and effect. Assignee of certificates of sale to acquire title and receive conveyance. Notices of assignee valid

4. *And be it enacted*, That all acts and parts of acts, so far as they conflict herewith, be and the same are hereby repealed, and that this act shall take effect immediately. Repealer.

Approved March 16, 1893.

CHAPTER CCXII.

A Further Supplement to an act entitled "An act to establish in this state boards of health and a bureau of vital statistics and to define their respective powers and duties," approved March thirty-first, one thousand eight hundred and eighty-seven.

Inventory of personal goods made, value of goods destroyed certified to state treasurer.

1. BE IT ENACTED *by the Senate and General Assembly of the State of New Jersey,* That whenever the state board or any local board of health in order to prevent the spread of contagious disease, destroy, or order to be destroyed, personal effects or bedding, it shall be the duty of the said board to make or cause to be made an inventory of the said personal goods, and immediately thereafter to certify the value of said personal goods so destroyed to the state treasurer, in case they have been destroyed by the state board of health, and to the municipal authorities in case of local boards, and it shall be the duty of the state treasurer or municipal authority to pay over to the owner of said goods or his or her legal representatives, the sum so certified.

Repealer.

2. *And be it enacted,* That all acts and parts of acts inconsistent herewith be and the same are hereby repealed, and that this act shall take effect immediately.

Approved March 17, 1898.

CHAPTER CCXIII.

A Supplement to an act entitled "An act in relation to assessment in townships," approved March ninth, one thousand eight hundred and seventy-seven.

1. BE IT ENACTED *by the Senate and General Assembly of the State of New Jersey*, That section three of said act be amended so as to read as follows: Section to be amended.

3. *And be it enacted*, That as soon as may be after such appointment such commissioners shall proceed to make such re-assessment or assessment, and in so doing shall assess upon all the tracts or lots of land and real estate benefited by such improvement such proportion of such costs, damages and expenses as will be equal to the amount of benefits actually acquired by said lands and real estate from such improvement, proportioned equitably to the benefit each of such tracts or lots shall be deemed to acquire, and shall make a report of their proceedings and assessments to such court within thirty days after their appointment; *provided*, that if it shall appear to the satisfaction of said court, upon the application of such commissioners, that further time is necessary, said court may extend the time for making said report for a further period of not more than thirty days; and upon the coming in of any such report signed by the said commissioners, or any two of them, the said court shall cause notice to be given as it shall direct of the time and place of hearing any objection that may be made to such assessment, and after hearing any matter which may be alleged against the same the said court shall, by rule or order, either confirm the said report or refer the same to the same or to new commissioners, to be appointed by the said court, to reconsider the matter thereof; and the said commissioners to whom the said report shall be so re ferred shall return the same report corrected and revised, or a new report to be made by them in the premises, to the said court without unnecessay delay, and the same on

When commissioners appointed shall make report of proceedings.

Proviso.

being so returned, shall be confirmed or again referred by said court in manner aforesaid as right and justice shall require, and so from time to time until a report shall be made or returned in the premises which the said court shall confirm, and such report, when so confirmed by said court shall be final and conclusive, as well upon the said township as upon the owner of any land and real estate affected thereby; and the said court shall thereupon cause a certified copy of said report to be transmitted to the clerk of such township, with a certified copy of the rule of said court confirming said report, and the assessment so made shall be thereupon collected as authorized by the special law under which such costs, damages and expenses were incurred; and in case the said costs, damages and expenses shall exceed the amount of said benefits, such excess shall be a debt upon and paid by the township in which such improvement is made out of moneys raised by general taxation for that purpose.

2. *And be it enacted*, That this act shall take effect immediately.

Approved March 17, 1893.

CHAPTER CCXIV.

A Supplement to the act entitled "A supplement to the act entitled 'An act to establish an excise department in cities of this state,' passed April eighth, one thousand eight hundred and eighty-four," which supplementary act was approved February twenty-fourth, in the year of our Lord one thousand eight hundred and ninety-two.

Powers of boards of excise commissioners in cities and towns, except cities of the first class.

1. BE IT ENACTED *by the Senate and General Assembly of the State of New Jersey*, That every board of excise commisioners within and for any town or city of this state,

except in cities of the first class, heretofore appointed and organized, and which hereafter shall be appointed and organized, under and pursuant to the supplementary act to which this is a supplement, shall have the following powers, namely: to appoint a clerk of said excise board at an annual salary of not more than one hundred dollars; to employ counsel learned in law to advise them, and prosecute suits and actions brought by and defend suits and actions brought against them at an annual salary of not more than one hundred dollars; to purchase such books to be kept as records, and such blanks and other stationery as they shall consider necessary at an annual sum not exceeding twenty-five dollars; and to pay the salary of their clerk, the compensation to which their counsel shall be entitled; the purchase price for record books, blanks and stationery, and their own salaries prescribed by the supplementary act to which this is a supplement out of the license fees which may come into their hands.

2. *And be it enacted*, That the clerk appointed by any board of excise commissioners shall hold his office during the pleasure of the board by and for which he shall be appointed, and shall before he enters upon the execution of his office take and subscribe an oath or affirmation in the following form, to-wit: Term of office of clerk.

I, ———, clerk of the board of excise commissioners within and for the (town or city) of ———, do solemnly and sincerely promise and swear (or affirm) that I will faithfully and honestly keep all the papers, writings, books and records by virtue of my office committed, and which from time to time shall be committed to me, and that I will, in all things, to the best of my knowledge and understanding, perform the duties of said office of clerk without favor or partiality; Oath.

Which oath or affirmation may be subscribed and taken before any person authorized by the laws of this state to administer oaths and affirmations, and after the taking thereof shall be filed by said clerk and kept by him with the papers and writings pertaining to his office. Oath to be filed.

3. *And be it enacted*, That upon the death or expiration of the office of clerk of any board of excise commissioners all the papers, writings, books and records belonging to the said office shall be delivered to the successor in All papers, books, &c., at expiration of office delivered to successor, on oath.

office, on the oath or affirmation of the preceding clerk, or, in case of his death, on the oath or affirmation of his executors or administrators; and if any such clerk, his executors or administrators, shall refuse or neglect to deliver the same on oath or affirmation as aforesaid, being lawfully demanded, then every such person shall forfeit fifty dollars, to be recovered with costs, by action of debt, in any court having cognizance of that sum in the name of the board by and for which such clerk was appointed, for the same uses to which license fees received by said board are directed to be applied and used.

Penalty for refusing or neglect to deliver.

Power to designate newspaper to publish ordinances, &c.

4. *And be it enacted*, That every board of excise commissioners heretofore appointed and organized, and which hereafter may be appointed and organized within and for any town or city of this State, under and pursuant to the act to which this is a supplement, shall have the power to designate the newspaper or newspapers in which any ordinance, by-law or resolution passed or adopted by them shall be published, and shall pay the charges of such publication out of any license fees received by them.

When license fees received shall be paid to treasurer.

5. *And be it enacted*, That all license fees received by any board of excise commissioners which shall not be required by them to pay salaries or other matter or thing which by this act they are authorized and empowered to pay, shall, within ten days after the receipt thereof, be paid by said board to the treasurer of the town or city within and for which they are appointed for the use of such town or city.

How board shall publish annually statement of license fees received and payments thereof.

6. *And be it enacted*, That annually after the passage of this act, every board of excise commissioners within and for any town or city of this state shall publish in two newspapers publ shed in such town or city, if so many be published therein, and if so many be not published therein, then in one newspaper published in such town or city and one newspaper published in the county in which such town or city is, and circulated in such town or city, and if no newspaper be published in such town or city, then in two newspapers published in the county in which said town or city is and circulated therein, a detailed statement and account of the license fees received, and of the payments thereof, the expenses of

which publication shall be paid by the board of excise commissioners out of the license fees in or which shall come into their hands.

7. *And be it enacted*, That all acts and parts of acts, general and special, local and public, iconsistent with the provisions of this act be and the same are hereby repealed, and that this act shall take effect immediately. Repealer.

Approved March 17, 1893.

CHAPTER CCXV.

An Act to establish the rate of interest on arrears of taxes in cities of this state.

1. BE IT ENACTED *by the Senate and General Assembly of the State of New Jersey*, That it shall be lawful for the common council or other board having charge and control of the finances of any city in this state to fix and change, by resolution, the rate of interest on all past-due taxes which were due and unpaid prior to January first, one thousand eight hundred and ninety-two; *provided, however*, that such rate when adopted shall apply only to such taxes as are still due and unpaid to such city.

Lawful to fix rate of interest on past due taxes by resolution.

Proviso.

2. *And be it enacted*, That if any taxes shall have been paid within four months prior to the passage of this act the said common council or other proper board shall have power to refund any excess of interest and costs that may have been paid, over and above the rate of interest, that may be fixed under the authority of the first section of this act.

Power to refund excess of interest and costs.

3. *And be it enacted*, That all laws, general or special, inconsistent herewith be and the same are hereby repealed, and that this act shall take effect immediately. Repealer.

Approved March 17, 1893.

CHAPTER CCXVI.

A Further Supplement to an act entitled "A general act relating to factories and workshops, and the employment, safety, health and work-hours of operatives," approved April seventh, one thousand eight hundred and eighty-five.

When and where unlawful to manufacture coats, vests, &c.

1. BE IT ENACTED *by the Senate and General Assembly of the State of New Jersey*, That no room or rooms, apartment or apartments in any tenement or dwelling house shall be used for the manufacture of coats, vests, trousers, knee-pants, overalls, cloaks, furs, fur trimmings, fur garments, shirts, purses, feathers artificial flowers or cigars except by the immediate members of the family living therein; that no person, firm or corporation shall hire or employ any person to work in any room or rooms, apartment or apartments, in any tenement or dwelling house or building in the rear of a tenement or dwelling house at making in whole or in part any coats, vests, trousers, knee pants, overalls, cloaks, furs, fur trimmings, fur garments, shirts, purses, feathers, artificial flowers or cigars, unless such person, firm or corporation first shall have obtained a written permit from the factory and workshop inspector or a deputy inspector, which permit may be revoked at any time that the health of the community or of those employed as aforesaid may require it, and that such permit shall not be granted until due and satisfactory inspection of the premises affected shall have been made by the said inspector or deputy inspectors; that such permit shall be framed and posted in a conspicuous place in the room or each of the rooms to which it relates, shall be duly numbered and shall state the number of persons allowed to be employed therein.

When necessary to have permit from inspector of factories, &c.

Permit may be revoked.

Permit posted in conspicuous place.

Penalty for violation.

2. *And be it enacted*, That any person, firm or corporation being the owner, lessee or occupant of the room or

rooms to which this act relates shall for the violation of any of the provisions herein be liable to the same penalty or penalties as are now prescribed for violations of the act and supplements of the act to which this is a further supplement.

8. *And be it enacted*, That this act shall take effect immediately.

Approved March 17, 1898.

CHAPTER CCXVII.

A Supplement to an act entitled "An act to secure to mechanics and others payment for their labor and materials in erecting any building," approved March twenty-seventh, one thousand eight hundred and seventy-four, for the purpose of extending the rights and remedies under said act to the labor performed and materials furnished to and for the removal of any building or buildings or part or parts of a building from one curtilage to that of another; and further, to extend the lien for such removal to the land or curtilage to which the said building, buildings or part or parts of a building shall be removed and located under the contract.

When debt contracted for removing building shall be a lien thereon.

1. BE IT ENACTED *by the Senate and General Assembly of the State of New Jersey*, That every building or part or parts of any building which shall hereafter be removed and shall be located upon some other lot or curtilage, and which shall, when removed, constitute a complete structure or a part of a structure upon the curtilage to which the same shall be removed, shall be liable for the payment of any debt contracted and owing to any person for labor performed or materials furnished in the re-

moval of the same, which debt shall be a lien on such building so removed and the building to which the same shall be attached or incorporated and on the land whereon the building shall be removed, including the lot or curtilage whereon the same is located by such removal.

What shall be deemed labor performed and materials furnished.

2. *And be it enacted*, That all of the labor performed and materials furnished in erecting, constructing and repairing the foundation or super-structure, upon which such removed building shall be located upon or incorporated with some other building, shall be deemed and taken to be labor performed and materials furnished in the removal of the building.

3. *And be it enacted*, That this act shall take effect immediately.

Approved March 17, 1893.

CHAPTER CCXVIII.

An Act to repeal an act entitled "A supplement to an act entitled 'An act concerning savings banks,' approved April twenty-first, one thousand eight hundred and seventy-six," which supplement was approved April ninth, one thousand eight hundred and eighty-eight.

Repealer.

1. BE IT ENACTED *by the Senate and General Assembly of the State of New Jersey*, That an act entitled "A supplement to an act entitled 'An act concerning savings banks,' approved April twenty-first, one thousand eight hundred and seventy-six," which supplement was approved April ninth, one thousand eight hundred and eighty-eight, be and the said supplement is hereby repealed.

2. *And be it enacted*, That this act shall take effect immediately.

Approved March 17, 1893.

CHAPTER CCXIX.

A Supplement to an act entitled "An act to authorize the incorporation of rural cemetery associations and regulate cemeteries" (Revision), approved April ninth, one thousand eight hundred and seventy-five.

Number composing and manner of electing managers and trustees

1. Be it enacted *by the Senate and General Assembly of the State of New Jersey*, That the care and management of all cemetery associations incorporated under the provisions of the act to which this act is a supplement, or by virtue of any special charter, may be confided in a board of managers or trustees, which board shall consist of not less than three nor more than twelve managers or trustees, who shall be lot-holders, and shall be elected at the annual meeting of the association, at which time the number of the said board of managers or trustees shall be determined; and the president and secretary shall, immediately after such election, divide the managers and trustees, by lot, into three classes; those of the first class to hold their office one year, those of the second class two years, and those of the third class three years, but the managers or trustees of each class may be re-elected if they shall possess the requisite qualification at the time of their re-election; they shall also determine on what day in each future year the annual election of managers or trustees shall be held; the said board to have the exclusive superintendence of such association, with full power to appoint, employ, and discharge any or all of the officers or agents of said association, as they may deem expedient, and to fix the compensation of such officers or agents.

Divided into classes

Term of office

May be re-elected.

Duties of board.

Time and place of holding elections.

2. *And be it enacted*, That the annual election for managers or trustees to supply the place of those whose term of office expires shall be holden on the day selected, or at such time and at such hour and place as the managers or trustees shall direct, at which election shall be chosen

such number of managers or trustees as will supply the places of those whose term expires; the managers or trustees chosen at any election subsequent to the first shall hold their places for three years, and until others shall be chosen to succeed them; the election shall be by ballot, and every person of full age, who shall be proprietor of a lot or plat in the cemetery of the association, or if there be more than one proprietor of any such lot or plat, then such one of the proprietors as the majority of the joint proprietors shall designate to represent such lot or plat, may either in person or by proxy give one vote for each lot or plat; *provided*, that no one person shall vote for more than one hundred plats or lots; and the person or persons receiving the largest number of the votes given at such election shall be managers or trustees to succeed those whose term of office expires; and the managers or trustees shall have power to fill any vacancy in their number occurring during the period for which they hold their office; public notice of the annual election shall be given in such manner as the by-laws of the association shall prescribe.

Election by ballot.

Persons entitled to vote.

Proviso.

Not personally liable for debts contracted.

3. *And be it enacted*, That no such manager or trustee shall be personally liable or responsible for the debts or obligations of any such association contracted after the passage of this act.

Repealer.

4. *And be it enacted*, That all acts or parts of acts inconsistent with this act be and the same are hereby repealed.

5. *And be it enacted*, That this act shall take effect immediately.

Approved March 17, 1893.

CHAPTER CCXX.

AN ACT relating to assessment insurance.

1. BE IT ENACTED *by the Senate and General Assembly of the State of New Jersey*, That any corporation or association organized under the laws of any other state of the United States for the purpose of furnishing life insurance upon the assessment plan, or that is carrying on the business of life insurance upon the assessment plan, may be authorized by the commissioner of banking and insurance to transact business in this state when it shall have deposited with him a certified copy of its charter or articles of incorporation; a statement under oath, of its president and secretary, in the form required by the commissioner of banking and insurance, of its business for the year ending December thirty-first last preceding; a certificate under oath of its president and secretary, that it is paying, and for the twelve months then next preceding has paid, the maximum amount named in its policies or certificates in full, and that it does not issue policies or certificates of life insurance upon lives of persons more than sixty-five years of age, nor upon any life in which the beneficiary named has no interest; a copy of the application for membership or insurance and of the by-laws, also a copy of the form of policy or certificate of membership, and of each form thereof if more than one form is used; a certificate from the insurance commissioner or other like officer charged with the duty of executing the insurance laws of the state where said corporation or association is organized, certifying that it is legally entitled to do business; evidence satisfactory to the commissioner of banking and insurance that the corporation or association has accumulated and maintains a reserve or emergency fund not less than the proceeds of one death assessment or periodical call on all policy or certificate holders thereof, and at least equal to the amount of its maximum policy or certificate; that such accumula-

When, by whom authorized to transact business

Statement under oath of its business.

Certificate under oath that it pays policies in full.

Copy of application for membership.

Insurance commissioner to issue certificate authorizing to do business.

Reserve fund to be maintained

tion is permitted by the law of its incorporation, and is a trust for the benefit of policy or certificate holders only, and is securely invested.

Certificates issued to agents to be renewed annually.

2. *And be it enacted*, That after authorizing such corporation or association to do business in this state as provided in this act, the commissioner of banking and insurance shall issue certificates to agents thereof, to be designated by the corporation or association authorizing them to act as such agents, which certificates shall be renewed annually on the first day of January, or within sixty days thereafter.

Unlawful to do business or act as agent unless authorized by certificate of commissioner of banking and insurance.

3. *And be it enacted*, That it shall not be lawful for any corporation or association organized under other authority than the laws of this state, for the purpose of furnishing life insurance upon the assessment plan, to do any business in this state or for any person to act within this state as agent in soliciting, procuring, receiving or transmitting any application for membership or insurance, in or for, or on behalf of any such corporation or association, unless such corporation or association shall be authorized to do business in this state under this act, and such agent shall have received a certificate of authority from the commissioner of banking and insurance as herein provided.

When, by whom an examination to be made.

4. *And be it enacted*, That whenever the commissioner of banking and insurance deems it prudent, for the protection of the policy or certificate holders in this state, he may visit and examine, or cause to be visited and examined by some competent person or persons he may appoint for that purpose, any such foreign assessment insurance corporation or association applying for admission or doing business in this state, and the necessary expense of any such examination made or ordered to be made by said commissioner shall be certified to by him and paid by the corporation or association so examined; and if, upon such examination or otherwise, the commissioner of banking and insurance shall be satisfied that any such corporation or association is not paying in full the maximum amount named in its policies or certificates, or that it is conducting its business fraudulently, or that it is not carrying out its contracts with its policy or certificate holders in good faith, it shall be his duty to

By whom expenses paid.

When, by whom authority may be revoked.

refuse such application for admission or forthwith to revoke all authority previously given to such corporation or association and all its agents, to do business in this state, and shall publish such revocation in some newspaper or newspapers published therein, and no business shall be thereafter done by such corporation or association or its agents in this state.

5. *And be it enacted*, That the commissioner of banking and insurance is hereby authorized and empowered to address any inquiries he may deem proper to any corporation or association which may be authorized to do business in this state under the provisions of this act, in relation to its business or condition, and it shall be the duty of the officers of such corporation or association so addressed to promptly reply in writing to all such inquiries under the oath of its president or secretary or other like officers, and, in case of a failure or refusal of such officers to so reply, the commissioner of banking and insurance may suspend or revoke all authority to such corporation or association and all its agents, to do business in this state.

On failure to reply to inquiries under oath authority may be revoked.

6. *And be it enacted*, That every such corporation or association authorized to do business in this state under this act shall designate some place within the state as the principal office therein of such corporation, and some person residing in the same city, village or town where such office is located as a person upon whom service of legal process and papers may be made as upon such corporation; such designation shall be made by an instrument under the hand of the president and secretary or other duly authorized officers of the corporation, and shall be filed with the commissioner of banking and insurance; if the person so designated shall die or remove from such place another person shall be appointed in his place within thirty days; and such attorney or location of principal office may, at the option of the corporation, be changed at any time; notice of such change or of a new designation of a person upon whom service may be made as herein provided, under the hand of such president and secretary or other officer, shall be filed with the commissioner within thirty days after such change or new designation is made; upon failure to

To designate place of principal office, &c., and file same.

Upon failure to comply, shall cease to do business.

comply with any of the provisions of this section within thirty days after written notice by the commissioner of such default and requiring such compliance, the corporation shall cease to do business in the state until it has complied therewith.

Who deemed to be an agent

7. *And be it enacted*, That whoever solicits, procures, or receives in or transmits from this state any application other than his own, for membership or insurance in any corporation or association embraced by section three shall be deemed and held to be an agent of such corporation or association within the meaning of this act; and any person who shall transact business for any corporation or association embraced in section three, as an agent thereof within the meaning of this act, without first procuring and having a certificate of authority from the commissioner of banking and insurance to act as such agent, or after such certificate of authority has been suspended or revoked, shall be subject to a penalty of two hundred and fifty dollars, to be recovered by an action of debt, in the name of the state, on the complaint of the commissioner of banking and insurance, the first process in which action may be a capias ad respondendum and a defendant against whom a judgment shall have been rendered shall remain in custody until such penalty and costs shall be paid; and the expenses of such suit shall be paid by the said commissioner out of any moneys in his hands not otherwise appropriated.

Agent doing business without authority, or when certificate has been revoked, liable to penalty.

Penalty.

To file annual report, under oath.

8. *And be it enacted*, That every corporation or association which may be doing business in this state under the provisions of this act, shall on or before the first day of March in each year make and file with the commissioner of banking and insurance a report of its affairs and operations during the year ending thirty-first next preceding, in such form as the commissioner of banking and insurance may require, which shall be verified under the oath of the president and secretary, and shall be published, or the substance thereof, in his annual report, by the commissioner of banking and insurance.

Fees for filing certificate, &c.

9. *And be it enacted*, That every such foreign corporation or association admitted to transact business under this act shall pay for filing the certified copy of its charter or articles of incorporation twenty dollars; for filing

the preliminary statement on admission, twenty dollars; for filing the annual statement thereafter, twenty dollars, and for certificates of authority to agents, two dollars each.

10. *And be it enacted*, That this act shall not apply to secret or fraternal societies conducting their business on the lodge system, nor to associations organized solely for benevolent or charitable purposes. Societies exempt.

11. *And be it enacted*, That all acts and parts of acts inconsistent with the provisions of this act be and the same are hereby repealed, and that this act shall take effect immediately. Repealer.

Approved March 17, 1898.

CHAPTER CCXXI.

An Act to amend an act entitled "An act in relation to the temporary custody of dangerous lunatics," approved March twenty-third, one thousand eight hundred and eighty-eight.

1. BE IT ENACTED *by the Senate and General Assembly of the State of New Jersey*, That section three of an act entitled "An act in relation to the temporary custody of dangerous lunatics," approved March twenty-third, one thousand eight hundred and eighty-eight, be and the same hereby is amended so as to read as follows: Section to be amended

3. *And be it enacted*, That in case there shall be no friends or relatives of such lunatic who will make application to the court or a judge thereof for the admission of such lunatic into a lunatic asylum, or the removal to their places of legal settlement, it shall be the duty of the city attorney or the officer acting in that capacity in cities, and of the chairman of the township committee in townships in which such dangerous lunatics may be apprehended, or supposed to have a legal settlement, immedi- Application for admission of lunatic into asylum, &c., who to make in certain cases.

ately after the temporary confinement of such lunatic, to make application to the court or a judge thereof for the admission of such lunatics into a lunatic asylum, or their removal to their places of legal settlement; and such proceedings shall be had thereon as are now provided by law.

2. *And be it enacted*, That this act shall take effect immediately.

Approved March 17, 1893.

CHAPTER CCXXII.

An Act to amend an act entitled "An act to regulate and license pawnbrokers," approved March twenty-ninth, one thousand eight hundred and eighty-seven.

Section to be amended.

1. BE IT ENACTED *by the Senate and General Assembly of the State of New Jersey*, That section thirteen of an act entitled "An act to regulate and license pawnbrokers," approved March twenty-ninth, one thousand eight hundred and eighty-seven, be and the same is hereby amended so as to read as follows:

Penalty for violation of provisions of this act.

13. *And be it enacted*, That any person or corporation who shall violate the provisions of the first section of this act shall be liable to a penalty of one hundred dollars for each and every day of the continuance of said violation; and any person or corporation who shall violate any of the provisions of any other section of this act shall be liable to a penalty of fifty dollars for every such violation; the said penalties shall be recovered by complaint under oath before any criminal court, police justice or recorder in such city, upon which a warrant or summons may be issued and the case shall be summarily heard and disposed of without the filing of any pleadings; said penalties when imposed shall be collected, in the case of an individual, by a body execution, and in

How penalties recovered.

the case of a corporation, by an execution against the goods and chattels of said corporation.

2. *And be it enacted*, That this act shall take effect immediately.

Approved March 17, 1898.

CHAPTER CCXXIII.

An Act to repeal chapter two hundred and eighty-five of the laws of one thousand eight hundred and eighty-nine, entitled "An act amendatory of an act entitled 'An act concerning divisions of wards in cities of this state.'"

1. Be it enacted *by the Senate and General Assembly of the State of New Jersey*, That chapter two hundred and eighty-five of the laws of one thousand eight hundred and eighty-nine, entitled "An act amendatory of an act entitled 'An act concerning divisions of wards in cities of this state,'" be and the same is hereby repealed. Repealer.

2. *And be it enacted*, That this act shall take effect immediately.

Approved March 17, 1898.

CHAPTER CCXXIV.

An Act to provide for the issuing of additional county road bonds for the purpose of improving county roads.

Authorized to issue additional county road bonds not exceeding $350,000.

1. BE IT ENACTED *by the Senate and General Assembly of the State of New Jersey*, That in any county in this state in which the board of chosen freeholders have acquired and improved public roads or may hereafter acquire and improve public roads under the authority of an act entitled "An act to enable boards of chosen freeholders to acquire, improve and maintain public roads," approved March nineteenth, one thousand eight hundred and eighty-nine, and the supplements and amendments thereto, and have issued county road bonds by virtue or under authority of the said act and the supplements and amendments thereto, and by reason of authority granted in a certificate issued by the circuit court of that county in accordance with the provisions of the said act and the supplements and amendments thereto, it shall not be necessary to repeat the application to the said court provided for in section three of the said act, in order to issue an additional amount of county road bonds for the purpose of improving additional sections of the county road that may be acquired by such board of chosen freeholders subsequent to the making of the original application for the issuing of such county road bonds, but in no case shall any such board issue bonds under the said act and the supplements and amendments thereto, exceeding the sum of three hundred and fifty thousand dollars; *provided*, that no additional county road bonds shall be issued where the amount of such proposed issue in addition to existing debt shall raise the debt of the county for all purposes above three per centum of the assessed value of the real estate therein at the time of the issue of such bonds.

Proviso.

Repealer.

2. *And be it enacted*, That all acts and parts of acts, inconsistent with the provisions of this act be and the same

are hereby repealed in so far as their operation may affect the operation of this act.

3. *And be it enacted*, That this act shall take effect immediately.

Approved March 17, 1893.

CHAPTER CCXXV.

An Act amending an act to provide for the purchase, construction and maintenance of public parks by the cities and other municipalities in this state, approved March fourteenth, one thousand eight hundred and eighty-three.

1. BE IT ENACTED *by the Senate and General Assembly of the State of New Jersey*, That the first section of the act to which this is amendatory be and the same is hereby further amended to read as follows: Section to be amended.

1. BE IT ENACTED *by the Senate and General Assembly of the State of New Jersey*, That in any city or other municipality in this state, the common council, board of aldermen, board of trustees, or other board or body having control of the streets, highways and public parks and places therein, may by ordinance passed by a two-thirds vote of the members of such board or body, purchase, or condemn if unable to purchase, one or more tracts of land lying wholly or partly within or without the limits of said city or other municipality, for the use of the inhabitants of such city or municipality as a public park or parks, and may dedicate the same to such use, and may lay out, embellish, and maintain the same, and from time to time pass ordinances regulating and controlling the same, and providing for the proper and convenient use thereof by the inhabitants aforesaid. Common council, &c., may, by ordinance, purchase lands for public park.

2. *And be it enacted*, That such lands may be paid for as provided in the second section of said act, and in case How lands paid for.

of condemnation, the mode and method of procedure shall be that provided in an act entitled "An act to empower cities to acquire lands for public parks by condemnation," approved May twelfth, one thousand eight hundred and ninety.

Repealer. 3. *And be it enacted*, That all acts and parts of acts inconsistent with this act be and the same are hereby repealed, and that this act shall be deemed a public act and shall take effect immediately.

Approved March 17, 1898.

CHAPTER CCXXVI.

An Act to provide for the paving or macadamizing of streets, roads and avenues in cities of the third class.

Lawful, upon application to council, &c., for paving or macadamizing, to authorize by resolution said improvement.

1. Be it enacted *by the Senate and General Assembly of the State of New Jersey*, That in any city of the third class, whose charter provides that the council may by ordinance provide for the payment of one-third of the expense and cost of paving the streets of said city with Belgian blocks, macadamizing, or any other substantial material, that if any of the owners of lands on any street, road or avenue in said city shall make application, in writing, to the council or other governing body of said city, for the paving or macadamizing of any such street, road or avenue, that in such case it shall be lawful for the said council or other governing body, at any regular meeting at which such application shall be presented, or at any regular meeting thereafter, to authorize by resolution the carrying out of said improvement, and that in such case the said resolution so adopted as aforesaid shall have the effect of a petition or application signed by one-third of the owners of the lands fronting on said improvement, and in such case such preliminary steps shall be taken to carry out such improvement as is provided

for by the charter of such city; and that unless two-thirds of the owners of the lands fronting on said improvement remonstrate, as provided for by said charter, then in that case it shall be lawful for the said city council or other governing body to proceed to carry out said improvement mentioned in said petition according to the provisions of the said charter. Who may remonstrate.

2. *And be it enacted*, That all acts and parts of acts inconsistent herewith be and the same are hereby repealed. Repealer.

3. *And be it enacted*, That this act shall take effect immediately.

Approved March 17, 1893.

CHAPTER CCXXVII.

A Further Supplement to "An Act for the better preservation of the early records of the state of New Jersey," passed March twenty-ninth, one thousand eight hundred and seventy-two.

1. Be it enacted *by the Senate and General Assembly of the State of New Jersey*, That to enable the New Jersey Historical Society to complete the work of procuring material for, and arranging, collating, editing and printing the early records of the state, to the close of the Revolution, in the form known as the "New Jersey Archives," the sum of three thousand dollars, or so much thereof as may be required for said purposes, is hereby appropriated, to be paid by the state treasurer on the warrant of the comptroller, to the person or persons furnishing such material or doing said work, upon presenting to and filing with the comptroller vouchers approved under the hands of at least three members of Appropriation to complete the work $3,000. How paid

the committee heretofore appointed by said society to have charge of the publication of said archives.

2. *And be it enacted*, That this act shall take effect immediately.

Approved March 17, 1893.

CHAPTER CCXXVIII.

A Supplement to the act entitled "An act to empower cities to acquire land for public use by condemnation," approved March seventeenth, one thousand eight hundred and ninety-one.

Commissioners shall ascertain and report damages.

1. BE IT ENACTED *by the Senate and General Assembly of the State of New Jersey*, That whenever the land which any city or any of the boards or departments thereof require or desire to acquire for public use, has already been dedicated or used by the city for other public purposes, whether such dedication has been made by grant, devise or otherwise, such land may be acquired under the provisions of the act to which this is a supplement and the supplements thereto, and such former use diverted to and the said lands acquired and used by such city or board or departments as required, and any person who may have an interest, in any manner, in said lands or any part thereof, in law or equity, shall be notified and the commissioners shall ascertain and report the damages of such person by reason of the diversion of such use of said lands, and the amounts so allowed shall be paid, or paid into court in the same manner as provided in said act and supplements, and upon such payment, tender of payment or payment into the court of the amount as aforesaid, the city may take possession and use such lands as required and desired, freed and discharged from all former uses, trusts, interests and estates of every kind and of every person whatever, and in case the commissioners are unable to ascertain with certainty all

who are, in any manner, interested in said lands and so report, then said commissioners, or a majority of them, may ascertain and report the total value, in gross, of all the damages occasioned by such proposed diversion of the use of said lands of such person as may be interested therein, and the city may pay to the clerk of the circuit court of such county such gross sum, and thereupon may enter into and take possession of said lands and use and occupy them as desired, freed and discharged from all trusts, estates and interests of every person whatsoever, and said sum, so paid into court, shall be paid out, on order of said court, to such persons as are entitled thereto or placed in trust, as provided in said act and supplements.

Report total value in gross

To take possession of lands

2. *And be it enacted*, That the commissioners appointed under the said act shall estimate and assess the damages that any person or corporation may sustain by reason of the diversion of such land from its dedicated use or present use to the use desired by such city or its boards or departments, and shall in their report make a return of what in their judgment or in the judgment of the majority of them is a fair and just award for damages suffered in any manner whatsoever by such person or corporation by reason of the proposed different use of said land from that dedicated or used; and that the city shall pay the amounts so appraised and allowed for damages, and any such person or corporation or the city if aggrieved by said report may appeal from the said apraisement and award in respect to her, him or it in the manner and within the time in the said act to which this is a supplement provided, and the jury shall assess his, her or its damages in the premises, and all the provisions in relation to such appeal in said act provided not inconsistent herewith shall apply.

Appeal from appraisement.

Jury shall assess damage.

3. *And be it enacted*, That in case the land, or any part thereof, to be acquired for public use has been conveyed for a private special use or purpose to any person or corporation, or is so used, and the grantor or his heirs or other persons have, or claim to have, some interest in law or equity therein, and will be, or claim that they will be, damaged if said lands are devoted to or used for other purposes, the commissioners may ascertain and report the total value in gross of all the interests, estates and shares

When the commissioners may ascertain and report total value in gross of all interests.

in said lands or real estate, whether in possession, remainder, reversion or expectancy, and the total damages for the taking of the same, or may, if all the parties in interest can be ascertained, report the share of each such person and the award of damages to each, the aggregate amount of which shall be the gross sum, and such award and appraisement otherwise lawfully made shall bind all persons and corporations in any manner interested in said lands; and upon payment to the parties, if all can be ascertained and all are satisfied, or to the clerk of the circuit court of such county, of such gross sum, the city may enter upon and take possession of such lands freed and discharged from all trusts, estates and interests, and of every person whatsoever; and in all such cases the circuit court of such county may appoint a trustee, or pay and dispose of such money to the persons entitled thereto, as in said act and the supplements thereto provided; and an appeal from such report and award may be taken in the manner and within the time as in the said act to which this is a supplement provided, and all the provisions in relation to such appeal not inconsistent herewith shall apply

When city may enter and take possession.

Appeal, how taken

Repealer.

4. *And be it enacted,* That all acts and parts of acts, so far as they are inconsistent herewith, be and the same are hereby repealed and that this act shall take effect immediately.

Approved March 17, 1898.

CHAPTER CCXXIX.

An Act to amend an act entitled "An act for the form tion and government of boroughs," approved Ap second, one thousand eight hundred and ninety-one.

Section to be amended.

1. BE IT ENACTED *by the Senate and General Assembly the State of New Jersey,* That section two of an act e

titled "An act for the formation and government of boroughs," which act was approved April second, one thousand eight hundred and ninety-one, be and the same is hereby amended so as to read as follows:

How and by whom a special election called.

2. *And be it enacted*, That it shall be the duty of the law judge of the court of common pleas in and for the county in which said proposed borough is situated, and if such county have no law judge then it shall be the duty of the justice of the supreme court appointed to hold the circuit court in said county, upon presentation to him of a petition for that purpose, setting forth the name and boundaries of the proposed borough, signed by persons owning at least one-tenth in value of the taxable real estate in the limits of the proposed borough, as the same appears upon the assessor's duplicate, to call a special election, to be held at some convenient place within the proposed borough, by notice in writing under his hand, which notice shall contain an accurate description of the same and boundaries of the proposed borough and state the object of the said election to be to vote for or against the incorporation of the said proposed borough, under the provisions of this act; which notice shall be set up at least ten days previous to said proposed election in five of the most public places within the said proposed borough limits, and published at least twice in a newspaper printed and published within the said proposed borough limits, if any, or if none so published, then in a newspaper printed and published in the county wherein said proposed borough is situated.

Notice to be given.

Notice to be printed and published.

Section to be amended

2. *And be it enacted*, That section four of the same act be and the same is hereby amended so as to read as follows:

How and by whom objections made

4. *And be it enacted*, That any citizen of the district within the limits of which the proposed borough is to be created shall be allowed to appear before said judge and object to the making of the order for such special election, and that the said judge shall, on the same day or on some other day to which he may adjourn the hearing of said petition, proceed to hear the matter.

3. *And be it enacted*, That this act shall take effect immediately.

Approved March 17, 1893.

CHAPTER CCXXX.

A Further Supplement to an act entitled "An act regulating proceedings in criminal cases" (Revision), approved March twenty-seventh, one thousand eight hundred and seventy-four.

Section to be amended.

1. BE IT ENACTED *by the Senate and General Assembly of the State of New Jersey*, That section ninety-six of the act to which this a supplement be amended to read as follows:

Convicts to be conveyed to state prison.

96. *And be it enacted*, That every person sentenced to hard labor and imprisonment under the laws of this state, for any time not less than six months, shall within twenty days after such sentence be transported, at the expense of the state, by the sheriff of the county where such conviction may be had or by his lawful deputy, to the state prison and there delivered into the custody of the keeper of said prison, together with a copy of the sentence of the court ordering such punishment and of the taxed bill of costs of prosecution against such offender, certified under the hand and seal of the clerk of the court where such conviction was had, and said person so delivered to

And safely kept.

the keeper of said prison shall be safely kept therein until the time of his or her confinement shall have expired and the fine or fines and cost of prosecution be paid or remitted, or until he or she shall be otherwise discharged according to law; and every person sentenced

For less than six months, in county jail, or county workhouse or penitentiary.

to imprisonment for any time less than six months shall be confined in the common jail of the county where the conviction was had, or the county workhouse, or the county penitentiary, in the discretion of the court, and there safely kept until the term of his or her confinement shall expire and the fine and costs of prosecution be paid, or until he or she shall be discharged by due course of law.

2. *And be it enacted*, That this act shall take effect immediately.

Approved March 17, 1893.

CHAPTER CCXXXI.

A Supplement to an act entitled "An act to establish in this state boards of health and a bureau of vital statistics, and to define their respective powers and duties," approved March thirty-first, anno domini one thousand eight hundred and eighty-seven.

When police justice, &c., authorized to issue a warrant.

1. Be it enacted *by the Senate and General Assembly of the State of New Jersey*, That all police justices, recorders, justices of the peace and all other magistrates are hereby authorized on complaint founded on information and belief, supported by oath or affirmation of any officer or agent of the state board of health or of any local board of health that there is in any dwelling house, store, stable or any building of any kind whatsoever any nuisance affecting health or any person sick of any contagious or infectious disease, or any condition of contagion or infection which may have been caused by any one recently sick of any such disease in such dwelling house, store, stable or any other building, to issue a warrant directed to the sheriff of the county within which such complaint shall be made, or to any constable, marshal, police officer or to any officer or agent of such board of health, directing him, them or any of them to search in such dwelling house, store, stable or other building for such nuisance affecting health; or for any person sick of any contagious or infectious disease, or for any condition of contagion or infection which may have been caused by anyone recently sick of any such disease in such dwelling house or other place as aforesaid, and if such nuisance be found, to abate the same; and if such sick person be found to deal with him according to law and the ordinances of such board of health; and if such condition of contagion or infection be found to exist, to destroy the same by means of proper disinfection.

Search to be made.

2. *And be it enacted*, That the officer to whom such

To whom return made. search warrant shall be directed shall make return of his proceedings thereunder to the court or magistrate by which or whom such warrant may be issued.

Who are directed to assist officers. 3. *And be it enacted*, That the sheriff of the county and all constables, marshals and police officers of any county, city, borough or town, or such of them as shall be required are hereby directed if required by any officer to whom such warrant may be directed, to be present and assist in the execution thereof.

4. *And be it enacted*, That this act shall take effect immediately.

Approved March 17, 1893.

CHAPTER CCXXXII.

An Act amendatory of an act entitled "An act to amend an act entitled 'An act relative to the jurisdiction and practice of district courts in this state,' approved March twenty-seventh, one thousand eight hundred and eighty-two," which amendment was approved March eleventh, one thousand eight hundred and eighty-five.

Section to be amended. 1. BE IT ENACTED *by the Senate and General Assembly of the State of New Jersey*, That section three of said act, as amended, be and the same is hereby amended to read as follows:

Pleadings to be filed as in circuit courts, &c. 3. *And be it enacted*, That the pleadings to be filed in said district courts in any suit where the debt demanded, or damage claimed, actually exceeds the sum of value of two hundred dollars, shall be the same as those in the circuit courts of the several counties of this state, and the practice of such circuit courts, also, in so far as applicable, shall apply to said district courts in such cases, excepting, however, cases where there may be some express provision of law providing otherwise, and the declaration in any such suit shall be filed within ten days after the return day named in the summons, and the plea of demurrer of the defendant shall be filed within ten days after the time limited for filing the plaintiff's declaration; and each succeeding pleading, until the cause is at issue, shall be filed within ten days after the time limited for pleading by the opposite party; and every cause when at issue shall be noticed for trial within twenty days thereafter, and at least five days' notice of trial shall be given by the plaintiff and served in the same manner as in the circuit courts of the several counties of this state; and if the plaintiff shall neglect to notice his cause for trial within said time, judgment shall be awarded for the defendant as in case of a non-suit, with costs, unless the court allow further time; and the costs to be taxed in any such cause shall be the same to the attorney, court, clerk and sheriff as are taxable in the circuit courts of the several counties in this state; *provided, however*, that in case the plaintiff shall upon or within ten days after the return day of the summons file his declaration and serve a copy thereof on the defendant or his attorney, the defendant shall plead or demur thereto within ten days from the date of such service, and in default thereof the plaintiff may have judgment in the same manner that judgment by default is rendered in the circuit courts of the several counties of this state; and judgments by default in other cases for want of or failure to file plea or demurrer within the time above limited therefor, may be had and taken by the plaintiff in said district courts in the same manner as in such circuit courts. Proviso.

2. *And be it enacted*, That this act shall take effect immediately.

Approved March 17, 1898.

CHAPTER CCXXXIII.

A Supplement to an act entitled 'An act in reference to cities of the fourth class," approved April sixteenth, one thousand eight hundred and ninety-one, and to give the governing body the power to improve any of the streets or avenues therein at the expense of the city at large, and to provide for the payment of the same.

Additional powers conferred upon common council, &c.

1. BE IT ENACTED *by the Senate and General Assembly of the State of New Jersey*, That in addition to the powers conferred by the act to which this is a supplement, it shall be lawful, and the common council or other governing body empowered by the provisions of the act to which this is a supplement is hereby empowered and authorized to improve, pave, drain, curb, elevate or depress any street or avenue under its charge and control or any part or section thereof, at the expense of the municipality at large, whenever and in any case in which said common council or governing body shall deem it for the general interest of the municipality so to do.

To provide by ordinance to improve, pave, &c.

2. *And be it enacted*, That whenever it shall appear to said common council or other governing body that it shall be to the advantage of the municipality at large to improve, pave, drain, curb, elevate or depress any street or avenue, or part or section thereof, said council or governing body is empowered to provide by ordinance what particular street or avenue, or part or section thereof, shall be so improved at the general expense of the municipality at large, and shall further provide the specific kind or quality of improvement that is to be done, and shall further provide for letting the contract for such improvment to the lowest and best bidder for said work.

Authorized to issue bonds known as "Street improvement bonds."

3. *And be it enacted*, That it shall be lawful for said common council or other governing body of such city to pledge the credit of the city for the payment of any ex-

penditure for the improvements provided for in this act, by issuing bonds not exceeding the sum of three hundred thousand dollars, which said bonds are to be known as "street improvement bonds," shall bear interest not exceeding five per centum per annum, and shall not be issued for a shorter period than ten years nor a longer period than thirty years, which bond shall executed in the same manner as now provided by law.

Money required raised by taxation.

4. *And be it enacted*, That it shall be lawful for said common council or other governing body of such city to raise by taxation, in the manner and form as all other moneys for the use of said city are raised, annually so much money as may be required for the payment of interest on said bonds, and the principal as it may come due.

5. *And be it enacted*, That this act shall take effect immediately.

Approved March 17, 1893.

CHAPTER CCXXXIV.

An Act concerning cities of the fourth class.

Authorized to elect an assessor for each ward.

1. BE IT ENACTED *by the Senate and General Assembly of the State of New Jersey*, That it shall be lawful for cities of the fourth class, to elect an assessor for each of the respective wards in said city, whose duties shall be the same for his respective ward as are now imposed by law upon the assessor of the city at large.

Have equal representation at county board of.

2. *And be it enacted*, That each of the said ward assessors shall have equal representation at the county board of assessors and shall comply with the law in every respect as the assessor of the city now is required.

When ward assessors meet to revise duplicates.

3. *And be it enacted*, That the respective ward assessors shall meet in the council chamber of such city ten days before the meeting of the county board of assessors, and

shall then and there at the hour of ten o'clock in the forenoon of said day organize as a city board of assessors by electing one of their number chairman, and another one of their number secretary, and immediately after organization they shall proceed to examine and compare their respective duplicates, and if in the opinion of a majority of said assessors it shall appear that any duplicate may need revision or correction, such correction shall then and there be made.

Compensation.

4. *And be it enacted*, That the said ward assessors shall receive in addition to the fees now allowed to them by law, the sum of three dollars per diem during the session of said city board of assessors; *provided*, they shall not sit for a longer period than five days.

Proviso

Repealer.

5. *And be it enacted*, That all acts inconsistent with the provisions of this act are hereby repealed and that this act shall take effect immediately.

Approved March 17, 1898.

CHAPTER CCXXXV.

An Act to authorize township committees or other governing bodies of townships, villages or boroughs to appropriate moneys to establish or aid public libraries and free reading-rooms.

Authorized to appropriate $300, annually.

1. BE IT ENACTED *by the Senate and General Assembly of the State of New Jersey*, That it shall be lawful for the township committee or the board of trustees or other governing body of any township, or village, or borough in this state to appropriate from any moneys not otherwise appropriated such sum of money, not exceeding three hundred dollars annually, as may in their judgment be deemed necessary to establish or aid public

libraries and free reading-rooms in such township, or village, or borough in this state.

2. *And be it enacted*, That this act shall take effect immediately.

Approved March 17, 1893.

CHAPTER CCXXXVI.

A Supplement to an act entitled "An act to establish a bureau of statistics upon the subject of labor, considered in all its relations to the growth and development of state industries," approved March twenty-seventh, one thousand eight hundred and seventy-eight.

1. BE IT ENACTED *by the Senate and General Assembly of the State of New Jersey*, That the sum of five thousand dollars be and is hereby appropriated for the current expenses of said bureau. Appropriation.

2. *And be it enacted*, That the treasurer of this state it hereby authorized to pay from any money not otherwise appropriated the sum provided for in the first section of this act. State treasurer to pay.

3. *And be it enacted*, That this act take effect immediately.

Approved March 17, 1893.

CHAPTER CCXXXVII.

Supplement to act entitled "A further supplement to an act entitled 'An act concerning corporations,'" approved April seventh, one thousand eight hundred and seventy-five, which further supplement was approved May tenth, one thousand eight hundred and eighty-four.

Section to be amended.

1. BE IT ENACTED *by the Senate and General Assembly of the State of New Jersey*, That the first section of the act entitled "A further supplement to an act entitled 'An act concerning corporations,'" approved April seventh, one thousand eight hundred and seventy-five, which further supplement was approved May tenth, one thousand eight hundred and eighty-four, be and the same is hereby amended so as to read as follows:

How and when electric companies have power to use streets, &c.

1. BE IT ENACTED *by the Senate and General Assembly of the State of New Jersey*, That any company organized by virtue of the act to which this is a supplement, for the purpose of constructing, maintaining and operating works for the supply and distribution of electricity for electric lights, heat or power, shall have full power to use the public roads or highways, streets, avenues and alleys in this state for the purpose of erecting posts or poles on the same to sustain the necessary wires and fixtures, upon first obtaining the consent in writing of the owners of the soil; *provided, however*, no posts or poles shall be erected in any street of any incorporated city or town, or in any street of any township, without first obtaining from the incorporated city or town, or from the township committee of such township, a designation of the streets in which the same shall be placed and the manner of placing the same, and that the same shall be so located as in no way to interfere with the safety or convenience of persons traveling on or over the said roads and highways, and that such use of the public streets in any of

Proviso.

the cities, towns and townships of this state shall be subject to such regulations as may be so imposed by the corporate authorities or legislative bodies of said cities, towns and townships.

2. *And be it enacted*, That section two of said further supplemental act approved May tenth, one thousand eight hundred and eighty-four, be and the same is hereby amended so as to read as follows: Section to be amended.

2. *And be it enacted*, That any such companies be and they are hereby authorized and empowered to lay pipes and conduits and to lay wires therein beneath the public roads, highways, avenues and alleys as they may deem necessary; *provided*, that said pipes or conduits shall be laid at least two feet below the surface of the same and shall not in any wise unnecessarily obstruct or interfere with public travel, or damage public or private property and shall not be laid nearer than three feet, except as is hereinafter excepted, to any water or gas main; but no public street shall be opened for the purpose of laying any such pipes, conduits or wires without the consent of the board of aldermen, common council or township committee of such city, town or township; *and provided*, that such use of the public streets in any of the cities, towns and townships of this state shall be subject to such regulations and restrictions as may be so imposed by the corporate authorities and legislative bodies of such cities, towns or townships. Authorized to lay pipes, conduits, &c. Proviso

3. *And be it enacted*, That this act shall take effect im mediately.

Approved March 17, 1898.

CHAPTER CCXXXVIII.

A Supplement to the act entitled "A further supplement to an act entitled 'An act to regulate elections,'" approved April eighteenth, one thousand eight hundred and seventy-six, which supplemental act was approved May twenty-eighth, one thousand eight hundred and ninety.

Section to be amended.

1. BE IT ENACTED *by the Senate and General Assembly of the State of New Jersey*, That section twenty-six of said supplemental act be and the same is hereby amended so that henceforth said section twenty-six shall be and read as follows, to-wit:

By whom candidates may be nominated

26. *And be it enacted*, That any convention of delegates or nominating body of a political party as hereinafter defined, and also individual voters by petition, to the number and in the manner hereinafter specified, may nominate candidates for public office, whose names shall be printed, written or placed upon the ballots as hereinafter provided and directed; a "convention of delegates" or "nominating body of a political party" within the meaning of this act is an organized assemblage of delegates or voters, representing a political party which at the election for members of the general assembly next preceding the holding of such convention or nominating body polled at least two per centum of the total vote cast in the state, county or other division or district in and for which the nomination is made.

Terms defined.

Section to be amended

2. *And be it enacted*, That section twenty-eight of said supplemental act, approved May twenty-eighth, one thousand eight hundred and ninety, be and the same is hereby amended so that henceforth said section twenty-eight shall be and read as follows, to wit:

Nominations may also be made by petition.

28. *And be it enacted*, That besides the nomination of candidates by a convention of delegates or nominating body of a political party, as hereinbefore provided, can-

didates for public office may also be nominated by "petition" in manner following: such petition shall be addressed to the secretary of state or clerk of said county, city or other municipality as may be proper, pursuant to the requirements of this act hereinafter contained, and shall set forth the name or names and places of residence and post office addresses of the candidates for the offices to be filled, the office for which each candidate is named, that such petitioners are legally qualified to vote for such candidates; said petition may also designate in not more than three words, the title of the party or principle which the candidates therein named represent, and shall be signed by legally qualified voters of the state residing within the district or political division in and for which the officer or officers nominated are to be elected, equal in number to at least one per centum of the entire vote cast at the last preceding election for members of the general assembly, in the state, county, district or other division in and for which the nominations are made; *provided*, that when the nomination is for an office to be filled by the voters of the entire state, eight hundred signatures in the aggregate for each candidate nominated in said petition shall be sufficient; when the nomination by such petition is for an office to be filled by the voters of a district, county, city, township or other division less than the entire state, the petition shall be signed by qualified voters of such district, county, city, town or other division not less in number than one for every one hundred votes cast in such district, county, city, town or other division at the next preceding election for members of the general assembly; *provided, however*, that not more than one hundred signatures shall be required to any petition for any officers to be elected, say only such as are to be voted for by the voter of the state at large; in case of a first election to be held in a newly established election district, division, county, city or ward, the number of fifty signatures to a petition shall be sufficient to nominate a candidate to be voted for only in such election district or division, county, city or ward; every voter signing a petition shall add to his signature his place of residence, post office address and street number if any; such voter may sign one petition for each officer and no more, but all the names

Petition to be addressed to the secretary of state or clerk.

What to set forth

Proviso

Number of voters must sign petition.

Proviso.

Voter signing petition must add residence, &c

May sign one petition for each officer.

Before petition filed five voters to make affidavit thereto

need not be signed to one petition; before any petition shall be filed as hereinafter provided, at least five of the voters signing the same shall make oath before duly qualified officer that the said petition is made in good faith, that the affiants verily believe all the signatures thereto to be genuine and those of duly qualified voters, and a certificate that such oath has been taken shall be endorsed upon or annexed to the petition by the officer before whom the same is made.

Section to be amended.

3. *And be it enacted*, That section thirty-three of said supplemental act, approved May twenty-eighth, one thousand eight hundred and ninety, be and the same is hereby amended so that henceforth said section thirty-three shall be and read as follows, to wit:

What to be printed on back of ballots.

33. *And be it enacted*, That on the back of each of the said ballots to be provided by the county or municipal clerks shall be printed the words "official ballot for ———," after the word "for" in each case shall follow the designation of the assembly district for which the ballot is prepared, if at such election an assemblyman is to be chosen; if at such election no assemblyman is to be chosen, then after the word "for" shall follow the designation of the township, municipality, ward or other subdivision for which the ballot is prepared; then shall follow the date of the election and a fac-simile of the signature of the county or municipal clerk by whom such ballot shall be prepared;

Number of ballots to be provided.

the county or municipal clerk shall provide for each political party, for each election district or voting precinct in his county or municipality, two hundred and fifty ballots for every one hundred or fraction of one hundred of the total votes cast therein at the last preceding election for members of the general assembly;

Number of ballots to be provided for independent nominations.

in cases of independent nominations or of nominations by any party, organization or petitioners that cast no votes for any candidate or candidates at the last preceding election for members of the general assembly, the number of ballots to be provided and furnished at public expense shall be equal in number to double the total number of votes cast in the election district or precinct at the last preceding election for members of the general assembly; when an election district shall be divided or the boundaries changed, or a new district created, the county or municipal clerk shall ascertain as nearly as possible the number of voters in the new district or districts, and shall provide therefor a sufficient number of ballots in the above proportion. When new district is created or boundaries changed.

4. *And be it enacted*, That all acts and parts of acts inconsistent herewith be and they are hereby repealed, and that this act shall take effect immediately. Repealer

Approved March 17, 1893.

CHAPTER CCXXXIX.

An Act relating to county officers and employees appointed or to be appointed or elected by boards of chosen freeholders in the counties of this state.

1. BE IT ENACTED *by the Senate and General Assembly of the State of New Jersey*, That all the hereinafter mentioned county officers and employes, appointed or to be appointed or elected by any board of chosen freeholders, in any county of this state, namely, the county collector or county treasurer, the auditor or like officer, the clerk of the board, the counsel or legal adviser of the board, who shall have charge of suits and all legal business thereof, the county superintendent of buildings and works, and the like, the county engineer, or other like officer, the wardens, chief-keepers and head officers in charge of any of the county institutions or buildings, and all other heads of departments and county officers or employees whatever, who may be authorized to take, have, receive and hold county moneys or property, and who are not already required by law to give bond or security to the county to secure the moneys and property aforesaid, shall be required by such board, who are hereby authorized to exact the same, such bond which shall be in such sum as shall be reasonable with good and sufficient surety or sureties, as may be directed by such board; *provided*, County officers and employees required to give bond. Proviso.

however, that such bond may not be required from any of the county officers or persons before mentioned; who shall not have, receive or hold county moneys, or property as aforesaid; and all such moneys and property shall be duly turned over and accounted for to the county, and to the proper officers, officials or persons authorized by law to take or receive the same, and this shall be done in all cases as speedily as may be practicable to do so; in cases where such bond or like security has been or may be given, and the same is now required to be given by any existing law, this act shall not be taken or construed as applying to or affecting the same.

2. *And be it enacted*, That this act shall take effect immediately.

Approved March 17, 1898.

CHAPTER CCXL.

Supplement to an act entitled "An act to increase the powers of township committees," approved March eleventh, one thousand eight hundred and eighty.

Authorized to prohibit coasting

1. Be it enacted *by the Senate and General Assembly of the State of New Jersey*, That the township committees of the several townships of this state shall hereafter have the following powers in addition to the powers now vested by law in said township committees, viz.: to regulate or prohibit by ordinance in the manner provided in said act, to which this is a further supplement, coasting on or over the public roads, streets, avenues or sidewalks in said township or such of the same as in the judgment of said township committee may be thereby made unsafe for public travel.

Penalty for violation of act.

2. *And be it enacted*, That when a fine is imposed for a violation of the ordinances provided for by the act to increase the powers of township committees, approved

March eleventh, one thousand eight hundred and eighty, or by this supplement thereto, and the offender is unable to pay such fine he may be imprisoned one day for each dollar of fine so imposed in lieu thereof.

3. *And be it enacted*, That this act shall take effect immediately.

Approved March 17, 1893.

CHAPTER CCXLI.

Supplement to an act entitled "An act for the organization of the national guard of the state of New Jersey," approved March ninth, one thousand eight hundred and sixty-nine, and the various amendments thereto.

1. BE IT ENACTED *by the Senate and General Assembly of the State of New Jersey*, That the supplement to the act for the organization of the national guard, approved March ninth, one thousand eight hundred and sixty-nine, which supplement was approved March twenty-third, one thousand eight hundred and ninety-two, be and the same is hereby repealed. Repealer

2. *And be it enacted*, That all surgeons and hospital stewards of the national guard, and all the other persons who may hereafter be commissioned or warranted as surgeons, assistant surgeons or hospital stewards in the national guard, together with such "hospital and ambulance corps" as may hereafter be created in the national guard, shall constitute a department to be known as the medical department of the national guard, and shall be under the medical control and direction of the surgeon-general. Who constitute the medical department

3. *And be it enacted*, That the commander in-chief, on the recommendation of the surgeon-general, shall appoint two medical inspectors, each with the rank of Appointment and duties of medical inspectors

lieutenant-colonel, who shall act as assistants to the surgeon-general and be under his direction and control.

Hospital and ambulance corps to consist of, &c.

4. *And be it enacted*, That the surgeon-general may enlist a "hospital and ambulance corps" in each brigade, to consist of not more than one man for each company; they shall be attached to their respective brigade headquarters, and shall be under the immediate medical control of the brigade surgeons and under the general medical control of the surgeon-general. and the men so enlisted shall be assigned to companies as members thereof by the brigade commander.

Non-commissioned officer appointed, rank as sergeants, designated medical cadets.

5. *And be it enacted*, That from each "hospital and ambulance corps" there may be appointed by the surgeon-general one non-commissioned officer for each five men; they shall rank as sergeants, and may also be designated as medical cadets, and shall be warranted by the commandant of the regiment in which they are members.

Amount to be paid annually to be expended.

6. *And be it enacted*, That there shall be paid on the first Monday of April of each year to the brigade paymaster of each brigade of the national guard the sum of two hundred and fifty dollars, to be expended by the said brigade paymaster, on the approval of the surgeon-general, for the military support and maintenance of the "hospital and ambulance corps" attached to their respective brigades.

Quartermaster-general shall issue medical supplies, &c.

7. *And be it enacted*, That the quartermaster-general shall act as chief medical purveyor and storekeeeer, and shall issue medical supplies only upon requisitions regularly forwarded and approved, but not without the approval of the surgeon-general; the medical purveyor shall purchase, with the consent of the governor, only such medical supplies as the surgeon-general shall select and approve.

Surgeon-general shall have charge of examination of candidates for medical officers.

8. *And be it enacted*, That all candidates for appointment as medical officers in the national guard shall be examined as to their ability to discharge in a satisfactory manner all the duties of a surgeon, assistant surgeon or hospital steward, and the surgeon-general shall have the charge and regulation of such examination, and no person shall be commissioned or warranted with undergoing such an examination; the morals, habits, physical and

mental qualifications and general aptitude for military service shall be subjects for careful consideration; also physical or mental infirmity that will interfere with the proper and efficient discharge of a medical officer's duty; and the approval or disapproval of the surgeon-general must in all cases be noted on the certificate of a candidate for appointment or promotion, and no medical officer will be commissioned or warranted without the approval of the surgeon-general.

No medical officer commissioned without approval of surgeon-general

9. *And be it enacted*, That all assignments or details of medical officers for any special duty, or for any duty outside of the commands in which they are commissioned or warranted, will be made only upon the request or approval of the surgeon-general.

By whom medical officers detailed for special duty.

10. *And be it enacted*, That the surgeon-general shall submit annually to the commander-in-chief a report of the medical department, and that such report shall be published with that of the adjutant-general.

Report of medical department submitted annually.

11. *And be it enacted*, That to each regiment there shall be one colonel, one lieutenant-colonel and one major for each drill battalion constituting a part of the regiment; the regimental staff shall consist of one adjutant, with the rank of first lieutenant; one quartermaster, with the rank of first lieutenant; one paymaster, with the rank of first lieutenant; one surgeon, with the rank of major; one chaplain, with the rank of captain; one judge advocate, with the rank of captain; one inspector of rifle practice, with the rank of captain; one sergeant major, one quartermaster sergeant, one commissary sergeant, one principal musician, one color sergeant and one bugler, with the rank of sergeant; and the regimental staff shall also consist of one adjutant, with the rank of first lieutenant; one assistant surgeon, with the rank of first lieutenant; one sergeant major, one hospital steward, for each drill battalion constituting a part of the regiment.

Designation of officers of regiment.

12. *And be it enacted*, That special enlistments may be made for bands, field music, signal corps and gun detachments with the approval of the commandant of the regiment, and they may be assigned to companies as members thereof by the brigade commander.

Special enlistments for bands, &c., subject to approval of.

When and by whom troops of cavalry organized.

13. *And be it enacted*, That the commander-in-chief, whenever he shall deem it advisable for the public interest, may cause to be organized two troops of cavalry, the minimum of which organization shall be not less than three commissioned officers and forty enlisted men; which company shall be entitled to the rights, privileges and allowances of companies of the national guard.

Repealer.

14. *And be it enacted*, That all acts or parts of acts inconsistent with this act are hereby repealed.

15. *And be it enacted*, That this act shall take effect immediately.

Approved March 17, 1893.

CHAPTER CCXLII.

An Act to exempt from taxation real and personal property of exempt firemen's associations and of firemen's relief associations.

When exempt from taxation.

1. BE IT ENACTED *by the Senate and General Assembly of the State of New Jersey*, That the real and personal estate of any exempt firemen's associaion and of all firemen's relief associations incorporated under the laws of this state, and which is used exclusively for the purposes of such association, shall be exempt from all state, county and municipal taxation, so long as such property is used exclusively for such purpose.

Repealer

2. *And be it enacted*, That all acts or parts of acts ininconsistent herewith be and they are hereby repealed, and that this act shall be a public act and take effect immediately.

Approved March 17, 1893.

CHAPTER CCXLIII.

An Act to authorize the acquisition of real estate, and the erection of buildings thereon for the use of police and fire departments in cities of this state.

1. Be it enacted *by the Senate and General Assembly of the State of New Jersey*, That whenever in the opinion of the boards or authorities having the control of the police and fire departments in any city of this state, it shall be deemed desirable to dispose of any tract of land in such city whereon there are erected police station and fire station houses it shall be lawful for the authorities or other board having charge of the erection of public buildings in said city to purchase in the corporate name of the city two plots of land in such part of said city as may be required and indicated by such police and fire boards respectively, and to have erected upon one of said plots or parcels of land so purchased a proper precinct station house and upon the other of said plots a proper fire station house, as said boards respectively may deem necessary; *provided, however*, that the purchase of such real estate shall be only at such price or prices as shall be authorized by a concurrent vote of the board having charge and control of the finances of said city, and that such building shall be built only upon contract and after due advertising for proposals for such work shall be made in the manner and way now provided for by law in such city, and that such contract shall be awarded to those responsible bidders who offer the terms most advantageous to the city.

Board of public buildings authorized to purchase land and erect buildings.

Proviso.

2. *And be it enacted*, That the sum to be expended for each of said plots and buildings shall in no case exceed the sum of twenty thousand dollars; and that the plans therefor shall be subject to approval of said police and fire boards respectively.

Sum to be expended subject to approval of.

3. *And be it enacted*, That in order to provide moneys necessary to pay for said real estate and the erection of

Authorized to issue bonds.

the said buildings it shall be lawful for the board having charge and control of the finances of such city to sell said present police and station houses at public auction to the highest bidder after due advertisement according to the laws governing such cities, and also to issue bonds in the corporate name of the city not exceeding the amount required to be paid for said real estate and the erection of said buildings less the amount estimated by said board as likely to be realized from the sale of said present buildings, which bonds shall be issued under the seal of the city, signed by the mayor of said city and tested by the its clerk of such denominations as said board having charge and control of the finances of such city shall deem fit, bearing interest at the rate not exceeding five per centum and not redeemable in not more than twenty years from the date of the issue thereof, and to dispose of the same at the best price that can be obtained for the same, but at not less than par and accrued interest, and to provide for the redemption thereof and the payment of the interest thereon by taxation.

Rate of interest, &c.

Abandoned buildings and lands to be sold.

4. *And be it enacted*, That upon the completion of said two buildings it shall be the duty of said board having charge and control of the finances of the city to sell in the manner aforesaid, the said abandoned buildings and lands.

Repealer.

5. *And be it enacted*, That all acts and parts of acts inconsistent with the provisions of this act be and the same are hereby repealed, and this act shall take effect immediately.

Approved March 17, 1893.

CHAPTER CCXLIV.

An Act to provide for the appointment of assessors in certain cities of the second class.

1. Be it enacted *by the Senate and General Assembly of the State of New Jersey,* That in any city of the second class of this state having a population of less than thirty-five thousand inhabitants, wherein it is now provided by law that the assessors for such city shall be elected by the voters of such city, such mode and manner of election of assessors is hereby abolished; and hereafter it shall be lawful for the mayor of such city to nominate and by and with the advice and consent of the common council or other governing body of such city (to be expressed by a vote of a majority of all its members) appoint a board of assessors in and for such city to consist of one assessor in and for each of the wards of such city, who when so appointed, shall perform all the duties as now required by law of the assessors as heretofore elected in such city, and they shall hold office for the term of three years, and until their successors are appointed, and in case of vacancy in the office of any such assessors during such term, either by death or other cause, such vacancy may be filled by the mayor of such city in the manner aforesaid; and as compensation for the performance of their duties as such assessors, they shall receive a stated annual salary, which shall be fixed at the time of their appointment and shall not be increased or reduced during the term of their office, and such salary and compensation shall be in lieu of all fees heretofore allowed to assessors in such city for the performance of their duty.

Election of assessors abolished.

Mayor to nominate assessors, with advice and consent of common council, &c.

Term of office

Vacancy, how filled.

Salary.

In lieu of all fees.

2. *And be it enacted,* That the said assessors may be appointed by the mayor and common council or other governing body of such city, in manner aforesaid, at any time after the passage of this act, but shall not enter upon the discharge of their duties nor shall their term of office begin until the expiration of the term of office for which

When to enter upon discharge of their duties, &c.

the present assessors in such city were elected, and the appointment of said assessors by the mayor and common council or other governing body of such such city in manner aforesaid, shall be taken to be and is hereby declared to be the election of the successors of the before mentioned assessors elected in and for such city as aforesaid.

Repealer.

3. *And be it enacted*, That all acts and parts of acts inconsistent with this act be and the same are hereby repealed, and that this act shall take effect immediately.

Approved March 17, 1898.

CHAPTER CCXLV.

A Supplement to an act entitled "An act respecting conveyances" (Revision), approved March twenty-seventh, one thousand eight hundred and seventy-four.

Section to be amended.

1. Be it enacted *by the Senate and General Assembly of the State of New Jersey*, That the sixth section of the act to which this is a supplement be amended to read as follows:

If witness be dead, insane, or res dent out of United States, proof may be before circuit court.

6. *And be it enacted*, That if the grantor, or any of the grantors, of any deed or conveyance of lands, tenements or hereditaments, lying or being in this state, heretofore made and executed, and not already acknowledged or proved according to law, or hereafter to be made and executed, and which shall not be acknowledged or proved according to law, and the subscribing witnesses thereto be dead or of unsound mind, or resident without the United States of America, it shall be lawful to prove such deed or conveyance before the circuit court of the county in which such lands, tenements or hereditaments, or some part of the same, are situate, by proving the handwriting of such witnesses, or if there be no witnesses to said deed, by proving the handwriting of

such grantor or grantors, to the full satisfaction of said court, which proof may be made by affidavits in writing taken before any officer in this state authorized by law to take the acknowledgment and proof of deeds, and annexed to the said deed, and which proof shall be certified on or under such deed or conveyance in open court, by the judge holding the same; and such deed or conveyance, so proved and certified, shall be recorded by the clerk of the court of common pleas of the county in which such proof shall be made; and the said deed or conveyance, and the record thereof, shall be received in evidence, and shall have the same force and effect, but none other, as other deeds or conveyances, and the record thereof, when acknowledged or proved by the grantor or witnesses; *provided*, that before any deed or conveyance shall be proved as aforesaid, notice of the application to the said circuit court for that purpose, describing the same, and describing the lands, tenements or hereditaments contained therein, and the time and place of such application shall be given by advertisements, signed by the person or persons making such application, and set up in five, at least, of the most public places in said county, one of which shall be set up in the city or township in which such lands, tenements or hereditaments are situated, at least two calendar months before making such application, and also by a publication, for at least six weeks successively in some newspaper printed in said county, if any be printed therein, and if not, then in some newspaper circulating therein, and printed in an adjacent county, and due proof by affidavit annexed to said deed, if such notice shall be made to the said court, and certified by said judge in the aforesaid certificate of proof; *and provided, also*, that all deeds proved according to this section shall, when recorded be filed and kept as deeds which are recorded ten years after the date thereof are in this act directed to be kept; and a copy of such deed, so filed, duly certified, with copies of the certificates of proof or acknowledgment by the clerk in whose office it is filed, under his hand and seal, may be recorded in any other proper office in this state, in the same manner as the original deed might

Deed shall be recorded.

Proviso.

Notice of application to be given.

Proviso

Deed to be put on file.

Certified copies may be recorded in other counties.

have been, and the record of such copy shall be available and sufficient for notice only.

2. *And be it enacted*, That this act shall take effect immediately.

Approved March 17, 1893.

CHAPTER CCXVI.

An Act authorizing the board of chosen freeholders, in counties of the second class, to fill vacancies.

Vacancies, how filled

1. BE IT ENACTED *by the Senate and General Assembly of the State of New Jersey*, That it shall be lawful for the board of chosen freeholders, in counties of the second class, to fill vacancies occurring in said board, by reason of death, removal or otherwise by majority vote of said board, for the unexpired term.

2. *And be it enacted*, That this act shall be a public act and shall take effect immediately.

Approved March 17, 1893.

CHAPTER CCXLVII.

An Act to repeal an act entitled "An act to authorize and enable counties in this state to acquire and improve lands for public parks, and to maintain and regulate the same," approved March thirteenth, one thousand eight hundred and eighty-eight, with and including the several acts supplementary thereto, and providing for the disposition of moneys raised by virtue thereof in any county of this state.

Repealer

1. BE IT ENACTED *by the Senate and General Assembly of the State of New Jersey*, That "An act to authorize and enable counties in this state to acquire and improve land for public parks, and to maintain and regulate the same," approved March thirteenth, one thousand eight hundred and eighty-eight, with the several acts supplementary thereto, be and the same are hereby repealed.

Money on hand to be paid over to county collector, and statement to be made.

2. *And be it enacted*, That any moneys raised and procured by taxation and collected or obtained at any time under or by virtue of said acts, or either of them, in any county of this state, and which may now remain on hand, or in the custody, care or control of any commissioner, treasurer, officer or person named or referred to in either of said acts, or any other person whatsoever, shall be and hereby are ordered and directed to be handed over without delay, accompanied by a full statement relative to all such moneys, including what may have been expended thereof, as shall have come to the hands of any such commissioner, treasurer or person, to the county collector of such county, who is hereby authorized to receive the same and grant receipt and discharge therefor; all such moneys, together with any sums or balance of such moneys as such collector may have on hand undisposed of are hereby committed to the care and custody of such county collector, to be taken and received by him, and distributed and paid back by him as follows: he

How money distributed and paid back.

shall, after computing the whole amount of such moneys which shall have come to his hands, also compute and ascertain what share, portion or sum thereof each city, town, township or other municipality of such county, which shall have paid and contributed thereto, may be entitled to be credited with, on the basis of and in proportion to the amount thereof which each may have paid and contributed thereto in the first instance; and this portion, sum or balance, thus ascertained, credited, and remaining to the credit of each such municipality shall be paid over by such county collector to such municipality; and such tax money, portion or balance thereof so remaining shall be paid in each case to that officer in such city, town, township or municipality who may be authorized to take and receive other tax moneys therein; and such last-mentioned officer shall receive and give receipt in writing to such county collector therefor, as so much park tax money paid back by the county, in pursuance hereof, to such municipality for its benefit and uses.

To whom money to be paid

8. *And be it enacted*, That this act shall take effect immediately.

Approved March 17, 1898.

CHAPTER CCXLVIII.

An Act providing for the pensioning of firemen in certain cities of this state.

When retired on half pay.

1. Be it enacted *by the Senate and General Assembly of the State of New Jersey*, That in all cities of this state having a paid fire department any fireman having received permanent disability by reason of accident incurred at any time in the service shall be retired upon half pay.

2. *And be it enacted*, That in any city or municipality of this state in which this act shall become operative the board or authority having control of the finances of such

city or municipality shall borrow a sum sufficient to cover such pensions required during the remainder of the current fiscal year of such city or municipality, or may permit the same to be paid out of any money of said city or municipality not otherwise appropriated, and shall thereafter annually put in the annual tax levy raised in said city or municipality a sum sufficient to cover such pensions. Authorized to borrow sufficient money required current fiscal year, thereafter by taxation annually.

3. *And be it enacted*, That the board of fire commissioners or other body having the control of the fire department in any such city or municipality of this state shall and are hereby empowered to regulate the pensions under this act and make all requisite rules and regulations necessary therefor not inconsistent with this act. Board to make rules and regulations.

4. *And be it enacted*, That all acts or parts of acts inconsistent with the provisions of this act be and the same are hereby repealed. Repealer.

5. *And be it enacted*, That this act shall take effect immediately.

Approved March 17, 1898.

CHAPTER CCXLIX.

A Supplement to "An act respecting conveyances" (Revision), approved March twenty-seventh, anno domini one thousand eight hundred and seventy-four.

WHEREAS, foreign commissioners of deeds from New Jersey in some instances have, through inadvertence or mistake, taken acknowledgments and proofs of deeds, mortgages and other writings after they were appointed and commissioned by the governor and before their official oaths and seals were filed in the office of the secretary of state of New Jersey, and innocent persons may be subjected to loss or injury thereby; therefore, Preamble.

Acknowledgments and proofs of deeds, &c., validated.

1. BE IT ENACTED *by the Senate and General Assembly of the State of New Jersey*, That all acknowledgments and proofs of deeds, mortgages and other writings, and the certificates thereof, heretofore taken or made before or by any foreign commissioner of deeds for New Jersey who was appointed and commissioned by the governor, and before whose official oath and seal were filed in the office of the secretary of state of New Jersey, the records of such deeds, mortgages and other writings are hereby confirmed and made valid and legal and effectual to the extent that the same would have been valid, legal and effectual if the said official oath and seal had been filed in the office of the secretary of state of New Jersey.

2. *And be it enacted*, That this act shall take effect immediately.

Approved March 17, 1893.

CHAPTER CCL.

An Act relative to the jurisdiction and powers of district courts in this state.

Manner of prosecuting suits and actions against foreign corporations.

1. BE IT ENACTED *by the Senate and General Assembly of the State of New Jersey*, That hereafter suits and actions against foreign corporations may be commenced and prosecuted in any district court of this state, in the same manner that other suits and actions are commenced therein, except that service of the writs and process to be employed shall be made by the sheriff of the county in which shall be located the court in which the suit or action is commenced, in the same manner that writs and process are served in suits and actions against foreign corporations commenced in the circuit court of such county.

2. *And be it enacted*, That this act shall take effect immediately.

Approved March 17, 1893.

CHAPTER CCLI.

Further Amendment to an act to amend at act entitled "An act to regulate and establish the compensation of law or president judges of the courts of common pleas of the counties of this state," passed May eleventh, one thousand eight hundred and eighty-six, and amended May sixth, one thousand eight hundred and eighty-nine, and further amended March tenth, one thousand eight hundred and ninety-one.

Salary of law or president judges of the courts of common pleas.

1. Be it enacted by the Senate and General Assembly of State of New Jersey, That the law or president judges f the courts of common pleas of counties in the state hall be paid an annual salary in proportion to the population of said counties respectively as hereinafter pro'ded; that is to say, the annual salary of each law or 'esident judge aforesaid shall be fifteen hundred dollars counties where the population is not more than thirtyne thousand; three thousand dollars in counties where e population is more than thirty-nine thousand and not ore than fifty-nine thousand; forty-five hundred dolrs in counties where the population is more than fiftyine thousand and not more than sixty-nine thousand; rty-seven hundred dollars in counties where the population is more than sixty-nine thousand and not more an seventy-nine thousand; forty-nine hundred dollars counties where the population is more than seventyne thousand and not more than eighty-nine thousand; re thousand dollars in counties where the population is ore than eighty-nine thousand and not more than nety-nine thousand; five thousand two hundred dollars counties where the population is more than ninetyne thousand and not more than one hundred and nine ousand; five thousand six hundred dollars in counties here the population is more than one hundred and nine ousand and not more than one hundred and fifty

thousand; seven thousand five hundred dollars in cou ties where the population is more than one hundred fifty thousand.

Section to be amended.

2. BE IT ENACTED *by the Senate and General Assembly the State of New Jersey,* That the above section be the same is hereby further amended so as to read follows:

Annual salary of law or president judges of the courts of common pleas.

3. BE IT ENACTED *by the Senate and General Assembly the State of New Jersey,* That the law or president jud of the courts of common pleas of the counties of state, shall be paid an annual salary in proportion to population of said counties respectively as herein provided, that is to say, the annual salary of each law president judge aforesaid shall be fifteen hundred dol in counties where the population is not more than nn teen thousand; eighteen hundred dollars in coun where the population is more than nineteen tho and not more than twenty-nine thousand; twenty-hundred dollars in counties where the population is m than twenty-nine thousand and not more than thi nine thousand; three thousand dollars in counties wh the population is more than thirty-nine thousand not more than fifty-nine thousand; forty-five hund dollars in counties where the population is more fifty-nine thousand and not more than sixty-nine tho and; forty-seven hundred dollars in counties where population is more than sixty-nine thousand and more than seventy-nine thousand; forty-nine hund dollars in counties where the population is more seventy-nine thousand and not more than eighty-n thousand; five thousand dollars in counties where population is more than eighty-nine thousand and more than ninety-nine thousand; five thousand two h dred dollars in counties where the population is m than ninety-nine thousand and not more than one h dred and nine thousand; five thousand six hundred lars in counties where the population is more than hundred and nine thousand and not more than one h dred and fifty thousand; seven thousand five hun dollars in counties where the population is more than hundred and fifty thousand.

4. *And be it enacted,* That the annual salary to be

any of said judges under section one of said act, as above amended, shall be based upon the total population of the county as ascertained and determined by the last federal census, and the annual salary thus ascertained or determined shall be paid each judge, by the collector of the county, in equal monthly payments, and said salary shall be in lieu of all fees. On what annual salary based and by whom paid

5. *And be it enacted*, That this act shall only apply to law or president judges of the courts of common pleas whose term of office shall hereafter commence or to those now in office who may file their assent in writing under their hands to the provision of this act in the office of the clerk of the county, the law or president judge of which assents as above provided; and in case any judge now in office shall assent as above provided, the amount of his annual salary shall be ascertained and determined by the federal census of the year one thousand eight hundred and ninety, and shall be paid to him, under the provisions of this act, from and after the date of filing his assent as aforesaid by the collector of the county, in equal monthly payments. Who may file assent. When salary begins

6. *And be it enacted*, That all acts or part of acts, whether general, special or local, inconsistent or in conflict with the provisions of this act are hereby repealed, and this act shall be a public act and take effect immediately. Repealer

Approved March 17, 1893.

CHAPTER CCLII.

An Act in relation to free public libraries in cities of the second class in this state.

1. BE IT ENACTED *by the Senate and General Assembly of the State of New Jersey*, That it shall and may be lawful for the board of trustees of the free public library in any city of the second class of this state to build upon land Board of trustees authorized to build upon land owned or to purchase land and build thereon.

already owned by it, or to purchase land and build thereon a building or buildings, structure or structures, for the uses and purposes of a free public library within its corporate limits; *provided*, that the cost and expense of the land purchased, and the building or buildings, structure or structures to be erected shall not in the aggregate exceed the sum of fifty thousand dollars.

Authorized to issue bonds

2. *And be it enacted*, That to defray the cost and expense of such land and building or buildings, structure or structures to be erected under and in pursuance of the first section of this act, it shall be the duty of the common council or other governing body of any city of the second class in this state, at the request of the said board of trustees of the free public library within said city, to issue bonds in the corporate name of said city for the aggregate amount required by said board of free library trustees in sums of not more than one thousand dollars and not less than one hundred dollars, each to be signed by the mayor and countersigned by the clerk and sealed with the corporate seal of said city and to have written or printed thereon the words "free library construction bonds," said bonds to be disposed of at not less than their par value and shall be payable at the expiration of not more than twenty years after their date of issue, and to draw interest at a rate not exceeding five per centum per annum, payable semi-annually; and the common council or other governing body of such municipal corporation shall have the power to raise the money to pay the principal and interest of said construction bonds as the same mature, in addition to the tax they are now authorized by law to raise for the purposes of a free public library, and in the same manner as other taxes are assessed and raised by such municipal corporation; and the money so raised by the issuing of said bonds shall be paid to the said board of free library trustees, to be used by them for the purchase of any land and the erection of any building or buildings, structure or structures for the use of a free public library within the corporate limits of said city of the second class.

Bonds designated "free library construction bonds," disposition of same

Principal and interest to be raised by taxation.

When lawful to have commissioners appointed.

3. *And be it enacted*, That in case said board of trustees of the free public library of any city of the second class cannot agree with the owner or owners, or other

persons interested in any lands which said trustees may desire to take, use and occupy, or from which they may desire to take or divert, either in whole or in part, for the purposes of their building, or cannot agree with the owner or owners for the whole or any part of any lands as to the amount of compensation to be paid for such taking, use, diversion or occupation or interest, it shall be lawful for any justice of the supreme court of this state, upon application by said trustees, and upon two weeks' previous notice served in person or by leaving at the dwelling house or usual place of abode of such owner or owners, or, in case of absence from the state or legal disability, published in a newspaper published nearest to the lands in question, to appoint three disinterested commisioners, residents of the county in which said lands are situated, to assess and ascertain the value of the lands so proposed to be taken, used and occupied, which commissioners shall appoint a time and place at which they shall meet to execute the duties of their appointment, and shall cause two weeks' notice thereof to be given to the parties interested therein, either by personal service or by publication in a newspaper published in the county where such lands may be, at which time and place the said commissioners shall meet and view the premises, and hear the parties interested and take evidence, if any be offered, and for that purpose shall have power to administer oaths or affirmations, and to adjourn from day to day; and in case of the refusal or failure of either or any of said commissioners to attend and perform their said duties, the said judge shall have power to appoint another or other disinterested person or persons as commissioners to act in the place of such absent commissioner or commissioners; and the said trustees shall make and exhibit to the said commissioners at their meeting aforesaid, for the use of the parties interested, a statement and description in writing or by drawings or maps, or both, of the lands by them sought to be taken or diverted as aforesaid, and of the use, occupation of and excavations upon any lands by them sought to be made; and the said commissioners shall thereupon ascertain and assess the value and damages aforesaid, and shall execute under their hands and seals, or the hands and seals of a majority of them,

Commissioners shall appoint time and place of meeting and give notice thereof.

Upon refusal or failure to perform judge may appoint another commissioner.

Statement and description to be made.

and award to said trustees of the lands by them sought in the statements and description aforesaid, stating therein the amount of damages and compensation therefor by them assessed in favor of such owner or owners, which award shall be by them acknowledged and filed in the county clerk's office, and by him recorded; *provided, always*, that if any real estate, the owner or owners of which shall not have given his, her or their consent in writing to the diversion or to the taking of said land, shall not have been ascertained and paid pursuant to the direction of this act, shall be injured or damaged by the diversion or diminution of any said land, that the owner or owners thereof may have and maintain his, her or their action to recover damages for such injury which he, she or they may sustain by reason of anything done under this act, as if this act had not been passed; before taking possession of any such lands, or entering thereon for the purpose of making any excavation or occupation thereof, or taking any interest in land as aforesaid, the said trustees shall pay or tender to such owner or owners, or, in case of absence from the state or legal disability, shall deposit with the clerk of the circuit court of said county the value and damages so awarded; and the award of said commissioners and the payment or tender or deposit as aforesaid of the same, shall vest in said corporation the lands by them sought, described and set forth in said statement and description, in all respects the same as if the same had been conveyed to said trustees by said owner or owners under their hands and seals; if either party feel aggrieved by said assessment and award, such party may appeal to the next or second term of the circuit court of said county, by petition and notice thereof served upon the opposite party two weeks prior to such term, or published a like space in a newspaper published nearest the lands in question, which petition and notice so served or published shall vest in said courts full power to hear and determine said appeal, and, if required, they shall award a venire for a jury to come before them, who shall hear and finally determine the issue under the direction of the court, as in other trials by jury; and it shall be the duty of the said jury to assess the damages to the said lands as above mentioned,

Proviso.

When deposit made with clerk of circuit court

When appeal may be made.

Trial by jury.

nd the value of such lands as shall be absolutely taken; nd said court shall have power to order a struck jury, or a jury of view, or both, to try any such appeal, and also to order any jury which may be empaneled and sworn to try any such appeal, to view the premises in question during said trial; and the right of said trustees to appeal from and dispute the correctness of any award shall not be waived or taken away by the paying or tendering the amount of the award and taking possession of the land, or exercising the rights covered by such award; and the right of any owner of any such lands or rights in like manner to appeal, shall not be waived or lost by the acceptance of the amount so awarded, when tendered; and upon the final determination of any such appeal, the said court shall render such judgment in favor of the one party and against the other as the right and justice of the case shall require, and shall award to the party substantially succeeding and prevailing in said appeal, his, her or their costs of said appeal against the opposite party, and shall have power to enforce the judgment so rendered by execution, as other judgments are enforced, and also by summary proceedings and attachments for non-payment thereof.

Court may order a struck jury or a jury of view

By whom costs of appeal paid.

4. *And be it enacted*, That this act is a public act and that all acts and parts of acts inconsistent with this act be and the same are hereby repealed, and that this act shall take effect immediately.

Repealer

Approved March 17, 1893.

CHAPTER CCLIII.

An Act to enable second class cities in this state to improve and extend the water supply in said cities and to issue bonds for the payment thereof.

1. Be it enacted *by the Senate and General Assembly of the State of New Jersey*, That in any city of the second

When lawful to purchase additional land to extend water supply.

class in this state in which the water works are owned and operated by the city authorities it shall and may be lawful for the common council, board of aldermen, board of public works, or other governing body having control and management of such water works, by whatever name such governing body shall be called, whenever they shall deem it expedient, to purchase and acquire such additional land, property, water source, water rights and privileges as they shall consider advisable for the improvement and extension of the water supply of such city, either at or near the present water works or at any other place in this state within twenty miles of such city, and to sink wells and to erect thereon reservoirs, pumping stations and such buildings as may be deemed advisable by said common council, board of aldermen, board of public works or other governing body for that purpose, and to purchase and erect such pumps, machinery and other appliances as shall be deemed advisable, and to lay pipes for conduits therefrom to connect with the pipes now laid within said city and to lay additional pipes in and along the streets of such city for the purpose of extending the water supply therein, and that it shall and may be lawful for said city to acquire the said land, water rights or property, in fee simple or any lesser estate or right therein.

Lawful to acquire land in fee simple, &c.

When the common council, &c., may order or direct condemnation of lands.

2. *And be it enacted*, That whenever in the judgment of the common council, board of aldermen, board of public works or other governing body of any such city, additional water facilities are or may be desired for public use it shall and may be lawful for such council, board of public works or other governing body to authorize the chief engineer of the water department of such city, or other person or persons appointed by said council, board of aldermen, board of public works or other governing body, to treat with the owners of such lands and water rights as may be required to be used for water purposes; and in case it should, in any case, be found that suitable property cannot be purchased by agreement with the owner or owners, or in case the price demanded by such owner or owners is, in the judgment of the common council, board of public works or other governing body, in any case exorbitant and more than a fair equivalent therefor, then the said chief engineer or other person or

persons appointed be said common council, board of public works, board of aldermen or other governing power shall report the same with a description of the lands to the common council, board of public works or other governing body, and the said council, board of public works or other governing body may order or direct the condemnation thereof.

3. *And be it enacted*, That if the said common council, board of public works or other governing body shall in any case direct the condemnation of any lands or water rights, as provided for in the preceding section, it shall be the duty of the city council forthwith to apply to one of the justices of the supreme court of this state for the appointment of three commissioners to make an appraisement of the value of the lands or water rights so to be condemned for the purpose aforesaid, and of the damages which any owner or owners of such lands or water rights may suffer by reason of the taking thereof; *provided*, that at least four days previous notice shall be given by service, either personally or by leaving the said notice at the dwelling house or usual place of abode of each owner or owners, or in case of absence from the state, or legal disability of such owner or owners, such notice shall be published in two or more newspapers published and circulating near the lands or water rights in question, for two weeks.

When and by whom commissioners appointed.

Proviso.

4. *And be it enacted*, That the said commissioners appointed by said justice, having taken an oath faithfully and impartially to execute the duties of their office, shall forthwith proceed to estimate and determine the fair value of the lands and real estate or water rights to be taken and condemned as aforesaid, and the damage which the owner or owners thereof will suffer by reason of the taking thereof, first having given at least ten days' notice in writing to the said owner or owners, either personally or by leaving the same at his or her place of abode, of the time and place when and where they may be heard in relation to the matter; in case any owner shall be an infant, married woman, non compos mentis or absent from the city or place where such condemnation proceedings are taken, or be from any cause incapacitated to act in this behalf, then notice of the time

Commissioners take an oath

Notice to be given of time and place of meeting.

When notice shall be advertised.

and place and object of said meeting shall be advertised or other notice given as the said justice may direct, and said meeting or meetings may be adjourned from time to time at the discretion of said commissioners; as soon as they shall have determined upon said valuation, they shall make and sign a certificate thereof and file the same in the office of the city clerk of such city or such other place as the said justice may direct, immediately upon the payment to said owner or owners of the amount of said valuation, or in case he or they will not or cannot receive the same, upon the deposit of the same in such bank or institution as the said justice may direct, the title to and the right of possession of such property or water rights shall immediately become vested in such city or place; and any owner conceiving himself or herself aggrieved by the proceedings of said commissioners may appeal therefrom to the supreme court of this state at any time within sixty days after the filing of said certificate, and the said court shall thereupon order a trial by jury to assess the value of said property and the said damages, which trial shall be conducted in all respects as in other cases of trial by jury, and the final judgment of the said court upon the verdict rendered therein shall be conclusive upon all parties as to the said valuation and damages, and the amount already paid or deposited as aforesaid shall be increased or diminished accordingly.

When appeal may be made

Trial by jury

Judgment conclusive.

Compensation of commissioners, how paid

5. *And be it enacted*, That the commissioners so to be appointed by the said justice of the supreme court shall receive such compensation for their services as the said justice shall order and direct, and the same shall be paid, as well as all other expenses incident to the condemnation proceedings, from the funds provided as herein directed for the purchase of land and water rights and the erection of buildings and the laying of water pipes.

Authorized to issue additional bonds, to be denominated "water bonds"

6. *And be it enacted*, That the said common council, board of aldermen or other governing body having control and management of the finances of said city, and the application of the governing body having the control and management of the water supply of said city be and are hereby authorized and required, for the purpose of improving and extending such water supply and the purchase and acquisition of land and water rights therefor

and the construction of buildings and reservoirs thereon, and the purchase and erection of pumps, machinery and other appliances and the laying of pipes in and along the streets of such city, to issue bonds in the name and under the seal of the city, to be denominated on their face "water bonds," in addition to any heretofore authorized by law, to any amount not exceeding three hundred thousand dollars; such bonds may be registered or coupon bonds, and shall bear a rate of interest not exceeding five per centum, and shall be redeemable at any time not less than five nor more than thirty years from their date, in the discretion of said board, which bonds may be sold at public or private sale for the best price they can obtain for the same, but not under the par value thereof; all bonds issued as aforesaid shall be signed by the city treasurer and countersigned by the mayor of such city, and all the real estate within such city shall be liable for the payment of the principal and interest that may become due on the bonds to be issued by virtue of this act.

Term of bonds and rate of interest.

How issued.

7. *And be it enacted*, That such be and is hereby authorized to contract with the authorities of any other municipality for furnishing water to the citizens and the extinguishment of fires.

Authorized to contract.

8. *And be it enacted*, That any such city shall by ordinance create, establish, maintain and regulate a sinking fund for the redemption of the bonds created by this act, and define the powers and duties of the board or committee in charge thereof, to which shall be added annually not less than five per centum of the gross receipts from the water works of said city.

Sinking fund created for redemption of bonds, &c.

9. *And be it enacted*, That all acts and parts of acts, general, and special, inconsistent with the prov s ons of this act, be and the same are hereby repealed, and this act shall take effect immediately.

Repealer.

Approved March 21, 1898.

CHAPTER CCLIV.

A supplement to a act entitled "An act concerning corporations" (Revision) approved April seventh, eighteen hundred and seventy-five.

Power to increase or decrease number of directors.

1. BE IT ENACTED *by the Senate and General Assembly of the State of New Jersey*, That any company or association incorporated under any general law of this state or by special act of incorporation or otherwise shall have the power to increase or decrease the number of its directors by the assent in writing of stockholders representing two-thirds in value of the existing capital stock of said corporation, and a certificate signed by the president and secretary and under the corporate seal of the company, reciting that the assents of the said stockholders have been given, and also setting forth the number of directors as increased or decreased, shall be filed in the department of state, within ten days after the execution of said certificate, and a certified copy of said certificate by the secretary of state shall be taken and accepted as evidence of such increase or decrease of directors in any court of this state; *provided*, that in no case shall the number of directors in such company or association be decreased to less than three.

Certificate to be filed in department of state.

Proviso.

Capital stock may be paid wholly or partly in cash or in property.

2. *And be it enacted*, That subscriptions to the capital stock of any corporation organized or to be organized under the act to which this is a supplement, or any supplement thereto, may be paid wholly or partly in cash, or wholly or partly in property of the full value thereof, and the stock so issued shall be declared and be taken to be full-paid stock, and not liable to any further call, neither shall the holder thereof be liable for any further payments under any provisions of this act or the act to which this is a supplement.

When corporation deemed to be dissolved, procedure therefor.

3. *And be it enacted*, That it shall be lawful for the incorporators, or a majority of them, of any corporation incorporated or that may hereafter be incorporated under

the act to which this is a supplement, or any supplement thereto, to file in the department of state, a certificate stating that they have failed, and do not intend to perfect an organization of said corporation, and surrendering all the rights and franchises of said corporation, which certificate shall be sworn or affirmed to by the incorporators signing the same, and within ten days thereafter be filed in the department of state, and upon the filing of said certificate, the corporate powers of said corporation shall thereupon cease and the corporation therein named shall be deemed to be dissolved.

Certificate of dissolution issued by secretary of state required to be published.

4. *And be it enacted*, That the dissolution of a corporation as provided by the thirty-fourth section of the act to which this is a supplement, shall not be considered complete until an affidavit that the certificate of dissolution issued by the secretary of state has been duly published, as required by the act, shall have been filed in the department of state.

Meaning of terms "general stock" and "common stock."

5. *And be it enacted*, That whenever in the act to which this is a supplement, or any supplement thereto, the terms "general stock" and "common stock" occur, they shall be considered as synonymous; that either may be used, and they shall be construed interchangeably, and as both meaning ordinary unpreferred stock.

Lawful to amend original certificate of incorporation.

6. *And be it enacted*, That it shall be lawful for any corporation organized or that may be organized under any general law of this state, with the assent of a majority in interest of its stockholders, at a special meeting to be called for that purpose, to amend its original certificate of incorporation by a certificate which shall be duly signed by its president and attested by its secretary, under its corporate seal, and in all respects executed in the same manner as its original certificate of incorporation, which amended certificate shall be recorded in the office of the clerk of the county wherein the original certificate was recorded and filed in the department of state; and thereupon such amended certificate shall take the place of the original certificate of incorporation, and shall be deemed to have been recorded and filed on the date of the recording and filing of the original certificate; *provided*, that nothing herein contained shall permit the insertion of any matter not in conformity with the law un-

Amended certificate shall be recorded and filed.

Proviso.

der which such company was organized, and that nothing herein contained shall affect any suit or proceeding at the time of the filing of such amended certificate, pending by or against the said corporation, or impairing any rights of action accrued by or against its stockholders, corporators or directors; *and provided further*, that the total authorized capital stock of any such corporation shall not be increased or decreased in the amended certificate herein provided for.

Proviso.

Section to be amended.

7. *And be it enacted*, That section one of an act entitled "A supplement to an act entitled 'An act concerning corporations,' approved April seventh, eighteen hundred and seventy-five," which supplement was approved February twenty-first, eighteen hundred and seventy-seven, be amended so as to read as follows:

Lawful for corporations to change corporate name.

1. BE IT ENACTED *by the Senate and General Assembly of the State of New Jersey*, That it shall be lawful for any corporation existing under and by virtue of the laws of this state, whether created by special charter or otherwise, to change its corporate name by a two-thirds vote of the board of directors or managers of such corporation, who shall be present at a regular or special meeting called for that purpose; *provided*, that the corporation cause to be made and filed a certificate in writing, in manner hereinafter mentioned; such certificate in writing shall set forth:

Proviso.

Proceedings upon changing name of corporation.

I. The name of such corporation in use immediately preceding the vote and making and filing the said certificate;

II. The name assumed to designate such corporation and to be used in its business and dealings in the place and stead of that referred to in the last preceding paragraph, and which said certificate shall be signed by the board of directors, or a majority of said board, and recorded, in pursuance of the act to which this is a supplement in the office of the clerk of the county where the principal office or place of business of such corporation in this state shall be established; and after being so recorded shall be filed in the office of the secretary of state; and to which certificate shall be affixed the official seal of said board and the affidavit of the secretary or acting secretary of such corporation, that the said certificate is made by the authority of the board of directors or managers of such corporation, as expressed by a two-thirds vote of the members of present at a regular or special meeting of said board called for that purpose.

8. *And be it enacted*, That the thirtieth section of the act to which this is a supplement be and the same is hereby amended so as to read as follows: Section to be amended.

30. *And be it enacted*, That the president and the secretary or treasurer of such company, after the payment of the last installment of the total amount of capital stock as authorized by its certificate of incorporation shall make a certificate stating the amount of the capital so authorized and paid in, which certificate shall be signed and sworn to or affirmed by the president and secretary or treasurer; and they shall within ten days thereafter cause the same to be filed in the department of state. Certificate to be filed after payment of total amount of capital stock.

9. *And be it enacted*, That the thirty-first section of the to which this is a supplement be and the same is hereby amended to read as follows: Section to be amended.

31. *And be it enacted*, That if any of the said companies shall increase their capital stock as provided by this act or any supplement thereto the officers mentioned in the preceding section, after the payment of the last installment of such additional stock, shall make a certificate of the amount so added and paid in and sign and swear to or affirm the same, and cause it to be filed in the manner provided in the preceding section. Certificate of increase of capital stock to be filed.

10. *And be it enacted*, That section thirty-three of the act to which this is a supplement be amended so as to read as follows: Section to be amended.

33. *And be it enacted*, That every such company may, by a vote of two-thirds in interest ot the stockholders, in person or by proxy, at any meeting called for that purpose, change the nature of its business; and in such case a certificate of the proceedings, signed by the president and secretary under the corporate seal of the company, reciting that the assets of the said stockholders have been given, and also the change of the nature of its business shall be filed in the department of state within ten days after the the meeting of the stockholders as aforesaid, and a certified copy of said certificate by the secretary of state Certificate of change of nature of business to be filed.

shall be taken and accepted as evidence in any court of this state.

Section to be repealed.

11. *And be it enacted*, That section twenty-four of the act entitled "An act concerning corporations" (Revision), approved April seventh, eighteen hundred and seventy-five, be and and the same is hereby repealed.

Fees to be paid on filing any certificate

12. *And be it enacted*, That on filing any certificate or other paper, relative to corporations, in the department of state, the following fees and taxes shall be paid to the secretary of state, for the use of the state: for certificates of organization, one-fifth of a dollar (twenty cents) per one thousand dollars of the total amount of capital authorized, but in no case less than twenty-five dollars; increase of capital stock, one-fifth of a dollar (twenty cents) per one thousand dollars of the total amount authorized, but in no case less than twenty dollars; consolidation and merger of companies, one-fifth of a dollar (twenty cents) per one thousand dollars of capital authorized, beyond the total authorized capital of the companies merged or consolidated: *provided*, that the minimum fee shall be twenty dollars; extension or renewal of corporate existence of any corporation, the same as required for the original certificate of organization by this act; dissolution of corporation; change of name; change of nature of business; increase or decrease of number of directors; amended or supplemental certificates of organization other than those authorizing increase of capital stock; decrease of capital stock; increase or decrease of par value or of number of shares, twenty dollars; for filing list of officers and directors, one dollar; and for all certificates not hereby provided for, five dollars.

Proviso.

Fee for all certificates not hereby provided for.

Repealer

13. *And be it enacted*, That all acts and parts of acts inconsistent with this act be and the same are hereby repealed, and that this act shall take effect immediately.

Approved March 21, 1893.

CHAPTER CCLV.

An Act for the support and improvement of the New Jersey school for deaf-mutes.

1. Be it enacted *by the Senate and General Assembly of the State of New Jersey*, That the state board of education shall have power to order all necessary repairs and alterations to the grounds, buildings and furniture of the New Jersey school for deaf-mutes, to provide additional furniture and apparatus therein, and to keep said buildings and furniture insured; and the comptroller shall draw warrants upon the treasurer of the school fund for the payment of the same, upon the certificate of the president of said board, the amount to be expended annually not to exceed the sum of five thousand dollars.

State board of education authorized to order all necessary repairs, &c

How payment made.

2. *And be it enacted*, That all acts and parts of acts inconsistent with this act be and the same are hereby repealed, and that this act shall take effect immediately.

Repealer.

Approved March 21, 1893.

CHAPTER CCLVI.

An Act for the support and improvement of the New Jersey school for deaf-mutes.

1. Be it enacted *by the Senate and General Assembly of the State of New Jersey*, That to enable the state board of education to provide proper hospital accommodations for the New Jersey school for deaf-mutes for suitably taking care of the sick therein, and to improve the sanitary condition of the buildings of the school, and to continue the

Appropriation of $15,000 to provide hospital accommodations, &c.

work of establishing and maintaining a sytem of manual and industrial education in the school, there is hereby appropriated the sum of fifteen thousand dollars; and the comptroller shall draw warrants upon the treasurer of the school fund for the payment of the same, upon the certificate of the president of said board.

How payment made

Repealer.

2. *And be it enacted*, That all acts and parts of acts inconsistent with act be and the same are hereby repealed, and that this act shall take effect immediately.

Approved March 21, 1893.

CHAPTER CCLVII.

A Supplement to an act entitled "An act respecting executions" (Revision), approved March twenty-seventh, one thousand eight hundred and seventy-four.

Section to be amended.

1. Be it enacted *by the Senate and General Assembly of the State of New Jersey*, That section twenty-three of the act to which this is a supplement be and the same is hereby amended so as to read as follows:

Order for discovery if execution returned unsatisfied.

23. *And be it enacted*, That when an execution against the property of any debtor, individual, corporation, unincorporated company or voluntary association, upon a judgment recovered or docketed in the supreme court, or in the circuit court, or court of common pleas in and for any county in this state, or which now is or hereafter shall be docketed in the court of common pleas from any of the courts for the trial of small causes in this state, or from any of the district courts in any of the cities in this state, shall be returned by the officer to whom it is delivered unsatisfied, in whole or in part, it shall be lawful for any judge of the court out of which said execution issued in term time or vacation, on application by the

judgment creditor in manner hereinafter provided, to make order requiring the judgment debtor to appear and make discovery, on oath, concerning his, its or their property and things in action, before such judge or a supreme court commissioner, to be designated in said order, at a time and place in said order specified; *provided, nevertheless*, that no such order shall be made when the amount due on such judgment shall be less than twenty-five dollars. Proviso

2. *And be it enacted*, That this act shall take effect immediately.

Approved March 27, 1893.

CHAPTER CCLVIII.

A Supplement to an act entitled "An act to regulate the action of replevin" (Revision), approved March twenty-seventh, eighteen hundred and seventy-four.

1. Be it enacted *by the Senate and General Assembly of the State of New Jersey*, That whenever a warehouseman at the time any goods or chattels are placed on storage with him shall obtain from the party placing such goods or chattels on storage a statement in writing that such goods are the sole and absolute property of the bailor aforesaid, and in any action of replevin thereafter brought in any court for the recovery of such goods or chattels by any person other than the bailor aforesaid, no costs of suit shall be adjudged, taxed or recovered against said warehouse keeper in any action aforesaid, whenever judgment is obtained against the defendant in such action. When warehouse keeper not liable for taxed costs.

2. *And be it enacted*, That this act shall be deemed a public act and to take effect immediately.

Approved March 27, 1893.

CHAPTER CCLIX.

An Act to amend an act entitled "An act to incorporate the New Jersey Society for the Prevention of Cruelty to Animals," approved April third, one thousand eight hundred and sixty-eight.

Section to be amended.

1. BE IT ENACTED *by the Senate and General Assembly of the State of New Jersey*, That section two of the act to which this is amendatory shall read as follows:

Have power to appoint officers, &c., to sue and be sued, to use common badge.

2. *And be it enacted*, That the said society shall have power to elect and appoint officers and agents for carrying on the business of the same, also to make and use a common seal and alter the same; also to establish such by-laws and regulations as shall seem necessary and expedient for the government of said corporation, and by its corporate name shall be known in law, and have power to sue and be sued, and to defend and be defended in all courts, whether in law or in equity; the members of said society, in good standing, may use a common badge, which shall be authority for making arrests, and any person not a member using said badge shall be deemed guilty of a misdemeanor, and for every such offence shall, on conviction thereof, be punished by a fine not exceeding one hundred dollars nor less than fifty dollars.

When guilty of misdemeanor.

Penalty.

Section to be amended.

2. *And be it enacted*, That section three of the said act shall be amended to read as follows:

May purchase real estate, take by devise, &c.

3. *And be it enacted*, That this society shall not, in its corporate capacity, purchase and hold real estate exceeding in value, at any one time, the sum of seventy-five thousand dollars; but it may take by devise or gift any and all real estate or personal property, which is or may be devised or given it, without regard to value.

Approved March 27, 1893.

CHAPTER CCLX.

An Act to amend an act entitled "A supplement to an act entitled an act to incorporate the New Jersey society for the prevention of cruelty to animals, approved April third, one thousand eight hundred and sixty-eight, which supplement was approved March twenty-first, one thousand eight hundred and seventy-three.

Section to be amended.

1. BE IT ENACTED *by the Senate and General Assembly of the State of New Jersey*, That section one of the act entitled "An act for the prevention of cruelty to animals," be and the same is hereby amended to read as follows:

President may appoint persons to organize district societies, &c

1. BE IT ENACTED *by the Senate and General Assembly of the State of New Jersey*, That the president of the New Jersey society for the prevention of cruelty to animals may, from time to time, and at such times as he shall deem proper, appoint in the several counties in this state as many persons as he shall deem fit, to organize in the county where they reside a district society for the purpose of the enforcement of all laws which are now or may hereafter be enacted for the protection of dumb animals; such society shall be organized under and by virtue of a certificate of authority issued by the president of the New Jersey society for the prevention of cruelty to animals for that purpose, which certificate may be revoked by said president at any time for cause; said county district society may organize other societies in said county, by and with the approval of the president of the state society.

Certificate of authority, by whom issued.

Section to be amended.

2. *And be it enacted*, That section four of the said act shall be amended to read as follows:

District societies may purchase real estate, take by devise, &c.

4. *And be it enacted*, That said district societies may purchase and hold real estate, in the counties where they are organized, not exceeding in value at any one time the sum of ten thousand dollars; but the New Jersey society for the prevention of cruelty to animals and said district societies may take by devise or gift any and all

real estate and personal property, which is or may be devised or given to them without regard to value; the title, however, to all such real estate to be taken in the name of "the New Jersey society for the prevention of cruelty to animals," to its own proper use or as trustee for said district society, according to the will of the testator; but the disposition of the same in the latter case to be under the control of the president of said district society.

Title to be in name of.

Approved March 27, 1893.

CHAPTER CCLXI.

A Further Supplement to an act entitled "An act to authorize the board of chosen freeholders of any of the several counties of this state to lay out, open, construct, improve and maintain a public road therein," approved April seventh, one thousand eight hundred and eighty-eight.

Lawful to provide by resolution to further provide for further improvements of roads.

1. Be it enacted *by the Senate and General Assembly of the State of New Jersey*, That whenever the board of chosen freeholders of any of the several counties of this state acting under the authority of the above mentioned act to which this is a supplement, and the supplements thereto, and acts amendatory thereof, or either of them have laid out and opened, or shall lay out and open wholly or partially, and have improved, or proceeded to put in process of improvement, or shall improve or proceed to put in process of improvement in accordance with the provisions of said acts and supplements, the whole or any part of any such part of any such public road as is authorized and provided for in and by the provisions of said acts, including any branch or connecting roads, and whether such connecting roads or any of the same be now laid out and opened or shall be laid out and

opened in the future; it shall be lawful for said board of chosen freeholders of such county from time to time, when they shall deem it expedient, in order to provide for and secure to the people of such county desirable and serviceable roads of the character before mentioned, with the further improvement thereof as hereinafter provided, by resolution or resolutions, to be passed by at least a majority vote of said board at a regular or stated meeting, to further provide for the improvement and the further improvement of such roads, and to improve and further improve the same as follows: by paving or covering the whole or such portion of the roadway of such roads as they may by said resolution or resolutions designate, with suitable road material, but no stone block pavement shall be used, excepting in paving gutters or waterways, or at the intersection of streets devoted to heavy traffic; by setting curb stone and paving the gutters and waterways along and within said roads or any part thereof; by planting trees along said roads or any parts thereof; by providing a proper plant or plants for the lighting of said road or roads, as directed by the act to which this is a supplement or any of said acts supplementary thereto, and to do all other work necessary to make and provide good, well regulated public road or roads of the character before described, serviceable in all weather and seasons.

Resolution shall designate.

Planting trees, lighting said road.

2. *And be it enacted*, That all work herein authorized shall be performed and carried out as provided in said original act to which this is supplementary, or as near thereto as practicable, including the methods and officers already provided for supervision of the work and the proceedings necessary to enable the same to be done, together with the awarding and making of contracts therefor, upon advertisements for bids duly made; in all other things requisite and necessary to be done to carry out and meet the purposes and objects of this act, the same shall conform to the provisions of the said original act and the acts supplementary thereto and amendatory thereof, except in so far as changes, alterations in, or deviations therefrom may be rendered necessary by this act; *provided*, that the entire cost and expenses, together with and including all the original and other cost and expense whatsoever of the laying out, opening, con-

Work may be done by contract.

Proviso.

structing and improvement of such public road, in any county as aforesaid, shall not exceed, on an average of the whole length of such roads, the sum of one hundred and forty thousand dollars (including awards for all lands, real estate and property taken, and damages thereto) for each mile thereof, and a proportionate cost for each fraction of a mile of such roads actually laid out, opened, constructed and fully improved as before provided.

Average cost per mile.

Authorized to issue additional bonds.

3. *And be it enacted*, That said board of chosen freeholders is hereby authorized, in order to secure sufficient moneys to meet the requirements and purposes of this act, to provide for and make a new or additional issue or issues of bonds, over and above those provided for and authorized to be issued by the said act to which this is a supplement, and the supplements thereto and amendments thereof, to an amount or sum requisite and necessary to meet such requirements; *provided, however*, that the bonds or additional issue of bonds, authorized to be issued under under and by virtue of this supplementary act, shall not exceed the sum of one million dollars; and the bonds to be issued hereunder shall be of like tenor and effect to those authorized to be issued under the original act to which this is a supplement; no part of the moneys to be realized from the sale of such bonds shall be used for any purpose than as authorized and mentioned in said acts, or either of them.

Proviso.

Repealer.

4. *And be it enacted*, That all acts or parts of acts, general, special, local or otherwise, inconsistent with the provisions of this act, be and the same are hereby repealed, and this act shall take effect immediately.

Approved March 27, 1893.

CHAPTER CCLXII.

An Act to amend an act entitled "A supplement to an act entitled 'An act to authorize the board of chosen freeholders of any of the several counties of this state to lay out, open, construct, improve and maintain a public road therein,' approved April seventh, one thousand eight hundred and eighty-eight," which supplement was approved April fourteenth, one thousand eight hundred and ninety-one.

Section to be amended.

1. BE IT ENACTED *by the Senate and General Assembly of the State of New Jersey*, That section one of the aforesaid supplementary act be and the same is hereby amended to be and read as follows:

Authorized to construct roads or branches to connect or intersect at convenient point any city, town or township.

1. BE IT ENACTED *by the Senate and General Assembly of the State of New Jersey*, That the board of chosen freeholders of any county in this state, wherein the result of an election held or to be held upon the question whether a public road shall be laid out, opened, constructed, improved and maintained as provided for in the act to which this is a supplement, shall have been or shall be in favor of such public road, is hereby authorized and empowered, without any other or further election, to lay out, open, construct, improve and maintain, in accordance with the provisions of the act to which this is a supplement, one or more roads or branches which shall run to and from, and connect or intersect at any convenient point, line or place thereof, any city, town or township of said county, not already connected with the road, or intersected by the lines, or any of them, as already laid out and fixed, of the road provided for in the act to which this is a supplement; *provided, however*, that no such city, town or township shall be connected by any such road or branch, as provided for in and by this supplementary act, where the same, or the nearest point, points or boundary lines thereof shall be more than

Proviso.

one-half mile distant or away from the main road or original road provided for in the said act to which this is a supplement, measured on the shortest and most direct line between the side line of said road and any such boundary line of any city, town or township as aforesaid; *and provided*, that all said connecting or other road, roads or branches provided for in this supplement shall not, in the aggregate length, distance or like extent exceed one-third the length of the aforesaid main or original road provided for in the said act to which this is a supplement; such connecting or branch road or roads may be laid out, opened, constructed and improved either upon a direct line from said main or original road and the line of any street, road or avenue already laid out or in existence, or partly upon both, or otherwise, or by means of a road connection or branch road, which shall leave or branch off from said main public road at any point or place to be determined by said board of chosen freeholders by resolution thereof, and after running to or through any such city, town or township, or any part, portion or territory thereof, shall be extended along such line as said board of chosen freeholders may and hereby are authorized to determine by resolution as aforesaid; *provided further*, that not less than two-thirds of the total or aggregate length, between commencement and ending points of any and all such connecting road or roads, and for the full width thereof, shall be, if laid out, opened and built or made at all, through and over lands acquired or to be acquired by the said board of chosen freeholders for the purposes of such road, by gift, grant, or for a mere nominal consideration, and through and over streets, roads or avenues already laid out and dedicated to public use; it being hereby expressly provided and understood that not more than one-third of the total length of said connecting roads shall be through and over lands the title to which, for the purposes of said connecting road or roads, shall be requisite to be acquired, or shall be acquired by proceedings in condemnation, or by the payment of any but a mere nominal sum or consideration therefor, as aforesaid; *and it is further provided*, that such connecting road or roads shall be laid out, opened, constructed, improved and maintained in all other respects

Proviso.

Proviso.

Proviso.

(including the supervision thereof, which is to be by the engineer-in-chief heretofore appointed under said original act), and the money necessary therefor, as mentioned in this act, shall be raised and had in the manner and by the methods provided for the raising of moneys and the like, contained in said act to which this is a supplement; *and provided further*, that the entire cost of laying out, opening, constructing and improving all of such connecting road in any county of this state shall not exceed (including awards for lands, real estate and property taken and damage thereto) the sum of two hundred and fifty thousand dollars, and that the issue of bonds to raise money to pay the costs, charges and expenses in laying out, opening, constructing and improving such connecting roads shall not exceed the sum of two hundred and fifty thousand dollars; and in order to provide for the proper acquirement by said board of chosen freeholders of the land, real estate and other property necessary to be acquired by condemnation, or the like, to meet and carry out the purposes of this act, three commissioners, and not more than three, of the character and with the powers provided for in and by the sixth section of said original act, to which this is a supplement, shall be appointed therefor in the manner provided for the selection and appointment of such like commissioners in the said original act and the acts supplementary thereto; any vacancy occurring in this commission of three, by the declination of any commissioner named to serve, or by death, resignation or otherwise, to be filled in the manner provided for filling vacancies in the office of commissioners in and by said supplemental acts.

Proviso.

2. *And be it enacted*, That this act shall take effect immediately.

Approved March 27, 1893.

CHAPTER CCLXIII.

A Further Supplement to an act entitled "An act for the formation of borough governments," approved April fifth, one thousand eight hundred and seventy-eight.

Lawful for mayor and council, by ordinance, to order and cause to be constructed sewers or drains, &c.

1. BE IT ENACTED *by the Senate and General Assembly of the State of New Jersey*, That it shall be lawful, by ordinance, without other formality except as hereinafter required, for the mayor and council of any borough that now is or may hereafter be incorporated under the act to which this is a supplement, to order and cause to be constructed sewers or drains in any part of said borough; and to provide and maintain a general system of sewerage or drainage, with all the appurtenances thereof, for such borough, or any part thereof, conformably to which all sewers and drains shall be constructed; and to establish and maintain one or more main or outlet drains or sewers and outlets or places of deposit, within or without such borough, for sewerage or drainage; and to provide for the disposal of sewerage and drainage from such borough; and to repair and cleanse and maintain such sewers and drains; and when it shall be necessary to locate any of such sewers or drains, or any part of such system, upon any land other than public highways or streets, any such land, or any easement, right or real estate therein may be lawfully acquired by such borough; and the proceedings therefor and for the award and payment of damage therefor, shall conform to the proceedings now provided or that may hereafter be provided by law for acquiring land for opening streets in such borough; *provided*, that it shall be lawful to take any such lands without first making compensation therefor; and in case it shall be necessary to cross any lands of the state in the construction of said sewer for the purpose of obtaining an outlet, it shall be lawful to take and use such lands for the purpose.

Proceedings for acquiring land.

Proviso.

2. *And be it enacted*, That whenever a petition in writing of any owners of property interested shall be presented to the mayor and council of the borough, asking for the construction of a main outlet or lateral sewer or drain in any particular section of said borough, it shall be lawful for said mayor and council by resolution to declare its intention to cause such main outlet or lateral sewer or drain to be constructed; and the said mayor and council shall forthwith cause said resolution to be published by the borough clerk in two or more newspapers printed or circulated in said borough for the space of two weeks, together with a notice requesting such persons as may object thereto to present their objections in writing, at or before the expiration of two weeks from the date of such notice, to the officer signing the same; and if persons owning and representing more than one-half of the lineal frontage of land along all the streets through which it is proposed to construct any such sewer or drain shall so present their objections in writing, then such proceedings shall cease, unless the local or state board of health shall certify that such main outlet or lateral sewer or drain is necessary for sanitary purposes; but otherwise, and after the expiration of said two weeks, said board, the mayor and council may, by ordinance, order the construction of such main outlet or lateral sewer or drain, and by resolution award contracts for the same or any part or section thereof, and may take all other necessary steps for properly carrying into effect the proposed work by resolution.

Proceedings when owners of property petition mayor and council to construct outlet or lateral sewer.

3. *And be it enacted*, That upon the completion of any such main outlet or lateral drain or sewer, the mayor and council shall apply to the circuit court of the county wherein such borough is situated to appoint commissioners to estimate and assess the special benefits derived therefrom by any lands or real estate in the vicinity thereof; of the time and place of such application notice shall be given by two weeks' publication in two newspapers printed and circulated in said borough, at which time and place or at such other time and place as the court shall designate, said court shall without unnecessary delay appoint three commissioners, who shall be freeholders and residents of such borough, to estimate and

Commissioners appointed to estimate and assess special benefits.

Notice to be given.

Vacancy, how filled.

assess said benefits; and the said court shall have power to remove any commissioner and appoint another in his place and also to fill any vacancy that may occur from any cause.

Take and subscribe an oath.

4. *And be it enacted*, That the commissioners so appointed, before entering upon the execution of the duties required of them by this act, shall take and subscribe an oath or affirmation that they will make said estimates and assessments honestly according to law and the best of their ability, which oath or affirmation shall be attached to the report that they are hereinafter required to make.

Give notice of time and place of meeting.

5. *And be it enacted*, That having thus qualified said commissioners shall give the notice directed by the court of the time and place where the persons interested may present themselves and present such objections as they may have to the said assessment; the hearing before the said commissioners shall be a public one, and may be adjourned from time to time as they may deem necessary, or as may be directed by the court; the said commissioners shall have power to examine witnesses under oath, which may be administered by any one of them, and they may also in their discretion view the premises affected by the said assessment; they shall use diligent effort to ascertain the names of the owners of the lands and real estate benefited by the construction of such main outlet or lateral sewer or drain, and shall state the same in their report; but failure to ascertain such names, or to state the same correctly or the omission of any owner's name, shall not invalidate the assessment by them made nor bar the collection thereof; and the said commissioners shall cause to be made a map showing the location of said main outlet or lateral sewer or drain, and the lots of land and real estate especially benefited by the construction of the same, and they shall annex said map to their report.

Have power to examine witnesses.

Assessment not invalidated by failure to ascertain owner's name.

Map to be annexed to their report.

Report their estimate, &c., to court.

6. *And be it enacted*, That as soon after their appointment as may be, reference being had to all the requirements of this act in the premises, the said commissioners shall conclude their estimate and assessment, and report the same in writing, signed by them or any two of them, to the said court; the said report shall state the cost of the whole work, the portion, if any, assessed upon the borough at large, and shall give the names, as far as ascer-

Report shall contain.

tained, of the owners of said lots of land and real estate and the amount assessed to each owner for each lot of land and real estate, and shall be accompanied by such other documents as are required by this act; the estimate of benefits and the assessment thereof shall in each case be in proportion to the advantage acquired by the construction of such main outlet or lateral sewer or drain, and in no case shall any owner or property be assessed beyond the amount of benefit actually derived; in determining the cost and expense of said work the said commissioners shall include all expenses lawfully incurred in making the estimate, assessment and report, as well as the cost of the actual construction of said work, and in case the cost and expense as found exceed the amount of benefits assessed, the difference shall be assessed against the borough at large, to be raised and paid as hereinafter provided.

What shall be included in costs and expenses

When difference to be assessed

7. *And be it enacted*, That upon the coming in of the report the said court shall cause such notice to be given as shall be proper of the time and place of hearing any objections that may be made to such assessment, and after hearing any matter that may be alleged against the same the said court, either by rule or order, shall confirm said report or shall refer the same to the same commissioners for revision and correction, or to new commissioners to be appointed forthwith to reconsider the subject matter thereof; and the said commissioners to whom such report is so referred shall return the same corrected and revised or a new report, if so ordered, to the said court as soon as may be, and the same being so returned shall be confirmed or again referred by the said court in manner aforesaid as right or justice shall require, and so from time to time until a report shall be made and returned in the premises which the said court shall confirm; such report, when so confirmed, shall be final and conclusive as well upon said borough as upon the owners of any lands and real estate affected thereby, and the said court shall thereupon cause a certified copy of such report and the map accompanying the same, together with a certified copy of the rule or order confirming the same, to be forthwith transmitted to the clerk of such borough, who shall forthwith file the same in his office and deliver a trans-

Notice to be given of time and place to hear objections to report.

Court shall confirm report or refer same to commissioners.

Corrected and revised report to be confirmed by the court.

When confirmed final and conclusive.

By whom assessments collected.

cript of said assessments to the officer of such borough charged with the duty of collecting assessments for improvements.

When no certiorari allowed unless.

8. *And be it enacted*, That the court shall direct what notice shall be given of the confirmation of such report, and after such notice has been given as directed in said order no certiorari shall be allowed to review any of the proceedings authorized by this act, nor in any way to affect the assessment made by said commissioners, unless the same shall be applied for within thirty days after the time fixed for notice in the said order.

Assessments divided in ten installments.

Portion unpaid to be a lien.

When said lands may be sold.

Proviso.

Proviso.

9. *And be it enacted*, That all assessments made under the provisions of this act shall be divided into ten equal installments, and may be paid at the option of the property owner within ten years, one installment for each year or sooner if he wishes, and the said assessment, and any portion thereof remaining unpaid, shall be and remain a first lien upon the lands and real estate affected thereby from and after the date of said confirmation of the said report to the same extent as taxes are a lien under the general laws of the state, and they shall be collected in the same way that taxes are collected, and in case of non-payment of such assessment within ninety days after the expiration of the ten years within which the foregoing installments are permitted to be paid, then the said lands and real estate assessed therefor may be sold for the same, or for any balance thereof remaining unpaid of the same, in the same manner provided by such laws for the sale of land for unpaid taxes, and the sale of land for any unpaid balance shall be as effectual in all respects as would be the sale of land for the entire assessment; *provided*, that upon failure to pay any of the said annual installments when the same are due, the whole of said assessment shall become immediately due and payable; *and provided*, that in no case shall the interest on such assessments exceed the legal rate established by law at the time such report is confirmed.

Authorized to issue improvement certificates.

10. *And be it enacted*, That the mayor and council may pay the expense of any such improvement as is authorized by this act by issuing improvement certificates, bearing interest at a rate not exceeding six per centum per annum, and payable not more than five years from the

date of their issue; *provided*, that if because of the provisions of section nine of this act it becomes necessary, any of such certificates may be renewed, upon falling due, by the issue of other like certificates. Proviso

11. *And be it enacted*, That in case any such main outlet or lateral sewers or drains as are in this act described are now in process of construction in any borough of this state, or have heretofore been constructed and completed, and no assessment of the cost and expense thereof has been heretofore made, or has been heretofore by law authorized to be made, upon the property owners specially benefited or to be benefited thereby, and such borough has issued its bonds or other evidence of indebtedness whereby it has raised the money with which the cost and expense of said main outlet or lateral sewers or drains has been in whole or in part paid, the provisions of this act shall apply thereto in all respects as if this act had been passed and become a law before the construction thereof had commenced, and the proceedings had and taken therein shall not be invalidated or set aside by reason of any informality or failure to comply with the requirements of sections one and two of this act, or from any former lack of such lawful authority as is herein conferred on such borough by said sections, but the same shall be deemed and taken as in all respects lawful; *provided*, that no property shall be assessed but for special benefits derived, and that the amount chargeable to the borough at large shall not be assessed, but shall remain a liability as the same now by law is. When the provisions of this act applicable. When proceedings not invalidated Proviso

12. *And be it enacted*, That the mayor and council of any borough proceeding under this act may by resolution order to be incorporated in the annual tax levy in each year such amount as shall be required to be paid by such borough at large, on account of all assessments for such improvements as in this act are authorized, which have been made in the next preceding fiscal year, over and above the total amount of the assessments made against the land and real estate specially benefited, and the same shall be assessed and raised in the general tax. Amount required to be raised by taxation.

13. *And be it enacted*, That for the yearly cost and maintenance of such system of drains and sewers as is authorized by this act, and to provide for the payment of Authorized to raise by taxation for payment of indebtedness incurred.

all indebtedness that may be incurred by any borough in constructing such system, or any part thereof, whether such indebtedness be funded or unfunded, or be for principal or interest, the mayor and council thereof shall have power, by resolution, to cause to be assessed in the annual tax levy and collected such sum as they in each year shall find necessary.

How money received to be applied.

14. *And be it enacted,* That all moneys received in payment of the assessments in this act mentioned shall be received and retained by the collector of taxes, and by him set apart absolutely for the payment and redemption, or upon the direction of the mayor and council, for the purchase of all bonds issued, whether under this act or any other act, for the purpose of main outlet or lateral sewer construction, and also for all improvement certificates issued for the payment of work for which said assessments are levied, and for no other purpose whatsoever.

Compensation of commissioners.

15. *And be it enacted,* That the commissioners mentioned in this act shall be entitled to three dollars for each day's service.

Limit to increase of total indebtedness.

16. *And be it enacted,* That nothing in this act contained shall be deemed to authorize any borough in this state at any time to increase its total indebtedness on its bonds and improvement certificates of every kind beyond ten per centum of the assessed valuation of real and personal property within such borough.

17. *And be it enacted,* That this act shall take effect immediately.

Approved March 27, 1893.

CHAPTER CCLXIV.

An Act relative to the fire department of cities of the first class in this state.

1. Be it enacted *by the Senate and General Assembly of the State of New Jersey*, That it shall be lawful for the board of fire commissioners or board having charge and control of the fire department of any city of the first class in this state for the better efficiency of the fire department to increase the number of men attached to each company, so that the total number of men allotted to each company shall not exceed eight, one of whom shall be designated as captain and who shall receive a salary not exceeding twelve hundred dollars per annum. Lawful to increase the number of men. Salary of captain.

2. *And be it enacted*, That when the increase herein provided for shall be made the position or appointment of all men attached to said department and known and designated as foreman, hosemen at call and truckmen at call shall immediately cease and determine. When and what positions cease.

3. *And be it enacted*, That in order to take advantage of the provisions of this act and put the same in operation in any such city, such board of fire commissioners or other like board shall pass a resolution declaring an intention to take advantage of and put the same in operation in any such city, a copy of which resolution duly certified under the hand of the clerk of such board, together with an itemized statement of the sums or amount of money necessary to enable such board to carry into effect the provisions of this act shall forthwith be forwarded to the finance board, or other body in such city having the control of the finances and the control or making of appropriations of money to meet the needs of the several departments of any such city, to the end that such last named body shall have reasonable notice to provide the necessary moneys needed for the purposes aforesaid; and such last named body are hereby authorized and required to borrow such sum of money so certified as Board of fire commissioners shall pass resolution declaring. Certified copy, &c., to be forwarded to board of finance. Authorized to borrow money

aforesaid in anticipation of taxes to be thereafter levied, and to issue evidence of indebtness of such city therefor under the hand of the mayor and the corporate seal of such city at such rate of interest not exceeding five per centum per annum as said board may find necessary; *provided*, that any money borrowed as aforesaid shall be met and paid by an appropriation in the tax levy next thereafter to be levied in any such city; *and provided further*, that said board of finance or board having charge and control of the finances of any such city may in their discretion divide said sum so needed as aforesaid so that one-half thereof may be placed in the tax levy next thereafter to be levied and the remainder in the tax levy of the ensuing year.

Proviso

Proviso.

Board of fire commissioners prescribe new and additional rules.

4. *And be it enacted*, That it shall be the duty of said board of fire commissioners, or like board, as aforesaid, to prescribe new and additional rules and regulations to any existing or authorized, for or relating to the fire department of any such city, or the government and control thereof, with all the officers and members thereof under their jurisdiction; and in doing so, penalties or fines shall be prescribed for violation, inattention to or neglect of any duty or rule, and the fine may be in any sum not exceeding two months' pay or compensation of the offending party; for absence from duty without leave, a penalty or fine shall be invariably imposed; no person shall be appointed to any place in any such fire department who shall be physically incapable of performing the duty of the place to which he shall be appointed or elected; no person shall take or have charge of any steam engine or apparatus, as engineer or the like, in such department, unless he shall pass an examination before some competent board or authority, to be prescribed or designated by such board of fire commissioners, or like board, which shall demonstrate his fitness for the place sought, to be attested in a written certificate from such examining board or authority; such board of fire commissioners, or like board, are hereby clothed with power to require, by reasonable and proper regulations, as aforesaid, the said officers and men of their department to report as to the erection, location, placing or removal of any frame or other like dangerous building or structure likely to pro-

Penalties and fines prescribed.

Persons physically incapable not to be appointed.

Engineer shall pass examination, have certificate of fitness

Board of fire commissioners have power to require officers and men to report as to erection, &c., of buildings, condition of fire and water hydrants, &c.

duce, invite, spread, or contribute to the making or spreading of conflagration or fire within the city limits, and said force may also be required to look after and report the condition of fire and water hydrants, pipes, conduits, and other material and things used or controlled, either wholly or partially, by any such fire department.

5. *And be it enacted*, That all acts and parts of acts inconsistent or conflicting with the provisions of this act, are hereby repealed, and this act shall take effect immediately. Repealer.

Approved March 27, 1893.

CHAPTER CCLXV.

An Act to amend an act entitled "An act amend an act entitled 'An act concerning the fire department of this state, and to provide for the retirement of firemen and employees therein,'" approved March twenty-third, one thousand eight hundred and eighty-eight, which said amended act was approved May ninth, one thousand eight hundred and eighty-nine.

1. Be it enacted *by the Senate and General Assembly of the State of New Jersey*, That section one of an act entitled "An act to amend an act entitled 'An act concerning the fire department of this state, and to provide for the retirement of firemen and employees therein,'" approved March twenty-third, one thousand eight hundred and eighty-eight, which said amended act was approved May ninth, one thousand eight hundred and eighty-nine, be and the same is hereby amended to read as follows: Section to be amended.

1. Be it enacted *by the Senate and General Assembly of the State of New Jersey*, That the board of fire commissioners or other municipal authority having charge and control of any fire department in the state, shall have the

Board of fire commissioners empowered to retire officers or men from service for certain reasons.

power by resolution or ordinance, adopted by a two-third vote subject in cities where the fire department is not under the control of fire commissioners to the approval of the mayor of said city, in cities where the mayor has the veto power, to retire from all service in the said fire department any officer or man doing fire service or employed in such fire department who shall become unable, by reason of injury sustained or sickness caused in the discharge of his duties in said department, to perform the duties assigned to him, or who shall be found to be disqualified, physically or mentally, for the performance of his duties in such department, when such disqualification has been induced and caused through the discharge of or attempt to discharge said duties, or who, by reason of advanced age, is found unfit for service in said department;

Proviso.

provided, he shall have served therein at least twenty years, whether continuously or otherwise; and the said officer or man so retired from service may, from year to year, be allowed by said board of fire commissioners or other municipal authority having charge or control of such fire department, during such inability, disqualification or unfitness for service in said department, an annual allowance as pension, not to exceed one-half the yearly salary last received by such person so retired; unless said one-half is less than three hundred dollars, and in the case of volunteer firemen not to exceed one hundred dollars, and in the event that the salary or yearly allowance of such officer or man shall have been less than three hundred dollars, then to pay to such officer or man a yearly pension not less than one hundred and fifty dollars; and if any chief engineer, or other chief or any officer or man doing fire service, or employed in such fire department, shall be killed while doing such duty, or shall die as the result of his doing such duty, an annual allowance as pension or pensions may be made in every such case not exceeding one-third of the yearly salary or compensation last received by any such person for service in such department prior to death as aforesaid; and such allowance may be made and allowed by such board of fire commissioners or other municipal authority having charge or control of such fire department, and paid to the widow of such officer or man during her lifetime or widowhood;

Annual pension.

Pension to widow and children.

or, if he shall leave no widow, or in the event of her death or re-marriage, such allowance or pension may be paid to or for the support of the child or children of said deceased officer or man during their minority, in such manner as said board shall direct; *and provided*, that the same shall be paid in installments each year out of the appropriations of such fire department at the same time and in the same manner as the wages and salary of firemen in active service are paid, or in case of volunteer firemen, to be paid quarterly; and the appropriation each year to said fire department shall be made with a reasonable allowance for pensions as aforesaid, to be paid out of the same as occasion may require; and the provisions of this section relative to pensions to be paid after death may be applied to and is intended hereby to cover and include the case of any chief hereinbefore named, and also any member or employee of any such fire department who shall have been killed in the discharge of duty at any time within three years prior to the time this act shall take effect.

Proviso.

2. *And be it enacted*, That this act shall take effect immediately.

Approved March 27, 1893.

CHAPTER CCLXVI.

An Act to authorize the construction of sewers and drains in cities of the first class and to provide for the payment of the cost thereof.

1. BE IT ENACTED *by the Senate and General Assembly of the State of New Jersey*, That it shall be lawful for the board or body having control of the streets and sewers in any city of the first class in this state to order and cause sewers and drains to be constructed in any part of such city, and to provide, maintain and alter a system of sewerage and drainage for such city or any part thereof, and

Borad having control of streets and sewers empowered to provide for disposal of sewage and drainage.

to establish and maintain one or more
of deposit for such sewers and drains
such city; to provide for the disposal
drainage from such city and to repair an
sewers and drains.

Board empowered to purchase or condemn private land.

2. *And be it enacted*, That if in any case
judgment of such board or body necessary
so to do, it shall have power to purchase,
inability to agree with the owner or o
purchase price, to condemn private land and
the purpose of constructing such sewers and
other works and constructions authorized

Procedure to condemn private lands, &c.

and in case any proceedings shall be taken
private lands and property under the authori
the methods of procedure shall be the same
be taken for the condemnation of lands for
poses by the act entitled "An act to author
chase and condemnation of lands and the
buildings for market purposes in the cities o
and other places in which market facilities are
required for public use and to provide therefo
April twenty-second, one thousand eight h
eighty-six."

What shall be deemed to be part of cost of the works, &c.

3. *And be it enacted*, That the land property
by section two of this act to be purchased or c
shall be held to include only such lands and p
cannot lawfully be used or taken in any such cit
uses herein specified without purchase or conde
and that the cost of such lands and property and
penses incurred in condemning the same shall be
and taken to be part of the cost of the works a
provements herein authorized, and shall be inclu
such cost.

Authorized to issue temporary improvement certificates.

4. *And be it enacted*, That such board or body in
to pay the expense of the improvements herein auth
by this act may issue temporary improvement certi
from time to time as the work progresses in such form
the said board or body may prescribe, bearing interest
a rate not greater than six per centum per annum, to
made payable at the expiration of not more than thr
years from the date of their issue, and to regulate ti
same and use the proceeds for the purpose aforesaid.

[illegible] *enacted*, That all special and peculiar bene- [illegible] upon property in any such city by any im- [illegible] erein authorized shall be assessed thereon, [illegible]st lien thereon, and such assessments for [illegible] l be made and collected in the same manner [illegible] nefit assessments are now or hereafter made [illegible] for the construction of sewers therein, and [illegible] ns of money received from such assessments [illegible] ed to pay the bonds herein authorized to be [illegible] for no other purpose, and shall be paid to the [illegible] ners of the sinking fund of such city as col- [illegible] received. Assessments shall be made for special and peculiar, be a first lien. Money paid to commissioners of sinking fund.

[illegible] *be it enacted*, That when such board or body [illegible] solution request it, the board or body having [illegible] the finances of such city shall cause the bonds [illegible] ch city to be used for an amount sufficient to [illegible] he temporary certificates issued under the au- [illegible] f this act, such bonds to run for a period of [illegible] than thirty years from the date of issue, to be [illegible] le in form, to bear insterest at a rate not greater [illegible] per centum per annum, payable semi-annually, [illegible] e payable at such place as the said board or body [illegible] termine; all such bonds shall be signed by the [illegible] of such city and countersigned by the comptroller [illegible] ested by the city clerk and shall be issued under [illegible] of such city, and shall be negotiated and sold for [illegible] than their par value. Authorized to issue bonds to take up the temporary certificates. How executed.

[illegible] *nd be it enacted*, That it shall be the duty of the [illegible] or body which by law shall be authorized to make [illegible] tax levy in such city to insert therein and levy [illegible] collect annually such sum by taxation as will be [illegible] ient in additon to the benefits assessed for the im- [illegible] ement for the payment of which such bonds are [illegible] d to provide the interest due thereon and a sinking [illegible] of not less than two per centum thereof, the annual [illegible] est and sinking fund thus raised to be paid annually [illegible] e sinking fund commissioners to meet the interest [illegible] principal of such bonds. To collect annually by taxation sufficient sum to pay principal, interest, &c.

[illegible]. *And be it enacted*, That this act shall take effect im- [illegible] diately.

[illegible] Approved March 27, 1893.

By whom assessments collected.

cript of said assessments to the officer of such borough charged with the duty of collecting assessments for improvements.

When no certiorari allowed unless.

8. *And be it enacted*, That the court shall direct what notice shall be given of the confirmation of such report, and after such notice has been given as directed in said order no certiorari shall be allowed to review any of the proceedings authorized by this act, nor in any way to affect the assessment made by said commissioners, unless the same shall be applied for within thirty days after the time fixed for notice in the said order.

Assessments divided in ten installments.

9. *And be it enacted*, That all assessments made under the provisions of this act shall be divided into ten equal installments, and may be paid at the option of the property owner within ten years, one installment for each year or sooner if he wishes, and the said assessment, and any portion thereof remaining unpaid, shall be and remain a first lien upon the lands and real estate affected thereby from and after the date of said confirmation of the said report to the same extent as taxes are a lien under the general laws of the state, and they shall be collected in the same way that taxes are collected, and in case of non-payment of such assessment within ninety days after the expiration of the ten years within which the foregoing installments are permitted to be paid, then the said lands and real estate assessed therefor may be sold for the same, or for any balance thereof remaining unpaid of the same, in the same manner provided by such laws for the sale of land for unpaid taxes, and the sale of land for any unpaid balance shall be as effectual in all respects as would be the sale of land for the entire assessment; *provided*, that upon failure to pay any of the said annual installments when the same are due, the whole of said assessment shall become immediately due and payable; *and provided*, that in no case shall the interest on such assessments exceed the legal rate established by law at the time such report is confirmed.

Portion unpaid to be a lien.

When said lands may be sold.

Proviso.

Proviso.

Authorized to issue improvement certificates.

10. *And be it enacted*, That the mayor and council may pay the expense of any such improvement as is authorized by this act by issuing improvement certificates, bearing interest at a rate not exceeding six per centum per annum, and payable not more than five years from the

date of their issue; *provided*, that if because of the provisions of section nine of this act it becomes necessary, any of such certificates may be renewed, upon falling due, by the issue of other like certificates. Proviso

11. *And be it enacted*, That in case any such main outlet or lateral sewers or drains as are in this act described are now in process of construction in any borough of this state, or have heretofore been constructed and completed, and no assessment of the cost and expense thereof has been heretofore made, or has been heretofore by law authorized to be made, upon the property owners specially benefited or to be benefited thereby, and such borough has issued its bonds or other evidence of indebtedness whereby it has raised the money with which the cost and expense of said main outlet or lateral sewers or drains has been in whole or in part paid, the provisions of this act shall apply thereto in all respects as if this act had been passed and become a law before the construction thereof had commenced, and the proceedings had and taken therein shall not be invalidated or set aside by reason of any informality or failure to comply with the requirements of sections one and two of this act, or from any former lack of such lawful authority as is herein conferred on such borough by said sections, but the same shall be deemed and taken as in all respects lawful; *provided*, that no property shall be assessed but for special benefits derived, and that the amount chargeable to the borough at large shall not be assessed, but shall remain a liability as the same now by law is.

When the provisions of this act applicable.

When proceedings not invalidated

Proviso

12. *And be it enacted*, That the mayor and council of any borough proceeding under this act may by resolution order to be incorporated in the annual tax levy in each year such amount as shall be required to be paid by such borough at large, on account of all assessments for such improvements as in this act are authorized, which have been made in the next preceding fiscal year, over and above the total amount of the assessments made against the land and real estate specially benefited, and the same shall be assessed and raised in the general tax.

Amount required to be raised by taxation.

13. *And be it enacted*, That for the yearly cost and maintenance of such system of drains and sewers as is authorized by this act, and to provide for the payment of

Authorized to raise by taxation for payment of indebtedness incurred.

all indebtedness that may be incurred by any borough in constructing such system, or any part thereof, whether such indebtedness be funded or unfunded, or be for principal or interest, the mayor and council thereof shall have power, by resolution, to cause to be assessed in the annual tax levy and collected such sum as they in each year shall find necessary.

How money received to be applied.

14. *And be it enacted*, That all moneys received in payment of the assessments in this act mentioned shall be received and retained by the collector of taxes, and by him set apart absolutely for the payment and redemption, or upon the direction of the mayor and council, for the purchase of all bonds issued, whether under this act or any other act, for the purpose of main outlet or lateral sewer construction, and also for all improvement certificates issued for the payment of work for which said assessments are levied, and for no other purpose whatsoever.

Compensation of commissioners.

15. *And be it enacted*, That the commissioners mentioned in this act shall be entitled to three dollars for each day's service.

Limit to increase of total indebtedness.

16. *And be it enacted*, That nothing in this act contained shall be deemed to authorize any borough in this state at any time to increase its total indebtedness on its bonds and improvement certificates of every kind beyond ten per centum of the assessed valuation of real and personal property within such borough.

17. *And be it enacted*, That this act shall take effect immediately.

Approved March 27, 1898.

CHAPTER CCLXIV.

An Act relative to the fire department of cities of the first class in this state.

1. Be it enacted *by the Senate and General Assembly of the State of New Jersey*, That it shall be lawful for the board of fire commissioners or board having charge and control of the fire department of any city of the first class in this state for the better efficiency of the fire department to increase the number of men attached to each company, so that the total number of men allotted to each company shall not exceed eight, one of whom shall be designated as captain and who shall receive a salary not exceeding twelve hundred dollars per annum. **Lawful to increase the number of men. Salary of captain.**

2. *And be it enacted*, That when the increase herein provided for shall be made the position or appointment of all men attached to said department and known and designated as foreman, hosemen at call and truckmen at call shall immediately cease and determine. **When and what positions cease.**

3. *And be it enacted*, That in order to take advantage of the provisions of this act and put the same in operation in any such city, such board of fire commissioners or other like board shall pass a resolution declaring an intention to take advantage of and put the same in operation in any such city, a copy of which resolution duly certified under the hand of the clerk of such board, together with an itemized statement of the sums or amount of money necessary to enable such board to carry into effect the provisions of this act shall forthwith be forwarded to the finance board, or other body in such city having the control of the finances and the control or making of appropriations of money to meet the needs of the several departments of any such city, to the end that such last named body shall have reasonable notice to provide the necessary moneys needed for the purposes aforesaid; and such last named body are hereby authorized and required to borrow such sum of money so certified as **Board of fire commissioners shall pass resolution declaring. Certified copy, &c., to be forwarded to board of finance. Authorized to borrow money.**

year thereafter until the full amount of said issue of bonds be paid and satisfied; and that for the purpose of meeting the principal of said bonds at maturity as aforesaid, the board or body having control of the financial appropriations of said city shall annually appropriate, after the expiration of ten years from the date of issue of said bonds, a sum sufficient to meet said bonds when they mature, which sum shall be devoted to a sinking fund for the purpose aforesaid, and the said board of finance or other body in control of the appropriations in said city shall also appropriate annually sufficient moneys in the tax levy of each year to meet the current interest due on said bonds and the incidental cost of maintaining said sewer or sewers; *provided, however*, that it shall not be lawful for said common council, board of aldermen or other governing body to incur an indebtedness for or on account of the construction of such sewer or sewers or the appurtenances thereof to exceed one hundred thousand dollars in any year, or to issue bonds as aforesaid for or on account of said work for greater amount in any years than one hundred thousand dollars.

Shall appropriate annually after ten years for sinking fund.

Proviso.

Repealer.

7. *And be it enacted*, That all acts and parts of acts and charter provisions, general and special, inconsistent herewith, be and they are hereby repealed, and that this act shall be considered a public act, to take effect immediately.

Approved March 27, 1898.

CHAPTER CCLXVIII.

A Supplement to an act entitled "An act concerning corporations" (Revision), approved April seventh, one thousand eight hundred and seventy-five.

1. Be it enacted *by the Senate and General Assembly of the State of New Jersey*, That when any corporation heretofore or hereafter created under the act to which this act

is a supplement shall have heretofore or hereafter by the terms of its certificate of incorporation classified its directors in respect to the time for which they shall severally hold office pursuant to the provisions of the "Act concerning corporations' (Revision), approved April seventh, one thousand eight hundred and seventy-five, and the supplements and amendments thereof in that behalf applicable, then and in that event any such corporation shall have the power at a meeting of the stockholders of said company, called for that purpose under the provisions of this act by the vote of a majority in amount in interest of the total number of shares of the capital stock of said company then outstanding, however represented, whether by common or preferred stock, or one or more classes, each share of stock in said company of whatever class, if classified, being entitled to one vote under the provisions of this act, to repeal any or all of the provisions whereby said classification of directors in respect to the time for which they shall severally hold office has been or may hereafter be effected, and to repeal any and all provisions, if any, whereby the right to choose the directors of any class may have been heretofore or may hereafter be conferred upon any class or classes of stockholders to the exclusion of the others, and to thereupon determine and limit the term of office of any board of directors of said company then in office, so as to have the said term of office of said entire board then and there expire by limitation at such meeting; on the passage of such resolution, and thereupon and after the passage of such resolution so repealing said provisions as to classification of directors, or voting rights or both as aforesaid, said stockholders shall forthwith proceed to elect a new board of directors to hold office for one year or until the next annual meeting of said stockholders, if the time fixed for the next annual meeting is less than one year from the date of such meeting at which said repeal of said provisions is made, and until their successors are chosen and qualified in their stead, and thereafter the directors of said corporation shall be chosen annually by stockholders at such time and place as shall be provided by the bylaws of the company, and shall hold their offices for one

Stockholders empowered to repeal provisions, determine and limit term of office of any board of directors, &c.

Stockholders shall proceed to elect new board of directors

year and until others are chosen and qualified in their stead.

Time and place of meeting of all stockholders to be published in newspaper.

2. *And be it enacted*, That the persons holding in their own names on the books of the company a majority in amount in interest of the total capital stock, whether made up of one or several classes as aforesaid, then outstanding of any such corporation, and desiring to avail themselves of the privileges of this act, may call a meeting of all the stockholders of said company for the purpose of considering the question of the repeal of any such provisions as to classification of directors, or voting power of both as aforesaid, and of electing a new board of directors in case of such repeal under the provisions of this act, by signing a notice of such meeting specifying the time and place of holding such meeting and in general terms the object thereof, and publishing the same at least ten days prior to the date fixed therein for said meeting in a newspaper circulating in the county wherein the business of said company is conducted, or where their principal place of business is located.

Where meeting shall be held.

3. *And be it enacted*, That any such meeting so called shall be a legal meeting of the stockholders of the company, and shall be held at the office of the corporation, or if it has none, at the place in this state where its principal business has been transacted, or if access to such office or place is denied or cannot be had, at some other place in the city, village or town where such office or place is, or was located; at such meeting, the stockholders attending shall constitue a quorum, and each share of stock of any kind or classes, if classified, shall be entitled to one vote on all questions properly coming before said meeting, any provision to the contrary in the certificate or by-laws of said company notwithstanding; the stockholders attending may elect a chairman, secretary and inspectors of the vote on the consideration of said question of repealing any such provision as to the classification of directors or voting power or both as aforesaid, and of any election of new directors that may be held in case of such repeal, and may elect a new board of directors if such repeal is passed, and may adopt by-laws providing for future annual meetings and election of directors of the company, and may transact any other

What shall constitute a quorum.

Elect chairman, secretary and inspector.

Adopt by laws providing for future annual meetings.

business which may be transacted at an annual meeting of the members of the corporation, and it shall be the duty of the secretary of the company, on receipt of the minutes of said meeting from the secretary thereof, to file the same in the office of the company, and record the same in the book of minutes of the company. Minutes of meeting to be filed

4. *And be it enacted*, That in the absence, at such meeting, of the books of the corporation, showing who are stockholders thereof, each person voting shall present his sworn statement setting forth that he is a stockholder of the corporation and the number of shares of stock owned by him and standing in his name on the books of the corporation, and if known to him, the total number of shares of stock of the corporation outstanding, including all classes if classified; on filing such statement he may vote as a stockholder of said corporation on the shares of stock appearing in such statement to be owned by him and standing in his name on the books of the corporation, each share of whatever class entitling him to one vote; *always provided*, that in case of falsity or mistake in such statement and question arising as the validity of the passage or rejection of any such resolution by the votes then cast, any shares not owned by any party voting as aforesaid shall be deducted from the total vote on either side then cast or represented in thereafter determining the validity of the passage or rejection of any such resolution by the actual vote cast at such meeting by those actually entitled to cast votes thereat as above provided. When a stockholder shall present sworn statement of number of shares of stock owned by him, &c. Proviso.

5. *And be it enacted*, That in case of a resolution shall be duly passed at any such meeting pursuant to the provisions hereof repealing any such provisions as to the classification of directors or voting power or both, that then and from henceforth the term of office of all directors of said company then in office shall cease and determine, and a new election for directors of said company shall be held as aforesaid, and the new directors then elected shall be the lawful board of directors of said company, and shall be forthwith entitled to the possession and control of its property and franchise. New directors elected shall be the lawful board of directors.

6. *And be it enacted*, That in case of the repeal of any such provisions as to the classification of directors or

Certificate of chairman and secretary to be filed in office of secretary of state.

voting power or both, it shall and may be lawful for the chairman and secretary elected by the stockholders at any such meeting to make and sign a certificate under their hands, sworn to by them as true to the best of their knowledge, information and belief, and acknowledged as a deed to be recorded setting forth and specifying in general terms the proceedings taken for the purpose of holding such meeting, including the original or a copy of the notice of meeting so signed and the affidavit of the printer as to the publication of said notice as aforesaid, and the proceedings had or action taken at said meeting, and such certificate so made as aforesaid may be filed in the office of the secretary of state, upon the payment to the secretary of the state for the use of the state the sum of twenty (20) dollars, and a copy of any such certificate so made and filed as aforesaid, duly certified by the secretary of state under his official seal, shall be evidence in all courts and places of the facts therein recited, and of the right to issue the notice of such meeting and of the due issue and publication of such notice and the holding and action of such meeting in the premises, and generally that the foregoing provisions of this act have been fully observed and complied with.

Fee for filing.

7. *And be it enacted*, That this act shall take effect immediately.

Approved March 27, 1893.

CHAPTER CCLXIX.

A Further Supplement to an act entitled "An act for the formation and government of boroughs," approved April second, one thousand eight hundred and ninety-one.

Who constitute the council.

1. Be it enacted *by the Senate and General Assembly of the State of New Jersey*, That in all boroughs incorporated

under the act to which this is a supplement, having a population of three thousand inhabitants or more, there shall be a mayor and six members of council, who shall constitute the council and shall hold office for two years; *provided*, that at the first meeting of the council after the first election held under said act the members of council shall divide themselves, by lot, into two classes; the term of the first class shall be vacated at the expiration of the first year, the term of the second class at the expiration of the second year, so that three members of council shall be elected annually after the first election; and if vacancies happen by resignation or otherwise the person or persons elected to supply such vacancies shall be elected for the unexpired term only.

Term of office.

Proviso.

2. *And be it enacted*, That the council of any borough may select and designate a justice of the peace in the borough to try and determime all causes and complaints for violation of any ordinance of the council, and the justice of the peace so selected and designated shall have the same power and authority to issue process, try and determine said causes, and fine and imprison, upon conviction, in all respects as the mayors of boroughs are now given under said act.

Council may designate justice of the peace to try complaints for violation of ordinances.

Powers of such justices

3. *And be it enacted*, That this act shall take effect immediately.

Approved March 27, 1893.

CHAPTER CCLXX.

A Further Supplement to an act entitled "An act to establish and organize the state reform school for juvenile offenders," approved April sixth, one thousand eight hundred and sixty-five.

1. BE IT ENACTED *by the Senate and General Assembly of the State of New Jersey*, That the sum of four thousand

Appropriation of $4,000 for purchase of lands and laying water pipes.

dollars is hereby appropriated to be used exclusively in the purchase of the necessary lands and apparatus and for the purpose of laying and constructing the necessary water pipes to the lands of the New Jersey state reform school, to the end that a permanent water supply may be established for said school.

2. *And be it enacted*, That this act shall take effect immediately.

Approved March 27, 1893.

CHAPTER CCLXXI.

A Further Supplement to the act entitled "An act to establish and organize the state reform school for juvenile offenders," approved April sixth, one thousand eight hundred and sixty-five.

Appropriation of $5,000 for completion and furnishing new building.

1. BE IT ENACTED *by the Senate and General Assembly of the State of New Jersey*, That the sum of five thousand dollars is hereby appropriated to be used exclusively in the completion of the erection of a new family building and for furnishing the same, to provide better accommodations for the increasing number of boys committed to said institution.

2. *And be it enacted*, That this act shall take effect immediately.

Approved March 27, 1893.

CHAPTER CCLXXII.

A Further Supplement to an act entitled "An act concerning taxes," approved April fourteenth, one thousand eight hundred and forty-six.

Exempt from taxation all bonds, securities, &c., issued by state, county, &c.

1. Be it enacted *by the Senate and General Assembly of the State of New Jersey*, That all bonds, securities, improvement certificates, and other evidence of indebtedness heretofore or hereafter issued by this state, or by any county thereof, or by any city town, township, borough, school district, or other municipality of this state, shall be exempt from taxation for any purposes.

2. *And be it enacted*, That this act shall take effect immediately.

Approved March 27, 1893.

CHAPTER CCLXXIII.

A Supplement to an act entitled "An act to establish in this state, boards of health and a bureau of vital statistics, and to define their respective powers and duties," approved March thirty-first, one thousand eight hundred and eighty-seven.

Penalty prescribed for violation of any ordinance, &c.

1. Be it enacted *by the Senate and General Assembly of the State of New Jersey*, That any local board of health may prescribe a penalty for the violation of any ordinance, section of code, or amendment thereof, heretofore or hereafter passed by such board, not to exceed one hundred dollars and not less than two dollars.

Penalty left to the discretion of the court, &c.

2. *And be it enacted*, That such board shall not be required to provide a penalty specific in amount for the violations referred to in section one hereof, but they may provide that the penalty shall not be less than one given sum nor greater than another given sum, the amount of such penalty between the maximum and minimum inclusive, shall be left to the discretion of the court or magistrate before whom complaint may be made; *provided, however*, that this act shall not be construed so as to invalidate any ordinances now in force.

Proviso

Repealer.

3. *And be it enacted*, That all acts and parts of acts in conflict herewith be and the same, in so far as they may conflict, are repealed.

4. *And be it enacted*, That this act shall take effect immediately.

Approved March 27, 1893.

CHAPTER CCLXXIV.

An Act to allow municipalities to issue bonds for street improvements.

Lawful to issue corporate obligations for payment of cost of improvements not assessed.

1. BE IT ENACTED *by the Senate and General Assembly of the State of New Jersey*, That in all cases wherein commissioners of assessments, board of assessors or other persons having the power and authority by any act or acts of the legislature of this state, to assess the costs, damages and expenses of any improvements upon the lands or upon the owner or owners thereof benefited by such improvement, shall assess or have assessed upon the same an amount less than the total cost of any improvement, it shall be lawful for the authorities of any municipality wherein such assessment was, or shall hereafter be made, to issue the corporate obligations of such municipality for the payment of the amount of the cost of any such im-

provements not assessed upon the land or upon the owner or owners of land benefited by such improvement.

Corporate authorities by ordinance may issue bonds, &c., not exceeding $75,000.

2. *And be it enacted*, That for the payment of the costs of such improvements in excess of the amount so assessed as aforesaid, the corporate authorities of any such municipality may issue by ordinance, bonds or obligations of such municipality for the payment thereof, which said bonds shall in no case exceed the sum of seventy-five thousand dollars, and shall not bear more than five per centum interest, and to be sold for not less than par; said ordinance shall distinctly specify and provide the ways and means and the manner of payment of said bonds and the interest thereof, and shall be irrepealable until all of said bonds shall be paid.

Ordinance shall be irrepealable until all bonds paid

Bonds issued may be in excess of bonded indebtedness.

3. *And be it enacted*, That the amount for which bonds shall be issued by any municipality under the provisions of this act, may be in excess of any limitation in its charter or supplements thereto as to the amount of its bonded indebtedness.

4. *And be it enacted*, That this act shall be deemed a public act, and take effect immediately.

Approved March 27, 1893.

CHAPTER CCLXXVII.

An Act relative to the publication of the expenditures of the public moneys by the common council or other governing body in cities of the second class of this state.

Treasurer to prepare statement of expenditures of public moneys to be published monthly.

1. Be it enacted *by the Senate and General Assembly of the State of New Jersey*, That it shall be the duty of the common council or other governing body in cities of the second class, monthly, to publish in a newspaper printed and published in said city a detailed itemized statement

of the expenditures of the public moneys by said board for the preceding month; and it shall be the duty of the treasurer of every such city to prepare the statements of such expenditures for publication

Required to designate newspaper to publish expenditures.

2. *And be it enacted*, That it shall be the duty of the common council or other governing body in said cities of the second class, at their first regular meeting held after the passage of this act, to designate a newspaper in said city to publish the said expenditures of the public moneys as herein provided for, and which newspaper so designated shall publish the same for the period of one year, at the expiration of which year it shall be the duty of said common council or other governing body to again designate a newspaper for that purpose; and in like manner shall a newspaper be designated each succeeding year.

Repealer.

3. *And be it enacted*, That all acts and parts of acts inconsistent with this act be and the same are hereby repealed.

4. *And be it enacted*, That this act shall take effect immediately.

Approved March 28, 1898.

CHAPTER CCLXXVIII.

Supplement to an act entitled "An act for the oranization of the national guard of the state of New Jersey," approved March ninth, one thousand eight hundred and sixty-nine, and the various amendments thereto.

Two cavalry companies may be added to national guard.

1. BE IT ENACTED *by the Senate and General Assembly of the State of New Jersey*, That the commander-in-chief, whenever in his judgment it shall be advisable for the public interest, may cause to be added to the national guard of New Jersey, and mustered thereinto, cavalry companies, not more than two in number.

By-laws, &c., subject to approval of commander-in-chief.

2. *And be it enacted*, That any such company shall retain and be governed by such constitution, organization and by-laws as it may have adopted and which shall receive the approval of the commander-in-chief.

Subject to order of commander-in-chief.

3. *And be it enacted*, That every such company shall be subject to the orders of the commander-in-chief, and while by him ordered out, to the order of the commandant of the body to which they shall be attached.

Minimum number of men.

Entitled to and subject to.

4. *And be it enacted*, That the minimum of any such company shall be forty men; and any such company while so ordered out shall be entitled to the rights, privileges, pay and allowances, and be subject to the discipline, duties and service of the national guard of New Jersey.

Who issues arms and equipments.

5. *And be it enacted*, That the quartermaster-general shall issue to any such company, arms and equipments.

Term of enlistment.

Who may accept resignation.

6. *And be it enacted*, That the term of enlistment shall be five years; and the time any member of an organized cavalry company has served such company faithfully prior to being mustered in, may be applied on such members' term of enlistment; and in view of the great expense of members of such company and of the great labor attending cavalry service, the commandant of any cavalry company may, for reasons satisfactory to him, accept the resignation of any member of any such company while not in active service, or in contemplation thereof.

Commander-in-chief may cause such company mustered out.

7. *And be it enacted*, That the commander-in-chief may, at any time, by reason of any such company being deficient in or neglecting drill, or for any other reason, cause any such company to be mustered out of the national guard.

8. *And be it enacted*, That this act shall take effect immediately.

Approved March 28, 1893.

CHAPTER CCLXXIX.

An Act to amend an act entitled "An act to enable boards of chosen freeholders to acquire, improve and maintain public roads," approved March nineteenth, one thousand eight hundred and eightly-nine.

Section to be amended

1. BE IT ENACTED *by the Senate and General Assembly of the State of New Jersey*, That section five of the above act be and the same is hereby amended so as to read as follows:

Authorized to employ competent engineer to survey county roads.

5. *And be it enacted*, That the board of chosen freeholders shall employ a competent engineer, at a reasonable compensation, to survey the county roads or any part thereof, when necessary; to prepare specifications for pavements or other improvements intended to be made in pursuance of this act, and to supervise the work and materials used; after such improvements or any part thereof shall have been completed, the same shall be kept in repair at the expense of the county, and some competent person shall be employed by said board annually, at a fixed compensation, to inspect the condition of the county roads, from time to time, so far as the same may have been improved, and such inspector shall have the power to cause necessary repairs to be made to the pavements or other improvements made under this act; *provided*, the costs of any such repairs shall not exceed fifty dollars in any city, town, township or borough in any year; repairs costing more than fifty dollars and not more than one hundred dollars shall be made only by authority of a committee of the said board, and repairs costing more than one hundred dollars shall only be made by direct authority of said board; all bills or claims for making repairs or furnishing materials therefor, after being approved by the inspector, shall be rendered to the said board by the parties who performed the work or furnished the materials used or

Shall appoint an inspector.

Power of inspector.

Proviso.

to be used; and no bills or claims for repairs shall be paid unless the same shall have been made strictly according to the provisions and directions of this act; no tax shall be levied for the purpose of repairs under this act in any one year, in excess of five per centum of the costs of the improvements made; and no repairs shall be made with moneys raised except as aforesaid; the inspector, immediately after his appointment, shall give a bond to the said board in the penal sum of two thousand dollars, to be approved and held by the county collector, conditioned for the faithful performance of his duties. Inspector shall give bond in $2,000.

2. *And be it enacted*, That all acts inconsistent herewith be repealed and that this act shall take effect immediately. Repealer.

Approved March 28, 1898.

CHAPTER CCLXXX.

An Act authorizing the board of aldermen, common council or other governing body in cities of the second class to fix and determine by resolution the compensation of recorders.

1. Be it enacted *by the Senate and General Assembly of the State of New Jersey*, That the board of aldermen, common council or other governing body in the cities of the second class of this state shall have power by resolution to fix and determine the amount of compensation to be paid to the recorder of such city; *provided, however*, that in such cities of ten thousand but not exceeding twenty thousand inhabitants, the annual salary of the recorder shall not exceed one thousand five hundred dollars; and in all such cities of twenty thousand but not exceeding thirty-five thousand inhabitants, the annual salary of the recorder shall not exceed two thousand dollars; and in Empowered to fix compensation of recorder. Proviso. Salaries.

all the other of said cities of the second class the annual salary of the recorder shall not exceed two thousand five hundred dollars.

Salary shall not be increased or diminished.

2. *And be it enacted*, That the salary of any such recorder fixed, as authorized by section one of this act, shall not be increased or diminished during his term of office.

Repealer.

3. *And be it enacted*, That all acts and parts of acts, whether general, public, private or special, inconsistent with the provisions of this act be and the same are hereby repealed.

4. *And be it enacted*, That this act shall take effect immediately.

Approved March 28, 1898.

CHAPTER CCLXXXI.

A Supplement to an act entitled "An act in relation to the state house and adjacent public grounds," approved February twenty-first, one thousand eight hundred and ninety-three.

Superintendent authorized to appoint telegraph operator, &c.

1. Be it enacted *by the Senate and General Assembly of the State of New Jersey*, That in addition to the power conferred upon the superintendent of the state house and adjacent public grounds, he shall have and is hereby given authority to have fitted up in the said state house a suitable room to be used as an office for the transmission and reception of telegrams, and shall have and is hereby given authority to appoint a suitable person to transmit and receive telegrams therein, which person shall be appointed at a salary not exceeding one thousand dollars per annum, as shall be approved by the governor, attorney general and state treasurer or a majority of them.

Salary, approved by.

2. *And be it enacted*, That the comptroller shall draw his warrant for the salary fixed as above for said appointee, which shall be paid by the state treasurer upon its presentation, said salary to be paid in monthly installments. Salary paid monthly.

3. *And be it enacted*, That this act shall take effect immediately.

Approved March 28, 1898.

CHAPTER CCLXXXII.

An Act relative to the publication of the expenditures of the public moneys by the boards of chosen freeholders in the counties of the second class.

1. Be it enacted *by the Senate and General Assembly of the State of New Jersey*, That it shall be the duty of the board of chosen freeholders in counties of the second class monthly to publish in a newspaper printed and published in said county, a detailed itemized statement of the expenditures of the public moneys by said board for the preceding month. And it shall be the duty of the county collector of every such county to prepare the statements of such expenditures for publication. Monthly statement of expenditures to be published. County collector to prepare the statement.

2. *And be it enacted*, That it shall be the duty of the board of chosen freeholders in said counties of the second class, at their first regular meeting held after the passage of this act, to designate a newspaper in said county to publish the said expenditures of the public moneys, as herein provided for, and which newspaper so designated shall publish the same for the period of one year, at the expiration of which year it shall be the duty of the said board of chosen freeholders to again designate a newspaper for that purpose; and in like manner shall a newspaper be designated each succeeding year. Newspapers to be designated to publish monthly statement.

Repealer.

3. *And be it enacted*, That all acts and parts of acts inconsistent with this act be and the same are hereby repealed.

4. *And be it enacted*, That this act shall take effect immediately.

Approved March 28, 1893.

CHAPTER CCLXXXIII.

An Act to amend an act entitled "A further supplement to the act entitled 'An act concerning taxes,'" approved April fourteenth, one thousand eight hundred and forty-six, which supplement was approved April seventeenth, one thousand eight hundred and seventy-six.

Section to be amended.

1. BE IT ENACTED *by the Senate and General Assembly of the State of New Jersey*, That section one of the act entitled "A further supplement to the act entitled 'An act concerning taxes,'" approved April fourteenth, one thousand eight hundred and forty-six, which said supplement was approved April seventeenth, one thousand eight hundred and seventy-six, be amended so as to read as follows:

Mortgages not to be assessed unless a deduction claimed.

1. BE IT ENACTED *by the Senate and General Assembly of the State of New Jersey*, That hereafter no mortgage on real or personal property, or both, whether given by individuals or corporations, or the debt secured by such mortgage, shall be assessed for taxation unless a deduction therefor shall have been claimed by the owner of such mortgaged property, and allowed by the assessor.

2. *And be it enacted*, That this act shall take effect immediately.

Approved March 28, 1893.

CHAPTER CCLXXXIV.

An Act fixing the term of office of overseers of the poor in second class cities.

1. Be it enacted *by the Senate and General Assembly of the State of New Jersey*, That in cities of the second class the overseers of the poor shall hereafter be appointed for the term of three years and until the qualification of his successor; it shall be lawful for the common council, board of aldermen, the mayor, board of commissioners of police or other governing body of any such city having the appointment of such officer, to appoint him at any time after the passage of this act for the term of three years as aforesaid, notwithstanding any appointment heretofore made; upon the appointment of said officer under the provisions of this act the term of the overseer of the poor heretofore appointed shall cease; at the time of such appointment the salary of the overseer of the poor shall be fixed as now provided by law.

Term of office.

When appointment to be made.

Salary to be fixed.

2. *And be it enacted*, That all general, public or other acts of any kinds whatsoever or any part thereof inconsistent with the provisions of this act are hereby abrogated and repealed, and that this act shall take effect immediately.

Repealer.

Approved March 28, 1893.

CHAPTER CCLXXXV.

An Act to provide for the planting and care of shade trees on the highways of the municipalities of this state.

Commission appointed shall have control and power to plant, &c., shade trees.

1. BE IT ENACTED *by the Senate and General Assembly of the State of New Jersey*, That in all the municipalities of this state there may be appointed, in the manner hereinafter provided, a commission of three freeholders, who shall serve without compensation, and who shall have the exclusive and absolute control and power to plant, set out, maintain, protect and care for shade trees in any of the public highways of their respective municipalities, the cost thereof to be borne and paid for in the manner hereinafter directed.

Governing body or municipality by resolution direct commissioners to be appointed.

2. *And be it enacted*, That it shall be optional with the governing body of any municipality whether this act shall have effect in, and such commissioners shall be appointed in, such municipality; and whenever any such governing body shall by resolution, approve of this act, and direct that such commissioners shall be appointed, then, from that time, this act and all its provisions shall be in force, and apply to such municipality; and such commissioners shall be appointed for terms of three, four and five years, respectively; and on the expiration of any term, the new appointment shall be for five years, and any vacancy shall be filled for the unexpired term only; and in cities the said appointments shall be made by the mayor thereof, and in townships by the chairman of the township committee, and in villages and boroughs by the chairman or president of the board of trustees, or other governing body.

Term of office.

Vacancy filled for unexpired term only.

By whom appointments made.

Notice of contemplated improvement to be published.

3. *And be it enacted*, That whenever said commissioners shall propose to make any such improvements as setting out or planting any shade trees, or changing the same in any highway, they shall give notice of such contemplated improvement (specify the streets or portions thereof where such trees are intended to be planted) in one or

more of the newspapers of their said municipality, if there be any newspaper published in said place, for at least two weeks prior to any meeting in which they shall decide to make such improvement.

By whom cost of planting trees borne.

4. *And be it enacted*, That the cost of planting and transplanting any trees in any highway, and boxes or guards for the protection thereof, when necessary, shall be borne by the real estate in front of which such trees are planted or set out, and the cost thereof as to each tract of real estate shall be certified by said commissioners to the person having charge of the collection of taxes for said municipality; and upon the filing of said certificate, the amount of the cost of such improvement shall be and become a lien upon said lands in front of which said trees were planted or set out, and the said collecting officer shall place the assessment so made against any property in the annual tax bills rendered to owner or owners of such property, and the same shall be collectible in the same manner as the other taxes against said property are collected.

Cost of such improvement collected same as other taxes.

Cost and expense of caring for said trees, &c., paid by a general tax.

5. *And be it enacted*, That the cost and expense of caring for said trees, after being planted or set out, and the expense of publishing said notices, shall be borne and paid by a general tax to be raised by said municipality; said tax shall not exceed the sum of one-tenth of one mill on the dollar annually on all the taxable property of said municipality, and the needed amount shall be each year certified by said commissioners to the assessor and assessors of the said municipality, and be assessed and raised as other taxes.

6. *And be it enacted*, That this act shall take effect immediately.

Approved March 28, 1898.

CHAPTER CCLXXXVI.

A Supplement to an act entitled "An act relative to guardians and the estates of minors" (Revision), approved March twenty-seventh, one thousand eight hundred and seventy-four.

When lawful for chancellor to authorize a guardian to mortgage or sell real estate of minors.

1. BE IT ENACTED *by the Senate and General Assembly of the State of New Jersey*, That whenever it shall appear to the chancellor, in any proceeding before him, that the lands or real estate of any minor or minors are likely to be disadvantaged, imperiled or sacrificed by reason of any liens or incumbrances existing against the same, and there is other estate of such minor or minors, it shall be lawful for the chancellor to cause such other estate to be sold, converted or applied for the purpose of reducing or discharging such liens or incumbrances, and saving the said lands or real estate to such minor or minors; and it shall be lawful in such case for the chancellor to authorize the guardian of such minor or minors to mortgage any or all of the lands or real estate of such minor or minors to raise money wherewith to pay and discharge such liens or incumbrances.

2. *And be it enacted*, That this act shall take effect immediately.

Approved April 3, 1893.

CHAPTER CCLXXXVII.

An Act to enable the city council or other governing body of any municipality of this state to accept trusts and purchase property for the purpose of carrying out said trusts.

WHEREAS, There are a number of school societies and religious organizations of this state possessed of personal property and valuable real estate in cities of this state, which, owing to the establishment of numerous excellent free schools and public institutions of a like character, renders it impossible or impracticable for said societies and organizations to continue the maintenance of such society or organization for the purposes for which it was created, and which said societies or organizations are desirous of conveying to the municipality in which they are located, personal property and valuable real estate, for the purpose of public buildings and also for the purpose of maintaining a free reading room, library or institute for the benefit of the public; and also to sell to said municipality certain real estate adjoining property which they desire to donate or convey to said municipality for the purposes aforesaid, the income from which adjoining property, so to be sold, shall be used by said municipality for the purpose of carrying out the terms and conditions of said trust; *and whereas*, the said societies or organizations desire to make such conveyance of property to said municipality in order that there may be maintained a free reading room, library and museum, and a place for free lectures on philosophical, mechanical and kindred subjects, which tend to elevate the minds and morals of the people and be of special benefit to the community; *and whereas*, such purpose can only be accomplished by a trust which would be most likely to exist in perpetuity, and municipal corporations are the Preamble only form of corporations in this state which have any assurance of perpetuity, and therefore such objects can best be attained by the intervention of some municipality; therefore,

Lawful for city council, &c., to accept trusts, and appoint trustees.

1. BE IT ENACTED *by the Senate and General Assembly of the State of New Jersey*, That it shall and may be lawful for the city council or other governing body of any municipality of this state to accept any trusts for the purposes aforesaid, and to appoint any number of trustees designated by the terms and under the conditions of the deed or instrument creating the trust and conveying the real or personal estate, or both, to said municipality; and it shall also be lawful for the said city council or other governing body of said municipality to purchase lands belonging to said society or organization, adjoining the lands conveyed to said municipality for the purposes aforesaid, and to issue bonds to an amount not exceeding ten thousand dollars in payment for said lands so purchased; *provided*, that the interest accruing upon said bonds shall be used and devoted for the purpose of maintaining said trust and carrying out the purposes thereof.

Also lawful to purchase lands, and issue bonds in payment thereof.

Proviso.

Not liable for misappropriation of funds, &c.

2. *And be it enacted*, That nothing herein contained shall be construed to make any municipality liable for the misappropriation of the funds created by said trust, nor to make good any diminution thereof resulting from the wrongful acts of its agents or any person or persons appointed in conformity with the terms and conditions of the deed or instrument creating said trust; *provided*, however, should any agent or officer of said municipality be under bonds thereto and upon default, the municipality should recover from the sureties on said bond a sum sufficient to pay or make good the amount of misappropriation of said funds of said trust, then said municipality shall make good the same out of the amount so received; *and provided further*, that any misappropriation of the funds aforesaid shall in no wise affect the trust aforesaid.

Proviso.

Proviso.

Repealer.

3. *And be it enacted*, That all acts or parts of acts inconsistent with the provisions of this act be and the same are hereby repealed.

4. *And be it enacted*, That this act shall take effect immediately.

Approved April 3, 1893.

CHAPTER CCLXXXVIII.

A Supplement to an act entitled "A further supplement to an act entitled 'An act for the better enforcement in Maurice river cove and Delaware bay of the act entitled "An act for the preservation of clams and oysters,"'" approved April fourteenth, one thousand eight hundred and forty-six, and the supplements thereto, approved March eighth, one thousand eight hundred and eighty-two, which further supplement was approved February twentieth, one thousand eight hundred and eighty-six.

Section to be amended.

1. BE IT ENACTED *by the Senate and General Assembly of the State of New Jersey*, That the twelfth section of the act entitled "A further supplement to an act entitled 'An an act for the better enforcement in Maurice river cove and Delaware bay of the act entitled "An act for the preservation of clams and oysters,"'" approved April fourteenth, one thousand eight hundred and forty-six, and the supplements thereto, approved March eighth, one thousand eight hundred and eighty-two, be and the same is hereby amended so as to read as follows:

When unlawful to catch or take oysters within certain boundaries

12. *And be it enacted*, That it shall be unlawful for any person or persons to catch or take oysters from any of the natural oyster beds or natural oyster grounds in Delaware bay north of a line running direct from the mouth of Straight creek, to Cross Ledge lighthouse, from the fifteenth day of June in each year to the first day of April in the succeeding year, and from the fifteenth day of June until the first day of September in each year no natural oyster growth nor planted oysters shall be caught or taken from any of the grounds in Delaware bay, Delaware river, and Maurice river cove for any purpose whatever, and any person offending against any of the provisions of this section shall be deemed guilty of a misdemeanor, and

Penalty for violation.

upon conviction thereof shall for every such offense be punished by a fine not exceeding two hundred dollars or by imprisonment not exceeding one year, or both, at the discretion of the court; and any boat or vessel used or employed in the commission of such offence against the provisions of this section, with all her tackle, furniture and apparel, and the oysters thereon, shall be forfeited and the same seized, secured and sold in the manner prescribed in the ninth and tenth sections of the act entitled "An act for the preservation of clams and oysters," approved April fourteenth, one thousand eight hundred and forty-six, and the proceeds of such sale, after deducting all expenses, shall be paid to the said collector of the oyster fund.

Boats, vessels, tackle, &c., forfeited.

Where unlawful to stake up grounds, &c.

2. *And be it enacted*, That it shall be unlawful for any person, persons or corporation to stake up grounds or plant oysters north of a line running from the mouth of Straight creek to Cross Ledge lighthouse, and that any and all grounds staked up contrary to the provisions of this act, and all oysters planted thereon shall be deemed public property and shall be prosecuted according to the provisions of the twelfth section of an act entitled "A further supplement to an act entitled 'An act for the better enforcement in Maurice river cove and Delaware bay of the act entitled "An act for the preservation of clams and oysters,"'" Approved April fourteenth, one thousand eight hundred and forty-six, and the supplements thereto.

Repealer.

3. *And be it enacted*, That all acts or parts of acts inconsistent with the provisions of this act be and the same are hereby repealed.

4. *And be it enacted*, That this act shall take effect immediately.

Approved April 3, 1898.

CHAPTER CCLXXXIX.

An Act relating to the compensation to be given to the prosecutors of the pleas in the counties of the first class of this state.

1. BE IT ENACTED *by the Senate and General Assembly of the State of New Jersey*, That hereafter the annual salary of the prosecutors of the pleas in every county of the first class shall be eight thousand dollars, payable in monthly installments in lieu of all fees and allowances, which fees shall be paid into the county treasury; *provided*, that this act shall not take effect in any of said counties until the said prosecutor in said respective counties shall have filed in the office of the county clerk of said county his acceptance of the salary hereinbefore fixed, and a waiver of all fees now fixed by law. Salary, in lieu of fees. Proviso. Acceptance to be filed.

2. *And be it enacted*, That all acts and parts of acts inconsistent with this act be and the same are hereby repealed, and that this act shall take effect immediately. Repealer.

Approved April 4, 1898.

CHAPTER CCXC.

An Act to promote the propagation and growth of seed oysters and to protect the natural oyster beds of this state.

1. BE IT ENACTED *by the Senate and General Assembly of the State of New Jersey*, That for the purposes of promoting the propagation and growth of seed oysters and to protect the natural oyster beds of this state, the said Oyster beds divided in districts.

natural oyster beds shall be and they hereby are divided into seven districts, as follows:

District No. 1—Newark bay and adjacent waters;

District No. 2—Barnegat bay, north of Gunning river;

District No. 3—From Gunning river south to Rose's point;

District No. 4—From Rose's point south to the division line between Atlantic county and Ocean county;

District No. 5—The bays and waters of Atlantic county;

District No. 6—The bays and waters of Cape May county;

District No. 7—The waters of Delaware bay and Maurice river cove.

Commissioners appointed.

2. *And be it enacted*, That the following-named persons shall be and they hereby are appointed to act as commissioners in and for their respective districts for the term of

Term of office.

three years, to do and perform such duties as may hereinafter be prescribed, and who shall, before they enter upon the performance of such duties, take and subscribe

Take an oath.

to an oath or affirmation before the clerk of the county wherein they reside respectively to faithfully discharge the duties of their office: first district, George Rabenstein, William P. Wood; second district, George Everham, Isaac Worth; third district, Abraham J. Jones, Thomas Cramer; fourth district, Marshall A. Loveland, George A. Mott; fifth district, James A. Beckwith, Lewis H. Barrett; sixth district, Robert Corson, George Dickinson, Jr.; seventh district, Reuben Smith, Henry Long;

How vacancy filled.

and in case of any vacancy occurring by death, resignation, removal or otherwise, the governor shall have authority to appoint any competent resident of the district to fill such vacancy.

Duties of commissioners.

3. *And be it enacted*, That it shall be the duty of the said commissioners to make a careful inspection of the natural oyster grounds in their respective district, and wherever and whenever in their opinion it is expedient to cause a supply of shells to be spread on the grounds of the said natural oyster grounds in this state, which from any cause have become depleted, which said shells shall be purchased by said commissioners at the lowest price, and be spread between the thirtieth day of April and the first

day of September in each year for the period of three years, and until the appropriation hereinafter made for the purposes shall be exhausted.

When unlawful to rake, tong, &c

4. *And be it enacted*, That it shall not be lawful for any person or persons to rake, tong, dredge or in any manner whatsoever to remove any of the shells so as aforesaid spread upon the beds within two years thereafter; and any person or persons offending against the provisions of this act shall be punishable by a fine of twenty-five dollars, to be recovered in an action of debt to be brought by and in the name of the commissioners of the district before any justice of the peace of the county where the offence is committed, and the fine when so recovered shall immediately be paid to the treasurer of this state for the use of the state.

Penalty for violation.

Compensation.

5. *And be it enacted*, That each of the said commissioners above named shall be entitled to receive for each day's actual service in the discharge of their duties as aforesaid the sum of three dollars and no other compensation whatsoever, to be paid by the state treasurer upon warrant of the comptroller, the comptroller being hereby authorized to issue such warrant upon presentation to him of a statement duly verified by oath or affirmation by such commissioner that the service for which pay is demanded has been duly performed.

Appropriation of $5,000, and how to be distributed.

6. *And be it enacted*, That for the purposes of carrying out the provisions of this act there shall be appropriated the sum of five thousand dollars annually for the period of three years, which said sum of five thousand dollars shall be distributed as follows:

For waters north of Cedar creek point in the waters of Barnegat bay, in the county of Ocean, to Pennsylvania railroad bridge, the sum of seven hundred dollars;

For the mouth of Mullica river and adjacent waters, known as Graveling oyster beds, the sum of five hundred dollars;

For the mouth of Tuckerton creek and adjacent waters, the sum of one hundred and fifty dollars;

For the mouth of Parkerton creek and adjacent waters, the sum of two hundred dollars;

For the mouth of West creek and adjacent waters, the sum of one hundred and fifty dollars;

From Dinner point to north side of Cedar run, the sum of one hundred and fifty dollars;

From Delaware bay and Maurice river cove, in Cumberland county, the sum of five hundred dollars;

For Newark bay and adjacent waters, the sum of six hundred and fifty dollars;

For the mouth of Great Egg harbor river and adjacent waters, including Atlantic county, five hundred dollars, and for Cape May county, five hundred dollars;

The remaining ten hundred dollars shall remain as a reserve fund in the event that it may become necessary that any one particular district shall require a greater expenditure than above provided, in which case the said commissioners in meeting assembled may determine the proportion to be alloted to such district, and also for the purpose of meeting such other incidental expenses not herein specially provided for.

May employ assistants.

7. *And be it enacted*, That the commissioners herein named are authorized to employ such assistants as they may deem necessary to carry out the provisions of this act.

8. *And be it enacted*, That section four of this act shall not apply to Cumberland county.

9. *And be it enacted*, That this act shall take effect immediately.

Approved April 4, 1893.

CHAPTER CCXCI.

An Act to amend an act entitled "A supplement to an act to provide for the purchase of sites for and the erection and equipment of armories in cities of the first and second class and making appropriations therefor, and to provide for the taking of real estate for such sites by commission, in case the same cannot be purchased by agreement," approved March twenty-third, one thousand eight hundred and eighty-eight, which supplement was approved May fifth, one thousand eight hundred and ninety.

1. BE IT ENACTED *by the Senate and General Assembly of the State of New Jersey*, That the first section of the act of which this is amendatory be and the same is hereby amended so as to read as follows: Section to be amended

1. BE IT ENACTED *by the Senate and General Assembly of the State of New Jersey*, That the commission constituted by the act to which this is a supplement be and it is hereby authorized to enter into contracts and cause to be erected armories in cities of the first and second class in the manner prescribed by the said act in excess of the limitation in said act prescribed; *provided*, that the excess over and above such limitation shall be secured to be paid in such manner as said commission shall prescribe and in such manner that the state of New Jersey shall not be obligated to pay more than one hundred and thirty-five thousand dollars for the entire cost of erecting and completing any such armory as provided by said act. Authorized to enter into contracts and erect armories. Proviso.

2. *And be it enacted*, That the second section of the act of which this is amendatory be and the same is hereby amended so as to read as follows: Section to be amended.

2. *And be it enacted*, That it shall be lawful for said commission in entering into such contracts as aforesaid, to provide therein that no more than fifty thousand dol- Amount to be provided on account of each armory.

lars shall be paid from the state treasury in any one year on account of each armory so contracted for.

3. *And be it enacted*, That this act shall take effect immediately.

Approved April 4, 1893.

CHAPTER CCXCII.

An Act to defray the incidental expenses of the legislature of New Jersey for the session of one thousand eight hundred and ninety-three.

Treasurer authorized to pay certain amounts.

1. BE IT ENACTED *by the Senate and General Assembly of the State of New Jersey*, That it shall be lawful for the treasurer of the state of New Jersey to pay, upon the warrant of the comptroller, to the several persons hereinafter named, the following amounts, that is to say:

Item No. 1. To each clergyman, for opening sessions of the senate and house of assembly with prayer, during session one thousand eight hundred and ninety-three, ten dollars, $10 00

Item No. 2. To each officer of the senate and house of assembly of the session of one thousand eight hundred and ninety-two, for services in opening the session of one thousand eight hundred and ninety-three, ten dollars, $10 00

Item No. 3. To Naar, Day & Naar, for stationery furnished president of the senate, one hundred and seventy-six dollars and sixty cents, $176 60

Item No. 4. To Naar, Day & Naar, for stationery furnished judiciary committee of the house of assembly, fifty-one dollars and thirty-five cents, $51 35

Item No. 5. To Naar, Day & Naar, for stationery furnished the committee on fisheries of the house of assembly, fifty-four dollars and forty cents, $54 40

Item No. 6. To Naar, Day & Daar, for stationery furnished the committee on bill revision of the house of assembly, fifty-five dollars and twenty-five cents, $55 25

Item No. 7. To Naar, Day & Naar, for stationery furnished the engrossing clerk of the senate, one hundred and five dollars and sixty-five cents, $105 65

Item No. 8. To Naar, Day & Naar, for stationery furnished the secretary of the senate, one hundred and twenty-two dollars and ninety-five cents, $122 95

Item No. 9. To Naar, Day & Naar, for stationery furnished the journal clerk of the house, fifty-five dollars, $55 00

Item No. 10. To Naar, Day & Naar, for stationery furnished the engrossing clerk of the house of assembly, two hundred and twenty-two dollars and fifty-five cents, $222 55

Item No. 11. To Naar, Day & Naar, for index books furnished the secretary of the senate, six dollars, $6 00

Item No. 12. To Naar, Day & Naar, for advertising notice to present claims against the legislature, one dollar and twenty-five cents, $1 25

Item No. 13. To Naar, Day & Naar, for stationery furnished the reading clerk of the house, thirty-one dollars and ninety-five cents, $31 95

Item No. 14. To Naar, Day & Naar, for stationery furnished the clerk of the house of assembly, one hundred and ten dollars and fifty cents, $110 50

Item No. 15. To Naar, Day & Naar, for stationery furnished the assistant engrossing clerk of the senate, twenty dollars and forty cents, $20 40

Item No. 16. To Naar, Day & Naar, for stationery furnished the sergeant-at-arms of the senate, ninety dollars and fifteen cents, $90 15

Item No. 17. To Naar, Day & Naar, for blank books furnished the secretary of the senate, ninety-six dollars and twenty-five cents, $96 25

Item No. 18. To MacCrellish & Quigley, for

stationery furnished the speaker of the house of assembly, two hundred and seventy-seven dollars and fourteen cents, $277 14

Item No. 19. To MacCrellish & Quigley, for stationery furnished the clerk of the house of assembly, four dollars, $4 00

Item No. 20. To MacCrellish & Quigley, for stationery furnished the assistant secretary of the house of assembly, fifty-five dollars and ten cents, $55 10

Item No. 21. To MacCrellish & Quigley, for twine furnished the sergeant-at-arms of the house of assembly, three dollars and twenty cents, $3 20

Item No. 22. To MacCrellish & Quigley, for printed cards furnished the engrossing clerk of the house of assembly, two dollars and fifty cents, $2 50

Item No. 23. To MacCrellish & Quigley, for stationery furnished the bill clerk of the house of assembly, twenty-three dollars and fifty-five cents, $23 55

Item No. 24. To MacCrellish & Quigley, for stationery furnished the assistant secretary of the senate, fifteen dollars and five cents, $15 05

Item No. 25. To MacCrellish & Quigley, for stationery furnished the bill clerk of the senate, twenty dollars and seventy cents, $20 70

Item No. 26. To MacCrellish & Quigley, for stationery furnished the sergeant-at-arms of the senate, seventy-eight dollars and seventy-five cents, $78 75

Item No. 27. To MacCrellish & Quigley, for calendar, journals and blank books furnished the secretary of the senate, eighty-nine dollars, $89 00

Item No. 28. To MacCrellish & Quigley, for printed cards furnished the engrossing clerk of the senate, two dollars and fifty cents, $2 50

Item No. 29. To Jordan Stationery Company, for stationery furnished the sergeant-at-arms of the senate, three hundred and eighty-three dollars and forty cents, $383 40

Item No. 30. To Jordan Stationery Company, for stationery furnished the secretary, assistant secretary and assistant journal clerk of the senate, three hundred and twenty-seven dollars and fifty cents. $327 50

Item No. 31. To Jordan Stationery Company, for files furnished the members and officers of the house of assembly, seven hundred and thirty dollars, $730 00

Item No. 32. To Jordan Stationery Company, for engraved ivory gavel for speaker of the house of assembly, calendars for officers of the senate and house of assembly, and minute books for officers of the house of assembly, two hundred and seventy-three dollars and fifty cents, $273 50

Item No. 33. To Jordan Stationery Company, for stationery furnished the engrossing clerk of the house of assembly, thirty-two dollars, $32 00

Item No. 34. To Jordan Stationery Company, for towels, brushes, soap, brooms, etc., furnished the sergeant-at-arms of the house of assembly, four hundred and nine dollars and thirty-two cents, $409 32

Item No. 35. To Jordan Stationery Company, for stationery furnished the sergeant-at-arms of the house of assembly for the use of the members, four hundred and eighteen dollars and fifty cents, $418 50

Item No. 36. To Jordan Stationery Company, for stationery furnished the clerk of the house of assembly, four hundred and fourteen dollars, $414 00

Item No. 37. To Jordan Stationery Company, for stationery furnished the stationery committee of the house of assembly, for the use of members, officers and reporters of the house, seven hundred and eighty-seven dollars and fifty cents, $787 50

Item No. 38. To Jordan Stationery Company, for stationery furnished the chairman of committees of the house of assemby, two hundred and fifty-one dollars, $251 00

Item No. 39. To R. Gray, Jr., for engraved ivory gavels and cases furnished the president of the senate, session of one thousand eight hundred and ninety-two, and one thousand eight hundred and ninety-three, eighty dollars, $80 00

Item No. 40. To Daniel J. Bechtel, for stamped brass coat checks furnished the senate, fourteen dollars, $14 00

Item No. 41. To F. S. Katzenbach & Company, for locks, etc., furnished the sergeant-at-arms of the senate and the clerk of the house of assembly, twelve dollars and seventy-five cents, $12 75

Item No. 42. To G. B. La Barre, for furnishing parchment and preparing oaths of officers and members of the senate and the house of assembly, fifty dollars, $50 00

Item No. 43. To A. Kessler, for furnishing keys and locks and repairs to desks in the senate and the house of assembly, sixty-three dollars and twenty-five cents, $63 25

Item No. 44. To The John L. Murphy Publishing Company, for advertising notice to present claims against the legislature, one dollar and eighty-five ce[illegible] $1 85

Item No. 45. To C. Rittenhouse, for stationery, printed blanks, etc., furnished the secretary of the senate, one hundred and fifty dollars, $150 00

Item No. 46. To Charles L. Stryker, for stationery furnished the secretary of the senate, fifty dollars, $50 00

Item No. 47. To the Phœnix Iron Company, for brass railing furnished the house of assembly, four hundred and five dollars, $405 00

Item No. 48. To the Stoll Blank Book and and Stationery Company, for thumb tacks furnished the sergeant-at-arms of the house of assembly, five dollars and five cents, $5 05

Item No. 49. To the "New Jersey Staats Zeitung" Company, for printing three thousand copies of Governor Werts's inaugural address, sixty-nine dollars and fifteen cents, $69 15

Item No. 50. To the "New Jersey Staats Zeitung" Company, for printing three thousand copies of Governor Abbett's annual message, three hundred and twenty-eight dollars and sixty-four cents, $328 74

Item No. 51. To Thomas F. Noonan, Jr., for preparing index to house minutes, session of one thousand eight hundred and ninety-two, and for services in procuring calendars, journals, and gavel, one thousand eight hundred and ninety-three, one hundred dollars, $100 00

Item No. 52. To John J. Matthews, for furnishing one hundred and sixty copies of members' pocket calendars for the senate and the house of assembly, one hundred and sixty dollars, $160 00

Item No. 53. To the Foye Letter File Company, for transfer bill files furnished the house of assembly, fifty dollars, $50 00

Item No. 54. To The Foye Letter File Company, for bill files furnished the senate, three hundred and six dollars and eighty cents, $306 80

Item No. 55. To The "Blairstown Press," for furnishing printed notices of committee meetings for the house of assembly, forty-one dollars, $41 00

Item No. 56. To Elizabeth Kucker, for washing towels for use of the legislature, sixty-five dollars, $65 00

Item No. 57. To Thomas J. Nolan, for services as page in the house of assembly, session of one thousand eight hundred and ninty-three, two hundred dollars, $200 00

Item No. 58. To Michael Nathan, for postage and expressage and extra services as sergeant-at-arms of the senate, one hundred and seventy-one dollars and twenty-seven cents, $171 27

Item No. 59. To Fred. Kissam, for extra services and postage in the post office department, house of assembly, one hundred and fifty dollars, $150 00

Item No. 60. To John F. Martin, for services as page in the house of assembly, session of one thousand eight hundred and ninety-three, two hundred dollars, $200 00

Item No. 61. To Herman Emmons, for services as clerk to the committee on boroughs and borough commissions in the senate, three hundred dollars, $300 00

Item No. 62. To Charles D. Morgan, for services as page in the house of assembly, session of one thousand eight hundred and ninety-three, two hundred dollars, $200 00

Item No. 63. To Benjamin Godshalk, for services as page in the house of assembly, session of one thousand eight hundred and ninety-three, two hundred dollars, $200 00

Item No. 64. To James Vaughn, for services as page in the house of assembly, session of one thousand eight hundred and ninety-three, two hundred dollars, $200 00

Item No. 65. To Thomas O'Connor, for extra services as page in the clerk's department of the house of assembly, fifty dollars, $50 00

Item No. 66. To the New Jersey Deutche Zeitung Company, for printing three thousand copies of Governor Abbett's annual message and three thousand copies of Governor Werts' inaugural address, four hundred and thirty-seven dollars and ninety-two cents, $437 92

Item No. 67. To the "Freie Presse," for printing three thousand copies of Governor Abbett's annual message and three thousand copies of Governor Werts' inaugural address, four hundred and thirty-seven dollars and ninety-two cents, $437 92

Item No. 68. To Convery & Walker, for combs, brushes and brooms furnished the sergeant-at-arms of the house of assembly, seventy-nine dollars and seventy-five cents, $79 75

Item No. 69. To B. F. Methven, for furnishing "Keystone" bill files to the house of assembly, session of one thousand eight hundred and eigty-seven, two hundred and sixty-nine dollars and twenty cents, $269 20

Item No. 70. To B. F. Methven, for furnishing "Keystone" bill files to the house of assembly, session of one thousand eight hundred and eighty-eight, seventy-three dollars and seventy cents, $73 70

Item No. 71. To Furman Norcross, for services rendered to the engrossing clerk of the house of assembly, one hundred and fifty dollars, $150 00

Item No. 72. To John K. Cody, for extra services rendered to the engrossing clerk of the senate, one hundred and fifty dollars, $150 00

Item No. 73. To Samuel C. Thompson, secretary of the senate, for expressage paid on supplies for the senate, twenty-four dollars and forty cents, $24 40

Item No. 74. To Andrew J. Bale, for extra services as bill clerk to the house of assembly, two hundred dollars, $200 00

Item No. 75. To Lorenzo Mason, for extra services in carrying and attending to mail matter in the senate, fifty dollars, $50 00

Item No. 76. To Leonard Kalisch, clerk of the house of assembly, for money expended for postage and expressage, eight dollars, $8 00

Item No. 77. To John H. DeMott, for extra services as clerk to the committee on bill revision of the house of assembly, two hundred dollars, $200 00

Item No. 78. To Jeremiah O'Connell, for services as page in the senate, session of one thousand eight hundred and ninety-three, two hundred dollars, $200 00

Item No. 79. To Michael Hall, for services as page in the house of assembly, session of one thousand eight hundred and ninety-three, two hundred dollars, $200 00

Item No. 80. To Charles Hoffman, for services in attending to the ventilation of the senate chamber, three hundred and fifty dollars, $350 00

Item No. 81. To James Dugan, for services in attending to the ventilation of the house of assembly, three hundred and fifty dollars, $350 00

Item No. 82. To George Barlow, for services as doorkeeper of the house of assembly, three hundred and fifty dollars, $350 00

Item No. 83. To P. H. Murphy, for services as assistant to assistant clerk of the house of assembly, two hundred dollars, $200 00

Item No. 84. To Joseph O'Mara, for services as page in the house of assembly, session of one thousand eight hundred and ninety-two, fifty dollars, $50 00

Item No. 85. To James P. Larkins, for evtra services as calendar clerk in the house of assembly, fifty dollars, $50 00

Item No. 86. To Philip Muldoon, for extra services to the sergeant-at-arms of the house of assembly, fifty dollars, $50 00

Item No. 87. To John J. Hickey, for extra services to the clerk of the house of assembly, one hundred and fifty dollars, $150 00

Item No. 88. To Daniel McCarthy, for extra services to the journal clerk of the house of assembly, one hundred and fifty dollars, $150 00

Item No. 89. To Edward Sitgreaves, for extra services rendered the secretary of the senate, one hundred dollars, $100 00

Item No. 90. To William Atkinson, Jr., for extra services as assistant engrossing clerk of the senate, one hundred and fifty dollars, $150 00

Item No. 91. To "The Sunday Standard," for publishing the session laws, session of one thousand eight hundred and ninety-two, seven hundred and thirty-six dollars and eighty cents, $736 80

Item No. 92. To Warren Richards, for extra services as clerk to the committe on municipal corporations of the senate, one hundred dollars, $100 00

Item No. 93. To John Glenn, for extra services rendered as page of the senate, one hundred and fifty dollars, $150 00

Item No. 94. To Annie Gough, for services as typewriter to the secretary of the senate and the committee on railroads and canals, thirty-seven dollars and fifty cents, $37 50

Item No. 95. To Edward Taylor, for extra services to committee on revision of the laws, one hundred and fifty dollars, $150 00

Item No. 96. To George Haley, for services as page in the house of assembly, session of one thousand eight hundred and ninety-two, fifty dollars, $50 00

Item No. 97. To William Porter, for services as page in the house of assembly, session of one thousand eight hundred and ninety-one, ten dollars, $10 00

Item No. 98. To James Lillis, for services as page in the house of assembly, session of one thousand eight hundred and ninety-three, two hundred dollars, $200 00

Item No. 99. To William Kuntz, for services as page in the house of assembly, session of one thousand eight hundred and ninety-three, two hundred dollars, $200 00

Item No. 100. To Lewis Schriver, for services as page in the house of assembly, session of one thousand eight hundred and ninety-three, two hundred dollars, $200 00

Item No. 101. To George Gartner, for services as page in the house of assembly, session of one thousand eight hundred and ninety-three, two hundred dollars, $200 00

Item No. 102. To Charles Hayhurst, for services as page in the house of assembly, session of one thousand eight hundred and ninety-three, two hundred dollars, $200 00

Item No. 103. To William Murphy, for services as page in the house of assembly, session of one thousand eight hundred and ninety-three, two hundred dollars, $200 00

Item No. 104. To George B. McHall, page in the house of assembly, for car fare expended in coming to and from the capital, twenty dollars, $20 00

Item No. 105. To Bernard Kane, page in the house of assembly, for car fare expended in coming to and from the capital, twenty dollars, $20 00

Item No. 106. To Daniel J. Tierney, for hand bag and scales furnished the postmaster of the house of assembly, twenty-two dollars, $22 00

Item No. 107. To W. C. Hamilton, for expenses as witness and money expended for expressage on ballot boxes in contested election case of Stuhr vs. McDonald, one hundred dollars, $100 00

Item No. 108. To George Berger, for extra services rendered the sergeant-at-arms of the senate, one hundred and fifty dollars, $150 00

Item No. 109. To John Haggerty, for services as sergeant-at-arms and for serving notices for special senate committee appointed to investigate matters pertaining to the national guard of New Jersey, one hundred dollars, $100 00

Item No. 110. To Cornelius L. Honeyman, for extra services attending the lavatory of the house of assembly, one hundred dollars, $100 00

Item No. 111. To Alexander C. Young, for services as clerk to the committee on agriculture and agricultural college, also to special committee to investigate matters pertaining to the national guard of New Jersey, three hundred dollars, $300 00

Item No. 112. To John H Mattison, for extra services as assistant journal clerk of the senate, three hundred dollars, $300 00

Item No. 113. To M. J. Griffin, for glassware, cuspidors, soap, brushes and supplies furnished the sergeant-at-arms of the house of assembly, three hundred and ninety-four dollars and fifty-one cents, $394 51

Item No. 114. To William K. Devereux, for services as clerk to the committee on incidental expenses, one hundred dollars, $100 00

Item No. 115. To John L. Jacques, for extra services rendered as assistant to the private secretary of the president of the senate, two hundred and fifty dollars, $250 00

Item No. 116. To Albert Datz, for stationery furnished the secretary of the senate, one hundred and ninety-one dollars and fifteen cents, $191 15

Item No. 117. To Henry J. Earle, to postage furnished and extra services as bill clerk of the senate, two hundred dollars, $200 00

Item No. 118. To Daniel J. Tierney, for extra services as sergeant-at-arms of the house of assembly, two hundred dollars, $200 00

Item No. 119. To William S. Howell, for services rendered as acting engrossing clerk of the senate, three hundred and fifty dollars, $350 00

2. *And be enacted*, That this act shall take effect immediately.

Approved with the exception of items number 55, 59, 60, 62, 65, 69, 70, 74, 80, 84, 85, 86, 87, 88, 89, 92, 95, 96, 97, 98, 99, 103, 104, 105, 107, 108, 109, 110, 118.

April 11th, 1893.

Joint Resolutions.

JOINT RESOLUTIONS.

NUMBER I.

Joint Resolution relative to the arbitration of the claims of Robert S. Johnson against the state of New Jersey.

WHEREAS, a controvery exists as to the amount legally and equitably due from the state of New Jersey to Robert S. Johnson, of the city of Trenton, for work done and materials furnished under the terms of a contract made on the twenty-sixth day of July, one thousand eight hundred and eighty-six, between the commission constituted under and by virtue of an act of the legislature of this state, entitled "An act for the restoration of the state house," approved April seventh, one thousand eight hundred and eighty-five, and the supplements thereto, and the said Robert S. Johnson, and for extra work done and materials furnished in the erection and completion of the addition to the state capitol building, which extra work and extra materials were rendered necessary by alterations in the original plans for the erection and completion of said building; Preamble.

1. BE IT RESOLVED *by the Senate and General Assembly of the State of New Jersey*, That all matters in difference between the state of New Jersey and Robert S. Johnson shall be and the same are hereby submitted to the arbitration of three arbitrators, one of whom shall be chosen by the governor, one by the said Robert S. Johnson, and the third by the two so chosen; such arbitrators shall be duly sworn by a justice of the supreme court to thoroughly examine all matters in difference between the state of New Jersey and the said Robert S. Johnson, and to report what amount, if anything, is legally and equita-

How and by whom arbitrators chosen.

By whom sworn.

bly due to the said Robert S. Johnson for all work done and all materials furnished by him in the erection and completion of the addition to the state capitol building; the said arbitrators shall be chosen within sixty days after the passage of this resolution; they shall have power to swear and examine witnesses, and the necessary expenses of such arbitration shall be allowed by the comptroller, on the approval of the governor; the award of said arbitrators shall be in writing, and shall be submitted to the governor for his approval; if he disagrees with the conclusions reached by a majority of said arbitrators, he shall return their award for correction; when a majority of said arbitrators shall reach a conclusion which shall be approved of by the governor, he shall endorse his approval thereon, and the award so approved shall be final, conclusive and binding upon the state and upon the said Robert S. Johnson; any money found to be due the said Robert S. Johnson by the award approved as aforesaid shall be paid to him from any state moneys not otherwise appropriated.

Powers of arbitrators.

Award subject to approval of governor.

Award approved shall be final.

2. *And be it resolved*, That this resolution shall take effect immediately.

Approved March 28, 1893.

NUMBER II.

Joint Resolution to enable the state of New Jersey to take part in the ceremonies attending the unveiling, at Trenton New Jersey, of the monument to commemorate the battle of Trenton.

Preamble.

WHEREAS, a battle monument to commemorate the battle fought during the revolutionary war, in Trenton, on the twenty-sixth day of December, one thousand seven hundred and seventy-six, is now being erected, and it is expected that it will be fully completed during the present year; *and whereas*, it is eminently proper that a public work commemorative of so momentous an event in the struggle for independence, a work encouraged by both state and national legislation and standing on property deeded to this state, should be unveiled with such appriate ceremonies as its great national importance demands; therefore,

1. BE IT RESOLVED *by the Senate and General Assembly of the State of New Jersey*, That his excellency the governor, the state officers, members of the senate and house of assembly and such other officials of the state as seem proper, shall be invited to take part in the ceremonies attending the unveiling of said battle monument.

Who shall be invited to attend unveiling of battle monument

2. *And be it resolved*, That an appropriation of five thousand dollars is hereby made to meet the necessary and proper expenses of carrying out the provisions and intent of this resolution and that the comptroller is hereby authorized to draw his warrant for the same and the treasurer to pay the same to the treasurer of the Trenton battle monument association.

Appropriation of $5,000.

Warrant to be drawn on treasurer.

3. *And be it resolved*, That this joint resolution shall take effect immediately.

Approved April 4, 1893.

Proclamations.

PROCLAMATIONS.

PROCLAMATION BY THE GOVERNOR.

Whereas, by a joint resolution, approved June 29th, 1892, it was resolved by the Senate and House of Representatives of the United States of America, in Congress assembled:

"That the President of the United States be authorized and directed to issue a proclamation recommending to the people the observance in all their localities of the 400th anniversary of the discovery of America on October 21st, 1892, by public demonstration and by suitable exercises in their schools and other places of assembly;"

And Whereas, the President of the United States, in pursuance of said authority, did on the 21st of July, 1892, issue his proclamation;

And whereas, the Executive Committee of the National Columbian Public School Celebration has urged the issuing of proclamations by the Governors of the several States, recommending the people to observe said day for the purposes set forth in said joint resolution of Congress;

Now therefore, I, LEON ABBETT, governor of the state of New Jersey, in order to carry out the purposes of said resolution, do hereby recommend that October 21st, 1892, be observed by the people of this state as a general holiday, and day of thanksgiving; that our citizens cease from toil and devote themselves on that day as far as possible to such exercises in their schools and other places of assembly as will properly celebrate the day and carry out the purposes of said resolution.

[L. S.] In witness whereof I have hereunto set my hand and caused the great seal of the state to be hereunto affixed, at Trenton, this twentieth day day of August, eighteen hundred and ninety-two.

LEON ABBETT.

By the Governor,
HENRY C. KELSEY,
Secretary of State.

PROCLAMATION BY THE GOVERNOR.

STATE OF NEW JERSEY, EXECUTIVE DEPARTMENT.

Whereas, Thomas S. R. Brown, who, at a general election held on the first Tuesday after the first Monday in November, in the year eighteen hundred and ninety, was duly declared to have been elected a member of the senate of this state from the county of Monmouth, and subsequently thereto duly qualified as such senator, died on the fourth day of June, in the year one thousand eight hundred and ninety-two, whereby a vacancy has occurred in the representation of said county of Monmouth, in said state senate;

Therefore, I, LEON ABBETT, governor of the state of New Jersey, by the requirement of law, do hereby issue this my proclamation, commanding and requiring that an election be held according to law in said county of Monmouth on Tuesday, the eighth day of November next ensuing the date hereof, for the purpose of electing a member of the senate of this state to fill the said vacancy occasioned by the death of said Thomas S. R. Brown.

[L. S.] Given under my hand and the great seal of the state of New Jersey, at Trenton, the fourth day of October, in the year of our Lord one thousand eight hundred and ninety-two, and of the Independence of the United States the one hundred and seventeenth.

LEON ABBETT.

By the Governor,
HENRY C. KELSEY,
Secretary of State.

PROCLAMATION BY THE GOVERNOR.

State of New Jersey,
Executive Department,
Trenton, Nov. 15th, 1892.

In accordance with the law and established custom in this State, the Executive each year sets apart a day of Thanksgiving and prayer, on which the people may rest from their labor and assemble in their homes and places of worship, to acknowledge and return thanks to Almighty God for his goodness and mercy, and pray that he will continue to bless them with abundance and prosperity;

Therefore, I, Leon Abbett, Governor of the State of New Jersey, do hereby designate Thursday, the twenty-fourth day of November, instant, as a day of public thanksgiving and prayer, and recommend that the people of this State on that day abstain from all secular avocation, assemble in their usual places of worship, and give thanks to God for his infinite goodness in the past, and invoke for the future his blessings upon the nation, the state and the homes of our people.

[L. S.] Given under my hand and privy seal, at the Executive Chamber, in the city of Trenton, on this fifteenth day of November, in the year of our Lord, one thousand eight hundred and ninety-two.

LEON ABBETT,
Governor.

Attest:
Leon Abbett, Jr.,
Private Secretary.

JOINT RESOLUTIONS.

NUMBER I.

Joint Resolution relative to the arbitration of the claims of Robert S. Johnson against the state of New Jersey.

WHEREAS, a controvery exists as to the amount legally and equitably due from the state of New Jersey to Robert S. Johnson, of the city of Trenton, for work done and materials furnished under the terms of a contract made on the twenty-sixth day of July, one thousand eight hundred and eighty-six, between the commission constituted under and by virtue of an act of the legislature of this state, entitled "An act for the restoration of the state house," approved April seventh, one thousand eight hundred and eighty-five, and the supplements thereto, and the said Robert S. Johnson, and for extra work done and materials furnished in the erection and completion of the addition to the state capitol building, which extra work and extra materials were rendered necessary by alterations in the original plans for the erection and completion of said building; Preamble.

1. BE IT RESOLVED *by the Senate and General Assembly of the S'ate of New Jersey,* That all matters in difference between the state of New Jersey and Robert S. Johnson shall be and the same are hereby submitted to the arbitration of three arbitrators, one of whom shall be chosen by the governor, one by the said Robert S. Johnson, and the third by the two so chosen; such arbitrators shall be duly sworn by a justice of the supreme court to thoroughly examine all matters in difference between the state of New Jersey and the said Robert S. Johnson, and to report what amount, if anything, is legally and equita- How and by whom arbitrators chosen. By whom sworn.

Auburn Mineral Water Company,
Automatic Car Brake Starter and Propeller Company of Camden, N. J.,
Automatic Cigar Machine Company,
Automatic Spring Motor Car and Carriage Company,
A. W. Cox Cutlery Manufacturing Company,
Ball Anti-Induction Electric Wire Company,
Banning Brake Shoe Company,
Barnegat City Beach Association,
Barnegat Inlet Hotel Company,
Barnegat Land Improvement Company,
Barnegat Yacht and Steamboat Company,
Barnes Lumber Company,
Barred End Buttonhole Attachment Company,
Batopilas Central Mining Company,
Bayonne City Stage Line,
Berkeley Land and Improvement Company,
Binder Milling, Mixing and Manufacturing Company,
Blackburn Straw Braid Sewing Machine Company,
Black Rock and Pacific Company,
Blevney Manufacturing Company,
Block Pavement Company,
Boston Mining and Reduction,
Bower Slate and Pencil Quarry Company,
Bradley Western Fuel and Gas Company,
Bragdon Manufacturing Company,
Bridgeport Steamboat Company,
Bridgeton Steamboat Company,
Bridgeton Transportation Company,
Brighton Hotel Company,
British American Ranch Agency Company,
Brooks-Snider Consolidated Gold and Silver Mining Company,
Brown's Seamless Metal Company,
Brundage Nail Machine Company,
Bull Pen Mica Mining Company,
Bunker Hill Gold Mining Company,
Burnett Mining and Milling Company,
Cabinet and Review Publishing Company,
Cahaba Coal and Coke Company,
Camden Coal and Improvement Company,
Camden Manure Baling Company,
Camden Opera House Company,

Cape May City Land Company,
Cape May Driving Park Company,
Cape May Ocean Pier Company,
Cape May and New Jersey Improvement Company,
Carbonic Acid and Fire Proofing Company of New Jersey,
Car and Building, Heating and Ventilating Company,
Carlton's English Blended Tea Company,
Carroll Copper Company,
Carrousel and Toboggan Company,
Cary Kaolin Company,
Casa Grande Land Improvement Company,
Cassedy Coupling Company,
Champion Light Company,
Champion Shoe Burnishing Machine Company,
Charles F. Currie Company,
Chatauqua Gold Mining Company,
Chattan Manufacturing Company,
Chihuahua Mining Company,
Chinchorro Phosphate Company,
Chiricahua and Chihuahua Mining and Development Company,
Chlorine Soap Company,
Choptank Iron Ore Mining Company,
Chormann Mitchell Manufacturing Company,
Chormann Wood Carving and Novelties Company,
Cincinnati Gold and Silver Mining Company,
Citizens' Coach Company,
Citizens' Electric Company,
Citizens' Gas Improvement Company,
Citizens' Local Telephone Company,
Citizens' Telephone Company,
City Electric Light Company of Philadelphia,
City of Mexico Electric Light and Power Company,
Clayton Rink Company,
Clemons Self-Holding and Hoisting Gear Company,
Clermont Improvement Company,
Clymer Distilling Company,
Coast Defense Association,
Coleman Improved Window Company,
Coleman Manufacturing Company,
Collection Guarantee Company,

Columbia Construction Company,
Columbia Contracting Company,
Colombia and Panama Telephone and Telegraph Company,
Commercial Electric Company,
Como Land Company,
Campania Mexicana de Piedra Artificial del Penon-Mexico,
Conemaugh Chemical Works,
Connecticut and Rhode Island Gas Fuel Company,
Consolidated Telephone Company,
Consumers' Western Meat Company,
Continuous Underground Electric Company of the United States,
Co-operative Brick Manufacturing Company,
Cosmopolitan Electric Light Company,
Cosmopolitan Electric Underground Telegraph, Telephone and Electric Light Company,
Cosmopolitan Manufacturing Company,
Cottrell Fuel Gas Company,
Courtney Parlor Match Company,
Crane Brother's Cracker Company,
Creamery Manufacturing Company,
Crescent Corset and Clasp Company,
Crescent Safety Parlor and Sleeping Car Company,
Crist Engine Works,
Crockford Steam Generator Company,
Crystal Rolling Pin Company,
Cuba Manganese Company,
Cunningham Manufacturing Company,
Curry and Hager Evener Spring Company of New Jersey,
Daft Electric Power Company of Newark, N. J.,
Dakota Railway Construction Company,
Darling Electric Locomotive Company,
Day Sewed Shoe Manufacturing Company,
Dayton Company,
Davenport Consolidated Mining and Smelting Company,
Delanco Hall Association,
DeLaval Cream Separator Company of Canada,
Delaware Bay Treasure Company,
Delaware Coal and Ice Company,

Delaware River Transportation Company,
Diamond Band Saw and Stone Machinery Company,
Diamond Steam Engine Manufacturing Company,
Domestic Chemical Company,
Dominion Steamboat and Excursion Company,
Dosoris Mining Company,
Dowling International Telephone Company,
D. Rodgers & Company,
Duluth and Winnepeg Construction Company,
Eagle Printing and Publishing Company of New Jersey,
Eastern Development Company,
Eastern Dispatch Transportation Company of New York City,
East Newark Land Company,
Echo Telephone Company of New Jersey,
Eclipse Sash Balance Company,
Economic Cork and Stopper Company,
Economy Kindling Wood Stove Company,
Egyptian Crystal Casket Company,
Electrical Energy Company,
Electric Gas Light Company,
Electric Renovating Company of New Jersey,
Electron Manufacturing Company,
Elevating Clothes Drier Company,
Elmore Hand Rock Drill Company.
El Monte Gold Mining Company,
Enterprise Bronze Company,
Erie Construction Company,
Erie and Brooklyn Annex Company,
Eureka Electric Company,
Eureka Golden Alloy Company,
Eureka Golden Alloy Watch Case Company,
Eureka Lawn Mower Manufacturing Company,
Excelsior Athletic Association,
Excelsior Box Nailing Machine Company,
Fairbanks Telephone Company,
Five Mile Beach Improvement Company,
Flores Consolidated Gold Mining Company,
Florida Land and Improvement Company,
Florida Mutual Sugar Cane Grove and Mill Company,
Flying Target Company,
Forked River Cranberry Company of New Jersey,
Fort Lee Elevator Company,

Fountain Brush Manufacturing Company,
Franc Cattle Company,
Francklyn Land and Cattle Company,
Franklin Manufacturing Company,
Franklin Telephone Company,
Freese Electric Lighting and Steam Heating Company,
Fresh Butter Baking Powder Company,
Fuel Economy Company,
Garfield Land Improvement Company of Atlantic County, N. J.,
Gas Apparatus Manufacturing Company,
Gelatine Plate Engraving and Printing Company,
George F. Leland Refining Company,
George W. Stead Manufacturing Company,
Germania Bottle and Stopper Company,
Germania Publishing Company,
Getz Gossamer Company,
Girard Shipping Company,
Glen Ridge Mining Company,
Globe Flight Company,
Globe Manufacturing Company,
Globe Telephone Company,
Godwinville and Paterson Macadamized Road Company,
Gogebic Construction and Improvement Company,
Golconda Gold and Silver Mining Company,
Gorton Cocoa Mat Company,
Great Basin Mining and Smelting Company,
Guarantee Slate Company,
Gunsight Mining Company,
Haledon Silk Dyeing Company,
Hand Power Test Machine Company,
Hardwick Manufacturing Company,
Hardy Moore Manufacturing Company,
Harvey Manufacturing Company,
Hathaway Combination Lock Company,
Haven Shorthand and Typewriting Instruction Company,
Hayes Safety Shell Company,
Hemsley and Company,
Hercules Metal Company,
H. F. Richter Publishing Company,
Hindoo Salamander Paint Manufacturing Company,
Hien Gravity-Lock Car-Coupler Company,

Hill National Spark Arrester Company,
Historical Publishing Company,
H. McCully and Company,
Holly Beach City Turnpike Company,
Home Journal Publishing Company,
Hopkins Mower Company,
Horn Silver Mining and Milling Company,
Horton Type Writer Company,
Household Fire Extinguisher Company,
Hudson County Turf Association,
Hydro Carbon Gas Company of Pennsylvania,
Hydroleine Manufacturing Company,
Hygienic Society of Camden, N. J.,
Independent Telephone Company,
Illinois Hand Power Test Company,
Improved Hollow Ware Company,
Improved Pipe Joint Company,
International Automatic Car Coupler Company,
International Construction Company,
International Dolbear Electric Company,
International Land Company,
Inter-State Construction Company,
Iowa Improvement Company,
Iron Mountain Mining Company,
Island Beach Company,
Jasper Mining and Smelting Company,
Jersey City Base Ball Association,
Jersey City Exhibition Company,
Johnson Fire and Burglar Proof Safe Manufacturing Company,
Journal of Fabrics Company,
J. R. Bailey Edge Tool Company,
Kaler Food Specialties Company,
Kansas Construction and Improvement Company,
Kansas and Colorado Land and Improvement Company,
Kearny Watchman Printing and Publishing Company,
Keystone Electric Company,
Keystone Fire Escape Company,
Keystone Improved Gas Machine Manufacturing Company,
Keystone Rubber Company,
Keystone Spice Supply Company,

King Wheel Company,
Kitson Electric Company,
Knickerbocker Carpet Renovating and Storeage Company,
LaBar Iron Mining Company,
LaBar Mineral Paint Company,
Land and Construction Company of Guatemala,
Land and Construction Company of Mexico,
"LaReine" Mining Company,
Laurel Hill Slate Company,
Lawrence Mineral and Timber Company,
Lebanon Valley Smelting Company,
Ledger Association,
Lembeck and Hergraves Brewing Company,
Lenawee Mining Company,
Linolphene Soap Stock Oil Company,
Liquid Engine Company,
Little Wood River Mining and Smelting Company,
Lloyd Slate Company,
Locomotive Speed Gauge and Mileage Indicator Company,
Long Branch Ocean Supply Company,
Long Branch and Seabright Steamboat Company,
Lord Acoustic Telephone Company of New Jersey,
Lykens Valley Coal and Lumber Company,
Manhattan Liquid Fuel Company,
Manhattan Rubber Company,
Manufacturers' Agency Company,
Manufacturers and Farmers Homestead Company,
Marine Auxiliary Side Light Company,
Marshall Seamless Shoe Crimping Company,
Marter Safety Car Door Company,
Mason Metcalfe Primary Electric Company,
Mason Metcalfe Primary Electric Company, Metropolitan District,
Massachusetts State Gas Fuel Company,
Matlack and Harvey Printing Company,
Maxwilton Park and Land Improvement Company,
McGeary Patent Cornice Company,
Mekee Lead Mining and Milling Company,
McKean Car Coupler Company,
Medicated Tablet and Lozenge Company,

Merchants Telegraph Construction Company,
Merchants World Company,
Metallic Decorating Company,
Metallic Match Company,
Metropolitan Construction Company,
Metropolitan Underground Telegraphic, Telephonic and Electric Light Cable Company,
Metropolitan Ventilating Company,
Meucci Telephone company,
Mexican Pacific Telephone Company,
Mexican Pulque Company,
Mexican and United States Development and Operating Company,
Middle Valley Kaolin Company,
Milk Producers' Association of Sussex County, N. J.,
Mills Buttonhole Attachment Company,
Mineral Land Improvement Company,
Missouri Land and Guarantee Imvestment Company,
Mitstand Metal Company,
M. J. Yard Paper Ware Company,
Mohave Mining and Milling Company,
Monarch Parlor Sleeping Car Company,
Monserrat Gold and Silver Mining Company,
Moore Manufacturing Company,
Morestown and Mount Laurel Turnpike Company,
Morrell Manufacturing Company,
Morse Underground Conduit Company,
Mountainville Iron Company,
Moyer Metal Manufacturing Company,
Municipal Construction Company,
Mutual Construction Company,
Mutual Dry Dock and Wrecking Company,
Mutual Marble Company,
Mutual Novelty Manufacturing Company.
Nash County (N. C.) Gold Mining Company,
National Anti-Sewer Gas Company,
National Automatic Car Coupler Company,
National Car Starter Manufacturing Company,
National Chair Seat Company,
National Consumers' Meat Company,
National Electric Mail Box Manufacturing Company,
National Fertilizer Company,

National Hotel Company of New Jersey,
National Medical and Chemical Institute of the U. S. A.,
National Mica Mining and Manufacturing Company,
National Opera House Company,
National Optical Company,
National Railway Patent Waste Company,
National Street Sweeping Machinery Company,
Negotiating, Collection and Publishing Company of New York,
Neptune Land Company,
Neversink Lighterage Company,
Newark Beer Cooling and Preserving Company,
Newark Daily Journal,
Newark Land Company,
Newark Molecular Telephone and Telegraph Company,
Newark Skating Rink Company,
Newark Tap Valve Company.
Newark Vent Bung Company,
Newcomb Rapid Transportation Company,
New Jersey Building and Loan Improvement Company,
New Jersey Coal Saving Company,
New Jersey Coast Publishing Company,
New Jersey Construction Company,
New Jersey Cycling and Athletic Association,
New Jersey District Messenger and Telegraph Alarm Company,
New Jersey Exhibition Company,
New Jersey Freie Presse Company,
New Jersey Gas Light and Fuel Company,
New Jersey Gas Saving Company,
New Jersey Homestead Company,
New Jersey Land and Dock Company,
New Jersey Litgherage Company,
New Jersey Rink Company,
New Jersey Steamboat Transportation Company,
New Jersey Telephone Company,
New Jersey Tube Transportation Company,
New Jersey and Sonora Reduction Company,
New York Arms Company,
New York Exhaust Ventilator Company,
New York, Florida and Havana Construction Company,
New York Petracrete Company,

New York, Pittsburg and Chicago Construction Company,
New York Standard Hydro-Carbon Company,
New York and Boston Short Line Railway Construction Company,
New York and Gogebic investment Company,
New York and New Jersey Terminal Dock and Warehouse Company,
New York and Pennsylvania Construction Company,
New York and Western Lumber and Manufacturing Company,
New Ultra Marine Blueing Company,
Norfolk Blanket Company,
North American Construction Company,
North American Construction Company of Puerto Cabello,
North Jersey Printing Company,
North Jersey Water Company,
North State Construction Company,
North Western Hand Power Test Company,
North and South American Steam Navigation Company,
Novelty Cane Company,
Novelty Glass Manufacturing Company of Philadelphia,
Noyes Steam Damper Regulator Company,
Occidental Improvement Company,
Omega Copper Mining Company,
Orange County Stock Farm Company,
Orange Mountain Land Company,
Orange Riding Club,
Orne Car Axle Company,
Osborne Company,
Pacific Placer Mining Company,
Package Express Company,
Palisade Hotel Company,
Panunco Gold and Silver Mining and Smelting Company, of the state of Coahuila, Mexico,
Paradise Valley Land and Improvement Company,
Park Rink Company of Jersey City,
Passaic Bleaching Company,
Passaic Co- operative Society,
Passaic County Iron Ore Company,
Passaic Manufacturing Company,

Passaic Printing and Publishing Company,
Passenger Railroad Locomotive Manufacturing Company,
Patent Motive Power Company,
Paterson Burglar Alarm and Messenger Telegraph Company,
Paterson Co-operative Commercial Association,
Paterson Industrial Co-operative Association,
Paterson Temperance Hall Association,
Paterson and New York Plank Road Company,
Pato Placer Gold Mining Company,
Pavonia Roller Skating Rink of Jersey City,
Paynter Garbage Fertilizer Company,
Pennock Underground Conduit and Surface Telegraph Company of New Jersey,
Penn Fibre Plaster and Moulding Company,
Penn Lead and Zinc Company,
Penn Overland Telephone and Telegraph Company,
Penn Pulverized Coal Company,
Pennsylvania Coal Saving Company,
Pennsylvania Evener Spring Company,
Pennsylvania Kaolin and Iron Mining Company,
Pennsylvania Mining and Milling Company,
Pennsylvania Rock Drill Company,
Pennsylvania and New England Construction Company,
People's Gas Improvement Company,
People's Market Company,
People's Telephone Company,
Pepuannock Iron Company,
Pequest Manufacturing Company,
Philadelphia City Electric Light Company,
Philadelphia Creamery Company,
Philadelphia Fertilizer Company,
Philadelphia Fruit Company,
Philadelphia Nail Driver and Lathing Company,
Philadelphia Sectional Electric Underground Company,
Philadelphia Time Telegraph Company,
Philadelphia and New Mexico Land and Cattle Company,
Philips Electric Cable Manufacturing Company,
Phœnix Electrical Company,
Phœnix Roof Coating Company,
Pine Creek Mining Company,

Pima Silver Company of Arizona,
Pino Palmine Company,
Pioneer Manufacturing Company,
Plainfield District Telegraph and Fire Alarm Company,
Plainfield Improvement Company,
Pneumatic and Electric Underground Conduit Company,
Poetsch Sooysmith Freezing Company,
Police Electric Assistance Company,
Polochic Valley Land and Construction Company of Guatemala,
Potter and Company,
Press Publishing Company,
Pure Brewers' Yeast Company,
Rae Electric Amalgamating Company,
Rae Electric Metallurgy Company,
Raleigh Transparent Ice Company,
Randolph Mining Company,
Rapid Transit Construction Company,
Real Estate Record and Manual Company,
Red Chief Gold Mining Company,
Regenerative Gas Lamp Company,
Regenerative Gas Light Company,
Renault Land Company,
Rennselaer Manufacturing Company,
Relief Gold Mining Company,
Reporter and Tribune Printing Company,
Requa Burner Company,
Rhode Island Lord Acoustic Telephone Company,
Richman Fire Escape Company,
Riley Railway Construction Company,
Rio Grande Copper Company,
Rockland Silk Company,
Royal Silver Mining Company,
Rowan Gold Mining and Milling Company,
Russell Consolidated Copper Company,
Sabastian Loan and Development Company,
Sachem Printing and Publishing Company,
Saergerville Slate Quarrying and Manufacturing Company,
Safety Automatic Car Heating Manufacturing Company,
Safety Barb Wire Fence Guard Company,

Salem Lecture Hall Company,
San Andreas Copper Mountain Mining Company,
San Carlos Mining and Smelting Company,
Saxonia Mining and Reduction Company,
Sea Isle City Lot and Building Association, No. 1,
Sea Shore Construction Company,
Sea Shore Improvement Company.
Security Construction and Trust Company,
Security Contract Company,
Selvage Sewing Machine Company,
Shongum Company,
Shriver Bartlett Company,
Sierra Construction Company,
Solar Gas Light and Heating Company,
Solenoid Cable and Electric Construction Company,
Somers Point and Ocean City Steamboat Company,
Southern Gold Mining and Manufacturing Company,
Southern States Lumber and Navigation Company,
South Jersey Electric Light Company,
Sparrow Kneader and Mixer Company,
Sparta Iron and Zinc Company,
S. R. Kennedy Manufacturing Company,
Standard Construction Company,
Standard Fuel Manufacturing Company,
Standard Gas Saving Company,
Standard Machine Company,
Standard Printing and Publishing Company,
Standard Railroad Construction and Equipment Company
Standard Soap and Chemical Company,
Standard Syphon Gas Machine Company,
Star Pipe Company,
Starr Electric Storage Company,
Steel Clad Cooperage Company,
Steel Wire Belt and Hose Company,
Stewart Medicine Company,
Sudsena Manufacturing Company,
Summit Sanitary Company,
Surgical Dilating Syringe Company,
Taylor Color Printing Press Company,
Taymans Disinfection and Fumigating Company,
Temiscouata Railway Contracting Company,

Texas Land and Cattle Company,
Thayer's Safety Wedge Elevator Company,
Thermostatic Steam Heating Company,
Thomas Tunis Manufacturing Company,
Tobacco Age Publishing Company,
Tortilita Gold and Silver Mining Company,
Transparent Ice Company,
Travis Metal Tie Company,
Tropical Fibre Machine and Manufacturing Company,
Twilight Club,
Underground Railway Construction Company,
Union Construction Company,
Union Development Company,
Union Electric Company,
Union Electric Light and Manufacturing Company,
Union Hand Power Test Company,
Union Metallic Fastening Company,
Union Mutual Investment Company,
Union Phosphate, Mining and Land Company,
Union Zinc Company,
Union Manufacturing Company,
United Railway Construction, Equipment and Improvement Company,
United States Automatic Electric Protector Company,
United States Baking Company,
United States Cable Motor Construction Company,
United States Construction and Improvement Company,
United States Fish Oil and Fertilizer Company,
United States Jensen Electric Bell and Signal Company,
United States Land and Investment Company,
United States of America Arc and Incandescent Electric Light Company,
United States Rail Road Construction Company,
United States Spring Car Motor Construction Company,
United States Trading Company,
United States Transportation Company,
United States, Foreign and Domestic Fruit Company,
Universal Concentrating Company,
Universal Cooking Crock Company,
Universal Insulating Company,
Victor Caloric Engine Company,
Victoria Copper Mining Company,

Vigo Bay Treasure Company,
Villaldama Development Company,
Vineland Gas Company,
Virginia Tide Water Coal Company,
Vulcan Asbetos Company,
Water Repellant Shoe and Leather Company,
Watnong Valley Poultry and Stock Breeding Association,
Weaver Electric Mail Box Manufacturing Company,
West Chester Construction Company,
West End Brick and Tile Company,
West Jersey Gas Company,
West Side Driving Park Association,
West Side Glass Company,
West Side Machine Company (Limited),
West Virginia Construction Company,
Wheatland Manufacturing and Improvement Company,
Wheeler Light Company of New Jersey,
Wide Awake Oil Can and Gas Machine Manufacturing Company,
William Penn Harrow Manufacturing Company,
Wolfe Contracting Company,
Wood-Bailie Ice Machine and Refrigerating Company,
Woolson Disc Car Brake Company,
World Travel Company,
Yellowstone Cattle Company, and the
Yellowstone National Park Improvement Company,
are repealed and declared null and void.

I direct that this proclamation shall be filed in the office of the Secretary of State, and published for one week in the following newspapers, to wit, the *True American*, of Trenton, N. J., and the *State Gazette*, of Trenton, N. J.

[L. S.] In Witness Whereof, I have hereunto set my hand and caused the great seal of the state to be hereunto affixed, at Trenton, this seventh day of January, one thousand eight hundred and ninety-three.

LEON ABBETT.

By the Governor.
HENRY C. KELSEY,
Secretary of State.

PROCLAMATION BY THE GOVERNOR.

WHEREAS, the Comptroller did, on the first day of May, eighteen hundred and ninety-two, under a provisions of an act entitled "An act to amend 'An act concerning corporations,' approved April seventh, one thousand eight hundred and seventy-five," approved March 20th, 1891—report to the Governor a list of all corporations coming within said act;

AND WHEREAS, the following corporations so reported had, on the first day of May, 1892, for two consecutive years, failed, neglected or refused to pay the state the taxes which had been assessed against them for the year 1889, under the laws of New Jersey, and made payable into the state treasury;

AND WHEREAS, under the provisions of said act the charters of said corporations are made void and all powers conferred by law upon such corporations declared inoperative and void unless the Governor gives further time for payment;

AND WHEREAS, the Governor has not given further time to the corporations so reported and herein after named, for the payment of such taxes, and the same are still unpaid.

THEREFORE, I, LEON ABBETT, Governor of the State of New Jersey, in pursuance of the provisions of the said act of the legislature, do hereby issue this proclamation under said act of the legislature that the charters of the following corporations so reported and in default, to wit:

Ætna Mineral Refining Company,
Allentown Slate Company,
American Drying and Seasoning Company,
American Flouring Mill Company,
American Gas Improvement Company,
American Hoop Driving Machine Company,
American Illuminating Company of Bayonne,
American Land and Cattle Company,
American Lighting Company,

American Reduction Company,
Argus Printing Company,
Atlantic City Amusement Company,
Automatic Coal Handling Company,
Automatic French Loom Company,
Automatic Mirror Company,
Automatic Opera Glass Company,
Auxiliary Fire Alarm Company,
Bache Safety Car Heater Company,
Beach Hale Manufacturing Company,
Blue Ridge Corundum Company,
Boluss Air Brake Company,
Bozrah Mineral Spring Company,
British-American Splice Bar Company,
Brooklyn Automatic Alarm Company,
Brooks Gas Process Company,
Brotherhood of the Union Publishing Company,
Brunswick Land Reclamation Company,
Canales Silver Mining and Smelting Company,
Cape Island Gas Company,
Cape May Lot Association,
Cape May Steamboat Company,
Cape Shore Bay Club,
Card and Merchandise Delivery Company,
Celebrities Photographing Company,
Central American Reduction Company,
Ceralvo Mining and Smelting Company of Ceralve Nuevo Leon, Mexico,
Chariton Coal and Mining Company,
Cinderlithic Pavement and Construction Company,
City Railway Contract Company,
City Railway Improvement Company,
Cold Water Kalsomine Company,
Commercial Electric Company,
Commercial Oil Company,
Composite Cell Company,
Continental Wine Company,
Crist Engine Company,
Cuba Marble Company,
Cyclist Printing Company,
Dodd Shutter-Worker Company,
Domestic Water Still Company,

Ella Stopple Company,
Empire State Manufacturing Company,
Empire Ventilator and Smoke Flue Company,
Englewood Dock and Turnpike Company,
Englewood Driving and Fair Ground Association,
Essex Finance and Investment Company,
Essington Buttonhole Finishing Machine Company.
Evans Coal and Iron Mining Company,
Excelsior Dynamite Company,
Fox Electrical Manufacturing Company,
Fraxine Manufacturing Company,
F. R. Rapp Company,
Fuel Gas Burner Company,
Fulton County Cold Mining Company,
Galloway Land and Improvement Company,
Gem Knitting Mills Company,
Georgia Railway Development Company,
Georgia and Florida Improvement Company,
Globe Powder Works,
Gonzales Onyx Company of Mexico,
Grand Central Slate Company,
Guerdon Group Gold Mining Company,
Guyape Mining Company,
Gustavus Storm Glass Company,
Hall Novelty Manufacturing Company,
Hauss Electric Company,
Haworth Land Company,
Hoboken Free Stores Company,
Homœpathic Medical Tablet Company,
Hopatcong Canal Company,
"Hough's,"
Household Machine Manufacturing Company,
Howard Coal Company,
Hudson County Superheated Water Company,
Illuminating and Fuel Gas Company,
International Etcher's Publishing Company,
International Express Company,
James Brick Horse Blind Fold Company,
J. M. Moore and Company,
John S. Worman Company,
Julien Electric Traction Company,
Knapp Real Estate Manual Company,

La Ignatable Mining and Smelting Company of Ceralvo, Nuevo Leon, Mexico.
La Incomparable Mining and Smelting Company of Ceralvo, Nuevo Leon, Mexico.
Lake Rheaumo Phosphate and Mica Mining and Milling Company,
Lake View Home Company,
LaReina Real Mining and Smelting Company of Ceralvo, Nueve Leon, Mexico,
L. E. Tree Company,
Lugo Laboratory Company,
Magneto-Electric Machine Company (Limited),
Manhattan Lumber Company,
Markets Refrigerating Company,
Maryland Improvement Company,
Metal Shaft, Tug and Harness Improvement Company,
Metropolitan Real Estate Company,
Mexican Land and Development Company,
Mexican Land and Improvement Company,
Miller Eyeless Pick Company,
Monserrat Mining Company,
Moorestown Agricultural and Industrial Society,
Morison, Allen & Company,
Mutual Accumulator Company,
Mutual Electric Construction Company,
National Electrical Conduit Company,
National Gas Improvement Company,
National Splice Bar Company,
Newark Oil Company,
Newark Patent Chair Company,
New Jersey Electric Company,
New Jersey Lumber Company,
New Jersey Medicinal Company,
New Jersey State Archer Gas Fuel Company,
New Jersey Superheated Water Company,
New Jersey Trotting Association,
New Jersey Unionist Publishing Company,
New Process Light and Fuel Company,
New York Automaton Company,
New York Cordage Company,
New York Electric and Automatic Exhibiting Machines Company,

New York Flexible Conduit Company,
New York and New England Telephone Company,
Nightingale Floor Company,
North Alaska Mining Company,
Novelty Air Ship Company,
Passaic Falls Paper Company,
Pennsylvania Pneumatic Tool Company,
Railroad Manual Company,
Railway Electric Car-Lighting and Signal Company,
Ramel Conley Iron and Steel Company,
Rey de la Plata Mining and Smelting Company of Ceralvo, Nuevo Leon, Mexico,
Richmond Tunnel and Railroad Construction Company,
Rocky Mountain Construction Company,
Rose Gas Generator Company,
Roseville Rink Company,
Ross Stone Dressing Machine Manufacturing Company,
Scott and Bitting Paper Company,
Sea Haven Improvement Company of New Jersey,
Sea Isle City Gas, Water and Sewerage Company,
Sea Isle City Lot Association,
Shear Mower Company,
Solid Rock Asphalt Company,
Southern Electric Construction Company,
Southern Railroad Construction Company,
Standard Metal Tie and Construction Company,
Standard Pressed and Ornamental Brick Company,
Stanley Electric Company,
Steel Mantel and Metal Manufacturing Company,
St. Louis, New Orleans and Ocean Canal and Transportation Company of New Jersey,
Theodore C. Knauff Company,
Thomas Hall Company,
Townsend Inlet Hotel Company of Seven Mile Beach, N. J.
Trenton Manufacturing Company,
Tropical American Telephone Company,
"Turn-Her" Fire Extinguisher Company,
Union Land Association of Passaic County,
Union Manufacturing and Trust Company,
Union Mercantile Agency,
United States Commercial and Trading Company,

United States Machine Company,
United States and South American Financial and Construction Company,
Upper San Quintin Land and Improvement Company,
Vance Manufacturing Company,
Vaughn Manufacturing Company,
Vermont Manufacturing Company,
Vulcan Manufacturing Company,
Wall Street Electro Pneumatic Tube Company,
Washington Construction Company,
Weequahick Lake Association,
Weil Gas Enriching Company,
Werts Adjustible Stopper and Bottle Manufacturing Company,
Wesler Shutter Worker Company,
West India Telegraph and Telephone Company (Limited),
Westray's Point Land and Improvement Company,
Wheeler Bluestone Company,
Williamson Patents Company,
Yale Manufacturing and Laundering Company
are void, and all powers conferred by law upon such corporations are hereby declared inoperative and void.

I direct that this proclamation shall be filed in the office of the secretary of state and published for one week in the following newspapers: The *True American*, of Trenton, N. J., and the *State Gazette*, of Trenton, N. J.

[L. S.] In witness whereof, I have hereunto set my hand and caused the great seal of the state to be hereunto affixed, at Trenton, this seventh day of January, one thousand eight hundred and ninety-three.

LEON ABBETT.

By the Governor.
HENRY C. KELSEY,
Secretary of State.

PROCLAMATION BY THE GOVERNOR.

Whereas, It has been satisfactorily made to appear that in the list of New Jersey Corporations reported to the Governor of said state on the first day of May, eighteen hundred and ninety two, was inadvertently included the corporation known as the Cape Island Gas Company, as one of such corporations which had for two consecutive years failed, neglected and refused to pay the state taxes which had been assessed against them for the year eighteen hundred and eighty nine under the laws of the said state of New Jersey, and made payable into the State Treasury;

And Whereas, It appears that all taxes due from said Cape Island Gas Company have been paid by the said last named company to the proper officers of the state of New Jersey, and that said company is not liable to the penalties set forth in the proclamation of the Governor of said state bearing date on the seventh day of January, eighteen hundred and ninety three, although said corporation known as the Cape Island Gas Company is included in the list of corporations specified therein;

Now, therefore, I, George T. Werts, Governor of the said state of New Jersey, do hereby issue this my proclamation, revoking so much of the said proclamation of January seventh, eighteen hundred and ninety-three, above referred to, as applies to the said corporation named therein as the Cape Island Gas Company, and said last named company is hereby delared to be restored to all of its corporate rights, powers, privileges and franchises as fully as if said proclamation of January seventh, eighteen hundred and ninety-three, had not been issued and published as aforesaid. And I further direct that this proclamation be filed in the office of the secretary of state of the state of New Jersey.

[SEAL.] In witness whereof, I have hereunto set my hand and caused the great seal of the said state of New Jersey to be hereunto affixed, at the city of Trenton, this twenty fifth day of January, A. D. eighteen hundred and ninety-three.

GEORGE T. WERTS.

By the Governor.
HENRY C. KELSEY,
Secretary of State.

PROCLAMATION BY THE GOVERNOR.

STATE OF NEW JERSEY.

Pursuant to the authority vested in me by a joint resolution of the legislature, relative to the planting of forest trees, approved February twenty-first, one thousand eight hundred and eighty-four, I do hereby set apart Friday, the twenty-eighth day of April, one thousand eight hundred and ninety-three, for the planting of forest trees, and recommend that the day be devoted by the people to that purpose.

[L. S.] In witness whereof, I have hereunto set my hand and caused the great seal of the state to be hereunto affixed, at Trenton, this twenty-eighth day of March, one thousand eight hundred and ninety-three.

GEORGE T. WERTS.

By the Governor.
HENRY C. KELSEY,
Secretary of State.

Special Public Acts.

SPECIAL PUBLIC ACTS

PASSED BY THE

ONE HUNDRED and SEVENTEENTH LEGISLATURE

CHAPTER XV.

An Act to establish a new township in the county of Bergen, to be known as the township of Bergen.

Portion to be established as a new township.

Boundaries.

1. BE IT ENACTED *by the Senate and General Assembly of the State of New Jersey*, That all that portion of the township of Lodi, in the county of Bergen, lying within the following boundaries, to wit, beginning at the intersection of the northerly boundary of the township of Boiling Springs, in the county of Bergen, with the middle of the Passaic river; running thence easterly along the northerly boundary of said township of Boiling Springs to the middle of the Hackensack river; thence, northerly along the middle of the Hackensack river to a point opposite the mouth of a creek emptying into said river, commonly known as the Upper Mudabock creek; thence, westerly in a straight line to a point where the northerly line of the public road leading from Moonachie to Woodridge, commonly known as the Mousetown road, intersects the westerly line of the public road commonly known as the Moonachie road; thence, westerly along the northerly line of the Mousetown road to the westerly line of the Riser ditch; thence, northerly along the westerly line of said ditch to the northerly line of lands now or formerly belonging to the estate of Richard Vreeland; thence, westerly along said line of lands to the Polifly road; thence, still westerly in the same course as

last described, along the northerly line of lands now or formerly belonging to the estate of Benjamin Cox to a line commonly known as the Polifly line; thence, northerly along said line to the southerly line of the public road leading from said Polifly road to the public road commonly known as the River road; thence westerly along the southerly line of said road leading from the Polifly road to the River road; thence, still westerly in line with the last course of the southerly line of said road to the middle of the Saddle river; thence, down stream through the middle of the Saddle river to the middle of the Passaic river; thence, down stream through the middle of said river to the place of beginning, shall be and hereby is set off from the township Lodi, in the county of Bergen, and made a separate township, to be known by the name of the township of Bergen.

Name of the new township.

Made a body politic and corporate.

2. *And be it enacted*, That the inhabitants of the said township of Bergen shall be and are hereby constituted a body politic and corporate in law, and shall be styled and known by the name of "the inhabitants of the township of Bergen, in the county of Bergen," and shall be entitled to all the rights, powers, authority, privileges and advantages, and subject to the same regulations, government and liabilities as the inhabitants of the other townships in said county of Bergen are or may be entitled or subject to by the laws of this state.

When and where first election to be held.

3. *And be it enacted*, That the inhabitants of the township of Bergen, aforesaid, shall hold their first town meeting or township election on the day now fixed by law for holding the annual town meeting or township elections in the several townships in the county of Bergen, and at such suitable room within such township as shall be designated by the township clerk thereof.

Officers of election.

4. *And be it enacted*, That said election and all matters relating thereto shall be regulated and conducted by a board of registry and election, to be appointed by the board of registration of the county of Bergen, in the same manner and to be constituted and qualified as boards of registry and election have been appointed and are now constituted and qualified in the several townships in said county of Bergen, which township board of registry and election shall perform the same duties in

preparing a registry and poll list as are required of boards of registry and election in cases of the creation or establishment of new or additional election districts in a township.

5. *And be it enacted*, That the officers elected at said town meeting or township election shall be elected to their respective offices and hold the same for the terms now provided by law. Term of officers.

6. *And be it enacted*, That the township committees of the townships of Bergen and Lodi, aforesaid, shall meet on the first Tuesday next after the said first town meeting or township election, at Zimmerman's hotel at Carlstadt, in the township of Bergen, in the county aforesaid, at ten o'clock in the forenoon of that day, and then and there proceed, by writing signed by a majority of the members of said committees present, to allot and divide between the said townships all the property, real and personal, moneys on hand, due or to become due, in proportion to the taxable property and ratables as assessed by the assessor of the said township of Lodi within the limits of the respective townships of Bergen and Lodi at the last assessment, and may adjourn said meeting from time to time, as a majority of those present may deem proper; and the inhabitants of the respective townships shall be liable to pay their just proportion of the debts, if any there shall be; and a majority of the persons comprising the township committee of said two townships shall constitute a quorum, and may proceed to make said division, and the decision of a majority of those present shall be final and conclusive; *provided*, that it shall be lawful to adjourn said meeting to such a time and place within either of said townships as a majority of those assembled as aforesaid may think proper. Division and valuation of property

7. *And be it enacted*, That August Kuntz shall be and is hereby appointed and constituted the clerk of said township of Bergen until his successor shall be elected and qualified, and it shall be his duty as such clerk to set up the notices required by law for holding said town meetings or township elections, together with all the several duties of a township clerk. Township clerk hereby appointed. Duties of clerk.

8. *And be it enacted*, That nothing contained in this act shall be so construed as to interfere with or impair the Commissions of justices of the peace and com-

missioners not impaired.

Rights of said township not impaired.

commissions of justices of the peace, or commissioners of deeds, or to impair the rights of the said township of Bergen in and to its just proportion of the surplus revenue of the general government and the interest thereon.

Said township part of second assembly district.

9. *And be it enacted*, That the said township of Bergen shall form a part of the second assembly district of the county of Bergen, as said assembly district is now formed.

10. *And be it enacted*, That this act shall take effect immediately.

Approved February 21, 1893.

CHAPTER CCLXXV.

An Act to annex to the township of Northampton, in the county of Burlington, a part of the present township of Lumberton, in said county.

Description of tract set off and annexed to Northampton township.

1. BE IT ENACTED *by the Senate and General Assembly of the State of New Jersey*, That all that portion of the township of Lumberton, in the county of Burlington, lying and being north and northeast of the following boundaries to wit: beginning at a stone in the south side of the "South Pemberton Road," said stone being a corner to the townships of Lumberton and Eastampton as heretofore, and runs thence (1) north sixty-nine and three-quarters degrees west one hundred and twenty-five chains and sixty links to a stone in the road leading from Mount Holly to Lumberton and a corner between said townsips of Lumberton and Northampton; thence (2) north thirty-nine degrees, west fifty-four chains and fifty links to a point in the middle of the road leading from Mount Holly to Hainesport; thence (3) north eleven degrees west to a point in the Rancocas creek, be and the same is hereby set off from said township of Lumberton, in the said county of Burlington, and

annexed to and made a part of the township of Northampton, in said county.

2. *And be it enacted*, That this act shall take effect immediately.

Approved March 28, 1893.

CHAPTER CCLXXVI.

An Act to set off the township of Randolph, in the county of Burlington, into the township of Washington, in said county.

Randolph township to become part of Washington township

1. Be it enacted *by the Senate and General Assembly of the State of New Jersey*, That from and after the passage of this act the township of Randolph, in the county of Burlington, shall become and be a part of the township of Washington, in said county.

When and where the township committees shall meet.

2. *And be it enacted*, That the township committee of Washington and the township committee of the township of Randolph, as now constituted, shall meet on the fourth Tuesday next after the date upon which this act shall take effect at the home of Augustus E. Koster, in the township of Washington, in the county aforesaid, at ten o'clock in the forenoon of that day, and then and there proceed by writing, signed by a majority of those present, to find and determine the amount of the indebtedness of the township of Randolph, and also the amount of the assets of the said township, and if the said township committee shall find that the indebtedness of the township of Randolph exceeds its assets, then such action shall remain and be a lien against the taxable property in the township of Randolph to be collected by taxation upon said property and not be made in any way a lien against the property in the township of Washington as said township is now constituted.

Proceedings of said committees.

Act repealed.

3. *And be it enacted*, That the act entitled "An act to create from the township of Washington, in the county of Burlington, and state of New Jersey, a new township to be called the township of Randolph," approved March seventeenth, one thousand eight hundred and seventy, be and the same is hereby repealed.

Repealer.

4. *And be it enacted*, That all acts or parts of acts inconsistent with the provisions of this act be and the same are hereby repealed, and that this act shall take effect immediately.

Approved March 28, 1893.

Private Acts.

---

(565)

PRIVATE ACTS

PASSED BY THE

ONE HUNDRED and SEVENTEENTH LEGISLATURE

CHAPTER LVI.

An Act to release the title and interest of the people of the state of New Jersey in and to certain real estate of which William Brown (colored) died seized, in the town of Mount Holly.

WHEREAS, One William Brown (colored), late of the town of Mount Holly, Burlington county, New Jersey, departed this life in the year one thousand eight hundred and fifty, seized of a certain lot of land at Mount Holly, which was conveyed to him by Joseph Estill and wife by deed recorded in the clerk's office at Mount Holly, in book Z four of deeds, page five hundred and sixty-one, without having made any will and leaving no wife, children or other known kindred; and that prior to his death he gave to one Sarah E. Tilghyman (colored) the said lot of land, without making any deed of conveyance for the same to her however, but by passing over to her, with the possession of said lot of land, the original deed which he had received from Joseph Estill, supposing that that made a complete transfer of the title to her; and that the said Sarah E. Tilghyman departed this life on the twenty-seventh day of March, one thousand eight hundred and seventy-three, without having made any will, but leaving her surviving as her heirs-at-law Henry Tilghyman, her son, and Ella Summer, her granddaughter; and that Preamble undisputed possession of the said premises since the death of said William Brown has been had by the said Sarah E. Tilghyman in her lifetime, and since her death by the said Henry Tilghyman and Ella Summer; therefore,

Title of the state of New Jersey released.

1. Be it enacted *by the Senate and General Assembly of the State of New Jersey*, That all the estate, right, title and interest of the people of the state of New Jersey in, to and upon all the above recited lot or tract of land whereof the said William Brown died seized, with the appurtenances thereunto belonging or in any wise appertaining, is hereby released unto and vested in the said Henry Tilghyman and Ella Summer, the heirs-at-law of the said Sarah E. Tilghyman, and their heirs and assigns forever.

2. *And be it enacted*, That this act shall be deemed a public act and take effect immediately.

Approved March 8, 1893.

CHAPTER LXXI.

An Act approving of the union, consolidation and merger of the New York and New Jersey underground railway company and the New York, New Jersey and Eastern railroad company.

Approval of consolidation and merger.

1. Be it enacted *by the Senate and General Assembly of the State of New Jersey*, That the scheme of union, consolidation and merger of the New York and New Jersey underground railway company and the New York, New Jersey and Eastern railroad company, submitted to the legislature of this state for its consideration (a copy of which is attached hereto and made a part hereof), is hereby approved by this act passed for that purpose.

2. *And be it enacted*, That this act shall take effect immediately.

Approved March 8, 1893.

SCHEME OF CONSOLIDATION AND MERGER.

THIS INDENTURE made and entered into this day of in the year one thousand eight hundred and ninety-two, by and between the directors of the New York, New Jersey and Eastern Railroad Company, and the directors of the New York and New Jersey Underground Railway Company. Witnesseth:

WHEREAS, The New York, New Jersey and Eastern Railroad Company is a corporation organized and existing under and pursuant to the laws of the state of New York to build, maintain and operate a line of railroad from some point in the city of Brooklyn, in the county of Kings, and state of New York, at or near the junction of Flatbush and Atlantic avenues in said city, and running from thence by the most convenient and eligible route underground to and under the waters of the East river, to and under the city of New York, in the county New York, and the waters of the Hudson river to some convenient and eligible point in the state of New York at the boundary line between the state of New York and the state of New Jersey under the waters of the Hudson river at some point in said boundary line lying opposite the city of Jersey City, in the state of New Jersey, which two points shall be the terminii with a branch or branches running from the boundary line aforesaid to some convenient and eligible point at or near the Battery in said city and county of New York; the said New York, New Jersey and Eastern Railroad Company has authorized capital stock of one hundred thousand dollars, divided into one thousand shares of the par value of one hundred dollars each, and its line and route has been located, but not yet constructed; and,

WHEREAS, The New York and New Jersey Underground Railway Company is a corporation organized and existing under and pursuant to the laws of the state of New Jersey for the purpose of constructing, maintaining and operating a railroad for the public use from some convenient and eligible point within or near Jersey City or Hoboken, in the county of Hudson and the state of New Jersey, and to run thence by the most direct and feasible route under the bed of the Hudson river and the bay of New York to a convenient and eligible point in that part of the boundary line between the states of New Jersey and New York lying between said Jersey City or Hoboken, in the said state of New Jersey, and the city of New York; the said New York and New Jersey Underground Railway Company has an authorized capital stock of one hundred thousand dollars, divided into one thousand shares of the par value of one hundred dollars each, and its line of route has been located but not yet constructed; and

WHEREAS, The railroads of the said company above named, or the lines and routes of said railroad as adopted form a continuous or connected line of railroad with each other, and do not run on parallel or competing lines, and such line of railroad being less than five miles in length; and

WHEREAS, The said corporations and the directors thereof have agreed to merge, unite and consolidate their capital stock, franchises, roads and property, forming one company, under the terms, conditions, provisions and restrictions and with the powers mentioned and contained in the laws of the state of New York and the state of New Jersey in such case made and provided;

Now therefore this Agreement Witnesseth:

For and in consideration of the premises and of the sum of one dollar by each of the said companies paid to the other, the said parties hereto have united, merged and consolidated and do hereby unite, merge and consolidate their capital stock, franchises, roads and property, forming one company, and the said directors have prescribed and do hereby prescribe the terms and conditions thereof, and the mode of carrying the same into effect, as follows, that is to say:

First. The name of the new corporation shall be The Brooklyn, New York and Jersey City Terminal Railway Company.

Second. The board of directors of the new corporation shall be composed of nine members, who shall be elected and possess such qualifications as shall be prescribed by law, and in and by the by-laws of the new corporation hereby adopted and such other by-laws as shall be adopted from time to time; the officers of the new corporation shall be a president, a vice-president, a secretary and a treasurer and such other subordinate officers as the board of directors may see fit to appoint; the said officers shall be elected at the time and in the manner provided in the by-laws, and perform such duties as shall be prescribed by the by-laws and the resolutions and orders of the board of directors; the following named persons shall be the first directors and officers of the new company, viz.:

1. William J. Hehre,	New York city, N. Y.;
2. Everett R. Reynolds,	New York city, N. Y.;
3. E. B. Gaddis,	Newark, N. J.;
4. C. B. Thurston,	Jersey City, N. J.;
5. B. M. Shanley,	Newark, N. J.;
6. W. A. Patton,	Radnor, Pa.;
7. O. J. DeRousse,	Philadelphia, Pa.;
8. Arthur. E. Sandford,	Newark, N. J.;
9. Thomas F. Brice,	Newark, N. J.;

OFFICERS:	RESIDENCE:
C. B. Thurston, President,	Jersey City, N. J.;
B. M. Shanley, Vice-President,	Newark, N. J.;
W. A. Patton, Sect'y and Treas.,	Radnor, Pa.

Which said directors and officers shall hold their respective offices until their successors are elected and qualified in accordance with the by-laws.

Third. The capital stock of the new corporation is hereby fixed and limited at two thousand shares at the par value of one hundred dollars each being the sum of the capital stock of the two constituent corporations, amounting to two hundred thousand dollars; *provided, however*, that the said new corporation shall possess all the powers to increase or diminish its capital stock granted to corporations in and by the statutes in such case made and provided.

Fourth. To the end that the different values of the stock, property, road and franchises of the said constituent companies shall be fairly and equitably adjusted, the said two thousand shares of capital stock of the new consolidated company shall be issued and distributed amongst the holders of the stock of the constituent companies share for share, that is to say, holders of stock in either of said constituent companies shall be entitled on surrender of their stock to the new consolidated company, to receive a similar number of shares in the said new company; the shares so surrendered, and all treasury stock uniissued in either of the constituent companies shall be forthwith cancelled by the consolidated company.

Fifth. The capital stock of the constituent companies shall become convertible into the capital stock of the new consolidated company, and immediately upon the adoption of this agreement by the stockholders of the consituent companies, and thereupon the holders of all the said stock shall be entitled to surrender the certificates representing the shares held by them respectively, and to receive therefor the proportion of the new capital stock to which they are entitled under the fourth paragraph of this agreement, and the new consolidated company shall cause such new certificates to be issued upon the presentation and surrender of the certificates representing the said shares in the said constituent company.

Sixth. The meetings for the election of directors shall be held at the office of the company on the second Tuesday in December, 1898, and annually thereafter, until the time for holding such meetings shall be changed by the by-laws and they shall be elected by ballot. Officers shall be elected and chosen by the directors at their first or some subsequent meeting after their election.

Seventh. The board of directors shall have power from time to time to adopt by-laws for the government of the business and the management of the affairs of the consolidated company not inconsistent with law or the provisions hereof and to add to, alter or amend the same, and until suitable by-laws shall be adopted the present existing by-laws of The New York and New Jersey Underground Railway Company shall, when applicable, be taken and observed as the by-laws of the new consolidated company.

Eighth. This agreement shall take effect at and immediately upon its adoption by the stockholders of the said constituent companies and the filing hereof in accordance with the statutes in such cases made and provided, and thereupon the directors and officers herein named shall assume absolute control and direction of the property and franchises of the said constituent corporations, as the property and franchises of the new consolidated company; and as soon as may be after the execution hereof by the directors of the said constituent companies, the said boards of directors shall cause this agreement to be submitted to the stockholders of the said companies in accordance with the provisions of the statutes in such case made and provided.

In witness whereof, the directors of the said corporations have subscribed this joint agreement under the corporate seal of each of the said companies the day and year first above written.

THE NEW YORK, NEW JERSEY AND EASTERN RAILROAD COMPANY,

by

Attest: President.

Secretary and Treasurer.

1.
2.
3.
4.
5.
6.
7.
8.
9.

} Directors.

THE NEW YORK AND NEW JERSEY UNDERGROUND RAILWAY COMPANY,

by

Attest: President.

Secretary and Treasurer.

1.
2.
3.
4.
5.
6.
7.

} Directors.

CHAPTER CXCVII.

An Act to repeal an act entitled "An act to incorporate the Red Bank and Eatontown Turnpike Company," approved February ninth, one thousand eight hundred and sixty-five, and the supplement thereto entitled "A supplement to an act entitled 'An act to incorporate the Red Bank and Eatontown Turnpike Company,' approved February ninth, one thousand eight hundred and sixty-five," which said supplement was approved March ninth, one thousand eight hundred and sixty-six.

Act repealed.

1. BE IT ENACTED *by the Senate and General Assembly of the State of New Jersey*, That the act entitled "An act to incorporate the Red Bank and Eatontown Turnpike Company," approved February ninth, one thousand eight hundred and sixty-five, and the supplement thereto entitled "A supplement to an act entitled 'An act to incorporate the Red Bank and Eatontown Turnpike Company,' approved February ninth, one thousand eight hundred and sixty-five," which said supplement was approved March ninth, one thousand eight hundred and sixty-six, be and the same are hereby repealed; *provided, always*, that nothing herein contained shall in any way effect any authority, permission or franchise to construct and operate a street railway on, along and upon the road-bed of said turnpike which may have been by said company granted, sold or conveyed prior to the passage of this act; but such authority, permission or franchise shall be as valid as if this act had not been passed.

Proviso.

2. *And be it enacted*, That this act shall take effect immediately.

Approved March 16, 1898.

Contents.

CONTENTS.

GENERAL PUBLIC LAWS.

JOINT RESOLUTIONS.

PROCLAMATIONS.

SPECIAL PUBLIC ACTS.

PRIVATE ACTS.

General Index.

GENERAL INDEX.

A.

G.

H.

I.

M.

P.

R.

S.

T.

U.

V.

W.

Lightning Source UK Ltd.
Milton Keynes UK
UKHW011541031218
333390UK00014B/912/P